RESTORATION AND REFORM
1153–1165

This book examines the processes by which effective royal government was restored in England following the civil war of Stephen's reign. It questions the traditional view that Stephen presided over 'anarchy', arguing instead that the king and his rivals sought to maintain the administrative traditions of Henry I, leaving foundations for a restoration of order once the war was over.

The period from 1153 to 1162, spanning the last months of Stephen's reign and the early years of Henry II's, is seen as one primarily of 'restoration' when concerted efforts were made to recover royal lands, rights and revenues lost since 1135. Thereafter 'restoration' gave way to 'reform': although the administrative advances of 1166 have been seen as a watershed in Henry II's reign, the financial and judicial measures of 1163–5 were sufficiently important for this, also, to be regarded as a transitional phase in his government of England.

GRAEME J. WHITE is Head of History, University College Chester.

Cambridge Studies in Medieval Life and Thought
Fourth Series

General Editor:

D. E. LUSCOMBE

Leverhulme Personal Research Professor of Medieval History, University of Sheffield

Advisory Editors:

R. B. DOBSON

Professor of Medieval History, University of Cambridge, and Fellow of Christ's College

ROSAMOND McKITTERICK

*Professor of Early Medieval European History, University of Cambridge,
and Fellow of Newnham College*

The series Cambridge Studies in Medieval Life and Thought was inaugurated by G. G. Coulton in 1921. Professor D. E. Luscombe now acts as General Editor of the Fourth Series, with Professors R. B. Dobson and Rosamond McKitterick as Advisory Editors. The series brings together outstanding work by medieval scholars over a wide range of human endeavour extending from political economy to the history of ideas.

For a list of titles in the series, see end of book.

RESTORATION AND REFORM,
1153–1165
Recovery from Civil War in England

GRAEME J. WHITE

CAMBRIDGE
UNIVERSITY PRESS

PUBLISHED BY THE PRESS SYNDICATE OF THE UNIVERSITY OF CAMBRIDGE
The Pitt Building, Trumpington Street, Cambridge CB2 1RP, United Kingdom

CAMBRIDGE UNIVERSITY PRESS
The Edinburgh Building, Cambridge CB2 2RU, UK   http://www.cup.cam.ac.uk
40 West 20th Street, NY 10011-4211, USA   http://www.cup.org
10 Stamford Road, Oakleigh, Melbourne 3166, Australia

First published 2000

Printed in the United Kingdom at the University Press, Cambridge

Typeset in Bembo 11/12 pt [VN]

A catalogue record for this book is available from the British Library

Library of Congress cataloguing in publication data

White, G. J. (Graeme J.)
Restoration and reform, 1153–1165: recovery from civil war in England / Graeme J. White.
p.   cm. – (Cambridge studies in medieval life and thought ; 4th ser.,)
Includes bibliographical references and index.
ISBN – 521 55459 4
1. Great Britain – Politics and government – 1154–1189.   2. Great Britain – History – Henry II,
1154–1189.   3. Great Britain – History – Stephen, 1135–1154.   I. Title.   II. Series.
DA206.W48   1999
942.08'1–dc21   99–19516   CIP

ISBN 0 521 55459 4 hardback

To F. M. J. and H. E. B.

CONTENTS

PREFACE

This is a study of government in England – of politics and especially of administration – in the years following the civil war between King Stephen and the Angevins. The period was one of both restoration and reform: on the one hand, the restoration of property, of orderly government and – it was claimed – of the customs of Henry I's reign, and on the other, administrative reform, particularly in the judicial system, prior to the more famous measures in and after 1166. The manner in which the kingdom was governed under Stephen is given close attention, as essential to an understanding of the subsequent period, but the focus is on recovery and reconstruction in the aftermath of war. The year of the peace settlement at Winchester, 1153, is an obvious starting-date, but cases could be made for continuing the work to 1163, 1170 or 1173–74. The date of 1165 has been chosen because by the following year – the year when the Assize of Clarendon and an assize concerning disseisins are known to have been operational, and when the barons had to submit lists of knights' fees – the king was clearly enlarging the scope of royal justice and seeking new sources of revenue, rather than merely regaining what had been lost under Stephen. It could be argued that 1163 would be a better terminal date. After spending nearly four and a half years on the continent, Henry returned to the kingdom and initiated various administrative reforms, some of which foreshadowed the developments of 1166. But by extending the study to 1165 it has been possible to include these initiatives and assess their significance.

The historian of this period is blessed with abundant charter material, since the *acta* of both kings have been collected together, although it has been essential to supplement these by reference to private charters in manuscript or print. From 1155 onwards, we also have the series of pipe rolls as a guide to governmental activity. But many of the narratives which illuminate the period of civil war fail us thereafter: John of Hexham's chronicle stops in 1153, the *Gesta Stephani* and Henry of

Huntingdon's *Historia Anglorum* in 1154, the 'E' recension of the *Anglo-Saxon Chronicle* in 1155. Robert de Torigni, a useful source for Stephen's closing years, kept his chronicle up-to-date until his death in 1186, but his account was brief and, naturally, better-informed on events on the French side of the Channel: as Howlett put it in his introduction for the Rolls Series edition, 'ours is but the thankfulness felt for moonlight when the sun is absent'. Despite contributions from monastic histories, from Welsh and Scottish annals and from Becket's biographers, we do miss a general survey of English history compiled during the early or middle years of Henry II's reign. Richard fitz Nigel claimed in his *Dialogus de Scaccario* to have written a 'history of England under Henry II' called *Tricolumnis*, but since his warning not to lose it has sadly not been heeded, we are bound to rely heavily on writers at work towards the end of the century. William of Newburgh's *Historia Rerum Anglicarum* explains and assesses policy, adding facts which would otherwise have been lost, but – for our period – is the work of a sexagenarian looking back to his late 'teens and twenties. Gervase of Canterbury and Giraldus Cambrensis also supplied details of the early phase of Henry's reign for which we have no other source, but Ralf of Diceto and Roger of Howden added little to the work of previous writers in their coverage of these years. Given the bias of the sources, therefore, this book has much to say on the recovery of property and on financial and judicial administration under Henry II, but it does not go into detail as a narrative of events.

Stephen's reign has recently received a good deal of scholarly attention, but only occasionally have Henry II's early years as king been accorded special treatment. Older books tended to pass over administrative developments prior to 1166; even such detailed studies as Boussard's *Le Gouvernement d'Henri II Plantagenêt* and Warren's *Henry II* , despite including sections devoted to this period, said less than they might have done on early financial and judicial measures. Legal historians, notably John Hudson, are now stressing the significance of some of Henry's legislative measures at this time, while an important contribution to our knowledge of landholding and finance came with the publication of Emilie Amt's *The Accession of Henry II* in 1993. It is the purpose of this book to offer more rounded treatment of the period: to set Henry II's work as king of England in the context of Stephen's and to examine closely his relations with his officials, his recovery and redistribution of property, his financial administration and his dispensation of justice, in the years before the better-known reforms of the middle and later phases of the reign. Obviously, it would be possible to approach this period from a different perspective, but it is not the intention here to give detailed coverage to issues of legal or ecclesiastical history, important though these are. There is no treatment of the reception of Roman law in England, for example, and the relationship between *ius, rectum* and *saisina* is not discussed at length. Nor is there fresh consideration of the Becket controversy, which is touched upon only where it impinges on the king's financial or judicial affairs. And the focus is firmly upon England, although no historian of this subject can ignore the importance of Henry II's responsibilities to his Angevin empire as a whole: indeed, the impact of the king's itinerary upon the timing of reform is one of the recurring themes in the chapters which follow.

As I complete this work, my first words of gratitude must go to scholars of an earlier generation, D. J. V. Fisher, R. C. Smail and R. H. C. Davis, none of whom is now with us: as thesis supervisor and examiners respectively, they were generous with their help and advice. More recently, I have to say that without the kindness and encouragement of Edmund King, the book would never have been written; he has read every chapter in one form or another, and I am very grateful indeed for his faith in the project, for his willingness to share his immense knowledge of subject-matter and sources, and for his careful and constructive criticism. Among other scholars whose expert advice has been sought and readily given are David Crouch, Paul Dalton, Judith Green, John Hudson and Thomas Keefe: I thank them all, as I do David Luscombe and the other editors of this series, alongside William Davies and his colleagues at Cambridge University Press, who have shown remarkable forbearance in the face of delays in the production of my typescript. I need hardly add that I take sole responsibility for the interpretations offered in the following pages; errors which remain are my own.

It has not been easy to combine the writing of this book with the fulfilment of my duties of head of department, but I do thank the principal and senior management of University College Chester for allowing me two sabbaticals, of a term and a semester, and must give special mention to my good friend Glyn Turton, who as Dean of Arts and Humanities insisted that I complete the work and watched over the History Department while I did so. My departmental colleagues, academic and secretarial, have given unfailing support. A succession of students, whom it has been a privilege to teach both in the W. E. A. Eastern District and at University College Chester, have contributed more to this book than they will ever know. My greatest debt however is to my family, to my parents and sister and especially to my wife Heather, daughter Elizabeth and son Benedict, whose interest and understanding have been deeply appreciated.

ABBREVIATIONS

Acta	*Acta of Henry II and Richard I*, ed. J. C. Holt and R. Mortimer (List and Index Soc., special ser., 21, 1986).
Amt, *Accession*	E. M. Amt, *The Accession of Henry II in England: Royal Government Restored, 1149–1159* (Woodbridge, 1993).
ANS	*Anglo-Norman Studies* (Proceedings of the Battle Conference).
ASC	*Anglo-Saxon Chronicle: a Revised Translation*, ed. D. Whitelock, D. C. Douglas, S. I. Tucker (rev. edn., London, 1965).
Baronies	I. J. Sanders, *English Baronies: a Study of their Origin and Descent, 1086-1327* (Oxford, 1960).
Becket Materials	*Materials for the History of Thomas Becket, Archbishop of Canterbury*, ed. J. C. Robertson, 7 vols. (RS, 1875-85).
[BI]HR	*[Bulletin of the Institute of] Historical Research*.
B. L.	British Library.
BNJ	*British Numismatic Journal*.
Boussard, *Le Gouvernement*	J. Boussard, *Le Gouvernement d'Henri II Plantagenêt* (Paris, 1956).
CCR	*Calendar of Charter Rolls preserved in the Public Record Office*, 6 vols. (Record Commission, 1903–27).
Chibnall, *Matilda*	M. Chibnall, *The Empress Matilda* (Oxford, 1991).
Chronicles	*Chronicles of the Reigns of Stephen, Henry II and Richard I*, ed. R. Howlett, 4 vols. (RS, 1884–9).
CP	*Complete Peerage of England, Scotland, Ireland, Great Britain and the United Kingdom*, ed. G. E.

	C(ockayne); new edn. by V. Gibbs, G. H. White et al. , 13 vols. in 14 (London, 1910–59).
Curia R. R.	*Curia Regis Rolls* (London, 1922– in progress).
Davis, *Stephen*	R. H. C. Davis, *King Stephen, 1135–1154* (3rd edn., London, 1990).
De Gestis Regum	William of Malmesbury, *De Gestis Regum Anglorum,* ed. W. Stubbs, 2 vols. (RS, 1887–9).
Dialogus	*Dialogus de Scaccario and Constitutio Domus Regis,* ed. C. Johnson, corrections F. E. L. Carter and D. E. Greenway (OMT, 1983).
Diceto	Ralf of Diceto, *Opera Historica,* ed. W. Stubbs, 2 vols. (RS, 1876).
EHR	*English Historical Review.*
EYC	*Early Yorkshire Charters,* i–iii, ed. W. Farrer (Edinburgh, 1914–16), iv–xii, ed. C. T. Clay (Yorks. Arch. Society, 1935–65).
Gervase	Gervase of Canterbury, *Opera Historica,* ed. W. Stubbs, 2 vols. (RS, 1879–80).
Gesta Regis	[Roger of Howden] *Gesta Regis Henrici Secundi Benedicti Abbatis,* ed. W. Stubbs, 2 vols. (RS, 1867).
Gesta Steph.	*Gesta Stephani,* ed. K. R. Potter, intro. R. H. C. Davis (OMT, 1976).
GF, *Letters*	*Letters and Charters of Gilbert Foliot,* ed. Z. N. Brooke, A. Morey, C. N. L. Brooke (Cambridge, 1967).
Green, *Henry I*	J. A. Green, *The Government of England under Henry I* (Cambridge, 1986).
HH	Henry, Archdeacon of Huntingdon, *Historia Anglorum,* ed. and transl. D. E. Greenway (OMT, 1996).
Hist. Nov.	William of Malmesbury, *Historia Novella,* ed. K. R. Potter (NMT, 1955).
HKF	W. Farrer, *Honors and Knights' Fees,* 3 vols. (London and Manchester, 1923–5).
Howden	Roger of Howden, *Chronica,* ed. W. Stubbs, 4 vols. (RS, 1868–71).
Itinerary	R. W. Eyton, *Court, Household and Itinerary of King Henry II* (London, 1878).
JH	'John of Hexham, *Historia*', in Symeon of Durham, *Opera Omnia,* ed. T. Arnold, ii (RS, 1885).

JW	*Chronicle of John of Worcester, 1118–1140*, ed. J. R. H. Weaver (Oxford, 1908).
JS, *Letters*	*Letters of John of Salisbury*, I, ed. W. J. Millor, H. E. Butler and C. N. L. Brooke (NMT, 1955); II, ed. W. J. Millor and C. N. L. Brooke (OMT, 1979).
King, *Anarchy*	E. J. King, ed., *The Anarchy of King Stephen's Reign* (Oxford, 1994).
Lawsuits	*English Lawsuits from William I to Richard I*, ed. R. C. van Caenegem, 2 vols. (Selden Society, 1990–91).
Monasticon	*Monasticon Anglicanum*, ed. W. Dugdale, new edn. by J. Caley, H. Ellis and B. Bandinel, 6 vols. in 8 (London, 1817–30).
Newburgh	'William of Newburgh, *Historia Rerum Anglicarum*', in *Chronicles*, I, II.
NMT	Nelson's Medieval Texts, London.
OMT	Oxford Medieval Texts, Oxford.
OV	Orderic Vitalis, *The Ecclesiastical History*, ed. M. Chibnall, 6 vols. (OMT, 1969–80).
P. R.	pipe roll.
PR 31 Hen. I	*P. R. 31 Henry I*, ed. J. Hunter (Record Commission, 1833).
PR2H, PR3H, PR4H	*P. R. 2–4 Henry II*, ed. J. Hunter (Record Commission, 1844).
PR5H, PR6H, etc.	*P. R. 5 Henry II, P. R. 6 Henry II*, etc. (P. R. Society, from 1884).
P. R. O.	Public Record Office.
RAH	*Recueil des Actes de Henri II*, ed. L. Delisle and E. Berger, 4 vols. (Paris, 1906–27) [*RAH, Intro.* = introductory volume].
RBE	*Red Book of the Exchequer*, ed. H. Hall, 3 vols. (RS. 1896).
Reg. Ant.	*Registrum Antiquissimum of the Cathedral Church of Lincoln*, ed. C. W. Foster and K. Major, 8 vols. (Lincoln Rec. Society, 1931–58).
RH	'Richard of Hexham, *Historia*', in *Chronicles*, III.
Richardson and Sayles, *Governance*	H. G. Richardson and G. O. Sayles, *The Governance of Mediaeval England from the Conquest to Magna Carta* (Edinburgh, 1963).

Royal Writs	*Royal Writs in England from the Conquest to Glanvill,* ed. R. C. van Caenegem (Selden Society, 1959).
RRAN	*Regesta Regum Anglo-Normannorum*, ii, ed. C. Johnson and H. A. Cronne (Oxford, 1956); iii, iv, ed. H. A. Cronne and R. H. C. Davis (Oxford, 1968–9).
RS	Rolls Series.
RT	'Robert de Torigni, *Chronica*', in *Chronicles*, iv.
Saltman, *Theobald*	A. Saltman, *Theobald, Archbishop of Canterbury* (London, 1956).
Select Charters	*Select Charters and Other Illustrations of English Constitutional History to the Reign of Edward I,* ed. W. Stubbs (9th edn rev. by H. W. C. Davis, Oxford, 1921).
Staffs. Colls.	*Collections for a History of Staffordshire,* 18 vols. in 20 (William Salt Archaeological Society, 1880–97) [further series thereafter].
Tractatus	*Tractatus de Legibus et Consuetudinibus Regni Anglie qui Glanvilla vocatur,* ed. G. D. G. Hall (2nd edn, OMT, 1993).
TRHS	*Transactions of the Royal Historical Society.*
VCH	*Victoria History of the Counties of England* (London, 1900–, in progress).
Warren, *Governance*	W. L. Warren, *The Governance of Norman and Angevin England, 1086–1272* (London, 1987).
Warren, *Henry II*	W. L. Warren, *Henry II* (London, 1973).
WN	William of Newburgh, *History of English Affairs,* i, ed. P. G. Walsh and M. J. Kennedy (Warminster, 1988).

Chapter 1

THE POLITICAL CONTEXT

At King Stephen's coronation mass on 22 December 1135, the arch-bishop of Canterbury forgot to include the kiss of peace.[1] The reign which followed was blighted by war: against the Scots and the Welsh, against Geoffrey count of Anjou in Normandy, and against rival con-tenders for the throne in England. In Geoffrey's wife Empress Matilda and their son the future Henry II, Stephen faced far more formidable challengers for his kingdom than William Rufus and Henry I had en-countered in the person of Robert Curthose, and in battling on to defend his position he showed that he was not without ability. His personal courage and skill as a soldier were acknowledged even by hostile com-mentators,[2] while those of more balanced judgement observed several kingly virtues in him, notably his generosity and fair-mindedness.[3] Settle-ments he negotiated can easily be condemned for giving too much away, but on closer scrutiny appear as the product of careful calculation: for instance, the first treaty of Durham in 1136 involved the surrender by the Scots of several recent acquisitions,[4] while the charter of 1146 containing lavish grants to the earl of Chester was largely confined to properties he already controlled and envisaged that some might eventually be restored

---

[1] The story seems to have become well known: JH, 286–7; Howden, I, 189; Gervase, I, 94–5; *Chronica Regum Mannie & Insularum*, ed. G. Broderick (Manx Museum, 1979), f. 36 (probably composed at Rushen Abbey, daughter-house of Stephen's own foundation at Furness). The date follows *Hist. Nov.*, 15–16.

[2] HH, 738; Walter Map, *De Nugis Curialium*, ed. M. R. James, rev. C. N. L. Brooke and R. A. B. Mynors (OMT, 1983), 474.

[3] *Hist. Nov.*, 20; OV, VI, 544–5; *Gesta Steph.*, 22–3.

[4] Of the five castles seized by David king of Scots when he invaded England immediately following Stephen's coronation, four (Wark, Alnwick, Norham and Newcastle) were surrendered under the first treaty of Durham, although David retained Carlisle as the base for control of much of Cumbria (JH, 287; RH, 145–6; G. W. S. Barrow, 'The Scots and the North of England' in King, *Anarchy*, 231–53, esp. 246).

to the king.[5] Against Stephen, it must be said that his decision early in his reign to use earldoms as a cheap form of patronage played into the hands of barons eager to assert their independence, leading to the fragmentation of government once the civil war began;[6] he was perceived as being open to manipulation[7] and his penchant for suddenly arresting those in his peace seriously damaged his reputation, probably contributing to his failure to win over Angevin loyalists in the later stages of the war. But, as will be argued in the next chapter, he maintained the administrative traditions of Henry I through the 1140s and early 1150s, albeit within a reduced area of the kingdom, and once the peace settlement came he applied them in parts of England previously out of his control. To preserve the apparatus of Henry I's government through fourteen years of civil war was no mean achievement. It provided Henry I's grandson with the foundations upon which the restoration of royal authority could be built.

Of course, Henry II gave Stephen no credit. It suited his purposes to present himself as the continuator of Henry I's reign, not that of his immediate predecessor, so that he could be free to recover the estates and reclaim the rights lost by the crown since 1135. This was the theme of his coronation charter, which confirmed the grants his grandfather had made and abolished the evil customs he had condemned.[8] Such thinking lay behind the edict, apparently issued soon after his accession, ordering sworn inquests into the former extent of royal demesne, so that losses could be restored to the crown.[9] It was apparent in the countless royal writs and charters which sought to restore, for the beneficiaries, the situation as it was either in Henry I's reign generally, or specifically at his death.[10] It also informed the Constitutions of Clarendon in 1164, with their claim to be setting out the customs of Henry I.[11] Chroniclers of Henry II's time or later took up the message that prerogatives ceded and concessions wrought during Stephen's reign had no validity, and so reinforced the impression that he was a usurper and his time one of uniform 'unpeace'. Accordingly, the sufferings of his reign were seen to have lasted the full nineteen years, with a breakdown in law and order following hard upon Henry I's succession by a weak and worthless

[5] *RRAN*, III, no. 178; G. J. White, 'King Stephen, Duke Henry and Ranulf de Gernons, earl of Chester', *EHR*, 91 (1976), 555–65; P. Dalton, 'Ranulf II and Lincolnshire' in A. T. Thacker, ed., *The Earldom of Chester and its Charters* (Journal of Chester Archaeological Society, 71, 1991), 109–34; P. Dalton, '*In neutro latere*: the armed neutrality of Ranulf II earl of Chester in Stephen's reign', *ANS*, 14 (1992), 39–59 (esp. 45–7).

[6] G. J. White, 'Continuity in government' in King, *Anarchy*, 117–43 (at 124–9, 133–5) and below, ch. 2; cf. *Hist. Nov.*, 23.   [7] *Ibid.*, 20 (cf. near the end of the reign, HH, 772–4).

[8] *Select Charters*, 158.

[9] *Gesta Abbatum Monasterii Sancti Albani*, I, ed. H. T. Riley (RS, 1867), 123; Warren, *Henry II*, 218, n. 1.   [10] Warren, *Henry II*, 217–20, 262.   [11] *Select Charters*, 163–4.

king.[12] But the depiction of the whole of the reign, rather than merely part of it, as a time of chaos does less than justice to such continuity in government as Stephen was able to maintain, and from which Henry II was able to profit.

The personality of the new king is not easy to summarise, despite there being three good contemporary assessments by members of his household. As his biographer Lewis Warren recognised, Henry II 'was a complex man, of contradictory qualities'.[13] His reputation as an industrious 'legislator king' with a genius for administrative proficiency, which persisted for over a hundred years following the publication of Stubbs's *Constitutional History of England*, has now been challenged but continues to influence modern scholarly opinion.[14] In fact, it is not difficult to find evidence – in the verdicts of contemporary observers and in reports of his conduct during specific episodes in his life – to support two contrasting views of Henry II: on the one hand, that he was an intellectual who hated warfare, a gifted judge and a painstaking administrator, and, on the other, that he was a man of action who loved fighting and hunting, had little time for judicial affairs and preferred to leave routine business to others.[15] But conflicting statements of this nature are not irreconcilable. In the course of Henry's long reign, all of them were true at some time or other: with the changing circumstances of the passing years, different qualities surfaced at different times.

Since our concern is with the earliest phase of Henry's reign, it is important to stress that he came to the English throne at the age of twenty-one already accustomed to political success. Early in 1150 his father, Geoffrey Plantagenet count of Anjou, had abdicated Normandy to him; in September 1151 he had succeeded to Anjou, Maine and Touraine on his father's death; in May 1152 he had acquired Poitou and Aquitaine through marriage to the duchess Eleanor, former wife of Louis VII king of France; by the close of 1153 he had been promised the kingdom of

---

[12] *ASC*, 199; HH, 774. Cf. Newburgh, I, 103 and *Chronicle of Battle Abbey*, ed. E. Searle (OMT, 1980), 212–13: below, ch. 2, nn. 15, 16.

[13] Warren, *Henry II*, 208.

[14] Henry II's concern with judicial administration is played down in J. Gillingham, 'Conquering kings: some twelfth-century reflections on Henry II and Richard I' in T. Reuter, ed., *Warriors and Churchmen in the High Middle Ages* (London, 1992), 163–78, but (with due credit to the king's advisers) is stressed in e.g. P. A. Brand, '"Multis vigiliis excogitatem et inventam": Henry II and the creation of the English common law', *Haskins Society Journal*, 2 (1990), 197–222, and J. G. H. Hudson, *The Formation of the English Common Law* (London, 1996), 144–6.

[15] Warren, *Henry II*, 207–17, summarises the verdicts of several contemporaries, with full references. M. T. Clanchy in *Tractatus*, lxxvii–lxxix, surveys the range of modern opinion. Cases heard before Henry II early in his reign, narrated in detail in *Chronicle of Battle Abbey*, 176–218, suggest that it was difficult to gain access to the king, but that he could be most attentive to proceedings once they had reached him (cf. below, ch. 5, nn. 54–5).

England.[16] He had also shown himself to be a decisive and effective military commander, skilfully defending his continental lands against the king of France and his allies – including Stephen's son Eustace – in the successive summers of 1151 and 1152.[17] This was a young man blessed with abundant energy, good fortune and self-confidence, a king who liked to keep on the move and who expected to get his own way. Accordingly, the assertion of his political authority, by negotiation where possible but by military force when necessary, was not only the most urgent governmental requirement but also the task for which – in this phase of his life – he was ideally suited by temperament.

It is hard to avoid the impression that the young Henry II relished the excitement of leading armies against recalcitrant vassals, to demand the surrender of former royal lands and castles: the recovery of royal rights enjoyed under Henry I became a convenient, readily understood justification for this endeavour. He could only be diverted from this task by the prospect of even greater adventures. A more mature statesman would not have contemplated a conquest of Ireland within a year of succeeding to England, a project abandoned – apparently – because of Empress Matilda's opposition. A more cautious king would not have embarked in 1159 on the costly and unsuccessful military expedition to Toulouse, in pursuit of Eleanor's claims to that county.[18] Neither enterprise could be validated by reference to Henry I, and in neither case had some fortuitous circumstance presented an opportunity which could not be allowed to pass. Henry II was responsible for the timing of these expansionist plans and they serve to underline the point that, at this stage, he was not yet the studious administrator who 'had at his fingertips . . . a great store of practical wisdom', as depicted by his later admirers.[19] In general, he was content to leave routine responsibility to his officials: it was their task to ensure that the machinery of royal government functioned as efficiently, and over as wide an area, as it had done under Henry I, while he concentrated on securing (and if possible extending) his frontiers, re-claiming lost lands, castles and revenues, and cowing the barons. Yet if this is the dominant impression left by Henry II in the first decade of his

---

[16] See esp. RT, 161–71, 177; Warren, *Henry II*, 41–8. On the date of Henry's accession as duke of Normandy, see Davis, *Stephen*, 107, n. 27.   [17] RT, 161, 165–6.

[18] *Ibid.*, 186, 201–4; Chibnall, *Matilda*, 163; Warren, *Henry II*, 81–7, 195–6. Warren was sceptical about Henry's intentions regarding Ireland in 1155 and regarded the similarly dated papal bull *Laudabiliter*, which encouraged him 'to enlarge the boundaries of the Church' as inspired by Archbishop Theobald. However, the text of the bull as we have it suggests that the pope was responding to Henry's initial proposal, and there is no good reason to doubt Robert de Torigni's report of the council which deliberated on the planned invasion.

[19] Giraldus Cambrensis, *Opera*, ed. J. S. Brewer, J. F. Dimock and G. F. Warner (RS, 1861–91), v, 306; cf. (on his studiousness) Peter of Blois in *Becket Materials*, VII, 573. For this interpretation of Henry II, see Gillingham, 'Conquering kings'.

reign, it still does not tell the whole story. Despite the hectic lifestyle and competing priorities of these early years, he did find the time to preside at lawsuits.[20] Although Clarendon and Woodstock were much-frequented hunting-lodges, Henry despatched a good deal of business while staying there.[21] Among the administrative initiatives he authorised were the issue of a new coinage[22] and the introduction of legislation to protect seisin and prohibit unsupported criminal accusations, all accomplished before the start of his third visit to England as king, in January 1163.[23] It was during this visit that – with the immediate political problems arising from the civil war now resolved – Henry was to give detailed attention to financial and judicial affairs.

However, when he landed in England on 8 December 1154, his immediate priority was to reaffirm his position as king. He received the fealty of several barons at Winchester and then proceeded to his coronation at Westminster, with Queen Eleanor, eleven days later.[24] The coronation would be followed over the next few years by ceremonial crown-wearings at St Edmunds, outside Lincoln, and at Worcester, the last probably at Easter 1158 when Eleanor again took part.[25] Steps were also taken at a council held at Wallingford in April 1155 to establish the succession to the throne, barons being required to swear fealty to the king's infant sons William and Henry.[26] William died in the following year, but the oaths to Henry the Younger would be renewed on the occasion of the king's return to England in January 1163.[27]

It was greatly to Henry II's advantage that no serious rival emerged to challenge his right to the English throne. Of his two brothers, the youngest, William, was certainly with him in England early in the reign.[28] Plans to reward him with the kingdom of Ireland or with the Warenne estates in marriage to the heiress Isabel came to naught, but he received the *vicomté* of Dieppe and estates in fifteen English shires, only to die

[20] E.g. *Lawsuits*, II, nos. 360, 371, 377; *Coucher Book of the Cistercian Abbey of Kirkstall*, ed. W. T. Lancaster and W. P. Baildon (Thoresby Society, 1904), no. 266. For further discussion on these and other cases determined in the king's presence, see below ch. 5.

[21] *Itinerary*, e.g. 14, 30, 34–5, 37, 63, 66–70. [22] Diceto, I, 283; Warren, *Henry II*, 265–6.

[23] J. G. H. Hudson, *Land, Law and Lordship in Anglo-Norman England* (Oxford, 1994), 256–7; below, ch. 5.

[24] RT, 182; Gervase, I, 159–60; Newburgh, I, 95–6, 101. Archbishop Theobald appears to have headed the government in England in the period between Stephen's death and Henry II's arrival: HH, 774; Saltman, *Theobald*, 41.

[25] *Chronicle of Battle Abbey*, 174–6; PR3H, 107; Newburgh, I, 117–18; Howden, I, 216; Diceto, I, 302.

[26] RT, 184.

[27] Diceto, I, 306; RT, 189, 216. A gold crown was prepared for Henry the Younger during 1161–2 (PR8H, 43).

[28] *RAH*, I, nos. 56–8; CCR, IV, no. 257 (at Westminster, 1154x58) and *Ancient Charters*, ed. J. H. Round (P. R. Society, 1888), nos. 34, 36 (both at Nottingham, 1155x58). He was in the king's company at Colchester in May 1157 (*Chronicle of Battle Abbey*, 176; *Itinerary*, 26–7).

without issue in January 1164, so ensuring that the grants had no lasting effect.[29] The other brother, Geoffrey, was more troublesome, resenting Henry's succession to the county of Anjou and taking up arms against him in both 1152 and 1156; evidence that he came to England is very limited, and the king may deliberately have kept him away, finding him a convenient apanage instead in the county of Nantes. In the event, any possible threat from this quarter was soon removed when Geoffrey, in his turn, died childless in July 1158.[30] The only other potential challenger to the throne was Stephen's surviving son William, who had negotiated his own terms with Henry in 1153 and had been compensated accordingly, becoming the wealthiest lay magnate in the kingdom.[31] Henry moved against him in May 1157, requiring him to surrender his English and Norman castles, several former royal manors in Surrey, and the holdings in Pevensey and Norfolk conceded to him under the peace settlement: he was left with all that Stephen had held at Henry I's death, with the honour of Warenne in right of his wife, and with the comital titles which accompanied these lands.[32] Friction in East Anglia involving William and Hugh Bigod, who also forfeited his castles, seems to have prompted these measures, but it was a sign of the times – and probably also of William's personality – that there was no vengeful 'flight to arms' as there might have been in the previous reign. William evidently appealed in vain to the pope[33] but was sufficiently in Henry's favour to be knighted by him at Carlisle in June 1158 and to accompany him on the Toulouse campaign in the following year. It was while returning from Toulouse, in October 1159, that he died. He was yet another who conveniently left no heirs, allowing Stephen's old baronial lands to pass to the crown and the Warenne heiress, honour and earldom to be given in 1164 to the king's illegitimate half-brother Hamelin.[34]

One is bound to reflect upon Henry's good fortune. In the second half of the 1160s, both his brothers were in their graves while his own sons, born in 1155, 1157 and 1158, were as yet too young to assume personal control.[35] Had Henry II died in this period, Queen Eleanor would

[29] RT, 186, 221; *Becket Materials*, III, 142; 'Draco Normannicus' in *Chronicles*, II, 67; Warren, *Henry II*, 195, 449; Chibnall, *Matilda*, 163–4.

[30] RT, 165–70, 186–90, 196; Geoffrey appears as a witness, above William, to *Ancient Charters*, no. 34, issued at Northampton probably in 1155 (cf. *Acta*, no. 205; T. A. M. Bishop, *Scriptores Regis* (Oxford, 1960), 57 and plate xxvi b, the scribe being one active *c*.1155); Warren, *Henry II*, 65–6.

[31] Richardson and Sayles, *Governance*, 253; J. H. Round, *Studies in Peerage and Family History* (Westminster, 1901), 147–80.

[32] RT, 192–3; *PR3H*, 94 (where the proportionate allowance to the sheriff for the Surrey manors suggests that they were resumed in May); cf. Warren, *Henry II*, 67 and n. 5, where the surrenders are assigned to the council of May 1157 reported in *Chronicle of Battle Abbey*, 174–6.

[33] JS, *Letters*, I, 82.   [34] RT, 196, 206, 221; Warren, *Henry II*, 365.

[35] The births of Henry the Younger, Richard and Geoffrey are noted in RT, 183, 195, 197.

doubtless have governed on behalf of Henry the Younger, to whom the barons had done homage, but the king would have had great cause for concern on his deathbed if a representative of the house of Blois had still been waiting in the wings: one, moreover, who had a territorial base even larger than Stephen's had been in 1135. If the series of deaths in 1153 had been a sign of God's blessing upon the Angevin cause,[36] the same might be said of the subsequent failure of Stephen's line: by 1160, both his legitimate sons were dead, and neither had left progeny with ambition for the throne.

Even so, Henry deserves full credit for his forceful assertion of authority when occasion required it. In the summer of 1157 Malcolm IV king of Scotland surrendered territories gained under Stephen with no more than token protest, but the Welsh princes only submitted after a dangerous and costly military campaign later in the year.[37] One of Henry's first acts as king, at Christmas 1154, was to order the expulsion of foreign mercenaries and the rasing of castles built since his grandfather's death, although the best were to be surrendered instead: measures with a significance as much psychological as physical, in signalling that the time for conflict had passed.[38] Security was also addressed through a major castle-improvement programme, which included work on those at Scarborough and Southampton, previously in the hands of William of Aumale and the bishop of Winchester. There was further expenditure on other royal buildings (*domus regis*) at Clarendon, Westminster, Woodstock, Brampton and elsewhere, including 66s. 8d. apparently to repair the exchequer buildings.[39] All this bears out Robert de Torigni's account of the building or upgrading of castles and royal houses, 'not only in Normandy but also in

[36] *Gesta Steph.*, 239.
[37] RT, 192–3, 195; Newburgh, I, 105–9; Gervase, I, 165–6; *Brut y Tywysogion: Red Book of Hergest*, ed. and transl. T. Jones (2nd edn, Cardiff, 1973), 134–9; Warren, *Henry II*, 68–71, 161–2, 182.
[38] RT, 183; Gervase, I, 160–1; Newburgh, I, 101–2. On the fate of Stephen's mercenary leader William of Ypres, see *PR3H*, 101–2; *Becket Materials*, III, 19; JS, *Letters*, I, nos. 23, 24 and pp. 258–60; Amt, *Accession*, 87–91. For the destruction of castles formerly belonging to the bishop of Winchester and Geoffrey de Mandeville, see *PR2H*, 54; *PR4H*, 132; 'Annales de Wigornia' in *Annales Monastici*, ed. H. R. Luard (RS, 1864–9), IV, 380.
[39] For work on Southampton castle, see *PR2H*, 53; *PR3H*, 107; *PR4H*, 179; *PR5H*, 50. For similar work at Scarborough, see *PR4H*, 146; *PR5H*, 29–31; *PR6H*, 14; *PR7H*, 36; *PR8H*, 50; *PR9H*, 57–8; *PR10H*, 12. Among other castles on which Henry II's early pipe rolls record work are Berkhamstead, Cambridge, Wark and Winchester (*PR2H*, 14, 21; *PR3H*, 96, 108; *PR4H*, 152, 165, 175, 177; *PR5H*, 7, 13–14, 48, 53; *PR6H*, 12, 56–7; *PR7H*, 23; *PR8H*, 37, 49). Some of these references do not appear in R. A. Brown, 'Royal castle-building in England, 1154–1216', *EHR*, 70 (1955), 353–98. Other building or repair is mentioned as follows: Clarendon, *PR2H*, 56–7; *PR3H*, 77, 104, 106; *PR4H*, 115; *PR6H*, 16; *PR7H*, 8; *PR8H*, 12; *PR9H*, 45; *PR10H*, 14; *PR11H*, 56; Westminster, *PR2H*, 4; *PR8H*, 67; *PR11H*, 31–2; Woodstock, *PR2H*, 36; *PR10H*, 7; Brampton, *PR3H*, 95; *PR6H*, 32. The expenditure 'in reparatione domorum de Scaccario' (*PR2H*, 4) is discussed (with suggested reinterpretation) in J. A. Green, 'Financing Stephen's war', *ANS*, 14 (1992), 91–114 (at 110–11).

the kingdom of England, the duchy of Aquitaine, the county of Anjou, Maine, Touraine'.[40]

A statement such as this reminds us that the restoration of orderly government in England was but part of a process which embraced Henry's Angevin empire as a whole. Here was a king of England whose heart lay in Anjou and who spent less than a third of his life in the country which gave him his throne.[41] The well-known summary of his itinerary in *Cambridge Medieval History* volume v shows that, of his thirty-five years as king of England, some fifteen were passed in Normandy, seven elsewhere in France and the remaining thirteen in England, Wales or Ireland; in the first eight years of his reign, only two and a half were spent in his kingdom, but he was then in England or Wales for all but a few weeks between January 1163 and March 1166.[42] England gave him a status equal to that of his Capetian rivals and was potentially an invaluable resource, but the challenges it posed had to await their turn on Henry's busy agenda and could be addressed only intermittently. It should of course be said that, whichever territory he was in, the king received suitors from all parts of his empire and issued writs and charters accordingly,[43] but a link between his itinerary and the timing of major political and administrative initiatives is unmistakable. In Normandy, for example, the issue of an edict prohibiting unsupported criminal accusations, the re-enforcement of the decrees of the council of Lillebonne defining the limits of ecclesiastical jurisdiction, and the launch of an enquiry by sworn inquest into customary royal and baronial revenues, all belong to the period between Christmas 1159 and the beginning of 1163; these were years when Henry spent the bulk of his time in the duchy and seems to have taken personal control of its government following the retirement and death of the seneschal Robert de Neufbourg.[44] In England, likewise, the most pressing governmental problems were tackled while Henry was in the country: when he was away there was not the same drive for reform.

[40] RT, 209–10 (assigned to 1161).

[41] Henry was born in Le Mans and returned to Chinon to die at the age of fifty-six. He spent about three and a half years on the English side of the Channel prior to his accession, over the four visits of 1142–4, 1146–7, 1149 and 1153–4 (A. L. Poole, 'Henry Plantagenet's early visits to England', *EHR*, 47 (1932), 447–52; *RRAN*, III, xlvi–xlviii) in addition to his thirteen as king.

[42] D. M. Stenton, 'England: Henry II' in *Cambridge Medieval History*, v, ed. J. R. Tanner, C. W. Prévite-Orton and Z. N. Brooke (Cambridge, 1929), 554, n. 1. *Itinerary*, 77–9, shows that Henry's sojourn in Normandy early in 1165 was of uncertain duration, beginning in Lent (17 February to 3 April) according to RT, 224 and ending about the middle of May.

[43] Warren, *Henry II*, 93–4. As examples may be cited the sequence of charters attributed to 1159 in *RAH*, I, nos. 124–32, which show Henry in Chinon, Poitiers, Saintes, Tours and Le Mans dealing with issues from various parts of England and western France.

[44] RT, 203–4, 212, 217; 'Continuatio Beccensis', *ibid.*, 324, 327; cf. C. H. Haskins, *Norman Institutions* (New York, 1918), 170–1, 329–30; Boussard, *Le Gouvernement*, 421–2; Warren, *Henry II*, 94–6, 434 n. 4.

Henry had devoted the months immediately before his accession as king of England to the recovery of lost ducal demesnes in Normandy, the suppression of rebellion both there and in Aquitaine, and the negotiation of an agreement whereby Louis VII king of France would cede two border castles. Between January 1156 and April 1157 he was in France again, doing homage for his continental territories to Louis VII, forcing his troublesome younger brother Geoffrey to come to terms, and consolidating his position in Aquitaine.[45] Then from August 1158 a series of diplomatic and military endeavours were to keep him away from England for a further four and a half years. The second half of 1158 was taken up with the negotiation of the marriage alliance involving his son Henry – now heir to the throne following the death of his elder brother William – and Louis VII's daughter Margaret, with the enforced submission of Conan IV duke of Brittany, and with the recovery of border castles from Theobald count of Blois and Rotrou count of Perche. Preparations for the Toulouse campaign, including the negotiation of an alliance with the count of Barcelona, occupied much of the spring of 1159, the expedition itself the whole of the summer, only for Henry to abandon his siege of the city towards the end of September; the only territorial gain from the enterprise was the border county of Quercy.[46] With hindsight, the enterprise could be seen as the start of forty years' warfare between the kings of England and France[47] – it brought Louis VII in person to the defence of Toulouse and led Henry in the autumn to campaign on Normandy's frontiers with the French royal domain – but in the short term a truce had developed by May 1160 into a full peace settlement, the opening clause of which underlined Henry II's consistent purpose in this opening phase of his reign: Louis VII 'restored to the king of England all the rights and tenements of King Henry his grandfather, which he held on the day he was alive and dead'. The only exception was the Vexin, much of which was to remain under the lordship of the king of France unless the marriage negotiated in 1158 took place with the Church's consent within the next three years; in the event, Henry was able to outmanœuvre Louis by obtaining that consent, which meant that the marriage had been concluded and the Vexin had been occupied and fortified, by the close of the year.[48] Meanwhile, various castles in Normandy, Brittany, Maine, Blois and Aquitaine were forcibly surrendered to Henry, and Waleran of Meulan was temporarily deprived of his

---

[45] RT, 179–81, 186–92.
[46] *Ibid.*, 196–203; 'Continuatio Beccensis', *ibid.*, 318–23; Newburgh, I, 121–6; Gervase, I, 166–7; Warren, *Henry II*, 71–7, 82–7.   [47] Newburgh, II, 491.
[48] *RAH*, I, no. 141; RT, 205–8; 'Continuatio Beccensis', *ibid.*, 324; Diceto, I, 303–4.

Norman estates.[49] Eventually, a fresh peace was concluded between the kings of England and France, reinforced when together they met Pope Alexander III in the late summer or autumn of 1162. This at last gave Henry sufficient security to leave his continental territories. 'Having settled his affairs, including his castles in Normandy, Aquitaine, Anjou and also Gascony, Henry came to Barfleur at Advent, wishing to cross over, if possible, before Christmas.' In fact, contrary winds meant that he was obliged to spend Christmas at Cherbourg, but he eventually landed at Southampton on 25 January 1163.[50]

The central administration in England had by now settled into a routine, but the king's arrival was to inject fresh dynamism into the search for additional sources of finance and to the identification, recovery and advancement of royal rights. Political problems remained: between 1163 and 1166 Henry twice led armies into Wales, secured a renewal of homage from Malcolm IV king of Scots, negotiated the marriage of two daughters with German princes[51] and, most famously, became embroiled in conflict with his archbishop of Canterbury. But the Becket controversy arose out of Henry's insistence on asserting his rights and reclaiming royal jurisdiction – in this case at the expense of the Church – and should be seen in the context of wide-ranging efforts made in these years to enhance the authority of the king. The measures taken in this period were to lead to significant changes in the governance of the country, going far beyond the initially declared aim of recovering for the crown what had been enjoyed under Henry I.[52] Yet – characteristically – having prompted reform Henry left its detailed implementation to others, for after his departure from Southampton in March 1166 conflicts with the king of France and with rebels in Brittany and Aquitaine were to keep him out of England for the next four years.[53] This was an approach to administrative development in the kingdom which was to be repeated several times during the course of the reign. Initiatives such as the launch of the 'Inquest of Sheriffs' in 1170, the issue in 1176 of the Assize of Northampton and provision for its enforcement by six teams each of

[49] RT, 209–12; Warren, *Henry II*, 95, 100–3; D. B. Crouch, *The Beaumont Twins* (Cambridge, 1986), 77–8.

[50] RT, 215–16.

[51] *Ibid.*, 216–26; Newburgh, I, 139–46; Diceto, I, 308–18; *Brut y Tywysogion: Red Book*, 142–7; Warren, *Henry II*, 96–100, 492–3. One of the proposed marriages, that of Henry's daughter Matilda to Henry the Lion duke of Saxony, duly took place in 1168.

[52] The extent to which there was an 'Angevin leap forward' in judicial administration has been reconsidered, e.g. in Hudson, *Land, Law and Lordship*, esp. 253–81, and *English Common Law*, esp. 118–56. However, it is clear that a series of measures taken from the mid-1160s onwards had the effect of changing the conduct of lawsuits and transforming the operation of the king's government in this field. The issues are discussed more fully in ch. 5.

[53] RT, 226–44; Warren, *Henry II*, 100–10.

three justices, the reorganisation in 1178 of the judiciary so that five justices would be based at Westminster, the devising of the Grand Assize and the assize of *darrein presentment* both probably in 1179, the decision on a recoinage in 1180, the passing of the assize of the forest in 1184: all can be dated to periods when Henry was resident in his kingdom.[54] While he was overseas his officials governed on his behalf without his routine intervention; whenever he visited England there was the prospect of their having to adjust to change.

The chapters which follow include studies of patronage and of the restitution of estates, of financial reorganisation and the administration of justice. These were the ingredients of the recovery in royal authority after the civil war of Stephen's reign. Yet it is clear that, for much of the period covered by this book, Henry II was preoccupied with political and military endeavours which focused his attention on his territories across the Channel. In his first eight years as king, he did not have much time for detailed involvement in the governance of England. This does beg the question of the extent to which royal authority in the kingdom, and the administrative structures which underpinned it, were really in need of restoration. If orderly government could be so effectively imposed by a king who spent most of his time elsewhere, had England truly descended into 'Anarchy'? And if, as suggested above, Stephen had sought to govern the kingdom much as Henry I had done, what exactly was the task which faced Henry II? In seeking answers to these questions, it is appropriate to turn now to the governance of England during the reign of King Stephen. The chapter which follows is a lengthy one and most of it is concerned with the years before 1153. But if we are to understand the process of recovery after the civil war, it is essential to look in detail at the extent to which customary forms of government had broken down.

[54] Henry II's itinerary (above, n. 42) included periods in England in 1170, 1175–7, 1178–80 and 1184–5.

Chapter 2

THE GOVERNANCE OF ENGLAND DURING STEPHEN'S REIGN

INTRODUCTION

Stephen's reign is so commonly associated with 'Anarchy' that it is worth reminding ourselves that no contemporary chronicler used the word. There were plenty of alternatives – *furor, caedes, rapina, perturbatio, miseria, tragœdia*[1] – but *anarchia* was not familiar to twelfth-century Latinists.[2] Seventeenth- and eighteenth-century writers also covered the troubles of this period without using the term, and although Henry Hallam's *View of the State of Europe during the Middle Ages*, first published in 1818, contained a dismissive reference to the reign as one of 'anarchy and intestine war', it was not until the closing decades of the century that the word came to be applied with any consistency.[3] This was largely the result of the work published during the 1870s by Edward Freeman and William Stubbs. For Freeman, this was a time of 'utter anarchy' and 'utter wretchedness, such as we may safely say that England never saw before and never saw again'. Stubbs's *Constitutional History* bemoaned 'that feudal anarchy which had sometimes prevailed abroad but never before in England', while his *Select*

---

[1] E.g. HH, 724; OV, VI, 535; JH, 302; *Hist. Nov.*, 41; *Gesta Steph.*, 154.

[2] The word is not found in classical Latin, being derived from the Greek ἀναρχία, 'lack of a leader (archon)' (H. G. Liddell and R. Scott, *A Greek-English Lexicon*, rev. edn by H. S. Jones and R. Mackenzie, Oxford, 1968, 120). The earliest references in R. E. Latham, *Revised Medieval Latin Word-List* (London, 1965), 19, and in *Dictionary of Medieval Latin from British Sources*, Fascicule I, A-B (British Academy, 1975), 82, are dated to 1523.

[3] Thus, R. B[urton], *England's Monarchs* (London, 1694), 34, and for his identification as Nathaniel Crouch, *Dictionary of National Biography*, ed. L. Stephen and C. Lee (London, 1885–1903), III, 466; D. Hume, *The History of England from the Invasion of Julius Caesar to the Revolution of 1688* (new edn, London, 1778), I, 355–69; H. Hallam, *View of the State of Europe during the Middle Ages* (2nd edn, London, 1819), II, 436. Sharon Turner, *The History of England during the Middle Ages* (5th edn, London, 1853), I, 180–93, mentioned 'disquiet', 'calamities', 'public ruin', 'civil fury' and the 'evils of rapine and violence', but never 'anarchy'. The first edition of J. R. Green's *Short History of the English People* (London, 1874) told of an 'outburst of anarchy' following the news of Henry I's death, but subsequently described the events of 1138–42 and the atrocities committed by the barons as a 'chaos of misrule' (97, 99); in the 'new edition, thoroughly revised' of 1888, the first phrase was repeated, the second was changed to 'feudal anarchy' (101, 103).

Charters showed how a mixture of disputed succession, misgovernment and baronial opportunism led to 'war, and anarchy succeeding war'.[4] The 1880s and 1890s were the decades when Anarchism as a social and political philosophy enjoyed brief notoriety in Britain, spawning a series of minority-interest journals and influencing the work of, among others, William Morris and Oscar Wilde,[5] and it was now that Stephen's 'anarchy' was consistently awarded a capital 'A'. Thus, in discussions of danegeld 'waste' in the 1156 pipe roll, where Madox in 1711 had blamed devastation 'by the long intestine wars moved between [Stephen] and the Empress' and Eyton as late as 1880 had seen 'the results of the recent Civil War', J. H. Round in 1888 cited 'the terrible devastation in the wars of the Anarchy'.[6] Four years later, he subtitled his *Geoffrey de Mandeville* 'A Study of the Anarchy'. Then in 1903, H. W. C. Davis published his article on 'The Anarchy of Stephen's reign', and the phrase has been with us ever since.[7]

The danger with the term 'Anarchy' is that the headline, so to speak, writes the story, predetermining the verdict on Stephen's government before the evidence is examined in detail. The word is particularly unhelpful because it accommodates different shades of meaning. At one level, it is simply a shorthand for lawlessness and mayhem, the widespread sense of insecurity which Henry of Huntingdon had in mind in his verses on the year 1140: 'a glimpse of the Styx and a comparable plague'.[8] But the sense closest to that of the original Greek is 'absence of government',[9] which as a characterisation of Stephen's reign does not bear scrutiny. Some parts of the country ceased to be ruled in any practical sense by the king of England, and various expedients were introduced to supplement

[4] E. A. Freeman, *History of the Norman Conquest* (Oxford, 1867–79), v, 242; W. Stubbs, *The Constitutional History of England* (Oxford, 1874–8), I, 327; *Select Charters*, 22 (cf. 1st edn, 1870, 20). Stubbs also inserted 'Anarchy' as a marginal subheading to his edition of Gervase of Canterbury for the Rolls Series in 1879 (Gervase, I, 142). There is an illuminating analysis of the intellectual background to Stubbs's views in the introduction to D. B. Crouch, *The Reign of King Stephen* (forthcoming); Revd Professor David Crouch very kindly allowed me to read this in advance of publication.

[5] G. Woodcock, *Anarchism* (Harmondsworth, 1962), 414–28; M. Bevir, 'The rise of ethical Anarchism in Britain, 1885–1900', *HR*, 69 (1996), 143–65. I am most grateful to Dr Christopher Lewis for suggesting this context to me.

[6] T. Madox, *History and Antiquities of the Exchequer of England* (London, 1711), 479–80; R. W. Eyton, 'The Staffordshire pipe rolls', in *Staffs. Colls.*, I, 22; J. H. Round, 'Danegeld and the finance of Domesday', in *Domesday Studies*, ed. P. E. Dove (London, 1888–91), I, 112.

[7] J. H. Round, *Geoffrey de Mandeville: a Study of the Anarchy* (London, 1892); H. W. C. Davis, 'The Anarchy of Stephen's reign', *EHR*, 18 (1903), 630–41; cf. (most recently) King, *Anarchy*, with comment, 4.

[8] HH, 724–5: a more accurate, but less resounding, translation of the verses than that in T. Forester, *Henry of Huntingdon* (London, 1853), 273, with the memorable conclusion 'all hell's broke loose and chaos reigns'! [9] *Oxford English Dictionary* (2nd edn, Oxford, 1989), I, 438.

customary governmental methods, but whether in the name of the empress or Duke Henry, the king of Scots or his son, or one of the magnates, a measure of administrative control persisted, in a form recognisable as that of the previous reign. Moreover, among ecclesiastical and lay magnates alike, there was no serious challenge to the principle that England should rightfully be governed as a single kingdom.[10] Despite the fact that regional political divisions had become entrenched by the second half of Stephen's reign, bishops from the west of England as well as the south and east continued to attend his court: as John of Salisbury explained 'although individual dignitaries followed different lords' at this time, 'the church as a whole recognised only one'. He was 'the prince approved by the papacy'.[11] And despite the loss of royal control over the mints during the 1140s, most earls who took over responsibility for the production of coins continued to ensure that a king's name appeared upon them, if not 'Stephen' then 'William' or 'Henry'.[12] It was this enduring respect for royal authority, coupled with the widespread survival of the traditional fabric of government, which eased the task of restoring order after the war was over. Indeed, it was a task that Stephen himself was able to embark upon in the last months of his life.

Much of the blame for conveying an impression of governmental collapse must rest with the 'classic description of . . . anarchy' under the year 1137 in the *Anglo-Saxon Chronicle*. The stories here of torture, extortion and pillage, of violence against clergy and common people, directly associated with castle-building and the 'devils' who inhabited them, are truly appalling, and have sufficient in common with accounts from elsewhere in the country to withstand the charge that they reflect merely local, temporary, conditions.[13] For the monk of Peterborough,

---

[10] This did not preclude acceptance of Scottish rule in the northern shires, which for most of Stephen's reign meant that the frontier between the two kingdoms was effectively moved south. On this, see e.g. Barrow, 'The Scots and the North', and K. J. Stringer, 'State-building in twelfth-century Britain: David I king of Scots and northern England', in J. C. Appleby and P. Dalton, eds., *Government, Religion and Society in Northern England, 1000–1700* (Stroud, 1997), 40–62. The subject is also discussed below, in the third section of this chapter.

[11] *RRAN*, iii, nos. 183 (Jocelin bishop of Salisbury and Gilbert Foliot bishop of Hereford at London, 1148x49), 511 (Robert bishop of Exeter and Robert bishop of Hereford at London, 1147x48), 760 (Robert bishop of Hereford at London, 1147x48); *Historia Pontificalis of John of Salisbury*, ed. M. Chibnall (OMT, 1986), 47–9.

[12] E. J. King, 'The anarchy of King Stephen's reign', *TRHS*, 5th ser., 34 (1984), 133–53 (at 150–1); M. Blackburn, 'Coinage and currency', in King, *Anarchy*, 145–205 (at 189–90). The discovery since these papers were written of coins minted in the name of Robert earl of Gloucester (E. J. King, 'Economic development in the early twelfth century', in R. Britnell and J. Hatcher, eds., *Progress and Problems in Medieval England* (Cambridge, 1996), 1–22 (at 16)) weakens but does not overturn this argument; other earls whose names (possibly) appear on coins are Patrick of Wiltshire and Robert of Leicester: see below, n. 259.

[13] *ASC*, 198–200; King, *Anarchy*, 1; C. W. Hollister, 'The aristocracy', in King, *Anarchy*, 37–66 (at 49–51).

writing in Henry II's reign, the root cause of all the misery which 'we suffered nineteen years for our sins' was not the civil war but the lamentable inadequacies of Stephen's government: 'when the traitors understood that he was a mild man, and gentle and good, and did not exact the full penalties of the law, they perpetrated every enormity'.[14] This view of Stephen's reign – that an outbreak of disruptive violence resulted from misgovernment by a weak and worthless king – was common among writers at work under his successors. It suited Henry II's purposes to present Stephen as a usurper who presided over uniform 'unpeace', so that concessions and property transfers belonging to his reign could be deemed to have no validity.[15] Accordingly, the troubles under Stephen lasted for the whole of the reign, with a breakdown in law and order following hard upon his accession to the throne.[16]

There was a rather different emphasis, however, among some of those writing during the course of Stephen's reign. In the *Historia Novella*, William of Malmesbury saw the atrocities as a vivid illustration not of weak government but of 'the brutalities of war'.[17] Orderic Vitalis, though more concerned with the sufferings in Normandy, observed that it was conspiracy and treason which plunged the kingdom into turmoil, 'bringing down ruin on the people'.[18] The *Gesta Stephani* repeatedly associated plunder and devastation with some form of military activity for or against the king, with those living in the vicinity of castles particularly vulnerable.[19] The point here is that several witnesses to events saw the civil war itself, rather than ineffective or non-existent government, as the principal reason for the troubles through which they lived. Obviously the two were intimately connected: the ability of Stephen and his officials to administer the country – or that of alternative rulers to do so – was badly affected by the prolonged military struggle, as local political and tenurial rivalries endemic in landed society found an opportunity to express themselves not only in armed conflict but also in resistance to higher authority. But once the civil war ended, so did many of the problems associated with it, for a king whose right to the throne was undisputed could call upon an administrative system which had survived sufficiently to need repair, but not wholesale reconstruction. The task of repair was to

---

[14] *ASC*, 198–9.

[15] Newburgh, I, 103 (The king ordered 'that all royal demesnes alienated through the weakness of King Stephen' should be surrendered 'for the charters of an intruder ought not to prejudice the rights of a legitimate ruler'.) Cf. below, ch. 3, n. 274.

[16] *ASC*, 198–200; HH, 774; *Chronicle of Battle Abbey*, 212–13 ('King Stephen succeeded, and in his time justice seldom prevailed . . . After King Stephen's death, the famous King Henry succeeded, grandson of the earlier Henry. He brought back the times of his grandfather').

[17] *Hist. Nov.*, 40–2.   [18] OV, VI, 494–5.

[19] *Gesta Steph.*, e.g. 94, 138, 144, 152–4, 198; all these references come from that part of the work believed to have been written during the course of Stephen's reign (*ibid.*, xviii–xxi).

span Stephen's last ten months as king and Henry II's first ten years.

Most of this chapter is concerned with the effectiveness of the government conducted in England, at various times, on behalf of King Stephen, the Angevin leaders, the king of Scots and his son, and some of the magnates. It attempts to identify those parts of the country subject to their respective authorities, relying on the testimony of coins, charters and chronicles which are, indeed, in broad agreement in so far as the regional pattern implied by one type of evidence is largely confirmed by the others. There are, however, two important qualifications to be made before this analysis is embarked upon. First, as already implied, any attempt to explain royal or Angevin control over the Church in terms of regional identity quickly falls down, for ecclesiastical leaders themselves recognised the importance of acting in concert.[20] Despite the withdrawal of royal influence over episcopal elections for most of the reign, which meant that local candidates were frequently installed, the bishops normally acted as a cohesive force, responsive to the leadership of the papal legate Henry of Winchester between 1139 and 1143 and thereafter of Theobald archbishop of Canterbury. Gilbert Foliot, for example, although a supporter of the Angevin cause, swore fealty to Stephen apparently on Theobald's instructions, following his consecration as bishop of Hereford; his kinship with Roger earl of Hereford did not prevent him from imposing an interdict on the diocese and recommending stern measures against the earl personally, on account of various acts of sacrilege committed by him.[21] Although the interdict promulgated by Theobald in September 1148 was ignored everywhere except in his own diocese of Canterbury, the bishops acted together in backing the archbishop's brave stance against Stephen's demands for the coronation of his son Eustace four years later.[22] The capacity of the bishops to transcend political and regional loyalties was valued by magnates negotiating *conventiones* during the civil war, and provided an essential safeguard for the peace settlement of 1153.[23] The second qualification concerns the degree of control exercised by one authority or another within a shire. Frequent

---

[20] *Councils and Synods and Other Documents relating to the English Church*, I, ed. D. Whitelock, M. Brett, C. N. L. Brooke (Oxford, 1981), ii, 803–4 (extract from canon 17 ascribed to the legatine council of 1143): 'God is one, and unless the pastors of the church are at one in him they will be unable to deliver justice properly for their subjects'.

[21] *Historia Pontificalis*, 47–9; GF, *Letters*, nos. 77, 93–6; Saltman, *Theobald*, 30, 109–10; D. M. Knowles, *Episcopal Colleagues of Archbishop Thomas Becket* (Cambridge, 1951), 38–43.

[22] Gervase, I, 135–6, 150; *Historia Pontificalis*, 45–6; HH, 758; Saltman, *Theobald*, 28–9, 36–8.

[23] F. M. Stenton, *The First Century of English Feudalism* (2nd edn, Oxford, 1961), 254; C. J. Holdsworth, 'War and peace in the twelfth century: the reign of Stephen reconsidered', in B. P. McGuire, ed., *War and Peace in the Middle Ages* (Copenhagen, 1987), 67–93 (esp. 84–6); E. J. King, 'Dispute settlement in Anglo-Norman England', *ANS*, 14 (1992), 115–30.

reference will be made in forthcoming pages to writs and charters addressed to shire officials, and to grants and confirmations of property identified, for convenience, by the shires in which they were located. But it is important to recognise that in so far as this evidence suggests some influence within a given shire, it does not mean control over the whole of it. There was hardly a shire in England where there was not some violent conflict during the course of the civil war; by the mid-1140s, most were divided communities with rival allegiances owed to king and empress. To present evidence of Stephen's government operating in Kent, for example, or Empress Matilda's in Wiltshire, is not to claim that every landholder in the shire would heed their commands. A good illustration of this is found in the meeting of the shire courts of Norfolk and Suffolk, which took place in the bishop of Norwich's garden under the presidency of Stephen's steward William Martel, probably in 1150. Although the king's controlling interest in the case is apparent, and is indicative of his exercise of authority in Norfolk and Suffolk, the assembly was composed almost entirely of men known to be his active supporters in the shires: there was no sign, for example, of Hugh Bigod, whom the empress recognised as her earl.[24] Royal government was being maintained in identifiable form, established institutions still functioned, but in circumstances of divided allegiance.

THE KING'S GOVERNMENT

The administrative system in England which passed from Henry I to Stephen in 1135 has been admirably explained by Judith Green.[25] At the centre, the royal *curia*, the king's household and close companions, was periodically augmented by large assemblies of magnates, the councils at which decisions of great moment in secular and ecclesiastical affairs were announced. The royal household, as described in the *Constitutio Domus Regis* which probably dates to the very beginning of Stephen's reign, comprised five departments. Two of these, the buttery and the steward's department, retained an essentially domestic role in provisioning the household. A third, the constabulary and marshalsea, supervised the household knights and specially recruited mercenaries (omitted from the *Constitutio*) and also embraced the hunting staff. The remaining departments had both outgrown the royal household. The chancery and chapel,

---

[24] *Lawsuits*, I, no. 331. For those attending, see *RRAN*, III, nos. 138, 177, 307, etc. (Reginald de Warenne); 35, 139, 201, etc. (Fulk d'Oilli); 427, 822 (Hugh fitz Eudo); 176, 183, 192, etc. (William de Chesney); 150 (Henry de Rye); 212 (Jordan de Blosseville); 34, 913 (Richard de Valderi). [25] Green, *Henry I*, esp. chs. 2–6.

covering scribes and chaplains, furnished a secretariat not only for the peripatetic king but also for the chief minister, Roger bishop of Salisbury at the Winchester treasury. The financial department, the chamber, included a chamberlain who travelled with the king, but there were at least two other chamberlains, plus a treasurer, whose duties spanned household and treasury.[26]

As for the king's finances themselves, he derived his income partly from the farms of boroughs and demesne manors – mostly grouped together into the 'sheriff's farm' of each county – partly from taxation, such as scutage, danegeld and various aids and *dona* (although it is possible that danegeld was not being levied in the last years of Henry I), and partly from what Green has called 'profits of jurisdiction', embracing customary payments by tenants, income from vacant bishoprics and abbeys, sums arising from the administration of royal justice, and miscellaneous offerings for the king's favour, including purchase of office. The money was rendered in silver pennies produced (towards the end of Henry I's reign) at about twenty-four mints, some as far afield as Carlisle and Launceston, the moneyers having to purchase their dies in London from the king's die-engraver as well as making other payments.[27] Financial accounts themselves were audited at the Easter and Michaelmas sessions of the exchequer and recorded annually in the pipe rolls; Winchester, home of the treasury, seems to have been the usual place for the exchequer to meet.[28]

Meanwhile, in the field of justice, the king dealt with the most serious crimes (the 'crown pleas'), with transgressions against his own rights, including royal demesnes and forests, and with cases between his immediate vassals, as well as having an appellate jurisdiction which brought a wide range of civil actions to his attention. He might also intervene either to protect a favoured individual or institution from impleading, or to order a hearing in an inferior court.[29] The availability of royal justice had been greatly increased in the second half of Henry I's reign by the despatch of itinerant justices to act on the king's behalf in different parts of

---

[26] 'Constitutio domus regis', in *Dialogus*, xlix–lii, 129–35.

[27] P. Nightingale, 'Some London moneyers and reflections on the organization of English mints in the eleventh and twelfth centuries', *Numismatic Chronicle* CXLII (1982), 34–50; Nightingale, '"The king's profit": trends in English mint and monetary policy in the eleventh and twelfth centuries', in N. J. Mayhew and P. Spufford, eds., *Later Medieval Mints: Organization, Administration and Techniques* (BAR International Series 389, Oxford, 1988), 61–75; M. Blackburn, 'Coinage and currency under Henry I: a review', *ANS*, 13 (1991), 49–81, and 'Coinage and currency' in King, *Anarchy*, 151–9.

[28] C. W. Hollister, 'The rise of administrative kingship: Henry I', in *Monarchy, Magnates and Institutions in the Anglo-Norman World* (London, 1986), 223–45 (esp. 232–5).

[29] *PR 31 Hen. I*, 11, 14, 18, 24 etc. (fines 'ne placitet de terra sua'); *RRAN*, II, nos: 530, 537, 577, 581, etc.; *Royal Writs*, nos. 6, 7, 10, 161, 164, etc.

the country; individuals could also be given special judicial commissions, and some shires had resident justices.[30]

All this was underpinned by a local governmental system which in its essentials was already well-established before the Norman Conquest, that of shires and their administrative subdivisions the hundreds (or in the north, wapentakes). Their courts, which met at regular intervals, retained an important local jurisdiction despite the increased activity of royal justices, and the shire was the basic unit for the accounting of the king's revenues, most of which were levied by the sheriff. There was not, of course, absolute uniformity in local government: some hundreds and wapentakes were in private hands, which meant in practice that a local lord enjoyed the profits of the relevant court, the royal forests were protected by their own custodians and laws, and there were various 'liberties', such as Cheshire, which the king's officials did not normally enter.[31] But by the standards of contemporary Europe, England – at least England as far north as the Mersey and the Humber beyond which more variable arrangements applied, – was a well-ordered kingdom, with a highly developed administration both in the centre and in the localities. The extent to which all this was undone as a result of the political crisis which followed Henry I's death is the issue which we may now turn to address.

Stephen's successful *coup* of December 1135 almost certainly owed a good deal to Henry bishop of Winchester, who would have looked forward to an era of Church–crown cooperation largely under his own control;[32] there was probably also an expectation that he would be a 'magnates' king', sympathetic to the aspirations of those from whose ranks he had emerged. Accordingly, in his 'Oxford charter of liberties' of April 1136, apparently a second 'coronation charter' which renewed promises made orally on that occasion, Stephen made various concessions to the Church and also addressed some of the lay barons' concerns. He surrendered the forests which Henry I had created, annulled illegal exactions imposed by sheriffs and other officials, and undertook to observe 'ancient and lawful customs' in the imposition of financial penalties.[33] Additionally, he bowed to pressure in restoring minting rights to boroughs which had lost the privilege as a result of reforms by Henry I, probably in 1125: no fewer than nineteen of the twenty-nine mints

---

[30] W. T. Reedy, 'The origins of the general eyre in the reign of Henry I', *Speculum*, 41 (1966), 688–724.

[31] For recent discussion of Cheshire's administrative position in the Anglo-Norman period, see J. W. Alexander, 'The alleged palatinates of Norman England', *Speculum*, 51 (1981), 17–27; B. E. Harris, 'The earldom of Chester: 1070–1301', in *VCH Cheshire*, II, 1–8.

[32] H. A. Cronne, *The Reign of Stephen, 1135–54* (London, 1970), 113–34.

[33] *RRAN*, III, no. 271; HH, 704–8.

suppressed before 1135 reopened to produce coins of Stephen's type 1, at least nine of them in the earliest years of the reign.[34] These seem to have been deliberately intended as popular measures to secure support for the new regime. But they do not tell the whole story, for Stephen's general intention at the beginning of his reign was to continue, not reverse, the administrative traditions of his predecessor.

It was in this spirit that his coronation charter undertook not only to maintain 'all the liberties and good laws' which Henry had granted, but also the 'good laws and good customs enjoyed in the time of king Edward', an echo of a similar promise made by his predecessor at the outset of his reign. Concessions to the Church, enshrined in the 'Oxford charter of liberties' in April 1136, had also been anticipated by Henry I in 1100.[35] The old king's chief minister, Roger bishop of Salisbury, a longstanding opponent of Matilda's succession, seems to have played a leading role in Stephen's progress to the throne;[36] he presumably expected to continue in office, and did so until his spectacular fall in June 1139. More than this, he secured promotion for two 'nephews', Roger le Poer as chancellor and Athelhelm as treasurer, doubtless as the price of supporting Stephen's *coup,* so entrenching his family in the new king's central administration even more effectively than he had done in Henry I's.[37] The compilation of the *Constitutio Domus Regis* itself suggests that Stephen intended to maintain his predecessor's household establishment, and of those in attendance upon him before June 1139, all four constables, the marshal, both chamberlains, a butler, two of the stewards and four of the scribes had previously served Henry I in these capacities.[38] Stephen's personal style contrasted with that of Henry I – he did not have the latter's commanding voice, and seems to have found it difficult to make the transition from count to king in his dealings with his barons[39] – but the fact that so many of the old king's servants survived in office helped to ensure continuity in administrative practice. Concessions on forests and minting rights notwithstanding, this was a regime initially intent on carrying on where the old one had left off. If proof were needed, it came towards the end of 1136 when Stephen went hunting at Brampton (Huntingdonshire) and impleaded his barons over forest offences. Henry

---

[34] Blackburn, 'Coinage and currency' in King, *Anarchy*, 153–9.

[35] *Select Charters*, 117–19; *RRAN*, III, nos. 270–1; J. Bradbury, 'The early years of the reign of Stephen', in D. Williams, ed., *England in the Twelfth Century* (Woodbridge, 1990), 17–30.

[36] E. J. Kealey, *Roger of Salisbury, Viceroy of England* (Berkeley, California, 1972), 154–9; C. W. Hollister, 'The Anglo-Norman succession debate of 1126: prelude to Stephen's Anarchy', *Journal of Medieval History*, I (1975), 19–39.

[37] *RRAN*, II, ix–x; *ibid.*, III, ix–x, xix; Kealey, *Roger of Salisbury*, 159, 272–4; Green, *Henry I*, 160, 167, 263.

[38] White, 'Continuity', 119, n. 9, and generally, 118–29, on the subject matter of this and the next paragraph.   [39] HH, 732; *Gesta Steph.*, 10, 22.

of Huntingdon claimed this as an early instance of his readiness to break promises, and implied that his levy of danegeld was another example: if so, the new king was demonstrating a determination to revive his predecessor's practices, whatever he might have sworn at the outset.[40]

The general picture of royal government in the first three and a half years of Stephen's reign is that, in financial and in judicial affairs, it was largely business as usual. Although we have no pipe rolls from Stephen's reign – those which existed having presumably been lost or destroyed along with all but one of Henry I's[41] – there is no reason to envisage an immediate collapse in the normal workings of the financial machinery. Several sheriffs seem to have continued in office,[42] presumably raising the king's revenues and accounting for them at the exchequer in the manner to which they were accustomed; the revolts of Baldwin de Redvers in Devon in 1136 and of William fitz Alan, sheriff of Shropshire, in 1138 may well have had a disruptive effect on the king's receipt of income from these shires,[43] but Stephen dealt swiftly with them both. As for the coinage, although several new or revived mints were involved in the production of Stephen's type 1 pennies, the weight of these coins compared very favourably with those of Henry I's last issue, at least until the early 1140s. Stephen's original intention seems to have been to maintain the policy of Henry I, introduced in 1125, of allowing coins of the same type to circulate long term, rather than declare a recoinage every few years, and minting of his type 1 coins has been interpreted as continuing until c.1145. Within this type, those showing the earliest inscription +STIFNE REX – which we can confidently regard as in production before 1139 – were minted in at least twenty-seven places, from York in the north to Cardiff in south Wales and Launceston in the south-west.[44] Meanwhile, those actually or potentially involved in lawsuits looked to the king to safeguard their interests. Among his writs – couched in similar

---

[40] HH, 704, 708.

[41] For discussion of possible reasons for the deliberate safe-keeping of the 1130 pipe roll, see J. A. Green, '"Praeclarum et magnificum antiquitatis monumentum": the earliest surviving Pipe Roll', *BIHR*, 55 (1982), 1–17.

[42] J. A. Green, *English Sheriffs to 1154* (P.R.O. Handbook 24, London, 1990), 13, 20 n. 49; cf. Green, 'Financing Stephen's war', *ANS*, 14 (1992), esp. 91–2.

[43] William fitz Alan's shrievalty of Shropshire is mentioned in OV, VI, 520. Baldwin de Redvers is not known to have been sheriff of Devon, at the time of his revolt or otherwise, but for the possibility cf. Green, *Sheriffs*, 35; *Charters of the Redvers Family and the Earldom of Devon, 1090–1217*, ed. R. Bearman (Devon and Cornwall Record Society, 1994), 6; Bearman, 'Baldwin de Redvers: some aspects of a baronial career in the reign of King Stephen', *ANS*, 18 (1996), 19–46 (at 23).

[44] Blackburn, 'Coinage and currency', in King, *Anarchy*, esp. 152–61, 194–200, although there is no consensus on the length of time during which Stephen's type 1 continued in production; cf. G. C. Boon, *Coins of the Anarchy, 1135–54* (Cardiff, 1988), 17 and M. M. Archibald, 'Dating Stephen's first type', *BNJ*, 61 (1992 for 1991), 9–21, where a shorter period is favoured.

phraseology to those of his predecessor – were several which prohibited or curtailed impleading;[45] he continued Henry I's practice of hearing cases in person, and royal justices acted on his behalf in all parts of the kingdom, from Kent through the Midlands to the Welsh and Scottish borders.[46]

Accordingly, it seems fair to say that, in this first phase of the reign, Stephen governed England substantially as Henry I had done, with a continuation of the financial and judicial systems and with many of the same personnel in both the central and the local administrations. In Wales and in Normandy his authority was seriously weakened by an inadequate response to the aggression of political rivals,[47] but in England his effective control was comparable to that enjoyed by Henry I towards the end of his reign, except that successive treaties of Durham in the early months of 1136 and 1139 ceded Carlisle and Northumberland respectively to the Scots, and outbreaks of localised revolt, mainly in the west, posed temporary problems.[48] His appointment of earls – possibly as many as twelve in the period before June 1139[49] – is one important aspect in which a contrast with Henry I's approach to government seems apparent, but it has been argued elsewhere, and will be suggested later in this chapter, that many of these appointments were originally intended to be honorific, and that their impact on local government in the early years of the reign is liable to be exaggerated.[50]

In his relations with the English Church, the king obviously wished to be conciliatory, and the three episcopal appointments of 1136–8 seem to have owed more to his brother Henry bishop of Winchester (Robert of Lewes to Bath), the local cathedral chapter (Robert Warelwast to Exeter) and the papal legate Alberic (John of Séez to Rochester) than to the exercise of traditional royal patronage. The legate also had a major part to play in the promotion of Theobald abbot of Bec to the archbishopric of Canterbury.[51] Yet the grant of 'liberties' to the Church at the outset of the reign was not in itself an innovation; Stephen was careful to qualify his concessions 'saving my royal and lawful dignity' and he continued to exercise jurisdiction over ecclesiastical disputes,[52] to secure the election of

[45] *RRAN*, III, nos. 133, 288, 350, 386, 886; cf. *Royal Writs*, nos. 161–4 and fines in the 1130 pipe roll 'ne placitet de terra sua' (above, n. 29).

[46] *RRAN*, III, nos. 134, 143, 257, 318, 382, 466, 506, 637, 656, 752, 883, 885; *Lawsuits*, I, no. 291, cf. nos. 163d, 168, 177, 179–81, etc.

[47] Chibnall, 'Normandy' and D. B. Crouch, 'The march and the Welsh kings', in King, *Anarchy*, 96–102, 256–73.

[48] E.g. Davis, *Stephen*, 19–24; K. J. Stringer, *The Reign of Stephen* (London, 1993), 14–18, 28–32.

[49] Davis, *Stephen*, 125–41. [50] White, 'Continuity', esp. 124–9, 133.

[51] F. Barlow, *The English Church, 1066–1154* (London, 1979), 92–5; Saltman, *Theobald*, 9–13.

[52] *RRAN*, III, no. 656.

his own nominees to important abbeys[53] and to restrict the number of bishops free to attend a papal council.[54] In this as in other respects, therefore, Stephen endeavoured to govern along the lines of his predecessor – while retaining, it might be added, good relations with most Church leaders, including Pope Innocent II and his legate Alberic.

The arrest at Stephen's court at Oxford in June 1139 of Roger bishop of Salisbury and his nephew Alexander bishop of Lincoln, soon followed by the capture of another nephew, the fugitive Nigel bishop of Ely, used to be seen as a cataclysmic end both to the smooth running of the royal administration and to the spirit of harmony between king and Church.[55] This interpretation was very effectively challenged by Kenji Yoshitake, who was able to demonstrate that between the arrest of the bishops and the battle of the Lincoln most of the episcopate, including Alexander, continued to give Stephen their support, and that much of the governmental routine carried on. Even he, however, was reluctant to dismiss the significance of the episode altogether: 'nobody can deny the impact of the arrest on the royal administration, and it is difficult to find positive evidence for the active continuity of the administration during this period'.[56] It is worth looking at its consequences again, before carrying this analysis of royal government forward through the 1140s and on to the peace settlement of 1153.

From June 1139 Roger bishop of Salisbury ceased to be the king's chief minister, and no successor was appointed. Of the 'nephews' whose promotions he had secured, Roger le Poer was arrested with him, and succeeded as chancellor by Philip d'Harcourt, while Athelhelm appears to have lost the treasurership; if he was replaced in the office, we do not know by whom.[57] The change of personnel signalled a shift of political power in favour of the Beaumonts, for the new chancellor was a protégé of Waleran of Meulan, one of those who had counselled Stephen against Bishop Roger and his associates prior to their arrest.[58] In adopting a new seal, for which the royal clerk Baldric had apparently been appointed keeper by the end of 1140, Stephen himself was apparently signalling a

---

[53] Stephen's illegitimate son Gervase and another relative, Robert, became abbots of Westminster and Winchcombe respectively during 1138 (D. Knowles, C. N. L. Brooke, V. C. M. London, eds., *The Heads of Religious Houses, England and Wales, 940–1216* (Cambridge, 1972), 77–9.

[54] Archbishop Theobald was accompanied to the second Lateran Council early in 1139 by only four bishops and four abbots, because Stephen did not wish to send any more on account of the state of his kingdom: RH, 176–7.   [55] Stubbs, *Constitutional History*, I, 326; *Select Charters*, 22, 135.

[56] K. Yoshitake, 'The arrest of the bishops in 1139 and its consequences', *Journal of Medieval History*, 14 (1988), 97–114 (quotation at 104).   [57] *RRAN*, III, x, xix, xxi.

[58] *Gesta Steph.*, 72–6; OV, VI, 530–4; cf. *Hist. Nov.*, 72–4; Kealey, *Roger of Salisbury*, 180–9; Crouch, *Beaumont Twins*, 43–5.

break with the former regime.[59] But while it is likely that the changes at the centre were mirrored in some of the localities, through measures such as the appointment of Beaumont associates as sheriffs, this cannot be demonstrated.[60] And despite the upheaval in personnel, there is no reason to suppose major disruption as a result. Four of the king's scribes appear to have worked for him both before and after the arrests, their styles and the formulae they followed showing no discernible changes as a result.[61] Stephen continued to be able to call on loyal administrators, among them his chamberlain Aubrey II de Vere who mounted a stout defence of the king's actions at the legatine council summoned to Winchester in August 1139.[62] Another was Roger archdeacon of Fecamp, who may have had financial expertise as a former treasurer of Normandy.[63] If the fall of the bishop of Salisbury had a detrimental effect upon the working of the exchequer, this is certainly not apparent from Stephen's grant to the canons of Huntingdon of his rent from the local mills, which dates to the period June 1139 to March 1140; the sum involved, 40 shillings, was duly entered in the pipe rolls from the first year of Henry II's reign, and may well, therefore, have been continuously recorded.[64]

It is difficult to assess the real impact of the arrest of the bishops, since Empress Matilda's invasion followed so soon afterwards. There is little doubt, however, that it was the empress's arrival, in September 1139, which was by far the more important setback to Stephen's government. Among his household administrators, one of the stewards, Humphrey II de Bohun, two constables, Miles of Gloucester and Brian fitz Count, and the marshal, John fitz Gilbert, deserted to Matilda almost immediately, and were not it seems replaced.[65] In the months which followed, the empress established an alternative administration based upon Bristol and Gloucester[66] and this in turn deprived the king of authority in, and

---

[59] *RRAN*, III, no. 478 and pp. xi, xv–xvii, but with amendments by T. A. Heslop in 'Seals', *English Romanesque Art, 1066–1200*, ed. G. Zarnecki, J. Holt and T. Holland (London, 1984), 303, accepted in Davis, *Stephen*, 86, n. 34.

[60] Green, *Sheriffs*, 12–13, 25–90.

[61] Scriptores XIV, XVIII, XIX, XX: Bishop, *Scriptores Regis*, 12–33; *RRAN*, III, xiv–xv; *ibid.*, IV, esp. 10–12; Cronne, *Reign of Stephen*, 217–18.   [62] *Hist. Nov.*, 30–4; *RRAN*, III, xix.

[63] Haskins, *Norman Institutions*, 110, but this is unproven (J. A. Green, 'Unity and disunity in the Anglo-Norman state', *HR*, 62 (1989), 120, n. 24.); his appearances in witness lists are frequently in association with the successive chancellors, Roger and Philip (*RRAN*, III, xii and nos. 27, 74, 189, 278, 468, 526, etc.). Yoshitake, 'Arrest of the bishops', 105–6, suggests that he was put in charge of the royal finances after the fall of the treasurer Athelhelm, but there is no direct evidence of this (cf. Green, 'Financing Stephen's war', 111).

[64] *RRAN*, III, no. 410; *RBE*, II, 653 (an allowance of 20 shillings for half the year ending at Michaelmas 1155); *PR2H*, 13, etc.

[65] *RRAN*, III, xviii–xxi, xxxi–xxxii. It is possible that John Marshal's allegiance was ambivalent between 1138 and 1140: D. B. Crouch, *William Marshal: Court, Career and Chivalry in the Angevin Empire, 1147–1219* (London, 1990), 12–13.   [66] Chibnall, *Matilda*, 81–4.

revenues from, the surrounding area. It is impossible to trace the transfer of power in the region with any precision, but (with rare exceptions) Stephen no longer addressed writs and charters after 1139 to his royal officials in a block of shires bounded by Shropshire to the north, Wiltshire and Dorset to the south-east and Cornwall to the west.[67] Among the mints responsible for Stephen's type 1 coins, those at Gloucester, Launceston, Shrewsbury and Wareham are not known to have used the latest dies (bearing the legend +STIEFNE) and so may not have been producing for the king by the early 1140s, although other mints in this region, including Exeter, Hereford and Wilton, seem to have carried on.[68] An indication of changing perceptions is to be found among charters in favour of religious communities. Both Salisbury Cathedral and Shrewsbury Abbey evidently abandoned the king as a source of confirmations after 1139, and subsequently turned to the Angevin leaders instead.[69] Hereford Cathedral appears not to have received a charter from Stephen after 1138, and the same is probably true of Bath.[70] Out of sixteen royal writs and charters known to have been issued during the reign in favour of Gloucester Abbey, none can be shown to belong to the period between the empress's invasion and the peace settlement of 1153.[71]

Elsewhere, however, the king's intervention continued to be sought. In the interval between the 'arrest of the bishops' and his own capture at Lincoln, he heard a sworn recognition at Oxford securing various rents and a fair in the borough for St Frideswide's Priory, safeguarded St Peter's Hospital, York, against impleading until a new archbishop was consecrated, and issued confirmations in favour of Alcester Abbey (Warwickshire), Ely Cathedral (Cambridgeshire) and Eynsham Abbey (Oxfordshire).[72] Yet a general review of the charter evidence datable with some confidence to late 1139 or 1140, and hence to the early months of civil war following the empress's invasion, leaves an unmistakable impression of growing disruption, even in that part of England which still looked to the king. He ordered the restoration of property in Essex, Hampshire and Wiltshire to Salisbury Cathedral and the canons of St Martin le Grand, London, following disseisins committed by his elder brother Theobald count of Blois.[73] A royal writ addressed to Hugh and Stephen de Scalers,

---

[67] Exceptions which apparently postdate 1139 include *RRAN*, III, nos. 1 (to Devon and Dorset), 344 (to Bristol) and 361 (to Gloucestershire); cf. nos. 192, 460, relating to property in Gloucestershire and Shropshire respectively. [68] Blackburn, 'Coinage and currency', in King, *Anarchy*, 158–60.

[69] *RRAN*, III, nos. 784–96, 819–21.   [70] *Ibid.*, III, nos. 382–5, 45–9.

[71] *Ibid.*, III, nos. 345–61 (discounting the first in the series as spurious). On the other hand, Stephen issued an important charter for the Gloucestershire abbey of Cirencester as late as Christmas 1139 (*ibid.*, III, no. 189). Cf. Yoshitake, 'Arrest of the bishops', 100, for the apparent withdrawal from Stephen's court between 1139 and 1141 of the bishops of Bath and Worcester.

[72] *RRAN*, III, nos. 640, 991, 16, 262, 293.   [73] *Ibid.*, III, nos. 543, 790.

ordering that they restore a 'farm' taken from the monks of Ely, had to be followed by a second one to Geoffrey II de Mandeville, who was to constrain them until they obeyed.[74] The bishop of Coventry may never have come into possession of the church of Wolverhampton, granted to him by Stephen 'ill-advisedly' (*inconsulte*) and subsequently restored to Worcester Cathedral; by the mid-1140s it was in the hands of neither, being controlled by various unnamed laymen.[75] These are the signs that civil war was beginning to undermine the effectiveness of royal government.

Stephen's defeat and capture at the battle of Lincoln, on 2 February 1141, turned a difficult situation into a catastrophe. He remained a prisoner, initially at Gloucester but mostly at Bristol, until his release on 1 November. The formalities involved in exchanging hostages took several more days, and it was another month before a legatine council at Winchester on 7 December, presided over by Stephen's brother Henry of Blois, formally restored the allegiance of the Church.[76] With his queen, he was ceremonially crowned by Archbishop Theobald at Canterbury during the Christmas festival.[77] He was therefore physically a captive for nine months, and royal authority might be regarded as in abeyance for at least ten. In the meantime, many of his supporters among the magnates, including Waleran of Meulan earl of Worcester, Roger earl of Warwick and Geoffrey II de Mandeville earl of Essex, came to terms with the Angevins,[78] and several household officials did likewise. The clerk Roger de Fecamp, three scribes (nos. XIV, XVIII and XIX), the constable Robert d'Oilli, the chamberlain William de Pont de l'Arche and the steward Robert Malet all seem to have left Stephen's service about this time, and do not appear to have worked for him after his release.[79] Any semblance of 'royal justice' presumably disappeared: the king was unable to authorise it, the empress was preoccupied in negotiations to secure her own position. Although she made several grants and confirmations during the year, there is no sign of her initiating any pleas.[80] On the other hand, probably at

[74] *Ibid.*, III, nos. 264–5.
[75] *Ibid.*, III, nos. 452–3, 962, 969; D. Styles, 'The early history of the king's chapels in Staffordshire', *Birmingham Arch. Soc. Trans and Proc.*, 60 (1936), 56–95; *Cartulary of Worcester Cathedral Priory*, ed. R. R. Darlington (P. R. Society, 1968), xlviii–xlix, nos. 263, 266–7.
[76] The fullest account of circumstances surrounding Stephen's release is in *Hist. Nov.*, 65–70.
[77] Gervase, I, 123–4, 524–7.
[78] For discussion of the dates of defections, see e.g. Crouch, *Beaumont Twins*, 50–1; Davis, *Stephen*, 131–6, 159.
[79] *RRAN*, III, xii, xiv–xv, xviii–xx, nos. 274, 897; *Gesta Steph.*, 116. In addition, Aubrey III de Vere, son of Stephen's chamberlain who died in 1140 or the first half of 1141 (cf. Round, *Geoffrey de Mandeville*, 81), received his father's office from the empress in July 1141 (*RRAN*, III, no. 634); here and elsewhere, the numbering of successive Aubreys de Vere follows that in Green, *Henry I*, 276.)   [80] Below, nn. 155–7.

Easter 1141, she renewed Stephen's gift to the canons of Oseney of 5s. 5¾d. from the farm of Oxford, and duly addressed a writ of *computate* to the barons of the exchequer. During the summer, she ordered the payment of annual pensions from the farms of London and Winchester to the nuns of Fontevrault and monks of Tiron respectively, at the customary exchequer terms of Easter and Michaelmas.[81] The empress was clearly doing what she could to ensure not only that the beneficiaries were properly rewarded but that borough farms would continue to be accounted for. But whether or not they were, and whether or not there was an exchequer session at any time in 1141, must remain a matter for conjecture.

Ten months without recognisable royal authority clearly opened the way for alternative governmental arrangements to be put in place in various parts of the country. To these we shall return. As for Stephen, at the end of the year he resumed control of an administration which, from now until the peace settlement of 1153, operated over a much reduced area of the kingdom. Coins of Stephen's type 2, probably minted in the mid- to late 1140s, and their successors of type 6, the last 'official' issue before the peace settlement, were of good weight and based on dies duly sent out from London. But only seventeen mints are at present known to have produced type 2 coins, all (with the exception of Bedford and Oxford) in the south-east and East Anglia. The same is true of the twenty mints from which type 6 coins have been found, except that Bedford, Stamford and Northampton form a small 'Midlands' group. In the whole of northern and western England, and in the north-west Midlands, where over half Stephen's type 1 mints had been located, not a single coin of types 2 and 6 is known to have been produced.[82] As for royal writs and charters, if one confines attention to those in favour of religious houses which can be firmly dated to the years between the battle of Lincoln and the peace settlement, and plots the beneficiaries' geographical distribution, one finds the king's authority being invoked in a broad band of country from Yorkshire in the north through Lincolnshire, Nottinghamshire, Huntingdonshire, Cambridgeshire and East Anglia to the south-eastern shires, including Hampshire, Berkshire, Oxfordshire and Buckinghamshire; beyond this, there are only isolated cases, all single grants or confirmations, relating to churches in Gloucestershire, Shropshire, Staffordshire, Warwickshire and Worcestershire.[83] Within the same period, the king addressed royal officials (albeit often anonymously) in

---

[81] *RRAN*, III, nos. 628, 328, 899.
[82] Blackburn, 'Coinage and currency', in King, *Anarchy*, 154–7, 162–5, with ?Rochester added to the type 6 mints; Blackburn, 'A new mint for Stephen – RVCI', *BNJ*, 63 (1994 for 1993), 126–7.
[83] Exceptions are *RRAN*, III, nos. 192 (Cirencester Abbey, 1152x53), 246 (Coventry Cathedral Priory, 1145x53), 455 (see of Lichfield, 1149), 460 (Lilleshall Abbey, 1145), 969 (Worcester Cathedral Priory, 1144x52).

Yorkshire, Nottinghamshire, Lincolnshire, Norfolk, Suffolk, Essex, Kent, Sussex, Surrey, London, Hertfordshire and Oxfordshire.[84] When due allowance is made for the problems of dating writs and charters, and for the fact that most texts survive only in cartulary copies, such crude measures generally confirm the picture which emerges from the currency. Royal government was at its most effective between the end of 1141 and the close of 1153 in parts of eastern, south-eastern and south Midland England, with only occasional intervention further afield.

In the conduct of the king's administration, many elements familiar from Henry I's reign persisted. Councils of magnates continued to be summoned: eight earls were apparently in attendance at Christmas 1141, when king and queen were crowned at Canterbury,[85] and during 1146 there seem to have been councils at Stamford, when Ranulf II earl of Chester was reconciled with the king, and at Lincoln, where Stephen celebrated Christmas and defied superstition by wearing his crown within the city.[86] The royal household, however, was scaled down. Taking the offices described in the *Constitutio Domus Regis* as a guide, we know of no one in Stephen's service with the titles of butler, chamberlain, treasurer or marshal after 1141. He relied heavily on a nucleus of trusted advisers, headed by Richard de Lucy, Richard de Camville, his steward William Martel and his constable Robert de Vere, the latter being succeeded on his death about 1151 by his son-in-law Henry of Essex. Of these, Richard de Lucy at Westminster and William Martel with the itinerant household probably had charge of the king's finances.[87] Meanwhile, at least until the closing years of the reign when he apparently went blind, William of Ypres commanded the Flemish mercenaries upon whom the king's military fortunes largely depended.[88] In the chancery there were probably only two scribes (at most) employed at any time, and only one, no. xx, can be identified as having had experience of royal service before the battle of Lincoln.[89] But while annual output fell, consonant both with reduced demand for confirmations once the king's initial years had passed and with the smaller area over which royal authority was being exercised, the scribes

---

[84] Examples from *RRAN*, III, include nos. 984 (Yorkshire, *c.*1141x53), 109 (Yorkshire and Nottinghamshire, *c.*June 1143), 738 (Nottinghamshire, 1146x49), 605 (Lincolnshire, 1143x52), 150 (Norfolk and Suffolk, *c.*1146), 229 (Suffolk, *c.*1148–52), 147–8 (Essex, 1143x52), 750 (Kent, 1152x53), 448 (Rape of Pevensey, Sussex, 1148x53), 957 (Surrey, 1147x52), 535 (London, 1149x50), 511 (Hertfordshire, 1147x48), 590 (Oxfordshire, ?1148). On the numerical preponderance of writs to Essex and Yorkshire, see White, 'Continuity', 133–4, n. 102.

[85] *RRAN*, III, no. 276 (nine earls if the beneficiary of the charter is included).

[86] *Ibid.*, III, nos. 494 (cf. 178), 736; *ASC*, 201; HH, 748; R. H. C. Davis, 'King Stephen and the earl of Chester revised', *EHR*, 75 (1960), 654–60. *Gesta Steph.*, 208, also refers to a council of *c.*1147 at which Stephen knighted his son Eustace and invested him with the county of Boulogne.

[87] *RRAN*, III, xviii–xxi; Green, 'Financing Stephen's war', esp. 112–13.

[88] Amt, *Accession*, 87–90.

[89] Bishop, *Scriptores Regis*, 30; *RRAN*, III, xv; Cronne, *Reign of Stephen*, 217–18.

maintained an accomplished standard. Stephen also had the benefit of a loyal and long-serving chancellor in the person of Robert de Gant; appointed probably in 1140 in succession to Philip d'Harcourt, he remained in office until the end of the reign.[90]

The king's income from traditional sources – farms, taxes, profits of jurisdiction – must have fallen significantly as the area under effective control was curtailed. Even so, there are signs of continuity in Stephen's second charter for Geoffrey II de Mandeville (evidently issued at the Christmas council following the king's release), which envisaged deductions for alienated royal demesne from the shire farms of Essex and Hertfordshire when accounted for at the exchequer, and in isolated references to the levy of danegeld in Kent, Hampshire and – apparently – Surrey, although only the first one can definitely be assigned to this phase of the reign.[91] The revenues he raised in Yorkshire in 1149, an amercement on the citizens of Beverley for receiving Henry Murdac as archbishop and an unnamed tax on York (which has all the appearance of a *donum*), both had precedents under Henry I.[92] But he also had to resort to a variety of other devices, including heavy borrowing from Flemings, Jews and merchant communities,[93] and the exploitation of the Church: the monks of St Augustine's, Canterbury, for example, made what appears to have been a 'forced loan' of 100 silver marks to the king some time in the 1140s, and were charged 500 marks in 1151 to conduct a free abbatial election and control their property during the vacancy.[94]

Evidence for the continued operation of the exchequer is problematical. Richard fitz Nigel's well-known comment that the *scientia* of the exchequer 'almost perished in the long civil war' is open to challenge because it is set in the context of a panegyric to his father Nigel bishop of Ely, 'almost the only man in England who so lived and died that the tongue of envy dared not blacken his character', to whom credit was accorded for the exchequer's subsequent restoration.[95] The allowance in the farm of London at Michaelmas 1156 *In reparatione domorum de Scaccario* can also be read in different ways, partly because it might indicate either the repair or the refurbishment of the exchequer's buildings, partly because the sum involved (66s. 8d.) was not substantial in any case. Judith Green has suggested that the exchequer may have switched from Win-

---

[90] Bishop, *Scriptores Regis*, 13–14, plates xxi–xxii; *RRAN*, iii, x; *ibid.*, iv, plates xxvii(b)–xxxvii.
[91] *RRAN*, iii, nos. 276, 934; *Lawsuits*, i, nos. 340, 343; cf. Green, 'Financing Stephen's war', 104.
[92] JH, 323–4 (cf. *Gesta Steph.*, 218); *PR 31 Hen. I*, 65, 114, for *donum* owed by the burgesses of Grantham, and for payments due from the burgesses of Dover and Lincoln apparently arising from offences.   [93] Green, 'Financing Stephen's war', 105–6; Amt, *Accession*, 94–109.
[94] *RRAN*, iii, no. 163; *Historia Pontificalis*, 86; cf. *Hist. Nov.*, 40, for a payment made by the monks of Malmesbury in 1140 ostensibly for the right to conduct a free abbatial election.
[95] *Dialogus*, 50.

chester to Westminster as its normal meeting place during the course of Stephen's reign, as a result of the former's insecurity from 1141 and as part of a general shift towards the south-east as the focus of royal government.[96] Whatever the truth of this,[97] it is clear that Westminster was the established meeting place early in Henry II's reign, and it seems reasonable to suppose that some accounts had been rendered there, albeit from a limited geographical area, during the later years of Stephen. The evidence of Henry II's early pipe rolls, to be examined later in chapter 4, suggests that, while exchequer clerks employed at that time were unfamiliar with some of their tasks, they did have a model to follow in the presentation of accounts, handed down from Henry I's financial administration via that of Stephen. Most sheriffs' farms in the earliest years of Henry II's reign appear to have been accounted for on the basis of totals established before his accession, and so presumably had been recorded on some form of 'exactory roll' or 'roll of farms' bequeathed from Stephen's exchequer.[98] As we shall see, there was certainly some exchequer activity at the very end of Stephen's reign, in the months following the peace settlement,[99] and this alone suggests that there had been foundations upon which to build.

In the field of justice, Stephen continued after 1141 to deal with a customary range of suits. He was concerned with crown pleas, such as the trial of Simon de Novers for the murder of the Jew Eleazer, heard in his presence in Norwich and London, and the case of two vassals of Bury St Edmunds Abbey accused of treason in plotting the king's death, which was delegated to William Martel as a royal justice but subsequently claimed by the abbot under the liberties of his church.[100] The canons of St Martin le Grand, London, where Stephen's brother Henry bishop of Winchester was dean, benefited repeatedly from the king's enduring readiness to intervene in judicial affairs. A dispute with Richard fitz Hubert over half a hide of land at Mashbury (Essex), which both parties appear to have claimed to hold in chief, was resolved in the canons' favour in the presence of king and queen; a marsh at Maldon (Essex), of which they had been disseised, was the subject of a sworn recognition by the men of three hundreds, held by Richard de Lucy as justice and Maurice de Tiretot as sheriff of Essex on the orders of the king; the sheriff and justices of London and Middlesex – with Richard de Lucy again featuring as a justice – were ordered to ensure that they held their land

---

[96] *PR2H*, 4; Green, 'Financing Stephen's war', 110–11.
[97] Two writs issued from Westminster early in the reign by Roger bishop of Salisbury may have been authorised in his capacity as presiding officer at the exchequer, since both enforce allowances from the king's revenues: *RRAN*, III, no. 397; Kealey, *Roger of Salisbury*, 259–60; White, 'Continuity', 122. If so, they suggest that the exchequer was already meeting at Westminster by 1139.
[98] *Ibid.*, 139–42.　　[99] Below, nn. 331–4.　　[100] *Lawsuits*, I, nos. 321 (?1148), 331 (?1150).

outside Cripplegate, as they had proved according to their charters; and their lands at Norton and Good Easter were specifically acquitted of 'pleas and assizes of assarts', which implies that, at least in Essex, forest pleas were still being heard.[101] Several other plaintiffs continued to look to the king for redress. Robert and William de Stuteville moved a plea in the king's court against a rival tenant-in-chief, Roger de Mowbray, claiming land in Coxwold (Yorkshire) which had been given for the foundation of Byland Abbey.[102] St Frideswide's Priory, Oxford, recovered the island of Medley of which it had been disseised, after a recognition by the burgesses of Oxford in the presence of the king.[103] Walter de Lucy abbot of Battle brought a claim to exemption from the jurisdiction of the bishop of Chichester before the king at St Albans and London, and duly won his case.[104] Stephen also initiated pleading in other courts. Robert earl of Leicester presided in his honorial court over the settlement of a dispute between St Frideswide's Priory and a knight Edward, concerning a hide of land in Oxfordshire, begun by a royal writ; Gilbert Foliot bishop of Hereford responded to the king's order to hear a complaint by Gilbert de Lacy against Roger earl of Hereford for breach of sanctuary, although the case then proceeded on appeal to the archbishop of Canterbury.[105] Conversely, the king might still grant the favour of a prohibition on impleading except in his presence, as ceded to the priors of St Frideswide's, Oxford, and St Botolph's, Colchester.[106] These are scattered references, but they serve to reinforce the point that in the south-eastern sector of the kingdom, and occasionally beyond, the king was still a force in the dispensation of justice.

The phrasing of several of Stephen's writs bears comparison with those of Henry II, in the precision with which they address points at issue. One witnessed by Robert de Gant as chancellor, and hence of 1140 at the earliest, commanded William earl of Warenne to restore to the monks of Reading their land of Catshill (Surrey) and anything taken from it; if he had any claim therein he was to 'come to my court and I will do you full right in the matter'. This has been interpreted as 'a decisive advance in the development of originating judicial writs': the opening instruction had

---

[101] *RRAN*, III, nos. 550 (1143x47), 546–7 (1147x52), 534 (1143x52), 559 (1143x47).

[102] *Lawsuits*, I, no. 323 (1147x49).

[103] *RRAN*, III, no. 639 (c.1150x52 following the dating in *Lawsuits*, I, no. 336).

[104] *Ibid.*, I, no. 320; *Chronicle of Battle Abbey*, 150–2 (late 1148).

[105] *Lawsuits*, I, nos. 316 (c.1147), 327 (c.1150); *Royal Writs*, 206–7; GF, *Letters*, no. 95. Crouch, *Beaumont Twins*, 161–2, favours a date in the 1160s for the suit in the earl of Leicester's court, because of the reference in the St Frideswide's cartulary to its initiation by a writ of right ('per breve de recto'); however, as Professor van Caenegem points out, this may well be an anachronistic use of the term, and the remainder of the text suggests *c.*1147. On the issue of royal writs 'to do right' prior to Stephen's reign, see *Royal Writs*, 195–234; Green, *Henry I*, 102–3.

[106] *RRAN*, III, nos. 650 (1148x53), 210 (1140x43).

become little more than a prelude to the summons to a royal court, and so the writ can be seen as a stage in the formulation of Henry II's writ *praecipe*.[107] Similarly, Stephen's writs concerning disseisin repeatedly defined the period within which the offence must have occurred, showing far more consistency in doing so than equivalent writs issued by his predecessors: although it is fair to add that surviving examples seem to date to 1141 at latest. Thus, orders that the canons of St Martin le Grand, London, be reseised of property of which they had been disseised – in the aftermath of the 'arrest of the bishops' – duly specified their previous tenure 'on the day King Henry was alive and dead' and seisin 'before the bishop of Salisbury was taken at Oxford'. Others referred to seisin 'on the day when King Henry last crossed the sea to Normandy', 'on the day when their abbot [of St Edmunds] left for Rome' and 'on my first coronation day'.[108] This location in time of a seisin no longer enjoyed was to be an essential ingredient of the later writs of *novel disseisin*. One might also cite in this connection the writ sent by Stephen to a court of Alexander bishop of Lincoln, probably in 1147, ordering the men of Luton to recognise whether (*utrum*) certain land pertained to the church of Luton and should be held in free alms. Unfortunately, the text survives only in paraphrased form in the *Gesta Abbatum Sancti Albani*, where there is certainly some confusion over narrative details, but we do seem to have here a precursor of Henry II's assize *utrum*, first set out in clause ix of the Constitutions of Clarendon.[109] Clearly, there was some innovative vitality to Stephen's administration of justice, even in the 1140s and early 1150s, despite the limited geographical area over which it applied.

Control of local government through loyal sheriffs and other officials was obviously crucial to the enforcement of the king's will, as well as to the collection of his revenues. Discussion of this subject inevitably involves consideration of the role – in intention and in practice – of the various earls created during the reign, and of their power within the shires from which they took their titles, a matter addressed later in this chapter. Suffice it to say here that, in the period from his second coronation to the

[107] *Ibid.*, III, no. 692; *Royal Writs*, 243 and no. 45; M.Chibnall, *Anglo-Norman England, 1066–1166* (Oxford, 1986), 178.

[108] *RRAN*, III, nos. 286, 354, 525, 527, 766; *Royal Writs*, nos. 61, 82–4, 87. Although the editors of *RRAN*, III, give 1136x41 as the date of no. 286, the reference to 'my first coronation day' implies that there had been a second; if the re-coronation of Christmas 1141 was in mind here, the writ would obviously have been issued later, possibly in the period after the peace settlement as Stephen reasserted his authority over the kingdom as a whole.

[109] *Gesta Abbatum Sancti Albani*, I, 113–18 (royal writ at 114); *Lawsuits*, I, no. 296; *Royal Writs*, 327–8. The case is dated by van Caenegem to 1138x39 because of the intervention of Alberic bishop of Ostia, 'then legate in England'; on the other hand, Robert earl of Gloucester is said to have died (31 October 1147) and 'not long afterwards' Earl Gilbert withdrew from his allegiance to Stephen, another event of 1147 (*Gesta Steph.*, 200–2). Alexander bishop of Lincoln died on 20 February 1148. See also Saltman, *Theobald*, no. 229; *RRAN*, III, nos. 745–6.

peace settlement, the political, military and administrative support which Stephen received from his earls was at best spasmodic, and that the most convincing evidence that sheriffs responded to the king's directives comes from shires in the east, south-east and south Midlands where he did not recognise an earl. Over twenty writs and charters are known to have been addressed by Stephen to royal officials in Essex in the years following the demise of Earl Geoffrey de Mandeville, the king's close adviser Richard de Lucy frequently appearing (sometimes as justice) alongside the sheriff, Maurice de Tiretot.[110] Stephen's good relations with the citizens of London are reflected in several writs addressed among others to their sheriff, again with Richard de Lucy featuring as one of the justices.[111] In Norfolk and Suffolk, where the empress recognised Hugh Bigod as earl but (until the peace settlement) the king did not, the shrievalties were held for much of the 1140s and early 1150s by Stephen's own tenants, John and William de Chesney and Roger Gulafre:[112] it was at a meeting of the shire court of Norfolk and Suffolk in 1150 that the king's steward William Martel heard the accusation of treason against two vassals of St Edmunds, in the presence of another steward, Walter fitz Robert, the constable Robert de Vere, and other leading royalists.[113] There was never an earl of Berkshire, while in Oxfordshire Stephen appears not to have acknowledged the earldom created by the empress for Aubrey III de Vere, despite the latter's return to the king's allegiance by 1145.[114] Here we find one sheriff, Jordan de Podiis, who campaigned with Stephen's army, and another, Atsor, who summoned the portman-moot of Oxford on the king's instructions and reported their verdict to him in person.[115] Nor did Stephen appoint an earl for Kent. The sheriff in the 1140s and 1150s, Ralf Picot, was associated in witness lists with the king's closest advisers, although his background had been as constable to Archbishop Theobald; he is found in 1153 holding a shire court at which it was proved that he had levied danegeld and other royal dues on land held by the monks of Christ Church, Canterbury, which should properly have been exempt.[116] It is fair to add, however, that the dominant power

---

[110] White, 'Continuity', 133–4 and n. 102.

[111] *RRAN*, III, nos. 532–6, 563, 693, 930 (although not all can be firmly dated after 1141); cf. Green, 'Financing Stephen's war', 106–10.

[112] Green, *Sheriffs*, 21, n. 54, and 61–2, 77; on Hugh Bigod, see Davis, *Stephen*, 138–9, and A. Wareham, 'The motives and politics of the Bigod family, *c.*1066–1177', *ANS*, 17 (1995), 234, which discusses the possibility that Hugh originally owed his comital title to Stephen.

[113] Above, n. 24.   [114] Davis, *Stephen*, 137–8, 140.

[115] *RRAN*, III, no. 89 (cf. no. 2); *Lawsuits*, I, no. 336; cf. *ibid.*, II, no. 363 (*RRAN*, III, no. 13) for Henry of Oxford responding to Stephen as sheriff of Berkshire, but probably not before 1154; Green, *Sheriffs*, 27, 70.

[116] *Ibid.*, 51; *RRAN*, III, nos. 142, 151, 163; *Lawsuits*, I, no. 340; Saltman, *Theobald*, nos. 55, 161, 174, 225, and p. 542.

in Kent was the mercenary leader William of Ypres, described by two chroniclers as having custody of the shire.[117] Stephen certainly relied upon him to discharge his commands, and in the one writ in which they both appeared – an order that Canterbury Cathedral Priory hold its lands in peace – he took precedence over Ralf Picot and other shire officials.[118]

The presence of William of Ypres does indeed sound a warning against too optimistic a view of the efficacy of royal government between 1141 and 1153, even in the region where the king apparently enjoyed most authority. The 1156 pipe roll shows that William had been receiving over £400 per annum from royal manors in Kent – halving the king's income from his demesnes in the shire – with control of hundredal jurisdiction in Canterbury, Milton, Dartford and Eynesford.[119] He had clearly acquired an entrenched position in the administration of the shire, and although much of his income must have been spent on the mercenaries who fought on Stephen's behalf, he would have been very difficult to dislodge had he turned against the king. Elsewhere, Berkshire was, as Edmund King has pointed out, a frontier shire with 'royal authority mediated . . . through two sets of masters', and with several royal manors being alienated to leading adherents of one or other party in the war.[120] Much the same might be said of Oxfordshire, where both king and empress granted away royal demesne, and the hundredal manors of Bampton and Headington came into the hands of the count of Flanders and Hugh de Plugenoi respectively.[121] Otherwise, most of the grants or confirmations of private hundreds known to have been issued by Stephen in the 1140s and early 1150s were in Norfolk, Suffolk, Essex and Kent.[122] Such privileges were, of course, already well established before his accession, but the king's readiness to concede jurisdiction, even in the area he most closely controlled, can scarcely have strengthened his hand: if those who held the hundreds saw themselves wielding authority on the king's behalf, his power might be buttressed, but everything depended on their remaining loyal. It must be said that the early pipe rolls of Henry II's reign give the impression that Norfolk and Suffolk were in a state of administrative and tenurial confusion, with perfunctory references to danegeld collections in 1156 and accounts for less than half the sums due as shire

---

[117] *Chronicle of Battle Abbey*, 144; Gervase, II, 73 (cf. I, 121, where he is said to have abused the shire).

[118] *RRAN*, III, no. 145; cf. nos. 165, 228.

[119] *PR2H*, 65; for the association of allowances 'blanch' with the grant of hundredal jurisdiction, see *Dialogus*, 85. On William of Ypres's decline, see above, n. 88.

[120] King, 'Anarchy of King Stephen's reign', 146–7.

[121] *RRAN*, III, e.g. nos. 366–8, 370, 627, 629–31; *PR2H*, 36, *PR3H*, 82, etc.; Chibnall, *Matilda*, 124. Oxfordshire's situation as 'a divided community' is examined in detail in Amt, *Accession*, 46–63.

[122] *RRAN*, III, nos. 34–6, 177, 183, 402–3, 758–9, 761, 845–7 (cf. nos. 4, 285, 592, 669, 722–3, 784, 817, 964).

farms before 1158.[123] The coinage, likewise, points to some loss of royal control even in the east and south during the 1140s, in the later stages of Stephen's type 1: there are isolated examples of irregular pennies minted at Pevensey, Canterbury and London, and a more substantial group struck from defaced, altered or locally cut dies at several East Anglian mints.[124]

The southern and eastern shires of England also harboured divided political loyalties. We have seen that the shire court of Norfolk and Suffolk at which William Martel presided about 1150 was an assembly apparently confined to the king's active supporters. Brian fitz Count's honour of Wallingford remained a bastion of Angevin loyalty in Berkshire and Oxfordshire, and several other opponents of the king, such as John Marshal and John of St John, had major interests in these shires.[125] Royal control in Kent was inhibited by the fact that nearly half the landed area was in ecclesiastical hands, especially those of the archbishop and monks of Canterbury; among lay barons there were defections to the Angevins around 1150–1, by such as William de Crevequer and William Patrick, to add to the earlier declarations for the empress on the part of Walchelin Maminot and William Peverel of Dover.[126] Even in Essex, Turgis d'Avranches the castellan of Walden revolted during 1144, Aubrey III de Vere having returned to the king's allegiance by the mid-1140s offered little active support, and the sons of Geoffrey II de Mandeville, though absent, remained a potential threat to security.[127]

In the administration of justice, episodes showing royal involvement in the south-east have to be set against evidence such as that presented by the celebrated Anstey case. Although the lands at issue lay in Essex, Richard of Anstey waited eighteen years, until 1158, before seeking a royal writ to begin proceedings to recover his inheritance; it was his adversary Mabel de Francheville who may have provided an explanation for the delay, when she asserted that under Stephen 'justice was banished from the realm'.[128] Similarly, despite his abbey's success before Stephen against the bishop of Chichester, the Battle chronicler repeatedly bemoaned the 'lack of justice' at this time, 'when he who was strongest got most'; the manor of Barnhorn (Sussex) was one of the properties which

---

[123] *RBE*, II, 651–2; *PR2H*, 6–10; *PR3H*, 75–6; *PR4H*, 125–31; totals between 1155 and 1157 were consistently below £350, but exceeded £700 from 1158 (cf. below, appendix I).

[124] Blackburn, 'Coinage and currency', in King, *Anarchy*, 154–5, 178–80.

[125] *RRAN*, III, e.g. nos. 366, 632, 644; *PR2H*, 34, 37; Chibnall, *Matilda*, 126, 131–2.

[126] R. G. Eales, 'Local loyalties in Norman England: Kent in Stephen's reign', *ANS*, 8 (1986), 88–108.   [127] *Gesta Steph.*, 174–6; *RRAN*, III, nos. 277, 460; HH, 746; Amt, *Accession*, 69–70.

[128] JS, *Letters*, I, 231; P. M. Barnes, 'The Anstey Case', in P. M. Barnes and C. F. Slade, eds., *An Early Medieval Miscellany for Doris Mary Stenton* (P. R. Society, 1960), 1–24.

the monks had to wait until Henry II's reign to recover.[129] The longest lists of complaints in the 1166 *cartae baronum* about knights' fees in dispute come from the west country and East Anglia, again suggesting that a good deal of self-help had gone unredressed not only in Angevin-held shires but also in those substantially loyal to the king.[130] And in ecclesiastical affairs, the loss of royal jurisdiction over advowson, criminous clerks and land held in free alms, which the Constitutions of Clarendon sought to redress, seems to have applied over the whole of the kingdom.[131]

All this helps to paint a picture of a king continuing to govern, and of loyal administrators answering to him both in the centre and in the localities, but also of frustration, disruption and obstruction at every turn. The area in which the king's government operated was restricted, and even here, in eastern, south-eastern and south Midland England, while royal grants and confirmations were sought, writs issued, courts held, coins minted and revenues collected, the king's administration was often ineffective. Beyond this region, Stephen was called upon occasionally, or not at all. Here, much of the administrative structure passed down from Henry I persisted, but it served not the king but those who claimed royal authority in his place. Yet these rivals to the king faced major problems of their own in imposing their alternative governments.

GOVERNMENT BY EMPRESS MATILDA, HENRY OF ANJOU AND THE SCOTS

Weak though Stephen's position was for much of the reign, it was always stronger than that of Empress Matilda, with the obvious exception of the year 1141. Charters, chronicles and coins combine to show that, both in geographical extent and in depth of control, there were severe limitations to the authority exercised either by the empress herself or by Robert earl of Gloucester on her behalf. After her arrival in England in 1139 – once she had extricated herself from Arundel – the empress made her base first at Bristol, then at Gloucester; from June 1141 until December 1142 her principal residence was in Oxford, and thereafter she stayed mostly at Devizes until she left England early in 1148.[132] These boroughs are as good an indication as any of the region answerable to her. From the outset, the marcher lordship of Robert earl of Gloucester provided her

---

[129] *Chronicle of Battle Abbey*, 212 (translation adapted), cf. 142, 238.

[130] References to disputes specifically associated with the recent war occur in *RBE*, I, 237 (Wiltshire), 251 (Devon), 298 (Gloucestershire), 351 (Essex), 401 (Norfolk), 408–9 (Suffolk). Cf. below, ch. 5, nn. 29–36.

[131] For ecclesiastical disputes in Stephen's reign resolved by the Church's own processes, see Saltman, *Theobald*, 66–9 (exemption, including advowson and presentation to churches), JS, *Letters*, I, 26 (criminous clerk, despite Stephen's initial attempt to claim the case), and *Lawsuits*, I, no. 338 (free alms).   [132] *RRAN*, III, xliv; Chibnall, *Matilda*, 82–4, 118.

most secure territory. William of Malmesbury was cautious in his assessment of the extent of her control by the end of 1139: he mentioned a few early transfers of allegiance, but otherwise would go no further than to say that 'the whole district around Gloucester as far as the depth of Wales, partly under compulsion and partly from goodwill' submitted to her in the closing months of the year, adding the town of Hereford a couple of sentences later. Gloucestershire was to remain one of her most closely controlled shires throughout her time in England. From 1141, largely as a result of gains made during Stephen's captivity which Robert earl of Gloucester refused to surrender when negotiating his release, she also enjoyed substantial authority in Wiltshire and – until she lost Oxford itself at the end of 1142 – the neighbouring county of Oxfordshire.[133] Control of Herefordshire was less secure: Josce de Dinan lost Ludlow to the king's adherents, and although Matilda granted the earldom of Hereford to Miles of Gloucester, his son Roger failed to make good his claims against Gilbert de Lacy to the estate of Payn fitz John.[134] Berkshire was another hotly disputed shire, where Wallingford castle held out for the Angevins throughout the civil war but where Stephen had many supporters of his own.[135] Beyond, in counties fringing this heartland to the north and east, and in the four shires of the south-west peninsula, the empress could fairly be said to have had influence rather than power. The realities of her position occasionally broke through in the phraseology of her charters: a confirmation of the gift of Kingswood (Gloucestershire) to Tintern Abbey – possibly the first charter she issued following her arrival in England – limited its address to those clergy and laity who were subject to her, while her elaborate treaties with Geoffrey II de Mandeville and Aubrey III de Vere in 1141 invoked the support of the Christian community of England but only in that part which was under her authority.[136]

One indication of the regional focus of the empress's authority is the distribution of her ecclesiastical patronage. Her confirmation of Kingswood was followed – apparently around the middle of 1140 – by the

---

[133] *Hist. Nov.*, 36, 69–70; Chibnall, *Matilda*, 123–7.

[134] *Ibid.*, 123–5; *Fouke le Fitz Warin*, ed. E. J. Hathaway, P. T. Ricketts *et al.* (Anglo-Norman Texts, 1975), xii (n. 3), 17–20; R. W. Eyton, *Antiquities of Shropshire* (London, 1856–60), v, 244–8; D. Walker, 'The 'Honours' of the earls of Hereford in the twelfth century', *Trans. Bristol and Glos. Arch. Soc.*, 79 (1960), 174–211 (esp. 186–8); W. E. Wightman, *The Lacy Family in England and Normandy* (Oxford, 1966), 180, 187.

[135] King, 'Anarchy of King Stephen's reign', 146–7; for a contemporary perception of Berkshire as embracing the frontier between the two parties in the civil war, see GF, *Letters*, no. 85.

[136] '[O]mnibus sancte matris ecclesie filiis tam clericis quam laicis sue subjectionis': *RRAN*, iii, no. 419; 'Christianitas Angliae quae est in potestate mea': *ibid.*, iii, no. 275; 'Christianitas Anglie que in potestate mea est': *ibid.*, no. 634. Cf. on these and the preceding charter, Chibnall, *Matilda*, 110–11, 129, and 'The charters of the Empress Matilda' in G. Garnett and J. G. H. Hudson, *Law and Government in Medieval England and Normandy: Essays in Honour of Sir James Holt* (Cambridge, 1994), 276–98 (esp. 283, 286–7).

presentation of the earl of Chester's chaplain John to the church of Trentham, on royal demesne in Staffordshire.[137] During 1141 charters were issued for the religious houses at Bordesley (Worcestershire), Glastonbury (Somerset), Haughmond (Shropshire), Oseney, Cowley and St Frideswide's, Oxford (Oxfordshire), Reading (Berkshire), and Salisbury (Wiltshire), plus Llanthony across the border from Gloucestershire.[138] Even in this year when she looked set to take the throne, the only houses elsewhere in the country known to have received her charters were those of St Benet's Holme (Norfolk), Holy Trinity and St Martin le Grand in London, Luffield (Northamptonshire) and Waltham (Essex).[139] Charters issued in subsequent years, or which cannot be closely dated, went again to several of those listed above – Bordesley, Haughmond, Oseney, St Frideswide's, Reading, Salisbury – but also to the houses at Cirencester (Gloucestershire), Eynsham and Godstow (Oxfordshire), Lilleshall and Shrewsbury (Shropshire), Monkton Farleigh and Stanley (Wiltshire), Missenden (Buckinghamshire) and Radmore (Staffordshire).[140]

If we look at the lands and revenues Matilda gave away – as opposed to those renewed or confirmed following donations by others – there is also an emphasis upon Gloucestershire, Herefordshire, Oxfordshire, Berkshire and Wiltshire, although the picture is blurred by the special circumstances of 1141 when her grants extended to property in London, Winchester and elsewhere in the south Midlands and south-east.[141] Royal demesne alienated by the empress included the manors of Mawarden, Lugwardine and Wilton (Herefordshire) to Miles of Gloucester, of Great Barrington (Gloucestershire) to Llanthony Priory, and the pool of Aldewere (Oxfordshire) to Oseney Abbey;[142] in addition, the *terrae datae* of Henry II's early pipe rolls show several Angevin adherents installed in former royal manors, among them Josce de Dinan at Lambourn (Berkshire), Hugh de Plugenoi at Headington, Henry of Oxford at both Headington and Bensington (Oxfordshire), John Marshal, Humphrey II de Bohun, Patrick of Salisbury and Jocelin de Balliol all in Wiltshire.[143] A

[137] 'Chartulary of the Augustine priory of Trentham', ed. F. Parker, in *Staffs. Colls*, XI, 322 (a confirmation by Roger bishop of Chester, d.1148, of the presentation by 'Domine nostre Matilde, filie Regis bone memorie Henrici, in plena sinodo Lichf' post Pentecost, anno quo aplicuit prenominata domina ad castrum Arundel de quo, tam prudenter quam sapienter, venit Bristol, et evasit de obsidione Regis Stephani'). Although the reference to Matilda as *Domina* indicates a date for the document after April 1141, Pentecost in the year following her escape from Arundel to Bristol fell on 26 May 1140; if this dating is correct, it suggests contact between the empress and Ranulf II earl of Chester some months before the battle of Lincoln.

[138] *RRAN*, III, nos. 115, 343, 377, 497, 628–9, 644, 646, 648, 697–701, 791, 854.

[139] *Ibid.*, III, nos. 400, 518, 529, 571, 918.

[140] *Ibid.*, III, nos. 116, 378, 630–2, 645, 647, 702–3, 792–4; 190, 295–6, 369–72, 461, 820–1, 836, 587, 839; Chibnall, 'Charters of Empress', 294–5.   [141] *RRAN*, III, nos. 274, 899, cf. 275, 316, 648.

[142] *Ibid.*, III, nos. 393, 497, 629.

[143] *PR2H*, 34, 36, 57; *PR3H*, 77–8, 80, 82, etc.; cf. Chibnall, *Matilda*, 118–27.

similar story emerges from attestations to her charters. The year 1141 was exceptional, with the archbishop of Canterbury, the king of Scots, and other ecclesiastical and lay magnates from various parts of the country figuring as witnesses.[144] But throughout her time in England, even in 1141, there was a regional basis to the composition of her court. To the earls of the south-western shires, principally those of Gloucester, Hereford and Cornwall, may be added the holders of household titles – especially Brian fitz Count, Humphrey II de Bohun, John Marshal, Robert d'Oilli all with interests focused on Berkshire, Oxfordshire and Wiltshire – and men such as Stephen de Mandeville lord of Erlestoke (Wiltshire), the Worcestershire baron Ralf Paynel, and another of Henry I's illegitimate sons, Robert *filius Regis*, whose holdings were in Devon and Somerset.[145] It must be acknowledged that there were a few exceptions to this south-west/south Midlands bias. Among those who accompanied Empress Matilda in and after 1141 were the Kent barons Walchelin Maminot and William Peverel of Dover, who had revolted in 1138 in sympathy with Robert earl of Gloucester; elsewhere, Ilbert II de Lacy of Pontefract, Geoffrey II Ridel of Great Weldon (Northamptonshire) and Geoffrey III de Mandeville son of the rebellious earl of Essex all sought confirmations of their holdings from the empress in preference to the king.[146] But the rarity of these exceptions underlines how limited was the impact of Matilda's authority within the kingdom at large, even at the height of her power in 1141.

The evidence of coins bears this out. The production of pennies in the name of Empress Matilda seems to have been confined to the region from Oxfordshire westwards, and less than a score of these coins have been found in hoards elsewhere in the country. Her first type, modelled on Stephen's type 1, is known from Bristol, Cardiff, Wareham and Oxford, the last mint presumably operating during her residence in the city from July 1141 to December 1142. There are grounds for believing that the other three mints did not begin to produce coins in her name until after the battle of Lincoln, their initial response to the assertion of Angevin authority in the region having been to issue pennies naming 'Stephen' but from locally cut dies. A second type in Empress Matilda's name was minted at Bristol and Cardiff, probably in the mid-1140s.[147] The type 1 coins with the inscription +PERERIC (or +PERERICM), based on dies sent out by the official London die-cutter and known to have been minted at

---

[144] *RRAN*, III, e.g. nos. 274, 328, 377, 393.

[145] *Ibid.*, III, e.g. nos. 111, 274, 277, 393–4, 581; for the holdings of Robert *filius Regis*, see *PR4H*, 122, 159, and for those of Stephen de Mandeville and Ralf Paynel, see *Baronies*, 42, 113.

[146] *RRAN*, III, nos. 68, 111, 274, 393, etc.; 429, 43, 277; Eales, 'Local loyalties', esp. 88–91.

[147] King, 'Anarchy of King Stephen's reign', 148–50; G. C. Boon, *Welsh Hoards 1979–81* (Cardiff, 1986), esp. 42–52; Blackburn, 'Coinage and currency', in King, *Anarchy*, esp. 187–8, 202–3.

Bristol, Canterbury, Ipswich, Lincoln, London, Stamford and Winchester, are now thought to have been issued on the empress's authority, but only during her brief ascendancy in and around London in the summer of 1141.[148] The striking of coins in the name neither of the king nor of the empress, a development of the 1140s observable at mints mainly in the north and south-west, is a reflection upon the limited authority of them both.[149]

But within that part of the kingdom where she resided, and where coins were minted in her name, how substantial was the empress's governmental control? The political problems were formidable. William of Malmesbury, as a writer sympathetic to her, conveys an impression of precarious support. On landing in 1139, Robert earl of Gloucester found in England that 'the nobles were either hostile or gave no help, apart from a very few who had not forgotten the faith they once swore'; in 1142 he was reluctant to cross to Normandy because 'it would be dangerous for his sister, whom others could hardly protect when he was away, men who had practically abandoned her when he himself was captured, without confidence in their own cause'.[150] Those who betrayed her trust included not only the mercenary captains Robert fitz Hubert and Robert fitz Hildebrand but also William de Mohun her earl of Somerset and Dorset, and Philip son of Robert earl of Gloucester.[151] Stephen brought troops into Cornwall in 1140, Dorset in 1142 and 1143, Gloucestershire in 1139, 1142 and 1144, Herefordshire and Worcestershire in 1139 and 1140, and Berkshire, Oxfordshire and Wiltshire on several occasions.[152] The king retained active supporters in Devon, where Henry de Tracy seems to have harassed the Angevins from Barnstaple for most of the civil war, and for a time in Dorset, where William Martel held Sherborne castle until its surrender in 1143. Well might the author of the *Gesta Stephani* describe Angevin rule in south-western England as bringing, at best, 'a shadow of peace but not yet peace complete'.[153]

One indication of the modesty of the empress's position is that, despite her efforts to maintain a household which paralleled that of the king, and her employment of a chancellor who frequently witnessed her writs and charters, she principally relied on beneficiaries' scribes to produce documents for her: only one scribe, no. XIV, worked for her regularly, apparently between 1141 and 1144, in a career which had previously seen

---

[148] *Ibid.*, 173–5; Archibald, 'Dating Stephen's first type', 13–17.
[149] Boon, *Welsh Hoards*, esp. 52–5 and *Coins of the Anarchy*, esp. 28–30 ; Blackburn, 'Coinage and currency', in King, *Anarchy*, 167–73, 182–93.   [150] *Hist. Nov.*, 35, 72.
[151] JW, 61–2; *Hist. Nov.*, 43–4; *Gesta Steph.*, 104–6, 150–2, 186; H. W. C. Davis, 'Henry of Blois and Brian fitz Count', *EHR*, 25 (1910), 279–303 (at 300–1); Davis, *Stephen*, 90–1, 138.
[152] These campaigns are covered most extensively in *Gesta Steph.*, 90–175.
[153] *Ibid.*, 82–4, 146–50, 210–12, 222 (quotation at 150, transl. 151).

service for Henry I and Stephen and would go on to embrace Archbishop Theobald and Henry II.[154] A more substantial sign of weakness is the paucity of evidence, among over seventy writs and charters which she issued during her eight-and-a-half years in England, of any active intervention in judicial proceedings. There are no writs to initiate impleading, and none which prohibit it in specific cases either.[155] In 1141, she ordered that the canons of St Martin le Grand, London, be reseised of houses they had lost, and that William fitz Otho be seised of land in Benfleet (Essex) as on the day King Henry was alive and dead.[156]. She also confirmed to Oseney Abbey the island of Langeney as Geoffrey de Clinton had quitclaimed it in her presence, and various other lands in Oxfordshire as conceded before her by Henry d'Oilli and John of St John.[157] Various disputes presumably lay behind these arrangements, but while the empress's authority was invoked to confirm their resolution, we can only speculate on whether she had played a significant part in bringing about a settlement. Elsewhere, a prevailing 'lack of justice' in the area where the empress held sway is implied by Gilbert Foliot's appeals to the relevant bishops in the mid-1140s to proceed against the Flemings Henry and Ralf de Caldret on the one hand, against John Marshal and Walter de Pinkeny on the other, whose depredations in Gloucestershire and Wiltshire respectively had gone unpunished.[158] A sense of personal insecurity is also apparent from the story of the Gloucestershire baron Roger de Berkeley, who by 1146 had a 'compact to keep the peace' with his kinsman Walter of Hereford and an agreement that Philip son of the earl of Gloucester would protect him. Little good did they do him, as he was captured and tortured by Walter of Hereford, in a vain attempt to secure the surrender of Berkeley castle.[159]

As for the empress's finances, she would presumably have received some customary royal revenues – farms at the very least – in those shires where she controlled the royal demesnes and which had sheriffs loyal to her. Her charter announcing the gift of Great Barrington to Llanthony Priory strongly suggests that she had formerly received an income from the manor, since she reserved an annual farm of £4 still to be rendered, and mentioned the consent of William of Buckland who had previously held at fee farm.[160] Other references to payments due to her, such as a writ

---

[154] Bishop, *Scriptores Regis*, plate xvii(b); *RRAN*, III, xiv–xv, xxx; *ibid.*, IV, 19–20 and plates xiii–xv; Chibnall, 'Charters of Empress', 291–2.

[155] General prohibitions on impleading were issued in favour of Geoffrey II de Mandeville and Humphrey II de Bohun (*RRAN*, III, nos. 274–5, 111).

[156] *Ibid.*, III, nos. 529, 316; neither writ qualified the order with the word 'juste', which could serve as an invitation to hold a preliminary hearing (cf. below, ch. 5). [157] *Ibid.*, III, nos. 629, 632.

[158] GF, *Letters*, nos. 27, 32 (cf. *Gesta Steph.*, 168, 178, 188). [159] *Ibid.*, 190.

[160] *RRAN*, III, no. 497.

of *computate* notifying the barons of the exchequer of her gift to Oseney Abbey of 5s. 5¾d yearly from the farm of Oxford (a sum already granted by Stephen), and the promises to Geoffrey II de Mandeville that he would hold Essex and Hertfordshire for the customary farms paid by his grand-father,[161] are better regarded as statements of her entitlement to royal revenues in the months of Stephen's captivity than as evidence that she actually received them, although it is quite possible that she did enjoy the farm of the borough of Oxford during her residence there in 1141 and 1142. But it is difficult to know how effectively she controlled those responsible for the collection of revenue, the sheriffs, at any stage be-tween 1139 and 1148. Some shrievalties were certainly held late in the reign by men who had been her close associates. Wiltshire's sheriff from 1153 at the latest was Patrick of Salisbury, who had witnessed for her at Devizes as a constable, and by 1147 had become her earl in that shire.[162] Henry of Oxford, who as sheriff of Berkshire answered to Stephen in 1154, was in receipt of instructions from the empress (in Rouen) during 1150–1, when she made arrangements for the foundation of a religious house for the canons of Wallingford.[163] But if these men were in office during the 1140s, they would have struggled to uphold the empress's rights against the king, particularly in the 'frontier shire' of Berkshire. Elsewhere, although Roger earl of Hereford had a grip on the shrievalties of both Gloucestershire and Herefordshire in the later years of Stephen's reign,[164] it is by no means clear that he exercised that control in the empress's interests rather than his own – a point taken up in the next section of this chapter. In Worcestershire, William de Beauchamp was granted the shrievalty hereditarily by the empress in July 1141; but he had fled the shire at the time, and he subsequently answered as sheriff not to Matilda but to Waleran of Meulan.[165] Although she addressed charters of the early 1140s in favour of Shropshire religious houses to William fitz Alan, sheriff at the time of his revolt against Stephen in 1138, he was in no position to implement her commands in that shire because he had taken refuge in her court. Another charter of 1141x42, concerning her restoration to Cirencester Abbey of land pertaining to the church of Frome

---

[161] *Ibid.*, III, nos. 626, 628, 275, with comment p. xxxi.

[162] *Ibid.*, III, no. 839 (cf. nos. 704, 795); Davis, *Stephen*, 137; Green, *Sheriffs*, 86; Crouch, *William Marshal*, 14.

[163] *Lawsuits*, II, no. 363 (taking this stage in the proceedings to belong to the year of Stephen's death, despite the dating suggested in *RRAN*, III, no. 13); *ibid.*, III, no. 88; K. S. B. Keats-Rohan, 'The making of Henry of Oxford: Englishmen in a Norman world', *Oxoniensia*, 54 (1991), 287–309.

[164] Although Earl Roger does not appear to have acted as sheriff of either county, his control in both is implied by 'Charters of the earldom of Hereford, 1095–1201', ed. D. Walker in *Camden Miscellany XXII* (Camden Society, 1964), nos. 17, 18, 37, 39; but cf. Green, *Sheriffs*, 42, 45–6.

[165] *RRAN*, III, no. 68; H. W. C. Davis, 'Some documents of the Anarchy', in *Essays in History presented to R. L. Poole* (Oxford, 1927), 170–1; Crouch, *Beaumont Twins*, 50–1.

(Somerset), was addressed to the earl and sheriff of Somerset, but while the former was named as William [de Mohun], the sheriff was anonymous.[166] We can only guess at the administrative consequences for the empress in Dorset and Somerset of William de Mohun's desertion of her cause a year or so later, or – conversely – of Robert earl of Gloucester's acquisition in 1143 of Sherborne castle, which allegedly brought the whole region 'from sea to sea' under Angevin control, because she did not address any other known writs or charters to officials in these shires: the discovery within the Box hoard of coins minted in the name of Robert earl of Gloucester reinforces the impression conveyed by the *Gesta Stephani* that it was the earl, rather than the empress, who was the effective power in much of the south-west peninsula.[167] Nor are there any surviving writs from the empress to the earls or sheriffs of Devon and Cornwall: despite the consistent support she enjoyed from Earls Baldwin and Reginald, her involvement with these shires was very slight, confined (on the evidence available) to a single confirmation of Baldwin's gift of St James's chapel, Exeter, to the priory of St Martin-des-Champs, Paris, issued in 1141x42.[168] Neither king nor empress had much power in the four counties of the south-west peninsula, at any stage of the civil war.

A key point, however, is that despite the severe limitations on Empress Matilda's practical authority, it was clearly in her interests to uphold the principle of royal government over the kingdom. Her original intention, when invading England in company with her half-brother Robert earl of Gloucester in September 1139, was to secure the throne through coronation as queen. After that ambition had been thwarted by the revolt of the Londoners on 24 June 1141, and the royalist success at the battle of Stockbridge twelve weeks later, her purpose became one of survival so that her son might eventually inherit the kingdom.[169] In both contexts, it was important that she presented her own authority as a credible alternative to the king's. Accordingly, most of her writs and charters were modelled on those produced by the royal chancery: addressed as was customary to clergy, barons and officials either of particular shires or of 'all England'; referring to royal demesne manors and borough farms as 'mine'; and in one case imposing the £10 forfeit traditionally set by kings for disobeying their orders.[170] She presented herself as in the line of kings,

---

[166] *RRAN*, III, nos. 378, 820,190; OV, VI, 520; Chibnall, *Matilda*, 123, 125.

[167] *Gesta Steph.*, 148–50; Davis, *Stephen*, 138; King, 'Economic development', 16 and n. 99.

[168] *RRAN*, III, no. 651.

[169] Chibnall, *Matilda*, esp. 114–15, 120; R. Hill, 'The battle of Stockbridge, 1141', in C. Harper-Bill, C. Holdsworth, J. L. Nelson, eds., *Studies in Medieval History presented to R. Allen Brown* (Woodbridge and Wolfeboro, 1989), 173–7; J. Bradbury, *Stephen and Matilda: the Civil War of 1139–53* (Stroud, 1996), 110–12.

[170] *RRAN*, III, e.g. nos. 68, 190, 259, 295, 316, 343, 368–9; 497, 629, 899; 253; for examples of looser drafting, see nos. 391, 419.

normally being styled 'daughter of King Henry' as well as (from April 1141) 'lady of the English' and from 1144 taking opportunities which arose to associate her son Henry in the patronage she bestowed.[171] She also maintained a small court akin to the royal household, and was attended by officers bearing the same titles as those they had enjoyed in the service of the king. Among the men who transferred to her allegiance on or soon after her arrival in England were several who had held office under Henry I and Stephen in succession: the constables Brian fitz Count and Miles of Gloucester, the marshal John fitz Gilbert, and the steward Humphrey II de Bohun. In addition, Robert de Courcy, steward to Henry I but not to Stephen, witnessed for her at Falaise before her invasion. Despite his devotion to the empress's cause, Brian fitz Count does not figure in any of her charters as a constable, but all the others seem to have brought their titles with them.[172] By the summer of 1141 she had various other officials: as chamberlains Aubrey III de Vere, William de Pont de l'Arche, William Mauduit and possibly Geoffrey de Clinton, as constables William de Beauchamp and Robert d'Oilli, and as chancellor William brother of John Marshal. All but the last had a claim to office dating from the previous reign, and two had been in Stephen's service.[173] Others who occur as her constables were William Peverel of Dover and Patrick of Salisbury, although these appointments may have come later.[174] And if she needed advice on the conduct of royal government beyond that which the more experienced of these office-holders could give, she could turn during 1141 to her father's former keeper of the seal, Robert de Sigillo (for whom she secured the bishopric of London), to the late king's former treasurer Nigel bishop of Ely, and both then and later to her mother's former chancellor Bernard bishop of St David's.[175]

Empress Matilda, then, while seeking in the long term to demonstrate her family's entitlement to the throne, was also in the short term exercising royal authority wherever she could. In the areas most directly under her control, around Gloucester, Oxford and Devizes, she treated the royal demesne both as a source of income and as a means of patronage.[176] Within a broader zone, as far north as Shropshire and as far west as Cornwall, she tried to set up an alternative shire administration, by

---

[171] Chibnall, 'Charters of Empress', esp. 277–80, 288–9, where possible use of the style *regina* in the spring and summer of 1141 is also discussed.

[172] *Hist. Nov.*, 36; *RRAN*, II, xii, xvi–ii; *ibid.*, III, xviii–xxi, xxx–xxxii, and no. 805. Brian fitz Count did not carry any title when issuing a charter in favour of Evesham Abbey, witnessed by the empress as *Domina* (B.L. Cott. MS. Vesp. B xxiv, fo. 17).

[173] *RRAN*, III, xix–xx (for the service rendered to Stephen by William de Pont de l'Arche and Robert d'Oilli), xxix–xxxii and no. 629; cf. *ibid.*, II, xiii–xvi.   [174] *Ibid.*, III, nos. 111, 839.

[175] Chibnall, 'Charters of Empress', 278.

[176] *RRAN*, III, nos. 296, 316a, 368, 370, 497, 628–9, 644; Chibnall, *Matilda*, 118, 122–34.

appointing her own earls or addressing her own sheriffs.[177] In 1141, she expressed her entitlement to a customary royal tax – the *donum* unwisely imposed on the Londoners – and assumed that the exchequer would respond to her commands as they had done to the king's.[178] All this was not an attempt to destroy royal government, but as far as possible to take it over and make it work. The same could obviously be said of her son Henry of Anjou, who took up the cause left to him by the empress when she retired to Normandy early in 1148. Yet with his arrival in her place, a change of emphasis can be discerned. Although Matilda's effective authority was confined to a small part of the country, except during 1141, within that area she could fairly claim to be maintaining an alternative royal administration. Henry's position was somewhat different. He was determined to pose as king-in-waiting, with a right to wield authority over the whole of England, but in practical terms his governmental control was weaker than his mother's. Grand political claims went with minimal administrative impact.

Henry's visit to England in 1149–50 was his third in all, but the first in which he had issued charters of his own. In one which carried a precise date, 13 April 1149, he notified the restoration of the manor of Bishop's Canning (Wiltshire) to the bishop and church of Salisbury, while retaining Devizes castle and the service of the knights of the manor 'on account of my necessity': a clear indication of the continuing importance of this locality to the Angevin cause, despite his mother's enforced surrender of Canning in the previous year on the orders of the pope. Another charter, issued on the same occasion, recorded the gift of Loxwell, also in Wiltshire, for the foundation of a Cistercian abbey on land formerly held by the empress's chamberlain Drogo.[179] Further grants which probably belong to this visit favoured Reading Abbey and the earl of Gloucester's vassal Fulk fitz Warin, who received the royal manors of Blewbury (Berkshire) and Alveston (Gloucestershire) respectively; these duly figured as *terrae datae*, still in the same hands, in the early pipe rolls of the following reign. Kingswood Abbey was another beneficiary, also apparently from royal demesne in Gloucestershire.[180] This was limited patronage, but it did at least serve to affirm the young Henry's authority in that part of the kingdom most committed to his mother, and to rally traditional supporters in the region, such as the earls of Cornwall, Gloucester, Hereford and Wiltshire, John Marshal and Humphrey II de Bohun,

---

[177] *RRAN*, III, e.g. nos. 190 (to Somerset), 378, 820–1 (to Shropshire), 793 (to Wiltshire), although a more extensive area was covered during her ascendancy in 1141; Davis, *Stephen* , 136–9.

[178] *Gesta Steph.*, 120–2; *RRAN*, III, nos. 328, 628, 899 (cf. nos. 327, 626 of Stephen).

[179] *RRAN*, III, nos. 794–5, 666; Chibnall, *Matilda*, 125, 134, 148–9.

[180] *RRAN*, III, nos. 704, 320 (correcting the identification suggested by the editors), 420; *PR2H*, 34, 49; *PR3H*, 80, 100, etc.

all of whom occur as witnesses to his charters at this time.[181]

Back in Normandy with the title of duke by the early months of 1150,[182] Henry maintained his stance as the prospective king, but to little immediate effect. He confirmed Reginald de St Valery's gift of £20 of Rouen money from the revenues of Dieppe as an annual pension to Fontevrault Abbey, promising to augment this to £20 sterling 'when, God willing, I shall have recovered my hereditary right in England' and the rents of the port had reverted to him.[183] A suspect charter in favour of Fontenay Abbey has him granting freedom from tolls in Normandy, Anjou and England 'through all my demesnes' on pain of £10 forfeit.[184] He was evidently sought out – in preference to the king – by the monks of Reading, in the hope of securing their tenure of the churches of Thatcham (Berkshire) and Berkeley (Gloucestershire), both the subject of previous grants by the empress but clearly under dispute. He duly issued writs to the offending parties, but also sent a letter asking Archbishop Theobald to intervene over Berkeley: the request, it would seem, of a man who did not expect to be obeyed.[185] The years before his final invasion of England witnessed considerable disruption within the region which had given the empress support. Gloucestershire and Wiltshire were ravaged by the king's adherents in 1149; Worcestershire fell victim both to assault by the king and to a violent dispute involving Waleran of Meulan and William de Beauchamp between 1150 and 1152; castles in Berkshire, including Wallingford, were besieged by the king, also in 1152.[186] By then, there was an air of desperation among Henry's supporters in the south-west, with Reginald earl of Cornwall crossing to Normandy in an effort to persuade him to invade, and Roger earl of Hereford sending a letter begging him 'if he . . . cared at all to recover the kingdom, to return to England with all speed and aid them . . . in their sore distress'.[187]

Many of the charters Henry issued in England in 1153–4 cannot be dated with any precision, but there are sufficient which can confidently be attributed to the period before the peace settlement for conclusions to be drawn about his administration at that time. He brought a new generation of household officials with him: the constable Richard du Hommet, the steward Manasser Bisset, and the chamberlain Warin fitz

---

[181] *RRAN*, III, no. 666 affords a glimpse of Henry's household in England during 1149–50, with Humphrey II de Bohun (formerly steward to Henry I, Stephen and the empress) attesting with Hubert de Vaux and Humphrey fitz Odo as constable, and a certain Gregory witnessing as steward (cf. nos. 392, 795).

[182] RT, 161; Gervase, I, 142; Davis, *Stephen*, 107, n. 27 with references there cited.

[183] *RRAN*, III, no. 329   [184] *Ibid.*, III, no. 326.   [185] *Ibid.*, III, nos. 698, 702, 705–10.

[186] *Gesta Steph*, 218–30; HH, 754–60; Davis, *Stephen*, 110–11.

[187] RT, 164; *Gesta Steph.*, 228–30.

Gerold. In company with William fitz Hamo who was certainly a member of the household but did not have a title, they were the most frequent witnesses to his charters in England, before and after the 'treaty of Winchester', and returned with him to France about Easter 1154. Some Angevin loyalists had their household titles acknowledged – Humphrey II de Bohun and Robert de Courcy as stewards, John fitz Gilbert as marshal – as did William Mauduit, whose chamberlainship was confirmed despite his apparent failure to discharge any duties until after Henry's accession as king.[188] There are references to Walter of Hereford, brother of Earl Roger, and to the Bedfordshire baron Walter de Odell as constables in August 1153.[189] Henry also had a chancellor, William, who seems previously to have served the empress, and a treasurer, Henry son of Robert fitz Harding, who was based at Bristol.[190] One scribe, no. XXIII, appears to have worked for him regularly in England during 1153.[191]

Henry's patronage in that year ranged widely, as was to be expected since his military campaign embraced much of the Midlands, and was uninhibited in its treatment of royal demesnes and revenues. A charter for St Augustine's Abbey, Bristol, apparently of January to May 1153, extravagantly remitted 'all revenues pertaining to the crown of England' on all alms given to the canons by himself or others, past or future; not surprisingly, Stephen omitted this open-ended commitment when confirming the duke's charter after the peace settlement. A confirmation charter for Biddlesden Abbey (Buckinghamshire), probably of June 1153, acquitted the monks of murder-fines, taxes 'and all customs pertaining to my crown'. In a charter mentioning Kings William I and Henry I as 'my *antecessores*', the monks of Malmesbury were acquitted of toll 'throughout all England' and assured that no royal forester would enter their forests. Confirmations of assarts in favour of the bishop and church of Lichfield, and of the foundation of the abbey at Radmore (Staffordshire), both clearly datable to 1153, also referred to Cannock forest as 'mine'.[192] The beneficiaries doubtless hoped that he would proceed to the throne so that his gifts could take effect, but cannot have seen them other than as promises for the future. Henry's famous charter for Ranulf II earl of Chester, issued at Devizes in the early months of the year and in reality a treaty with the earl who had his own set of witnesses, granted 'all his inheritance of Normandy and England' and added a series of baronial estates and royal manors across the north Midlands. But both parties

---

[188] *RRAN*, III, xxxv–xxxviii and no. 582; G. J. White, 'The end of Stephen's reign', *History* 75 (1990), 3–22 (at 15–17 and n. 58).   [189] *RRAN*, III, no. 492; cf. *ibid.*, III, no. 962.
[190] *Ibid.*, III, xxxiv, xxxvii; White, 'End of Stephen's reign', 16–17 and n. 56.
[191] *RRAN*, III, xxxv; *ibid.*, IV, plates xl–xli; Bishop, *Scriptores Regis*, plate xxiii.
[192] *RRAN*, III, nos. 126–7, 104, 574, 459, 840.

knew that, while the Norman estates were under Henry's control, it was up to Ranulf to fight for what he had been given in England: Henry had to promise that, wherever he was unable at present to restore Ranulf's full inheritance, he would do so when he could.[193] When making recompense for damage to the canons of St Paul's, Bedford, about the end of August, Henry magnanimously offered to restore, protect, defend and guard their rights 'wherever they were in England'. But he also promised, more realistically, that if he could not guarantee the ten librates he had given them in Bedford, he would find them something of equivalent value, and would give more 'when, God willing, I shall have attained my right' in England.[194]

A search for evidence of active government by Henry during 1153 – the raising of revenues, the settlement of disputes, and the exercise of patronage intended to take immediate effect – rarely takes us far from Bristol, the seat of his treasury. Probably in the late spring, he confirmed Roger earl of Hereford's gift to Cirencester Abbey of two hides in Cirencester, Baunton and Chesterton (Gloucestershire), one of which was of 'my demesne' held by the earl at fee farm; the gift was made 'saving my farm which the same Earl Roger ought to render to me'.[195] Henry's charters in favour of Robert fitz Harding, supposedly recording grants during 1153 from the royal demesne in Bitton, Berkeley and Berkeley 'hernesse', also in Gloucestershire, were probably drawn up for the beneficiary to justify encroachments during the civil war, but appear to make reference to transactions which actually took place: 'on account of this gift, Robert fitz Harding became my man' and 'he gave me fifty marks in recognition'.[196] The only example of a Henrician writ addressed to the officials of a specific shire and definitely datable to 1153 also relates to Gloucestershire: Roger earl of Hereford, in company with an un-named sheriff and the burgesses of Gloucester, was the addressee in a writ ordering that Roger de Tockenham hold his land near the north gate as freely as he had held in Henry I's time.[197] Even if analysis of Henry's charters from this phase of the reign is extended to embrace those which cannot be closely dated, we still find property and beneficiaries in Gloucestershire dominating the picture,[198] and it seems clear that this was the shire in which he perceived his authority to be most secure. Of the other counties where his mother had apparently enjoyed some control, he seems to have had few direct dealings with Berkshire and Wiltshire,

[193] *Ibid.*, III, no. 180; White, 'Stephen, Henry and Ranulf'.
[194] *RRAN*, III, no. 81; Richardson and Sayles, *Governance*, 254.
[195] *RRAN*, III, no. 193; the hides appear to be those granted by Earl Roger in 'Charters of Hereford', ed. Walker, no. 29, but despite the attestation of this charter by Henry's chamberlain Warin fitz Gerold it has no reference to a fee farm obligation. [196] *RRAN*, III, nos. 309–10.
[197] *Ibid.*, III, no. 901. [198] *Ibid.*, III, nos. 306, 321, 362, 363a–365a, 997–1000.

none with Herefordshire or Oxfordshire.[199] In practice, therefore, his short-term position was weaker than his mother's. The region from which he collected revenues may very well have been confined to Gloucestershire. He only retained the empress's old headquarters at Devizes castle on sufferance from Jocelin bishop of Salisbury for a three-year term or until 'he should recover his right'.[200] And there is no firm evidence that even the mints which had struck coins in the name of Empress Matilda ever produced coins for Henry of Anjou.[201]

Of course this is only part of the story. The years since the empress's departure in 1148 had reinforced the independence of the earls in south-western England, and it was not in Henry's interests to threaten their positions. Henry's purpose was not to reassert authority in one part of the kingdom, but to wrest control of it all. Accordingly, most of the charters he issued during 1153 were addressed generally, to all his officers and faithful men French and English, or alternatively to those of Normandy and England, in conscious imitation of the royal chancery.[202] Moreover, his campaign during the summer through the Midlands was an ideal opportunity to present himself over a wide area as a live contender for the throne, responding to approaches by individuals and institutions seeking promises for the future, confirmations of holdings, or the redress of grievances. His favours to the bishop and church of Lichfield, and to the canons of Bedford, involving royal property far from the south-west and only redeemable after he had come to the throne, belonged to the summer of 1153. So did confirmations of the possessions of Haughmond Abbey (Shropshire) and Radmore Abbey (Staffordshire) issued at Leicester and Coventry respectively.[203] In August 1153, at the siege of Crowmarsh, he appears to have played a major part in facilitating Ranulf II earl of Chester's grants of Marston and Warkworth (Northamptonshire) in recompense for damage to Lincoln Cathedral. Ranulf made his donation, and the rival holder Walter de Odell quitclaimed his rights in the manors, in Henry's presence; the earl also undertook to resolve other claims to the property, or give the cathedral land of equivalent value, with Henry promising compensation from his own demesne if Ranulf failed to do so.[204] This was not the first time Henry had reinforced agreements between his barons, for at Gloucester, apparently in the spring, he had confirmed the *conventionem et concordiam* made between Stephen Gay and

---

[199] *Ibid.*, III, nos. 574–5, 710, 837; his charter in favour of the Oxfordshire abbey of Thame (no. 875) apparently postdates the peace settlement. [200] *Ibid.*, III, no. 796.

[201] King, 'Anarchy of King Stephen's reign', 150; Blackburn, 'Coinage and currency', in King, *Anarchy*, 188–90. [202] *RRAN*, III, e.g. nos. 44, 81, 126, 180, 193, 339, 379, 459.

[203] *Ibid.*, III, nos. 459, 81, 379, 841.

[204] *Ibid.*, III, no. 492; cf. no. 491, and for comment *Charters of the Anglo-Norman Earls of Chester, c. 1071–1327*, ed. G. Barraclough (Record Society of Lancs. and Ches., 1988), 119.

his stepson Gilbert regarding the inheritance of Gilbert's mother, now Stephen Gay's wife.[205] Through his involvement in settlements such as these, Henry was already contributing to a restoration of order after the civil war, and providing that security for baronial *conventiones* which had been lacking in earlier years, when hostages had had to be offered and it had been necessary to resort to the intervention of the Church.[206] This was a fine advertisement for the re-establishment of royal government throughout the kingdom.

There was, however, a third source of royal authority in England during Stephen's reign, that of David king of Scots and his son Henry. Under the first treaty of Durham of 5 February 1136, Henry of Scots received Carlisle, Doncaster and his father's earldom of Huntingdon; he also did homage to Stephen, though whether this was for all the territories is unclear. After further Scottish offensives, the second treaty of Durham (9 April 1139) confirmed all these to Henry and added the earldom of Northumberland, with certain exceptions, notably the castles of Bamburgh and Newcastle, probably in return for a renewal of homage.[207] The Scots subsequently made strenuous efforts to consolidate and extend their authority in the northern shires. In Northumberland, they came into possession of Bamburgh and Newcastle, despite the terms of the 1139 treaty, and treated Newcastle as a major royal residence.[208] In Cumbria, the Scottish noblemen William fitz Duncan (David's nephew) and Hugh de Morville were given lordships to reinforce the grip established by Henry of Scots at Carlisle.[209] In Durham, King David attempted in vain to secure the election of his chancellor William Cumin to the bishopric vacated by the death of Geoffrey Rufus in May 1141.[210] In Lancashire, David came to rule at least as far south as the Ribble, before receiving the homage of Ranulf II earl of Chester for the honour of Lancaster in 1149.[211] In Yorkshire, where he had extensive demesnes,

---

[205] *RRAN*, III, no. 339.
[206] Holdsworth, 'War and peace in the twelfth century', esp. 84–6; King, 'Dispute settlement', esp. 122–3.
[207] JH, 287, 300; RH, 146, 177–8; Barrow, 'The Scots and the North', 246–7; Stringer, *Reign of Stephen*, 32–3; P. Dalton, *Conquest, Anarchy and Lordship: Yorkshire 1066–1154* (Cambridge, 1994), 204–5.
[208] *Regesta Regum Scottorum I: the Acta of Malcolm IV, King of Scots*, ed. G. W. S. Barrow (Edinburgh, 1960), 109–10; Barrow, 'The Scots and the North', 247; Dalton, *Conquest, Anarchy and Lordship*, 206.
[209] Barrow, 'The Scots and the North', 241–2; Dalton, *Conquest, Anarchy and Lordship*, 206–7.
[210] A. Young, *William Cumin: Border Politics and the Bishopric of Durham, 1141–44* (University of York, Borthwick Paper 54, 1979), esp. 5–19.
[211] G. W. S. Barrow, 'King David I and the honour of Lancaster', *EHR*, 70 (1955), 85–9; J. A. Green. 'Earl Ranulf II and Lancashire', in Thacker, ed., *Earldom of Chester*, 97–108; the suggestion *ibid.*, 101, that Scots control in north Lancashire began as early as 1138 also appears (independently) in Dalton, *Conquest, Anarchy and Lordship*, 227–8.

probably including Doncaster and possibly part of Hallamshire for most of the reign,[212] the king of Scots helped to secure William fitz Duncan in possession of Skipton, and won considerable influence over the Church, cultivating close relations with leading Cistercian houses and seeking the election of a favourably disposed archbishop.[213] His attack on York in 1149, which was foiled by Stephen's prompt march to its defence, has been plausibly interpreted as a bid to incorporate the whole of Yorkshire into the Scottish kingdom.[214]

In Northumberland, Earl Henry immediately assumed the king's lordship as his own: a charter apparently predating the battle of Lincoln has him granting to Eustace fitz John all the lands in Northumberland previously held in chief from Henry I and Stephen.[215] Coins bearing his name soon appeared from the mint at Corbridge; these were modelled on Stephen's type 1 and were the work of a moneyer Erebald who also produced coins of King David at Edinburgh. Several other charters relating to his northern earldom show his control of sheriffs, his reservation of pleas, his right to levy castle-works, and his capacity to alienate property in the borough of Newcastle and the liberty of Tynedale; by the mid- to late 1140s a new type of coinage was being struck in his name, probably at Bamburgh.[216]

King David, on the other hand, seems at first to have kept a low profile. A few coins in his name, modelled on those of Henry I's type 15, were struck at Carlisle; these may be attributable to the weeks between his capture of the town at the beginning of 1136 and his reconciliation with Stephen under the first treaty of Durham, or they may be a little later, but in any event they appear to have been exceptional and rare.[217] The mints at Carlisle, Durham and Newcastle went on in the late 1130s to produce coins of Stephen's type 1, albeit from locally made dies except initially at Newcastle, or local variants still in the name of Stephen. Although Davidian coins were being minted during these years at Edinburgh and Roxburgh, it was not until the early 1140s that a new type (ivc) bearing his name began to be struck at Carlisle and Newcastle. Thereafter Carlisle, most conveniently situated for the Alston silver mines which helped to sustain this Scottish currency at a standard even better

[212] *Ibid.*, 220–1.
[213] JH, 326; Dalton, *Conquest, Anarchy and Lordship*, 214–19, 221–7 and ch. 5 for Scots influence in Yorkshire generally.
[214] *Ibid.*, 228–9; cf. Stringer, *Reign of Stephen*, 36–7 and 'State-building in twelfth-century Britain', 57–9. [215] *Regesta Regum Scottorum*, I, no.11.
[216] *Ibid.*, I, nos. 23, 28, 32, 43, 96–8, 103; *Early Scottish Charters*, ed. A. C. Lawrie (Glasgow, 1905) nos. 131, 146; Blackburn, 'Coinage and currency', in King, *Anarchy*, 191–3.
[217] I. Stewart, 'Scottish mints', in R. A. G. Carson, ed., *Mints, Dies and Currency* (London, 1971), 165–289 (esp. 191–3).

than Stephen's substantive issues, minted a further type in the name of
David and also of Henry late in the reign.[218] As for the charters, it is clear
that David did on occasion advertise his authority in England in the early
years of Stephen's reign, for he granted protection to Tynemouth Priory
while besieging Norham in June 1138; according to Richard of Hexham
he had joined with his son in giving similar protection to Hexham Priory
earlier in the year.[219] But with these exceptions, David seems at first to
have been reticent about displaying his kingship in the region, apparently
leaving other charters of Earl Henry unconfirmed.[220] The year 1141 may
well have been a watershed in this respect. Stephen's capture at the battle
of Lincoln was an event regarded as of some significance for dating
purposes by the Scots royal court, even after his release,[221] and King
David's lifestyle certainly changed dramatically during the course of the
year, taking in visits to Empress Matilda's courts at Westminster and
Oxford, and a narrow escape from the battle of Stockbridge, at which he
fought on her behalf.[222] These experiences possibly convinced the king of
Scots that he need no longer dissemble in his attitude to the northern
English shires, that there was no reason not to treat them as fully part of
his realm, and that he was free to extend his kingdom further by force if
he could. From hereon, he often associated himself with grants made by
his son, confirming to Tynemouth Priory, as 'my own alms', all held at
Henry I's death (as similar charters of King Stephen and Earl Henry had
done), granting Nostell Priory an annual render of three marks from 'my
silver mine of Carlisle' (identical words to those used by Earl Henry) and
reinforcing his son's foundation of Holm Cultram Abbey in Cumbria.[223]
Elsewhere, he made grants to Shrewsbury Abbey from what had become
his demesnes as far south as Bispham in Lancashire, and confirmed gifts by
his vassals to St Bees Priory in Cumbria, St Mary's Abbey and St

---

[218] R. P. Mack, 'Stephen and the Anarchy, 1135–1154', *BNJ*, 35 (1966), 38–112 (esp. 97–101);
Stewart, 'Scottish mints', 192–6; Blackburn, 'Coinage and currency', in King, *Anarchy*, 192–3.
The silver-mining boom around Alston following discoveries in 1133 is discussed in I. Blanchard,
'Lothian and beyond: the economy of the "English empire" of David I', in Britnell and Hatcher,
Progress and Problems, 23–45.   [219] *Early Scottish Charters*, no. 119; RH, 154.
[220] Neither the early charter of Earl Henry in favour of Eustace fitz John (above, n. 215) nor two of
his charters for Durham Cathedral Priory which probably predated the attempt to instal William
Cumin (*Early Scottish Charters*, nos. 129, 131) appear to have received confirmation from King
David.
[221] *Early Scottish Charters*, nos. 141–2, where the Friday after Ascension Day in the second year
following Stephen's capture was given as the date of a perambulation in the 'foundation charters'
of Melrose Abbey.
[222] *RRAN*, III, nos. 328, 377, 393, 629, 899; *Hist. Nov.*, 56, 59; *Gesta Steph.*, 120, 128. 134; HH, 740;
Chibnall, *Matilda*, 100–1; Hill, 'Battle of Stockbridge'.
[223] *Regesta Regum Scottorum*, I, no. 31 (dated 1141 at earliest because of attestation of Edward the
chancellor: *ibid.*, I, pp. 111–12); cf. no. 24 and *RRAN*, III, no. 906; *Regesta Regum Scottorum*, I, nos.
39–40 (cf. nos. 37–8); *Early Scottish Charters*, nos. 144–5; Stringer, *Reign of Stephen*, 37.

Leonard's Hospital, York, and Whitby Abbey, Yorkshire.[224] He used the style 'king of Scots' whatever the geographical location of his grants, was accompanied by a household of consistent membership, and held court not only in Edinburgh and Roxburgh but also at Newcastle (where he obliged the barons of Northumberland to acknowledge his grandson William as earl following Henry's death in July 1152) and Carlisle (where he died in May 1153).[225]

Such governmental activity obviously had the potential for the long-term establishment of a frontier between the English and Scottish king-doms much further south than it had been at Henry I's death: a prospect Henry II tackled head on when he met Malcolm IV at Chester in the summer of 1157 and told him that 'the king of England ought not to be defrauded of so large a part of his kingdom'. Northumberland, Cumber-land and Westmorland were surrendered as a result.[226] It must be ac-knowledged that King David and Earl Henry's relations with many of the northern barons were tenuous and that they encountered stiff resistance to their authority at times,[227] yet their government in northern England – certainly in Cumbria and Northumberland – was conducted with suffi-cient vigour to leave Henry II with a sound administrative legacy. The 1158 pipe roll, the first to include accounts from this region following Malcolm IV's surrenders of the previous year, shows the sheriff of Carlisle Robert fitz Troite, the custodian of the silver mines William fitz Erem-bald and the sheriff of Northumberland William de Vesci all meeting obligations on their farms in full.[228] The boroughs of Carlisle and New-castle were among the few to be charged a *donum* in this year, and both paid all they were charged without delay. The full amount of farm was also received from Doncaster, where the custodian was Adam fitz Swein. He was a Yorkshire landholder who had been associated with the king of Scots during Stephen's reign, witnessing one of David's charters and securing his royal confirmation of a gift to St Mary's Abbey, York.[229]

---

[224] *Early Scottish Charters*, nos. 138–40, 187, 254; *Regesta Regum Scottorum*, I, no. 76.

[225] *Ibid.*, I, p. 114 and nos. 30–2; *Early Scottish Charters*, e.g. nos. 121, 148, 155, 158, 168; JH, 327, 330; G. W. S. Barrow, 'The charters of David I', *ANS*, 14 (1992), 25–37.

[226] Newburgh, I, 105; *A Scottish Chronicle known as the Chronicle of Holyrood*, ed. M. O. Anderson (Scottish Historical Society, 1938), 32; Barrow, 'The Scots and the North', esp. 251–3.

[227] Dalton, *Conquest, Anarchy and Lordship*, 207–27, and 'Northern England in King Stephen's reign', in J. E. Hollinshead and F. Pogson, eds., *Studies in Northern History* (Liverpool, 1997), 1–35; cf. J. A. Green, 'Anglo-Scottish relations, 1066–1174', in M. Jones and M. Vale, eds., *England and her Neighbours: Essays in Honour of Pierre Chaplais* (London, 1989), 53–72 (esp. 63). Barrow, 'The Scots and the North', 248, 252, draws attention to the unwillingness of some Northumbrian magnates to accept Earl Henry and (in 1152) his son Earl William. Young, *William Cumin*, covers the enduring hostility to King David of the Durham cathedral chapter.

[228] *PR4H*, 119–20, 177; the sheriffs' farm accounts of Carlisle and Northumberland did in fact show a surplus.

[229] *Ibid.*, 179; *Early Scottish Charters*, nos. 140, 187; Dalton, *Conquest, Anarchy and Lordship*, 216–17.

Since Robert fitz Troite also had connections with the Scots royal house,[230] it is quite possible that, at least in Doncaster and Carlisle, the king of England was relying on the same administrators as had previously answered to the Scots.

The impression of orderly government in northern England under David and Henry of Scots is reinforced by the favourable verdicts they received from the chroniclers. John of Hexham, who experienced their rule of Northumberland, praised Earl Henry as kind and gentle, disciplined and reverent, devoted to acts of charity to the poor, adding that King David's memory would be blessed through all generations.[231] Ailred of Rievaulx's biographer Walter Daniel shared his abbot's admiration of David, a king worthy of the veneration accorded to him, compassionate, honest and steadfast.[232] William of Newburgh, who wrote towards the end of the century but with boyhood memories of Yorkshire in Stephen's reign, lamented the state of the country but made an exception of 'the northern region, which as far as the River Tees had fallen under the control of King David of Scotland'. Under David, 'a civilised king of an uncivilised race', and his son Henry, 'a young man of great renown . . . noted for his pleasant and honest disposition', the far north of England was a haven of peace.[233] There can be little doubt that, within much of this region, royal government, modelled on that of Henry I in whose court David had been raised,[234] was operating with fair efficiency. The task for Henry II was not to reconstruct it, but to transfer it to his own control.

To summarise, then, England in the reign of Stephen was a kingdom in which royal authority was exercised from rival centres. David and Henry of Scots effectively annexed the northernmost parts to their own separate kingdom, and threatened to make the arrangement permanent. Further south, Stephen on the one hand, Empress Matilda and her son Henry on the other, claimed rightfully to govern the whole of the kingdom, but in practice controlled limited areas while occasionally asserting themselves further afield. But these rival authorities all saw themselves as the lawful successors of Henry I,[235] and although the civil war meant that any local dispute was liable to erupt into violent disorder, each of them had a vested interest in maintaining as far as possible the systems of royal government he had left behind. 'Anarchy' in the sense of 'absence of government' is

---

[230] *Regesta Regum Scottorum*, I, 13 and n. 2.   [231] JH, 327, 330.

[232] *Life of Ailred of Rievaulx by Walter Daniel*, ed. F. M. Powicke (OMT, 1978), 2–8.

[233] WN, 98–103. For other panegyrics, see G. W. S. Barrow, *David I of Scotland (1124–1153): the Balance of New and Old* (University of Reading, 1985), 5–7.

[234] OV, IV, 274–5; *RRAN*, II, nos. 648, 689, 701, 706, 818a, 828, 832–3, 883; Barrow, *David I of Scotland*, 16–17; J. A. Green, 'David I and Henry I', *Scottish Historical Review*, 75 (1996), 1–19.

[235] *RRAN*, III, e.g. nos. 1, 4 (Stephen), 20, 43 (Empress Matilda), 44, 90 (Henry).

scarcely appropriate, therefore, as a description of Northumberland under David and Henry of Scots, or Gloucestershire before the empress's departure from England, or Essex once Geoffrey II de Mandeville had been removed from the scene. It is in relation to other parts of the country, where neither Stephen nor the Angevin leaders – let alone the Scots – could exercise much control in the 1140s and early 1150s, that the term arguably has more validity, despite the efforts of various magnates to govern these regions, independently of the king but also in imitation of him. This is the subject of the next section of this chapter.

GOVERNMENT BY THE MAGNATES

The image of England falling prey during Stephen's reign to the rapacity of local barons is a familiar one. William of Newburgh offered a good description.

Numerous castles had been raised in different regions through the eager activity of various factions; and in England there were in a sense as many kings, or rather tyrants, as there were lords of castles. Each minted his own coinage, and each like a king had the power to lay down the law for his subjects. As each of them sought predominance in this way, so that some could not stomach a higher authority and some not even an equal, they disputed with each other in deadly hatreds, they despoiled the most famous regions with plunderings and burnings, and in a country once most fertile they virtually wiped out the bread which is the staff of life.[236]

William of Newburgh immediately made an exception of David king of Scots and his son, but his general message was that non-royal government meant bad government. This was a sentiment shared by other twelfth-century writers. There were few good words, for example, for the earls appointed by Stephen and Empress Matilda in turn. Leading participants on both sides in the battle of Lincoln, all holders of comital titles, were vilified by Henry of Huntingdon, several Angevin-appointed earls were criticised as oppressors in the *Gesta Stephani*, and Stephen's creations were dismissed as 'pseudo-comites' by Robert de Torigni.[237] But condemnation was directed at others besides the earls. The wicked levy of *tenserie*, which if taken literally means 'protection money', was associated in the *Anglo-Saxon Chronicle*, in papal bulls in favour of Ely Cathedral and Sherborne Abbey, and in Theobald's legatine council of 1151, with men

---

[236] WN, 98–9 (translation adapted).
[237] HH, 728–34; *Gesta Steph.*, 102, 158–60, 164, 214; RT, 183. For a similarly dismissive reference to William de Mohun, appointed by the empress as earl of Dorset in 1141, see H. W. C. Davis, 'Henry of Blois and Brian fitz Count', *EHR*, 25 (1910), 300–1.

of no specific rank.[238] It was not only Stephen's earl of Sussex, William d'Aubigny, and the empress's earl of Hereford, Miles of Gloucester, who offended the Church with 'illegal' exactions, but also William de Beauchamp and John Marshal, who never held a comital title. Similarly, it was 'barons' in general, not earls in particular, whose hearing of crown pleas received legatine condemnation.[239]

But was this government by the magnates necessarily to be deplored? Should it not, in some circumstances, be seen as an essential response to the curtailment of effective royal authority in various parts of the country as a result of civil war? Magnates were happy to take this opportunity for self-aggrandisement, but in filling the vacuum left by a partial breakdown in royal government, they were not always working to the detriment of those subjected to their rule. In 1150, for instance, the leading baron in Staffordshire, Robert of Stafford, presided in his honorial court over the hearing of a dispute between Ernald fitz Enisan of Walton and the canons of Stone Priory concerning land in Walton and Stone. When some of this land had been in question during the previous reign, the matter had been settled in the king's court at Beckenham in the presence of Henry I, who had issued a charter of confirmation, but now there was neither a royal writ to initiate proceedings, nor a royal charter to confirm their outcome. Nevertheless, with the help of three archdeacons to represent the bishop and protect the Church's interests, and after careful scrutiny of documentary evidence, Robert of Stafford – 'mindful of the peace' – duly brought the parties to a compromise settlement.[240] Another relevant example, of about the same date, concerns Simon II de Senlis. When the monks of St Andrew's Priory, Northampton, required enforcement of a settlement in their favour reached in the court of the bishop of Lincoln, it was not the king but Simon as the local earl who brought the parties before him and issued the confirmation charter.[241] Magnates' charters, their addresses

[238] *ASC*, 199; *Papsturkunden in England*, ed. W. Holtzmann (Berlin and Gottingen, 1930–53), II, no. 36, III, no. 58; Saltman, *Theobald*, 547; Round, *Geoffrey de Mandeville*, 414–16; King, 'Anarchy of King Stephen's reign', 135–7.

[239] *Ibid.*, 133, 135–6; GF, *Letters*, nos. 3, 32; Saltman, *Theobald*, 547 (cap. ii). It is of course possible that some cases of recompense to religious houses following levies 'in my necessity' are the result of agreements entered into at the time of the exactions, with the churches striking a hard bargain: cf. Roger de Mowbray and Fountains Abbey in *Charters of the Honour of Mowbray, 1107–1191*, ed. D. E. Greenway (London, 1972), no. 103, and (from Henry II's reign) Geoffrey de Hay and Combe Abbey (Warwickshire) in Bodleian Dugdale MS. 12 (SC 6502), p. 114 (a gift to the monks from his wood of Brinklow, with reference to the fact that the monks in friendliness and affection 'per mea necessitate allevianda' had made over to him 41 silver marks).

[240] *Lawsuits*, I, no. 325 (cf. no. 275).

[241] *Ibid.*, I, no. 338. Two charters of Simon II de Senlis as earl of Northampton, in favour of Thorney Abbey, are also worth citing in this connection. Both offer protection to the monks' market at Yaxley (Huntingdonshire) and are included in the abbey's cartulary among a series of royal charters in similar terms. One charter, addressed to Simon's steward, officers and men, overtly

restricted to their own men, French and English,[242] obviously carried less weight than those of a king, but such intervention was better than nothing. So in approaching the subject of 'government by the magnates', we ought not to accept the sweeping generalisations of the chroniclers without qualification: it is important to take each case on its merits.

The proliferation of earldoms during Stephen's reign has received a good deal of scholarly attention, and it is appropriate therefore to give first consideration to the earls. This is not the place to rehearse arguments presented in detail elsewhere [243] but it seems fair to say that, with few exceptions, the king's main intention in his liberal distribution of earldoms (mostly between 1138 and 1140) was to pander to magnates' aspirations through what he perceived to be a cheap form of patronage. The outbreak of civil war following Empress Matilda's invasion was a turning point, as both parties came to appreciate the value of having their own military and administrative representatives in various shires, but neither Stephen's earls nor those created by the empress proved to be dependable in this role (especially through the traumas of 1141) and there were few new creations, by either side, thereafter. The address clauses of surviving writs and charters, issued by Stephen, the empress or Henry before his accession, show earls to have been called upon only occasionally to act on their leader's behalf: Simon II de Senlis in Huntingdonshire and Northamptonshire was exceptional in being addressed with some consistency.[244]

Yet if earls rarely proved effective as local representatives of royalist or Angevin government, it is clear that they did seek to enhance their own

reinforces the king's previous orders ('sicut carta Regis Stephani precepit') but seems indicative of a perception on the part of the monks that their best prospects of security lay, for the moment, with the earl. The other charter, addressed to Alexander bishop of Lincoln and the earl's barons and officers of Huntingdonshire, shows how fragile such security might be: although Simon confirms previous charters of Henry I and Stephen, he provides no sanctions and can only 'pray you that for the love of God and of me you will maintain the aforesaid market and all possessions of that place' (Cambridge University Library, Add. MS. 3020, fos. 21–21v.; King, 'Economic development', 12).

[242] Robert's address was to 'all his men and friends French and English', Simon's (for St Andrew's Priory) to 'all his men French as well as English of Northamptonshire'; cf. those for Thorney, above n. 241, and P. R. Hyams, 'The charter as a source for the early common law', *Journal of Legal History*, 12 (1991), 173–89.

[243] For discussion of the role of earls in Stephen's reign, in intention and in practice, see esp. Round, *Geoffrey de Mandeville*, 267–77; G. H. White, 'King Stephen's earldoms', *TRHS*, 4th ser., 13 (1930), 51–82; F. M. Stenton, *First Century of English Feudalism* (2nd edn, Oxford, 1961), 227–35; Davis, *Stephen*, 125–41; Warren, *Governance*, 92–5; P. Latimer, 'Grants of 'Totus Comitatus' in twelfth-century England', *HR*, 59 (1986), 137–45; Stringer, *Reign of Stephen*, 53–5; J. A. Green, *The Aristocracy of Norman England* (Cambridge, 1997), 298–305. This paragraph follows the interpretation in White, 'Continuity', esp. 124–9, 133, to be developed more fully in 'Earls and earldoms during King Stephen's reign', in D. E. S. Dunn, ed., *War, Government and Society in Medieval and Early Modern Britain* (forthcoming).

[244] *RRAN*, III, nos. 611, 657, 671, 884 (but cf. no. 660).

positions. There was a tendency, for example, to present their authority as similar to that of the king. A writ of Roger earl of Hereford ordered quittance of tolls on the whole corredy of the monks of Worcester in almost identical terms to those previously used by Henry I and Stephen, and subsequently by Henry II; he emphasised his own importance by adding that he had seen and read the charters of Edward the Confessor, Henry I and Stephen granting the quittance.[245] William earl of Gloucester and Ranulf II earl of Chester employed scribes whose handwriting was akin to that of the royal chancery, and both imposed forfeits of £10, commonly (though not exclusively) found in royal documents, upon any who presumed to infringe the terms of their charters.[246] Of more practical significance was the subordination of sheriffs to their local earls. Waleran of Meulan as earl of Worcester had apparently established control over the sheriff of Worcester as early as December 1139, and later addressed the holder of the office, William de Beauchamp, as 'his son'. Waleran's brother Earl Robert notified his sheriff of Leicestershire, Ralf, of a grant in recompense for damage to Lincoln cathedral; whether or not Ralf is to be identified as Ralf the butler, a long-serving member of the earl of Leicester's household, it is clear that the earl's steward, Geoffrey l'Abbé, son of Ralf the butler, had been installed as sheriff by 1155.[247] By that time, also, the counties of Gloucestershire, Herefordshire, Nottingham-shire, Derbyshire and Northamptonshire had sheriffs whose experience was as stewards to their local earls, while in Devon the sheriff was Earl Baldwin's son Richard de Redvers.[248] All these appear to be cases in which the sheriff had been appointed by the earl during the course of Stephen's reign, and had been answerable to him – had become, in effect, the earl's private official in the county. It should be added that several of Henry I's sheriffs had also been under the influence of local magnates;[249]

---

[245] *Cartulary of Worcester*, nos. 45–8.

[246] *Earldom of Gloucester Charters*, ed. R. G. Patterson (Oxford, 1973), nos. 29 and 89 (cf. no. 68); *Charters of Chester*, nos. 61, 109; T. Webber, 'The scribes and handwriting of the original charters', in Thacker, ed., *Earldom of Chester*, 148–9; J. G. H. Hudson, 'Diplomatic and legal aspects of the charters', *ibid.*, 172. For the £10 forfeit in contemporary charters of Stephen and Empress Matilda, see *RRAN*, III, e.g. nos. 170, 253, 349, 369, and in early charters of Henry II, *RAH*, I, e.g. nos. 30, 36, 82, 134.

[247] *Monasticon*, IV, 56; Davis, 'Documents of the Anarchy', 170–1; *Reg. Ant.*, II, no. 324; Crouch, *Beaumont Twins*, 39–40 and n. 54, 142 and n. 24; Green, *Sheriffs*, 53, 88. It is possible that Geoffrey l'Abbé did not become the earl's steward until after his tenure of the shrievalty.

[248] Green, *Sheriffs*, 21, n. 52; *Charters of Redvers*, 8. Robert Grimbald, steward to Simon II de Senlis, was certainly sheriff before Stephen's death (B.L. Add. ch. 6037; B.L. Cott MS. Vesp. E. xvii, fos. 8v–9v; B.L. Royal MS., 11 B. ix, fo. 12; *Facsimiles of Charters in the British Museum*, ed. G. F. Warner and H. J. Ellis (London, 1903), no. 26; *RRAN*, III, no. 611) and Maurice, steward to Roger earl of Hereford, almost certainly so ('Charters of Hereford', nos. 17, 18, 33, 43). Although the other appointments probably date to Stephen's reign, conclusive proof is elusive.

[249] Green, *Henry I*, 211–13, and *Sheriffs*, 16.

in some cases, Stephen may have formally granted the privilege, and it may have helped in the enforcement of the royal will. Thus, when Roger earl of Warwick early in the reign ordered his barons, sheriff, bailiffs, ministers and collectors of Warwickshire that the monks of Worcester should hold five hides in Alveston quit of gelds, murder-fines, and all other exactions, as Henry I and Stephen had ordered by their writs, he may genuinely have been acting on the king's behalf, rather than presuming that the royal revenues were his own to dispose of. Similarly, when Geoffrey II de Mandeville as earl of Essex ordered Aelard de Guerris (possibly his sheriff) to cause a recognition to be made on whether the canons of St Martin's London should hold five acres of which Walter Long had disseised them, and to restore their grain harvest, he may have been indulging himself to the extent of copying the formulae of royal writs on this subject, but he was not necessarily depriving the king of jurisdiction, since the offences appear to have involved his own men.[250] But usually – both in intention and in practice – the privatisation of sheriffs increased the authority of an earl at the expense of that of the king.

There can be no doubt that, during the course of Stephen's reign, several earls acquired regalian rights within their shires – rights normally reserved to the king – a process facilitated by their appointment of amenable sheriffs. Thus, Roger earl of Hereford, addressing his sheriffs (of Gloucestershire?) and foresters of Dean, announced the grant of a forge to the canons of Llanthony Secunda and protected them from impleading except before himself alone.[251] In his letter of the mid-1140s as earl of Worcester, addressed to 'his son' William de Beauchamp as sheriff, Waleran of Meulan pardoned the monks of Worcester their payments for Tibberton of 'king's geld which pertains to me' and also 'all customs, services and forest rights which were formerly the king's and afterwards mine'.[252] There were similar trespasses upon the king's rights in a charter issued by Miles of Gloucester, earl of Hereford, in 1141x43, in which he forbade the impleading of his chaplain Roger de Tockenham over property in Northgate 'except by my precept',[253] and also in an agreement between Reginald earl of Cornwall and Jocelin bishop of Salisbury in June 1152, whereby the earl would hear any crown pleas concerning the church's lands and men 'if my lord Henry, the lord of the land, orders me to do so'.[254] In 1151x53, Baldwin de Redvers earl of

[250] *Cartulary of Worcester*, no. 9, cf. nos. 6–8; *Lawsuits*, I, no. 309; *Royal Writs*, 84, 277.
[251] 'Charters of Hereford', no. 37.
[252] Davis, 'Documents of the Anarchy', 170–1; cf. E. J. King, 'Waleran count of Meulan, earl of Worcester', in D. Greenway, C. J. Holdsworth and J. Sayers, eds., *Tradition and Change: Essays in Honour of Marjorie Chibnall* (Cambridge, 1985), 165–81 (esp. 168–9).
[253] 'Charters of Hereford', no. 5.
[254] *Sarum Charters and Documents*, ed. W. D. Macray (RS 1891), 23–4.

Devon issued a charter in favour of the canons of Christchurch (Hampshire) which clearly assumed his right to hear crown pleas: the canons' men were to be judged for theft, homicide and other crimes only in the prior's court before the earl and his bailiffs. Significantly, this concession was missing from an earlier charter issued by Baldwin before he became earl, while in another by his son Richard, dating to 1161, the clause was amended to admit the presence of a royal official.[255] Several boroughs, with at least some of their revenues, also passed during Stephen's reign from the control of the king to that of the local earl, among them Derby, Exeter, Gloucester, Hereford, Huntingdon, Lincoln, Northampton, Worcester and York.[256]

As already acknowledged – for instance in the case involving Stone Priory in the court of Robert of Stafford [257] – not every lay magnate who took over some of the functions of royal government enjoyed the title of earl. Towards the end of the reign, the boroughs of Dover and (probably) Nottingham came under the direct control of Faramus de Boulogne and William Peverel of Nottingham respectively.[258] Some without a comital title – Eustace fitz John and Robert de Stuteville in York, Henry de Neubourg at Swansea, John (of St John?) at Cardiff – assumed responsibility for the production of coins bearing their own names, as did (with varying degrees of certainty) Robert earl of Gloucester, Patrick earl of Wiltshire and Robert earl of Leicester.[259] The irregular minting of coins was a singular demonstration of fragmented authority, involving new administrative arrangements because dies were no longer being sent out from the centre, and will be discussed further below. In other respects, however, the exercise by earls and other magnates of governmental duties hitherto associated with the king, while certainly undermining royal authority, did not in itself destroy the traditional administrative system. Just as Waleran of Meulan seems to have taken over the king's geld and other dues in Worcestershire, so Robert earl of Gloucester levied scutage in the west country; even Miles of Gloucester, excommunicated follow-

---

[255] *Charters of Redvers*, no. 34, cf. nos. 15, 49 with comment pp. 30–1.

[256] Derby: *Cartulary of Darley Abbey*, ed. R. R. Darlington (Derbys. Arch. and Nat. Hist. Soc., 1945), I, xlv–xlix, II, no. N3. Exeter: *Charters of Redvers*, 8, 31. Gloucester, Hereford: 'Charters of Hereford', nos. 5, 39, 42. Huntingdon: G. H. Fowler, 'The shire of Bedford and the earldom of Huntingdon', in *Publications of the Bedfordshire Historical Record Soc.*, 9 (1925), 23–35 (at 28–9). Lincoln: Dalton, 'Ranulf II and Lincolnshire', 111–12. Northampton: *VCH Northants*, III, 3–4. Worcester: Crouch, *Beaumont Twins*, 30. York: Dalton, *Conquest, Anarchy and Lordship*, 153–4.

[257] Above, n. 240.

[258] Eales, 'Local loyalties in Stephen's reign', 101; M. Jones, 'The charters of Robert de Ferrers, earl of Nottingham, Derby and Ferrers', *Nottingham Medieval Studies*, 24 (1980), 7–26 (at 9–10).

[259] King, 'Anarchy of King Stephen's reign', 150–1; Blackburn, 'Coinage and currency', in King, *Anarchy*, 180–5, 188–9; Boon, *Welsh Hoards*, 52–5; King, 'Economic development', 16. Cf. for comment H. R. Loyn, 'Numismatics and the medieval historian: a comment on recent numismatic contributions to the history of England, c.899–1154', *BNJ*, 60 (1991 for 1990), 36.

ing the imposition of a 'tyrannical exaction' upon the bishopric of Hereford, believed that he had a 'legal claim' to it, which implies that it was a well-established customary levy.[260] Income due to the king from boroughs came to the earls instead: the farm of Huntingdon, for example, was received by Henry of Scots as earl before his interests here passed to Simon II de Senlis.[261] Elsewhere, Reginald earl of Cornwall is known during the 1140s to have held a shire court without reference to the king.[262] Independence of royal control was clearly signalled by such arrangements, and the dangers of a long-term fragmentation of the kingdom through the growing autonomy of regional earls were real enough, but in seeking to imitate the king it was in the magnates' interests to keep his administrative system in working order.

An impression of the consequences, had earls and others been able to retain their grips on shire administration in the long term, may be gleaned from the experiences of Cornwall and the Isle of Wight. In 1130, their sheriffs had accounted for the royal revenues at the exchequer.[263] During Stephen's reign, the shrievalties and the revenues fell under the command of Earls Reginald and Baldwin, and were not restored to the king's control on Henry II's accession. Cornwall only reappeared in the pipe rolls, with a sheriff answerable to the king, after Reginald's death in 1175. The Isle of Wight remained, in effect, a 'private shire', figuring in the pipe rolls only in exceptional circumstances, its taxes and law-courts normally controlled by the earl not the king.[264] Yet even these cases should be seen as affirmations of shire government, not as attempts to undermine it. What made Cornwall and the Isle of Wight exceptional was that, when the civil war eventually came to an end, they were not restored to the king's direct control as a matter of urgency. In nearly every other shire, local earls were almost immediately deprived of their commands of their shire administrations, and their sheriffs made accountable

---

[260] *Gesta Steph.*, 150, 158–60, although it is fair to add that the author claims that the churches were forced to pay 'unprecedented levies' ('novae exactionis tributa'). One of Simon earl of Northampton's charters for Thorney Abbey (Cambridge University Library Add. MS. 3020, fo. 21; above, n. 241) includes the grant of exemption from 'tenseria'.

[261] *Early Scottish Charters*, no. 114.

[262] *Lawsuits*, I, no. 322. Cf. *ibid.*, I, no. 338 (*HKF*, II, 297–8, and above nn. 241–2), where Simon II de Senlis as earl of Northampton, when confirming a settlement before the bishop of Lincoln, addresses all his men French and English of Northamptonshire in a manner which suggests that the charter may have been intended to be read out in the shire court.

[263] *PR 31 Hen. I.*, 41, 158.

[264] *Cartulary of Launceston Priory*, ed. P. L. Hull (Devon and Cornwall Rec. Society 30, 1987), nos. 244, 415 shows the sheriff of Cornwall, Richard de Raddon, acting in association with Reginald earl of Cornwall; the first accounts from the shire in Henry II's pipe rolls occur in *PR22H*, 141, 151, 153. *Charters of Redvers*, 26–9 and nos. 18, 32, appendix I no. 10, shows the autonomy of the Isle of Wight; although Dr Bearman questions the assumption that this arose out of developments of Stephen's reign, the weight of evidence points to that conclusion.

to the king and his exchequer. When we see accounts in the pipe rolls from Earl Patrick as sheriff of Wiltshire between 1153 and 1160,[265] and similar renders in the 1155 roll from the sheriffs of Gloucestershire, Herefordshire, Leicestershire, Northamptonshire and Nottingham-shire–Derbyshire, close associates and almost certainly the appointees of their respective earls,[266] we catch a glimpse of this essential process taking place, as those who had previously enjoyed autonomy were now subjected to the king. It was a process which demonstrated that the restoration of effective royal government in the aftermath of civil war was a matter not only of repairing the administrative machinery, but also of transferring it to central control.

More serious as a challenge to the integrity of shire administration were the grants of *totus comitatus* to Robert earl of Leicester in Herefordshire, probably in 1140, to Ranulf II earl of Chester in Staffordshire in 1153, and to Stephen's son William de Warenne in Norfolk, also in 1153.[267] As Paul Latimer has argued, these did not convey earldoms, but they nevertheless gave each of the beneficiaries a largely independent position in his shire: possession of all royal demesnes and the lordships of several barons, in addition to key boroughs and castles from which to exert authority. But, to quote Latimer, the grant of 'powerful concentrations of lordship', albeit with many fiefs excluded, to 'men who held no royal office in the shires concerned' threatened to undermine the traditional authority of sheriffs and shire courts, whether or not these were under the control of the king. In the event, all these grants came to nothing, the earl of Leicester's designs on Herefordshire being rebuffed by the Angevins and neither of the favours given in 1153 being allowed to persist by Henry II.[268] Had such arrangements become established in any of the shires concerned, the restoration of royal authority through the customary shire administration would have been far from straightforward.

Even when due allowance is made for the difficulties posed by endemic warfare, we are bound to conclude that what made the government of earls, or other magnates, less effective than that of the king was that they failed to command the same level of respect. Although several earls chose to refer grandly to the areas under their authority as their *potestates*,[269] in

---

[265] *RBE*, II, 649; *PR2H*, 56–7; *PR3H*, 77, etc. to *PR6H*, 16; Green, *Sheriffs*, 86.

[266] *RBE*, II, 650, 653, 655; cf. above, n. 260.   [267] *RRAN*, III, nos. 437, 180, 272.

[268] Latimer, 'Grants of "Totus Comitatus"' (quotations at 144). Despite the challenge to some of Latimer's points in Davis, *Stephen*, 216, n. 1, the argument that such grants conferred 'all the king's rights in a county' but not specifically the earldom is persuasive.

[269] King, 'Anarchy of King Stephen's reign', 133–4. Use of the word was not, however, confined to earls: for example, from Bridgnorth in 1155 Henry II ordered Henry de Pommeraye, apparently a justice (*PR2H*, 15), to protect the land and holdings of St Andrew's Priory, Northampton, 'que in tua potestate sunt' (B.L. Cott. MS. Vesp. E. xvii, fo. 19v.; B.L. Royal MS.11 B. ix, fo. 21v).

reality they had difficulty not only in asserting themselves against rival tenants-in-chief, but also in maintaining control over honorial tenants. In part, this was the result of trends already apparent before Stephen's accession: when Gilbert de Gant, shortly before becoming Stephen's earl of Lincoln, prohibited the monks of Rufford from answering to his tenant Ralf fitz Wichard concerning land Gilbert had given from his demesne, he was protecting the jurisdiction of his seignorial court against mounting pressure from below.[270] In part, the difficulties arose from conditions of war, as when Robert earl of Leicester found no service forthcoming from Robert de Meppershall for his tenure of Biddlesden, so proceeded to disseise him.[271] The earls' failure to secure law and order is well attested by the career of Warin of Walcote, who made a living in Stephen's reign from plundering territory south of Rugby, and by Peter of Goxhill's opportunistic encroachments during the 1140s on Roumare and Benniworth estates in Lincolnshire, areas supposedly under the local authority of the earls of Warwick and Lincoln respectively.[272] The prevalent instability was such that some men turned to the Church for material as well as spiritual assistance: in the southernmost part of Northamptonshire, Osbert de Wanci arranged for the monks of Biddlesden to have custody of his livestock, 'if there shall be so great war that we cannot keep our animals in peace', and to mediate for himself and his family in the event of their capture, while from Leicestershire we have a charter of 1145 in which Robert of Burton announced the grant to Garendon Abbey of 3 carucates from his demesne at Ibstock, in recompense for the 30 silver marks which the monks had given to redeem him from captivity.[273] There is little sign here of any control over events by the earls of Huntingdon/Northampton and of Leicester. Although shire courts might persist, sheriffs still be appointed and customary dues continue to be levied, the earls were obviously struggling to enforce their authority.

Much has been made of the treaties entered into by the earls to ensure a measure of peace between them, but despite the impression they convey of 'a country divided into regions each under the control of, in the power of, the greater magnates',[274] they reveal several weaknesses in the participants' positions. The *confederatio amoris* between Robert earl of Glouces-

---

[270] *Lawsuits*, I, no. 324; Dalton, *Conquest, Anarchy and Lordship*, 264.

[271] Crouch, *Beaumont Twins*, 80.

[272] *Rolls of the Justices in Eyre for Gloucestershire, Warwickshire and [Shropshire], 1221, 1222*, ed. D. M. Stenton (Selden Society, 1940), no. 390; Poole, *Domesday Book to Magna Carta*, 151–3; Dalton, *Conquest, Anarchy and Lordship*, 186–8.

[273] Stenton, *English Feudalism*, 247–8; Cronne, *Reign of Stephen*, 162–3; J. G. Nichols, *History and Antiquities of the County of Leicester* (London, 1795–1815), III (pt. ii), 384.

[274] E. J. King, 'Mountsorrel and its region in King Stephen's reign', *Huntington Library Quarterly*, 44 (1980), 1–10 (quotation at 1), and on the treaties generally, Davis, *Stephen*, 108–24; King, 'Dispute settlement'; Green, *Aristocracy of Norman England*, 319–21.

ter and Miles earl of Hereford, of 1141x43, frankly acknowledged the detrimental effects of the current war between the empress and the king, for when it was over they would both 'have their lands and their rights again'.[275] The treaty between Robert earl of Leicester and Ranulf II earl of Chester, datable to 1148x53, included provision for their cooperation against William de Launay, a troublesome tenant whom the earl of Leicester feared he could not bring to justice.[276] The treaty of 1147x50 involving William earl of Gloucester and Roger earl of Hereford failed in one of its principal aims, the disinheritance of Gilbert de Lacy, and betrays throughout a lack of trust between the two parties:[277] Earl William possibly, and Earl Roger certainly, made overtures to Stephen during the early 1150s, although both backed Henry in 1153.[278] What seems clear from such manoeuvres is that earls' difficulties with recalcitrant vassals and acquisitive neighbours were further compounded by mistrust of one another's political intentions.

The readiness of earls towards the end of the civil war to treat with Stephen, Henry, or both in turn,[279] underlines the fact that there had never been a serious threat to the principle of royal government over the kingdom as a whole. It is true that the treaty between the earls of Chester and Leicester made no mention of the king, but the 'Angevin' earls of Gloucester and Hereford duly accorded Stephen his royal title in their *confederatio amoris* of 1141x43,[280] and Roger earl of Hereford repeatedly looked forward to the assertion of royal authority at some time in the future: one of his charters in favour of St Guthlac's Priory, Hereford, quitclaimed 17 shillings burgage rent from Hereford until they should have the 3 pence a day alms which they ought to have from the king, while another concerning the grant of fishing rights to St Peter's Abbey, Gloucester, promised an alternative if he was unable to uphold his gift because of violence on the part of the king or another magnate.[281] A

---

[275] *Sir Christopher Hatton's Book of Seals*, ed. L. C. Loyd and D. M. Stenton (Northants. Record Soc., 1950), no. 212 ('Et postquam guerra finita fuerit, et Robertus comes Gloecestrie et Milo comes Hereford' terras suas et sua recta rehabuerint . . . ').

[276] Stenton, *English Feudalism*, 249–56, 286–8; Cronne, *Reign of Stephen*, 179–80; Crouch, *Beaumont Twins*, 80–1.

[277] R. H. C. Davis, 'Treaty between William earl of Gloucester and Roger earl of Hereford', in Barnes and Slade, *Medieval Miscellany*, 139–46.

[278] *Gesta Steph.*, 228; R. B. Patterson, 'An un-edited charter of Henry Fitz Empress and earl William of Gloucester's comital status', *EHR*, 87 (1972), 755–7; D. B. Crouch, 'Earl William of Gloucester and the end of the Anarchy: new evidence relating to the honor of Eudo *Dapifer*', *EHR*, 102 (1988), 69–75; cf. *RRAN*, III, nos. 344, 746, which despite the editors' dating may precede the peace settlement and indicate a temporary reconciliation between king and earl.

[279] For possible negotiations early in 1153 between Henry and Earls William d'Aubigny, Aubrey de Vere and Roger of Clare, see White, 'End of Stephen's reign', 7.

[280] *Book of Seals*, no. 212 ('guerra que modo est inter imperatricem et regem Stephanum').

[281] 'Charters of Hereford', nos. 43, 30; *Historia et Cartularium Monasterii Sancti Petri Gloucestriae*, ed. W. H. Hart (RS 1863–7), no. 193.

latent respect for the authority associated with kingship is also apparent from much of the coinage of the reign, despite the collapse of royal control over the mints during the 1140s. For although one archbishop, possibly three earls and some 'men of the second rank' produced coins in their own names,[282] the majority of ecclesiastical and lay magnates held on to the idea that the issue of currency was a royal prerogative and ensured that the mints under their authority used dies which, though locally cut, bore the names of kings. Thus, pennies from the Midlands mints controlled by the earls of Derby, Leicester, Lincoln and Hunting-don–Northampton, while apparently proclaiming their independent provenance by departing from the style of Stephen's type 2, still carried the name and image of King Stephen. Much the same could be said of various irregular issues in the king's name from York, where William of Aumale was in control. In the south-west, the production of coins proclaiming Empress Matilda was confined, as we have seen, to the mints at Bristol, Cardiff, Oxford and Wareham, the first two being located in boroughs held by Robert earl of Gloucester, and the third reflecting her residence there in 1141–2. Otherwise, local earls seem to have preferred to use the names of previous kings, the mints at Bristol, Dorchester, Gloucester, Hereford, Ilchester, Malmesbury, Sherborne and Wareham all producing coins ascribed to William or Henry.[283] It is of course possible that some of the last group refer to the rising star Henry of Anjou, but in any event the political message which these coins convey is that a new generation in the west of England, men such as Roger earl of Hereford and William earl of Gloucester, while rejecting the empress as the figure to place on their coins, looked nevertheless for the eventual restoration of royal authority in their part of the country. That expectation provided a firm foundation on which Stephen as well as Henry II could eventually build, once a political settlement to the civil war had been achieved.

It remains to consider briefly the contribution of Church leaders to the maintenance of law and order during the civil war. A prevalent view among the chroniclers was that their efforts were futile. 'The bishops and learned men were always excommunicating them, but they thought nothing of it, because they were all utterly accursed and perjured and doomed to perdition.'[284] 'The legate, with the bishops, many times excommunicated all who broke into graveyards and outraged churches

[282] Archbishop Henry Murdac, Robert earl of Gloucester, probably Patrick earl of Wiltshire and Robert earl of Leicester, Eustace fitz John, Robert de Stuteville, Henry de Neubourg, John (of St John?): King, 'Anarchy of King Stephen's reign', 150–1; Boon, *Welsh Hoards*, 52–5; Blackburn, 'Coinage and currency', in King, *Anarchy*, 180–90; King, 'Economic development', 16.

[283] Blackburn, 'Coinage and currency' in King, *Anarchy*, 180–90; Boon, *Welsh Hoards*, esp. 43–52; King, 'Anarchy of King Stephen's reign', 150–1.   [284] *ASC*, 199.

and laid hands on men of a holy or religious order or their servants, but he accomplished hardly anything by these efforts.'[285] This seems unduly negative. It is true that excommunication appears to have had little impact upon Geoffrey II de Mandeville's conduct in the fens, nor as far as we can tell upon that of William de Beauchamp in Worcestershire.[286] But Reginald earl of Cornwall and Ranulf II earl of Chester were both induced to make recompense to churches they had damaged,[287] Miles of Gloucester earl of Hereford decided to return money levied from his local bishop and churches,[288] Robert de Broi acknowledged his unjust occupation of land belonging to Ramsey Abbey and duly restored it,[289] while Henry de Rye felt obliged to grant his manor of Deopham in Norfolk to Canterbury Cathedral Priory in recompense for another manor withheld from the monks.[290] The king himself acknowledged the value of the Church's contribution, for he was present at Archbishop Theobald's legatine council in March 1151 which dealt not only with baronial exactions and usurpations of crown pleas but also reinforced the sentence of excommunication by introducing additional penalties: anyone who had not sought reconciliation with the Church after one year's excommunication would lose their rights to plead in courts and suffer disinheritance.[291]

In the *Leges Henrici Primi*, the bishop appeared as a leading member of the shire court, alongside the earl and the sheriff, a position confirmed – repeatedly if not consistently – by the address clauses of Henry I's writs and charters.[292] Stephen continued to look to his bishops to fulfil this role. Representatives of every diocese in England – except Carlisle which was controlled by the Scots for all but the first few weeks of the reign – were addressed by Stephen in writs and charters directed to the officials of specified shires.[293] Several of these omitted earls known to have held their

---

[285] *Hist. Nov.*, 41; cf. the criticism of bishops' feeble sentences of excommunication in *Gesta Steph.*, 156.

[286] *Ibid.*, 164–6; *Chronicon Abbatiae Ramesiensis*, ed. W. D. Macray (RS, 1886), 329–32; GF, *Letters*, nos. 3, 94. Even in Geoffrey II de Mandeville's case, there was deathbed repentance and an order to his son to withdraw from Ramsay Abbey: cf. J. Bradbury, 'The civil war of Stephen's reign: winners and losers', in M. Strickland, ed., *Armies, Chivalry and Warfare in Medieval Britain and France* (Stamford, 1998), 115–32 (at 115–16).

[287] *Cartulary of Launceston*, xi, xix and nos. 12–13; *Gesta Steph.*, 198; *Charters of Chester*, nos. 96, 104, 106, 115.   [288] *Gesta Steph.*, 158–60.

[289] *English Episcopal Acta I, Lincoln 1067–1185*, ed. D. M. Smith (London, 1980), no. 225.

[290] Saltman, *Theobald*, 537–8; *Lawsuits*, I, no. 311.

[291] HH, 756; Saltman, *Theobald*, 35, 547–8 (cap. v); cf. C. J. Holdsworth, 'The Church', in King, *Anarchy*, 215.

[292] *Leges Henrici Primi*, ed. L. J. Downer (Oxford, 1972), 98; *RRAN*, II, e.g. nos. 501, 505, 531, 1064, 1415, 1465, 1657, 1659, 1940, 1969.

[293] *Ibid.*, III, e.g. nos. 1 (bishop of Salisbury, *Dorset, Devon*), 4, 5 (bishop of Salisbury, *Berkshire*), 14 (bishop of London, *London, Middlesex*), 15 (bishop of Norwich, *Norfolk, Suffolk*), 27 (bishop of Bath, *Somerset*), 30 (bishop of Lincoln, *Buckinghamshire*), 33 (bishop of Winchester, *Surrey*), 41

titles at the relevant dates, such as grants in favour of Reading Abbey, Newhouse Abbey and Holy Trinity Priory, York, addressed to Leicestershire, Lincolnshire and Yorkshire respectively.[294] After 1141 the geographical distribution of the bishops so addressed reflected the regional nature of the king's power and influence, for among writs and charters which can clearly be dated between 1142 and 1153, it was the archbishop of Canterbury and the bishops of Chichester, Lincoln, London and Norwich who figured repeatedly in his address clauses.[295] A glimpse of their continued involvement in the business of shire government can be found in the case of treason alleged against two vassals of Bury St Edmunds Abbey about 1150, to which reference has already been made; although the king's steward William Martel presided, the court was convened as an assembly of the shire communities of Norfolk and Suffolk, included the bishops of Ely and Norwich among those attending, and met in the latter's garden.[296] But even outside that part of England where the king retained a measure of control, bishops might continue to serve occasionally as his local representatives. In the late 1140s, he was still summoning the bishops of Exeter and Hereford to councils in London.[297] There is a single example from the later phase of the reign of an address to the bishop of Worcester, announcing a grant to Cirencester Abbey in 1152x53; the others notified were anonymous king's officials and faithful men generally, rather than those of any particular shire, a fact which implies that the bishop was the only figure of authority in the area to whom the charter could realistically be addressed.[298] At a more practical level, Gilbert Foliot as bishop of Hereford duly responded to a royal mandate when hearing a case between Gilbert de Lacy and Roger earl of Hereford arising from breach of sanctuary in 1150: this was a matter for canon law, which passed on appeal to the archbishop of Canterbury,[299] but at least it demonstrated that the king's

(bishop of London, *Essex*), 85 (bishop of Lincoln, *Lincs.*), 101 (archbishop of York, *Yorkshire*), 117 (archbishop of Canterbury, bishop of Rochester, *Kent*), 129 (bishop of Winchester, *Hampshire, Wiltshire*), 138–9 (bishop of Ely, *Cambridgeshire*), 166 (bishop of Durham, *Durham*), 219 (bishop of London, *Hertfordshire*), 350 (bishop of Worcester, *Gloucestershire*), 351 (bishop of Salisbury, *Wiltshire*), 376 (bishop of Chester, *Shropshire*), 398 (bishop of Hereford, *Herefordshire*), 435 (bishop of Exeter, *Cornwall*), 448 (bishop of Chichester, *Rape of Pevensey, Sussex*), 500 (bishop of Exeter, *Devon*), 519 (bishop of Rochester, *Kent*). [294] *Ibid.*, III, nos. 681, 605, 987.
[295] *Ibid.*, III, nos. 106 (Norwich, 1145x50), 147–8 (Canterbury, 1143x52), 150 (Norwich, 1146), 177 (Norwich, 1149x53), 223 (London, 1148x52), 229 (Norwich, 1148x52), 232 (London, 1153), 401 (Norwich, 1146x49), 402 (Norwich, 1147x49), 448–9 (Chichester, 1148x53), 501, 504 (London, 1147x52), 511 (London, 1147x48), 535 (London, 1149x50), 542 (Canterbury, London, 1145x47), 555 (London, 1145x47), 605 (Lincoln, 1143x52), 745 (Lincoln, 1151x53), 750 (Canterbury, 1152x53), 957 (Canterbury, 1147x52). The bishop of London between 1141 and 1150, Robert de Sigillo, had been the empress's choice: Chibnall, *Matilda*, 137–8. [296] *Lawsuits*, I, no. 331.
[297] *RRAN*, III, nos. 183, 402, 511–13, 760. [298] *Ibid.*, III, no. 192.
[299] GF, *Letters*, no. 95; *Lawsuits*, I, no. 327.

orders could still be heeded in a region dominated by Angevin sympath-isers. Here was an encouraging sign for any who saw that the best hope of resolving local disputes of this kind lay in the restoration of royal author-ity over the kingdom as a whole.

Stephen's accession to the throne of England came at a time when lords were increasingly looking to the king to confirm their inheritances and help resolve their tenurial disputes.[300] This enhanced dependence upon the intervention of royal authority sat uneasily with resentment of a government whose growing efficiency in the levying of taxes, fines and amercements was widely perceived as oppressive.[301] Although Stephen, despite initial concessions, apparently set out to govern much as Henry I had done, the civil war severely curtailed the extent of the kingdom under his effective control. It also excited a series of local conflicts, based on rival hereditary claims and territorial encroachments, while virtually destroying the capacity of royal justice over most of the kingdom to deal with them. An alternative 'Angevin' government established itself, but except in 1141 the empress's practical authority was confined to two or three shires, and before the peace settlement of 1153 her son Henry's covered even less. The northernmost region, under the king of Scots and his son, was effectively administered, but elsewhere, neither the govern-ment of the Angevin leaders, nor that of the various earls who claimed authority over their respective *potestates*, proved effective substitutes for that of the king, as unruly subordinates disrupted the countryside, 'castle-men' indulged in plunder and extortion, and low-weight coins were put into circulation. But where royal government did not function, some of its elements nevertheless persisted, including the appointment of sheriffs, the collection of customary farms and taxes, and the granting of privileges and confirmations in a style which deliberately echoed the king's. This shadow of royal government, however pale it must have become at times, at least kept traditions alive. Men continued to attend the shire and hundred courts, or to seek exemption from the obligation to do so.[302] To some extent, the king's dues continued to be paid, even if not to the king, and the records kept for this purpose were doubtless made available to the royal exchequer when sheriffs who had not accounted there during the civil war began to do so again. By the early 1150s, the restoration of royal

---

[300] See esp. Hudson, *Land, Law and Lordship*, 36–44, 131–53.

[301] HH, 698–700; R. W. Southern, 'The place of Henry I in English history', *Proceedings of the British Academy*, 48 (1962), 127–69; Hollister, 'Rise of administrative kingship'; J. A. Green, 'William Rufus, Henry I and the royal demesne', *History*, 64 (1979) 337–52 (at 350–1); Green, *Henry I*, 51–94.

[302] *RRAN*, III, e.g. nos. 104 (Henry in favour of monks of Biddlesden, probably 1153), 295 (empress in favour of abbot of Eynsham's men in Oxfordshire, 1141x42), 770 (Stephen in favour of monks of St Edmund in Essex, 1149x53).

government over the kingdom as a whole continued to await the political settlement which would bring the war to a close, but at least the means to achieve that restoration were still in place.

THE PEACE SETTLEMENT AND ITS SEQUEL

Henry's arrival in England in January 1153 brought to an end a relatively quiet phase in the civil war. Military campaigning had become intermittent – Henry's previous incursion in 1149, Stephen's attacks on Worcester in 1150 and 1151, the sieges of Newbury and Wallingford castles in 1152[303] – and although Ranulf II earl of Chester's ambitions remained a threat to the stability of the north Midlands[304] much of the southern half of England seems to have been remarkably peaceful. The description of Stephen in 1152 – he 'bore himself like a brave man and with success all over England' and 'held the upper hand everywhere and did everything in the kingdom as he willed'[305] – was an obvious exaggeration, but it may reflect a perception that in the months before Henry's last invasion the king's authority was already being reasserted beyond its former confines. There had been signs of this in Stephen's levy of taxes on the citizens of York and Beverley in 1149, and in his attendance at Archbishop Theobald's legatine council of 1151, which had gone on the offensive against those who usurped regalian rights.[306] The invasion of January 1153 not only challenged Stephen's enhanced authority, but threatened to upset such stability as had already been achieved, with the possibility that the young duke of Normandy and Stephen's son Eustace count of Boulogne would keep the civil war alive for another generation. This was an appalling prospect not only for Church leaders but also for most earls and lay magnates, whom we have seen struggling to maintain control at regional and local level, and whose treaties of peace, uneasily secured by hostages and the pledges of bishops, were vulnerable to shifts in the political climate. A settlement which guaranteed their hereditary estates, whatever their past allegiances, and promised some amelioration of local disorder, would be an ideal solution, and after two armed confrontations during 1153 when the barons declined to fight, and the timely death of the count of Boulogne, this is what Archbishop Theobald and Henry bishop of Winchester were able to negotiate.[307] With Stephen as king for life, and Henry doing homage as his son and heir for the kingdom of England, everyone had been on the 'right side' in the civil war. Newly

---

[303] *Gesta Steph.*, 214–30; HH, 754–60.
[304] *Gesta Steph.*, 198–202; Dalton, '*In neutro latere*', esp. 52–4. [305] *Gesta Steph.*, 226.
[306] *Ibid.*, 218; JH, 323–4; Saltman, *Theobald*, 33–6, 547–9.
[307] White, 'End of Stephen's reign', esp. 6–11.

built castles were to be destroyed – so ending the careers of petty tyrants who had challenged the authority of earls and bishops as well as that of the king. Royal justice was to be exercised throughout the whole kingdom. And inheritances were to be restored to their rightful holders.[308]

One clause in Stephen's Westminster charter of December 1153, the charter which announced the terms of the peace settlement, promised that 'in all the affairs of the kingdom I shall act with the advice of the duke'. This undertaking was not well observed. Stephen and Henry appear to have gone their separate ways, but to have met at a series of conferences, at Oxford, Dunstable, Canterbury and Dover, during January and February 1154. At the second of these, Henry complained that Stephen had not demolished some of his followers' castles as agreed, but was met with a rebuff from the king. At the fourth, according to the later testimony of Gervase of Canterbury, the duke learned of a plot against his life involving the Flemings and Stephen's surviving son William.[309] There is no sign that members of the ducal household were deputed to safeguard his interests by joining Stephen's court: Henry's constable, steward and chamberlain attested a royal charter at Dunstable, but this only confirmed a previous gift by Henry and almost certainly belongs to the conference there early in 1154.[310] Nor is there any evidence that one of Stephen's retainers acted as adviser to the duke; the only members of the king's household known to have attested a ducal charter of 1153x54 are Richard de Lucy and William Martel, who witnessed a confirmation for Cluny Abbey probably issued at the Westminster peace assembly. When Stephen and Henry gave separate charters at Dunstable, confirming various grants to Meaux Abbey in identical terms, the witness lists were completely different.[311]

In any case, about Easter 1154 Henry returned to Normandy. He spent much of the remainder of the year dealing with recalcitrant vassals there and in Aquitaine, and also negotiated a fresh settlement with Louis VII king of France, for whom he led an army into the Vexin.[312] His influence over affairs in England in the last months of Stephen's life must have been minimal. No member of the household he had taken to England in January 1153 appears to have stayed behind to represent him in the kingdom.[313] Reginald earl of Cornwall was described in a ducal charter of

---

[308] *RRAN*, III, no. 272; HH, 770; RT, 177; *Gesta Steph.*, 240; JH, 331; cf. WN, 126; Gervase, I, 156; Howden, I, 212; Diceto, I, 296. See also J. C. Holt, '1153: The treaty of Winchester', in King, *Anarchy*, 291–316.   [309] HH, 772; Gervase, I, 158–9; White, 'End of Stephen's reign', 13–14.

[310] *RRAN*, III, nos. 126–7 (cf. p. xix where, despite no. 126, it is suggested that Henry's chamberlain Warin fitz Gerold may have been seconded to Stephen's household).

[311] *Ibid.*, III, nos 206 (cf. no. 204), 583–4.   [312] RT, 179–81.

[313] *RRAN*, III, xxxv–xxxvii; from April to December 1154 all charter attestations by Richard du Hommet, Manasser Bisset, Warin fitz Gerold and William fitz Hamo were in north-west France (nos. 22, 29, 49, 64–5, 332, 900).

this period as the man 'who in this and in my other affairs holds my place in England' but witnessed this very charter, at Eu, and another of similar date at Rouen; unless his name was added in his absence, he clearly did not represent the duke continuously.[314] So Stephen's government of England between December 1153 and October 1154 should not simply be dismissed as 'by the favour of Duke Henry'.[315] The duke would one day return, but no one knew when, and no one knew how many years Stephen would survive on the throne. His attempts in the closing months of his life to implement the terms of the peace settlement do the king some credit, and twelfth-century chroniclers duly acknowledged his efforts.[316]

The promise to 'exercise royal justice' bore fruit in the appointment during the summer of 1154 of Robert bishop of Lincoln as local justice of Lincoln and Lincolnshire; the two previous bishops had held the office in their time, but although Robert had been elected and consecrated in December 1148, the king had not seen fit to grant him the justiciarship until now.[317] He occurs in the 1156 pipe roll as having imposed *placita* in Lincolnshire, and since he seems not to have been retained as local justice by Henry II, these may well have originated under Stephen.[318] It was also in the 'year when King Stephen and Duke Henry of Normandy were allied' that the king ordered the abbot of Abingdon to reseise Turstin fitz Simon of the church of Marcham and other property in Berkshire which he claimed by hereditary right. When the abbot prevaricated, Turstin complained to the king, who duly authorised his sheriff Henry of Oxford 'to deal with the case according to the royal law, and without any delay or scruple'; as a result, Turstin obtained seisin, but in the same year Stephen died, and the abbot was able in consequence to reopen the case with Henry II.[319] The phraseology used by the Abingdon chronicler leaves open the possibility that Turstin's original approach to the king predated the peace settlement, but there can be little doubt that the hearing before Henry of Oxford, an Angevin adherent in the civil war,[320]

---

[314] *Ibid.*, III, nos. 709, 49.

[315] Davis, *Stephen*, 124; cf. J. W. Leedom, 'The English settlement of 1153', *History*, 65 (1980), 347–64 (esp. 360).

[316] *Gesta Steph.*, 241 (Stephen died 'after he had reduced England to peace and taken the whole kingdom into his hand'); WN, 126–7, 130–1 (Stephen 'began to rule as if for the first time . . . traversing the provinces of England with regal pride . . . welcomed by all'); HH, 772–3 (the king 'now for the first time had the power . . . to gain possession of what was rightfully due to the royal dignity' although in this case his debt to his adopted son Henry is acknowledged).

[317] *RRAN*, III, no. 490.

[318] *PR2H*, 26. Henry II is not known to have confirmed the local justiciarship to Bishop Robert; royal writs of 1155×58 which suggest that the bishop of Lincoln and local justice of Lincolnshire were different people occur in *Reg. Ant.*, I, nos, 144, 148.

[319] *RRAN*, III, no. 13; *Lawsuits*, II, no. 363.

[320] *RRAN*, III, no. 88; Keats-Rohan, 'Making of Henry of Oxford', esp. 287–8, 306–8.

came after it. As such, this is an example of the extension of royal justice to what, if not strictly the 'duke's part' of the kingdom as envisaged in the Westminster charter, had certainly been a disputed frontier zone.[321] If we turn to the destruction of castles, we have the testimony of John of Hexham, Roger of Howden and William of Newburgh to show that Stephen's capture and subsequent demolition of Drax (Yorkshire) in summer 1154 was far from being an isolated case.[322] Several inheritances also appear to have been restored during the course of the year, although it is instructive to note that arrangements were consistently made for compromise or compensation. The fitz Alan family seem to have re-gained Mileham (Norfolk) from William de Chesney, to whom Stephen granted various other Norfolk manors in exchange. Robert de Gant was deprived of Drax so that a share of the estate could be restored to the Paynel family as alternative claimants. King and duke joined in reinstat-ing William Spileman in his hereditary serjeanty based upon Brocken-hurst (Hampshire) but provision appears to have been made for a rival as well.[323] Steps were also taken to recover the king's own inheritance, the royal demesne: the Northamptonshire manors of Kingsthorpe, Gedding-ton and Silverstone, almost certainly regained from Simon II de Senlis sometime after his death in August 1153, were apparently in crown hands by Michaelmas 1154, since a full year's farm was rendered for them twelve months later.[324]

Further indications both of reconciliation and of widespread acknowl-edgement of the king's new authority are to be found in charters and coins. The monks of Reading and the Knights of the Temple both saw fit to obtain confirmations from Stephen of all lands held at the Easter following the peace settlement, as if this might eventually have become a defining moment for purposes of determining right or seisin.[325] Early in 1154, the king was willing to confirm a ducal charter in favour of St Augustine's Abbey, Bristol, conceding portions of royal demesne in the south-west given away by Henry and others, without even claiming them as his 'own alms'.[326] Former Angevin adherents such as Eustace fitz John and Hugh Bigod now occurred as witnesses to royal charters, the latter with the comital title accorded him by Empress Matilda.[327] The

---

[321] GF, *Letters*, no. 85; King, 'Anarchy of King Stephen's reign', 146–7.

[322] JH, 331; Howden, I, 213; WN, 130; cf. *RRAN*, III, nos. 490, 817.

[323] *RRAN*, III, nos. 177, 130–1 (cf. no. 129 which appears to be compensation to a rival claimant); *EYC*, VI, 33; Davis, *Stephen*, 122; Hudson, *Land, Law and Lordship*, 150, n. 149.

[324] *RBE*, II, 655; the sums involved were identical to those rendered for full years subsequently, *PR3H*, 104, *PR4H*, 142, etc. For these properties as royal demesne, see *VCH Northants*, I, 305–6, 325, 344–6, 387 (although in Domesday Book it was the count of Mortain not the king who had a stake in Silverstone). Earl Simon's death is recorded in HH, 768; RT, 172; cf. *CP*, VI, 643.

[325] *RRAN*, III, nos. 696, 866.   [326] *Ibid.*, III, no. 127, cf. no. 126.

[327] *Ibid.*, III, nos. 664, 696, 896, 993; cf. no. 28 (also witnessed by Hugh Bigod as earl but not datable on

shire officials of Hampshire, Wiltshire, Lincolnshire and Yorkshire were all addressed by the king in this period, and the abbeys of St Benet's, Holme (Norfolk) and Rufford (Nottinghamshire) were among his beneficiaries,[328] but it may be significant that (with the possible exception of a writ to William earl of Gloucester which may predate the peace treaty in any case)[329] there were no addresses from Stephen to named earls: a conscious effort to regard all earldoms as no more than titular honours had perhaps already begun. As for the coinage, there is no reason to doubt that Stephen's last type, no. 7, was issued following, and in consequence of, the settlement between king and duke. The pennies were of good weight, and were produced from centrally cut dies at over forty mints in all parts of the kingdom except the far north still held by the Scots. Among these were at least fifteen which had not struck 'official' coins of the king since type 1, including Lincoln and Nottingham where 'Stephen' pennies in the meantime had been produced from local dies, and Cardiff, Gloucester, Hereford and Salisbury, which had yielded coins in the names of the empress or others. Henry II allowed these type 7 coins to remain in circulation until 1158, doubtless claiming to have given them his authority when peace had been agreed. Their success in replacing other issues is shown by the fact that, with rare exceptions, they are the only coins bearing Stephen's name to have been found in the same hoards as Henry II's.[330]

There are signs of recovery in the king's administration during the closing months of the reign. Analysis of the sheriffs' farms totals in Henry II's early pipe rolls suggests that an 'exactory roll' recording these totals was handed on from Stephen's exchequer to that of Henry II, although this does not demonstrate that Stephen had actually been in receipt of such farms.[331] There is, however, some evidence that by the end of his life Stephen was able to draw income from a wide area of the kingdom, in the transcript of the 1155 pipe roll preserved in the *Red Book of the Exchequer*. Several accounts entered here covered a full year back to Michaelmas 1154, nearly a month before Stephen's death, and while they do not prove that Stephen had secured control of these revenues before he died, that is their clear implication. Among these accounts were the sheriffs' farms of Berkshire, Dorset, Essex, Northamptonshire, Staffordshire, Sur-

other grounds specifically to 1154) and White, 'Stephen, Henry and Ranulf', 656 (which includes Earl Patrick as a witness and is probably also, therefore, to be dated after the peace settlement). On Hugh Bigod's comital style see above, n. 112.

[328] *RRAN*, III, nos. 129, 258, 490, 664, 797, 923, 993; 404, 739.

[329] *Ibid.*, III, no. 344; above, n. 278.

[330] F. Elmore Jones, 'Stephen type VII', *BNJ*, 28 (1958), 537–54; Mack, 'Stephen and the Anarchy', 101–7; Blackburn, 'Coinage and currency', in King, *Anarchy*, 154–7, 161.

[331] White, 'Continuity', 141–2; below, ch. 4.

rey and Wiltshire, and also the farm of Brian fitz Count's honour of Wallingford which, despite the castle's repeated resistance to the king throughout the civil war, had now apparently escheated to the crown.[332] The extent to which the king was in receipt of other revenues, and his exchequer active in handling accounts, must remain problematical. There is, however, an isolated reference in the 1156 pipe roll to a debt owing on the sheriff's farm of Wiltshire for 1153–4,[333] and it is clear from a charter in favour of St Peter's Hospital, York, that in summer 1154 Stephen expected the render of his 'farm of York' at the customary terms, Easter and Michaelmas.[334] As for the royal household, this seems to have continued during 1154 much as before, with heavy reliance upon Richard de Lucy and Richard de Camville, who were joined for the visit to Yorkshire in the summer by the king's nephew Hugh du Puiset bishop of Durham. William Martel appears to have been stayed in London, possibly to preside over a Westminster exchequer, and the constable Henry of Essex may also have remained in the south.[335] A relative newcomer to the king's regular entourage was Warner de Lusors, a minor landholder in Wiltshire who eventually found a place in Henry II's administration as sheriff of Dorset.[336] Robert de Gant continued as chancellor, Baldric de Sigillo as keeper of the seal; there is no sign that Stephen took on any new scribes to supplement the work of no. XXII, apparently the only chancery scribe in the last few years of the reign.[337]

Of course, Henry continued to keep his own household in England, for as long as he remained in the country, but after the peace settlement he no longer sought to challenge the administration of the king. The style of his charters, which persisted in treating royal estates and revenues as his own, can give the impression of enduring defiance of Stephen's authority, but for Henry their essential purpose was to advertise his regal status in making promises for the future.[338] The suggestion that the farm of Wiltshire due from 1153–4, entered in the 1156 pipe roll, had originally been accounted for in the duke's treasury is without foundation; the

---

[332] *RBE*, II, 648–58; White, 'End of Stephen's reign', 18–19 and n. 66.

[333] *PR2H*, 56 (for 'the third year' meaning 'the year before last', see H. G. Richardson, 'The exchequer year', *TRHS*, 4th ser., 8, 1925, 173–5). [334] *RRAN*, III, no. 993.

[335] Richard de Lucy and Richard de Camville witnessed e.g. *RRAN*, III, nos. 239, 358, 489, 490, 664, 817, 993, Hugh du Puiset all but the first two of these. William Martel witnessed nos. 258, 866 (both London), Henry of Essex these plus nos. 129, 583 (both Dunstable) and 896 (London). However, if William Martel stayed in London and Westminster while Richard de Lucy travelled with the itinerant royal household, this would be a reversal of roles (at least at the very end of the reign) from that suggested in Green, 'Financing Stephen's war', 112–13, and endorsed above, n. 87.

[336] *RRAN*, III, e.g. nos. 28, 129, 344, 583, 696, 896; Amt, *Accession*, 117 and n. 35; J. Boorman, 'The sheriffs of Henry II and the significance of 1170', in Garnett and Hudson, *Law and Government*, 255–75 (at 260–4). [337] *RRAN*, III, x–xi, xv.

[338] E.g. *RRAN*, III, nos. 582–4; cf. White, 'End of Stephen's reign', 15–16.

sheriff responsible, Patrick earl of Wiltshire, appears to have witnessed for Stephen in the period following the peace treaty, and must be presumed therefore to have rendered account to the king and his exchequer.[339] Nor is there any evidence that sheriffs whose former loyalty had been to the Angevins or their local earls were accounting to Henry rather than to the king in the period after the peace settlement. Three of the sheriffs known to us from the transcript of the 1155 pipe roll are Henry of Oxford in Berkshire, Richard de Raddon in Dorset and Robert Grimbald in Northamptonshire. The first had upheld the Angevin cause in his shire, the second was closely associated with Reginald earl of Cornwall, the third had been steward to the late earl Simon II de Senlis.[340] Yet all three accounted for their farms for the full year from Michaelmas 1154, evidently having acknowledged Stephen's authority before his death, and we know from other evidence that Henry of Oxford responded to Stephen's mandate in a judicial case in the last year of the reign.[341] It was in the future king's interests that royal authority should be extended as far as possible over the whole of the country, so – provided that Stephen abided by the treaty and did not live too long – there was no point in fomenting discord.

In the event, Stephen died on 25 October 1154, Henry crossing to England from Barfleur on 7 December to be crowned twelve days later.[342] At first sight, the task of reconstruction which he faced might seem formidable. The years of civil war had led to large-scale alienation of royal demesne, especially in East Anglia and in the region westwards from Oxfordshire and Berkshire.[343] Royal government had effectively been confined to parts of eastern England, the south-east and south Midlands, and even here there had been challenges to the king's control. Yet whatever chroniclers writing in Henry II's reign liked to say, was there really 'anarchy' in Stephen's reign? In the sense of lawlessness and disorder the answer must be 'yes', but the treaty ending the civil war removed the context in which such conduct could flourish, and the measures taken in 1154, many to be continued by Henry II, represented a response to the problem even before Stephen's death. In the sense of 'absence of government', we have to say 'no': there was plenty of government, not always in Stephen's hands, but much of it continuing to rely on sheriffs and shire courts, featuring taxes such as scutage and geld,

[339] Richardson and Sayles, *Governance*, 257; White, 'Stephen, Henry and Ranulf', 656.
[340] *RBE*, II, 655–7; *RRAN*, III, no. 88; *Cartulary of Launceston*, nos. 12, 13, 538; Green, *Sheriffs*, 21, n. 52, 27, 37, 64.   [341] Above, nn. 319, 332.   [342] HH, 774–6; RT, 181–2.
[343] This is most clearly demonstrable from the lengthy lists of *terrae datae* in Henry II's early pipe rolls, e.g. *PR2H*, 30 (Somerset), 33–4 (Berkshire), 36 (Oxfordshire), 49 (Gloucestershire), 57 (Wiltshire); full accounts for the farm of Norfolk and Suffolk were delayed until 1158, when the *terrae datae* ran to fifteen items (*PR4H*, 125). This subject is discussed further below, ch. 3.

and accordingly recognisable as that normally associated with the king. Moreover, lay magnates and Church leaders alike continued to think of the kingdom as rightfully under royal control. In these circumstances, the restoration of orderly royal government after 1154, while never easy, was far from being an unmanageable task. Had the anarchy of Stephen's reign been more deep rooted, devouring the very fabric of traditional administration, it is hard to see how a king who spent only two and a half of the first eight years of his reign in England could have coped with its aftermath as successfully as he did.

Chapter 3

PERSONNEL AND PROPERTY

INTRODUCTION

Henry II was conscious from the outset of his reign of the importance of upholding and enhancing the dignity of kingship. Although his first Easter court had been a glamorous affair, Stephen had often been too self-effacing: he 'commonly forgot a king's exalted rank' and 'saw himself not superior to his men, but in every way their equal, sometimes actually their inferior'.[1] Henry II, who was eventually to declare himself king 'by the grace of God',[2] was concerned to present a different image: the repeated crown-wearings of the early years of the reign and the pressure he applied on Pope Alexander III to secure the canonisation of Edward the Confessor were intended to add lustre to his kingship.[3] In subsequent years, he was at pains to keep his heir, Henry the Younger, above and apart from the baronial hierarchy – resisting demands to grant him a portion of his inheritance in his lifetime and refusing his homage 'quia rex erat'.[4] But effective kingship needed more than dignity. The goodwill, and active support, of Church leaders and of a fair proportion of the baronage – especially the richest among them, the magnates – was essential. So was loyal and efficient service by administrative officials. Both could be facilitated by patronage: indeed, decisions on who should receive patronage and from whom it should be withheld were among the most delicate facing any medieval king.[5] Henry II had to reckon with the additional problem that civil war had led to the loss of royal demesne and had created (or exacerbated) family rivalries for offices and estates: if he was to tackle all this, he was bound to favour some and give offence to

---

[1] *Gesta Steph.*, 22–3; HH, 706.
[2] On the adoption of the *Dei gratia* style (between May 1172 and February 1173), see *RAH Intro*, 12–28; Bishop, *Scriptores Regis*, 11–12, 19 and n. 1.
[3] *Chronicle of Battle Abbey*, 174 (cf. *PR3H*, 107); Newburgh, I, 117–18; Diceto, I, 302; Howden, I, 216; B. W. Scholz, 'The canonization of Edward the Confessor', *Speculum*, 36 (1961), 38–60.
[4] *Gesta Regis*, I, 41, 79.   [5] Cf. Green, *Aristocracy of Norman England*, 254–70.

others. This chapter, which looks at the king's relations with his adminis-trative personnel on the one hand and with lay and ecclesiastical land-holders on the other, addresses some of the issues involved.

Henry did at least start with the advantage of an unchallenged right to the English throne, amid widespread acceptance that the time for armed conflict had passed. The settlement which had ended the civil war in November 1153 had not only promised him the kingdom on Stephen's death, but had set the agenda for pacification: 'arms should be finally laid down and peace restored everywhere in the kingdom, the new castles demolished, the disinherited restored *ad propria*, and laws and enactments made binding on all according to the ancient fashion'. Property was to be restored to the 'ancient, legitimate holders' of Henry I's time, and castles built since that king's death were to be destroyed.[6] Stephen had imple-mented some of these provisions in the remaining months of his life, but his successor brought a new political authority, an essential prerequisite to the long-term restoration of orderly government. The new climate was already apparent to those who lived through the six weeks between Stephen's death and Henry II's crossing from Normandy. This was a period when England 'by God's protecting hand did not lack peace, either through love or fear of the king who was about to come', a time when 'nobody dared do anything but good to another'.[7]

Baronial ambition did not, of course, disappear with the end of civil war. Unjust disseisins persisted as a problem: some of the disputes cited in the *cartae baronum,* for example, seem to have arisen after 1154, not before.[8] And claims to lost estates were liable to fuel further violence whenever the crown found itself in a vulnerable position. In 1173, Henry the Younger gathered support for his rebellion by promising Northum-berland north of the Tyne to William the Lion king of Scots, and Cambridgeshire to his brother David of Scots; both had been held by

---

[6] *Gesta Steph.*, 240–1; RT, 177. For the interpretation of *ad propria* as 'inheritances' (as opposed to acquisitions), see Holt, '1153', esp. 297; the arguments which follow are broadly in line with those of Sir James Holt, but more emphasis is placed here on Henry II's preference for treating each case on its merits. Other recent discussions of the fortunes of landholders who had participated in the civil war include Amt, *Accession*, 149–68, and Bradbury, 'Civil war of Stephen's reign', esp. 121–32.

[7] HH, 774–5; *ASC*, 202–3.

[8] For example, under Dorset, the *carta* of William fitz John of Harptree complained that Richard de Raddon was withholding the service of one knight due from Raddon. Richard may have been sheriff of Dorset under Stephen; he certainly was from the outset of Henry II's reign until 1158, and since the allegation made no reference to the recent war it may be that he had taken advantage of his position during Henry's early years as king (*RBE*, I, 248). Cf. *ibid.*, I, 188–9, 200, 212, 221–2, 224, 249–50, 279, 300, 306, 364, 392, 394 for claims by bishops or abbots to be wrongly deprived of demesnes or services, again without mentioning the circumstances of war. See below, ch. 5 n. 253, for a royal writ (possibly of *c.*1162) ordering restoration of tenure to the canons of Plympton as in the time of a former bishop who had died in 1155, terms which suggest that the disseisin had occurred since that date.

their father in Stephen's reign. Hugh Bigod was to have hereditary custody of Norwich castle, to which he had aspired under Stephen, as well as the honour of Eye to augment his position in East Anglia, while the counts of Flanders and Boulogne were led to expect territory formerly held by William of Ypres (Kent) and by Stephen himself (Mortain). The earls of Leicester, Chester and Derby were others who joined the rebels, asserting hereditary rights denied to them by Henry II.[9] Similarly, the claims made in 1215 by Saher de Quency to the castle of Mountsorrel, by William II de Forz count of Aumale to the manor of Driffield, and by Geoffrey IV de Mandeville to custody of the Tower of London, can be traced to their ancestors' tenures under Stephen, subsequently lost.[10] But the first half of Henry II's reign was not the time for barons to assert their rights by taking up arms. The young king could take nothing for granted, but in the absence of a rival prepared to bid for his throne, the disgruntled were deprived of the opportunity for violent self-help. Instead, there was patient resignation, recourse to the law courts, and the hope that fortunes might prosper through the favour of the king.

THE KING'S SERVANTS

In studying Henry II's administrators early in his reign, we encounter much that is familiar. Stephen, the empress and the king of Scots had all sought to maintain the governmental traditions of Henry I, and the new king was heir to those traditions. His household embraced the same departments, with the same titled officials, as those described in the *Constitutio Domus Regis*.[11] His exchequer set out to model itself on that of Henry I's reign and so needed a similar range of staff.[12] Earls, sheriffs, itinerant and local justices can all be identified representing the king's government in the shires, as they had done under Henry I.[13] In terms of personnel, many of the same families, even the same individuals, continued in office. There were striking similarities also in the methods of patronage: Henry I's 'new men' had profited from alienated royal demesne, gifts of wardship and of heiresses in marriage, undertenancies and tax exemptions, and so did Henry II's.[14] But it would be wrong to focus

---

[9] *Gesta Regis*, I, 44–9; K. J. Stringer, *Earl David of Huntingdon, 1152–1219* (Edinburgh, 1985), 21; Warren, *Henry II*, 121–3, 234–5.

[10] S. Painter, *The Reign of King John* (Baltimore, 1949), 330–4.   [11] *Dialogus*, 129–35.

[12] *Ibid.*, 50.   [13] Green, *Henry I*, 107–10, 118–22.

[14] Southern, 'Place of Henry I'; cf. D. B. Crouch, 'Geoffrey de Clinton and Roger earl of Warwick: new men and magnates in the reign of Henry I', *BIHR*, 55 (1982), 113–24; Green, *Henry I*, 171–93; C. A. Newman, *The Anglo-Norman Nobility in the Reign of Henry I* (Philadelphia, 1988), 114–48; J. E. Lally, 'Secular patronage at the court of Henry II', *BIHR*, 49 (1976), 159–84; R. V. Turner, *Men Raised from the Dust: Administrative Service and Upward Mobility in Angevin England* (Philadelphia, 1988), esp. 1–19.

exclusively on the parallels between one king and another in their handling of administrative officials. Henry II did not, in fact, reconstitute his household exactly on the pattern of his grandfather's day: it looks, for example, as if he had more chancery scribes but fewer constables and marshals.[15] In appointing Robert earl of Leicester and Richard de Lucy as chief justiciars, probably at the very beginning of the reign, he was reviving a position similar to that held by Roger bishop of Salisbury under Henry I and, initially, under Stephen: but to entrust responsibility to two men, not one, was innovative, and the office was allowed to develop and define itself thereafter in the light of changing circumstances.[16] Most significantly, we observe under Henry II a sharper distinction than hitherto between those officials whose titles were essentially honorific and those in active, routine service. The purpose of this section is not to offer a comprehensive, detailed survey of the king's servants as a whole, but to point to general trends and draw overall conclusions: the fact that, for some, an official title implied ceremonial service only, while for others it meant regular duties, is one phenomenon which merits fuller discussion here.

As far as the royal household is concerned, the young king clearly accepted the need to acknowledge hereditary claims to office. Hugh Bigod and Humphrey II de Bohun as stewards, William II Mauduit as a chamberlain and John fitz Gilbert as marshal were allowed to continue in titles accorded to them by Henry I.[17] Aubrey III de Vere, Geoffrey II de Clinton and William of Earley (chamberlains), William II d'Aubigny and Geoffrey Martel (butlers), William de Courcy (steward), Walter and

---

[15] Towards the end of his reign, Henry I had had four constables (serving in rotation) and five marshals, but evidence from the period 1154–66 suggests that only Richard du Hommet, Henry of Essex and Henry d'Oilli were styled constable and only John fitz Gilbert and William fitz Adelin marshal (*Dialogus*, 134; G. H. White, 'Constables under the Norman kings', *Genealogist*, new ser., 38, 1922, 113–27; *RRAN*, II, xv–xvii). On Henry d'Oilli, see *RAH*, I, no. 16; *CCR*, III, 418–19; *Acta*, no. 155; *RBE*, I, 305, and on William fitz Adelin, *PR8H*, 52; *PR11H*, 75, 98, 101; *RBE*, I, 209. The chancery, and the careers of certain individual scribes, are discussed in Bishop, *Scriptores Regis*, esp. 21–33 and 'A chancery scribe: Stephen of Fougeres', *Cambridge Historical Journal*, 10 (1950), 106–7; *RAH Intro.*, 96–8, 431–4; V. H. Galbraith, 'Seven charters of Henry II', *Antiquaries Journal*, 12 (1932), 169–78; C. Duggan, 'Richard of Ilchester, royal servant and bishop', *TRHS*, 5th ser., 16 (1966), 1–21; *Earldom of Gloucester Charters*, 13, 29; V. D. and R. S. Oggins, 'Richard of Ilchester's inheritance: an extended family in twelfth-century England', *Medieval Prosopography*, 12 i (1991), 57–128. The number of scribes concurrently at work in Henry II's chancery in the busy early years of his reign is put by Bishop as at least five, possibly more; although the figure may have dropped thereafter, it seems to have returned to five later in the reign. This compares with what appears to be a normal establishment of four under Henry I. None of Stephen's scribes is known to have been retained in the service of Henry II.

[16] F. J. West, *The Justiciarship in England, 1066–1232* (Cambridge, 1966), 13–45; cf. D. Bates, 'The origins of the justiciarship', *ANS*, 4 (1981), 1–12.

[17] Green, *Henry I*, 235–6, 248–9, 261–2; *Itinerary*, 3, 4, 9, 15, 29–30, 34, etc.

Henry of Hereford (constables) and Ralf fitz Wigan (marshal) all held titles under Henry II which their fathers had enjoyed under Henry I,[18] while in the cases of the chamberlain Robert fitz Herbert, the constables Henry of Essex and Henry d'Oilli, and the dispenser Turstin fitz Simon, descent was from other kinsmen in office at that time.[19] It should be stressed, however, that all these claims derived from the period before Stephen's accession. Most of these men had also served Stephen, the empress or both in turn,[20] but it was the fact that their titles had originated before 1135 which was critical to their persistence under Henry II. Conversely, offices newly acquired during Stephen's reign were not allowed to continue. For example, the stewardship held in 1136 (but not it seems before then) by Robert fitz Richard de Clare passed under Stephen to his son Walter fitz Robert but does not appear to have survived Henry II's accession.[21] Geoffrey Martel succeeded his father William as butler – the title enjoyed in the reign of Henry I – but not as steward, in which capacity William Martel had given devoted service to Stephen.[22] Although a grant by the empress in 1141 had restored William de Beauchamp to the constableship held by his father Walter, Henry I had not allowed that office to pass to William and so he was not accorded the title under Henry II.[23]

The respect for hereditary rights which predated 1135, the denial of those originating under Stephen, characterised Henry II's approach to the

---

[18] For holders under Henry I: Green, *Henry I*, 276, 239–41, 229–30, 242–3; *RRAN*, II, xi–xvi. For Aubrey III de Vere and William II d'Aubigny: *RBE*, II, 651; Map, *De Nugis Curialium*, 492–4. Geoffrey Martel: *RBE*, I, 217. Geoffrey II de Clinton: *Book of Seals*, nos. 194, 508; cf. *Cartulary of Oseney Abbey*, ed. H. E. Salter (Oxford Hist. Society, 1929–36), I, nos. 2–4, 488; Richardson and Sayles, *Governance*, 427. William of Earley: *RBE*, I, 235; Crouch, *William Marshal*, 195–6. William de Courcy: *Itinerary*, 78; *RBE*, I, 224–5. Walter and Henry of Hereford: 'Charters of Hereford', nos. 69, 73, 78, 80, 84. Ralf fitz Wigan: *RBE*, I, 304.

[19] Robert fitz Herbert was grandson of Herbert the chamberlain, who served during Henry I's reign (*Itinerary*, 4; Richardson and Sayles, *Governance*, 426–8; Green, *Henry I*, 32–3). Henry of Essex was son-in-law of Robert de Vere, constable under Henry I and Stephen (*RAH*, I, nos. 6–9, 26–8, 74; *Itinerary*, 2, 5, 11, etc.; Green, *Henry I*, 276–7). Henry d'Oilli's constableship (*Itinerary*, 6, 18, 34) was that held by his grandfather Nigel under Henry I and by his father Robert in Stephen's reign (*RRAN*, II, xv–xvi; III, xx). Turstin fitz Simon's dispensership is traced to his grandfather Hugh, early in Henry I's reign, in J. H. Round, *The King's Serjeants and Officers of State* (London, 1911), 186–97. When Henry of Essex lost his lands and constableship after defeat in trial by battle in 1163, the king did not grant them to the victor Robert de Montfort, even though he represented the family disinherited by Henry I in 1107 (*Baronies*, 120–1, 139); in this case, even the old king's forfeitures continued to be respected.

[20] Stewards Hugh Bigod and Humphrey II de Bohun; Chamberlains William II Mauduit, Aubrey III de Vere; Constable Henry of Essex; Marshal John fitz Gilbert (*RRAN*, III, xviii–xxi, xxxi–xxxii).

[21] *Ibid.*, III, xviii and n. 1; for Walter fitz Robert as a witness to Henry II's charters but without reference to the stewardship, see *Itinerary*, 16, 57.

[22] *Hist. Nov.* 55–6; *RRAN*, III, xviii; *RBE*, I, 217.

[23] *RRAN*, II, xvi; III, xx, xxxi and no. 68; William de Beauchamp occurs as a witness to Henry II's charters without reference to the constableship in *Itinerary*, 10, 12, 15.

succession to land, as we shall examine in more detail later in this chapter. The principle clearly applied to succession to household office as well: even grants made by his mother or himself between 1135 and 1154 were liable to be revoked.[24] It should be stressed immediately that there are cases which can be cited against the general rule. Robert de Pont de l'Arche appears never to have been accorded the title chamberlain, held by his father William under Henry I.[25] Conversely, William Malet, one of Henry II's most active household stewards, had a hereditary claim to the office derived from his father Robert, steward to Stephen in 1136 but not – on available evidence – to Henry I.[26] But the general picture is clear enough: household titles held prior to 1135 were normally allowed to pass by hereditary succession, those first granted during Stephen's reign were not.

However, by no means all these hereditary officials discharged their duties on a regular basis. Walter Map tells of an incident at Paris in September 1158 when William II d'Aubigny 'whom none of us had seen for three years past' because of his absence on pilgrimage, suddenly burst in on Henry II and Louis VII to assert his right as master-butler to serve the king's wine.[27] But like some others with inherited titles, including Hugh Bigod (steward) and Aubrey III de Vere (chamberlain), he did not attest royal charters with this style and his performance of household duties must have been confined almost entirely to ceremonial occasions.[28] Those with honorific positions of this sort did not normally enjoy the privilege of tax exemption: that went instead to men in active, routine service, or alternatively was a mark of very special royal favour.[29] Having appeased his grandfather's household servants, or their families, by acknowledging their titles, Henry II usually looked elsewhere for his key advisers and administrators, favouring especially those whose origins

[24] In addition to the constableship of William de Beauchamp, above n. 23, the stewardships held under the empress or Duke Henry by Geoffrey II de Mandeville and Reginald de St Valery did not persist (*RRAN*, III, xxx–xxxi). [25] *Ibid.*, II, xiv; Green, *Henry I*, 267–8.
[26] *RRAN*, II, xii; III, xviii and no. 944). His attestations for Henry II as steward include *RAH*, I, nos. 195, 268 and several charters in *Itinerary* (24, 33, 38, 55, 60, etc.)
[27] The story was told in relation to similar conduct by the hereditary chamberlain of Normandy, William de Tancarville, in 1182: Map, *De Nugis Curialium*, 488–94.
[28] For discussion of ceremonial court occasions under Henry I, see Green, *Henry I*, 20–4, and for ceremonial duties performed by Roger Bigod and the earls of Leicester, Arundel, Salisbury, Huntingdon and Essex in 1186 and 1189 see *Gesta Regis*, II, 3, 81.
[29] *Dialogus*, 47–56, but it is clear that this did not cover all who were exempt from taxes: e.g. *PR23H*, 3, 20, 24, 48, 99, 146–7, 149, 154, 158, 181–2; *PR24H*, 11–14, 37, 94, 96; *PR25H*, 45 (covering the years when the *Dialogus* was written) show the household chamberlains Ailward and Ralf fitz Stephen and the prominent *curiales* William de Lanvalein and Reginald de Courtenay also to have enjoyed pardons. Early in the reign, William the king's brother and Thierry count of Flanders were among those afforded this privilege (*PR2H*, 7, 9, 12, 14, 16, 37, 39, etc.). Cf. below, n. 79, for a similar concession in favour of earls.

had lain outside the ranks of established baronial families, as his grandfather had done. His most intimate counsellors early in his reign were
four who had been close to him prior to his accession – Richard du
Hommet (constable), Manasser Bisset (steward), Warin fitz Gerold
(chamberlain) and William fitz Hamo[30] – plus another two – Richard de
Lucy the joint chief justiciar and Thomas Becket the chancellor – drawn
from the service of King Stephen and Archbishop Theobald respectively.[31] They were in frequent, though not constant, attendance upon the
king and their services clearly transcended the offices they formally held:
Warin fitz Gerold, for instance, though nominally a chamberlain of the
treasury, spent much of his time supervising receipts by the chamber,
while both Thomas Becket and Richard de Lucy were sent on embassies
on the king's behalf.[32] Their most important contributions to Henry II's
government in England are largely hidden from us: it was doubtless their
prompting and advice which bore fruit in the various financial and
judicial measures, and in decisions on patronage, which are attributed to
the king in the pages which follow. And, of course, they had their
rewards. Richard du Hommet, for example, benefited not only from tax
exemptions but also from marriage to the daughter and heiress of Jordan
de Say, from the wardship of Bertram de Verdun, and from receipt of
royal manors, escheated lands and undertenancies of which one fee, held
of John de Port, was alleged in 1166 to have been 'deforced'.[33] Becket
seems to have profited from the vacant sees of Coventry, Exeter and
Worcester and from custody of the king's demesnes at Eye and Berkhamstead, although failures consistently to account for these holdings were
destined to be used against him by the king in 1164.[34]

   Those whose service to the king was not confined to one particular
office also included Richard de Camville, Jocelin de Balliol and William
de Lanvalein, who were often with Henry in England and France and
enjoyed extensive remissions of taxes, but who carried no formal titles; of

[30] *RAH Intro.*, 403–4, 429–30, 468–9, 479; *RRAN*, III, xxxv–xxxvii. Richard du Hommet and
   William fitz Hamo had been serving the Angevin cause since the mid-1140s: *ibid.*, III, nos. 58, 703.
[31] *RAH Intro.*, 434–6, 463–4; *Becket Materials*, III, 17; IV, 12; E. M. Amt, 'Richard de Lucy, Henry II's
   justiciar', *Medieval Prosopography*, 9 i (1988), 61–87 (where evidence is also adduced for Richard's
   previous service to Henry I).
[32] Only Becket and Richard de Lucy witnessed charters issued on the Toulouse campaign (*RAH*, I,
   nos. 125–8); on their embassy duties, see e.g. *Becket Materials*, III, 22, 29–33, 71–2, 176–7; IV, 13,
   57; V, 128. On Warin fitz Gerold, see H. G. Richardson, 'The chamber under Henry II', *EHR*, 69
   (1954), 596–611; Richardson and Sayles, *Governance*, 436–7.
[33] *RBE*, I, 202, 208; II, 630, 655–6; *PR2H*, 24, 40–2; *PR3H*, 83, 103,106, etc.; *Magni Rotuli Scaccarii
   Normanniae sub Regibus Angliae*, ed. T. Stapleton (Society of Antiquaries, 1840–4), I, cv, cxxxv;
   Monasticon, v, 662; *HKF*, II, 338; Boussard, *Le Gouvernement*, 96, n. 2.
[34] *Becket Materials*, II, 362; III, 20, 53–4, 299–300; IV, 11, 43; JS, *Letters*, I, no. 128 and p. 266, n. 1;
   PR2H, 21; *PR4H*, 152; *PR5H*, 7; *PR6H*, 12; *PR7H*, 68; *PR9H*, 34.

these, Richard de Camville had loyally served Stephen, Jocelin de Balliol the Angevins.[35] Others were sufficiently active as royal servants to merit pardons from taxes, but, as far as we can tell, their duties were normally limited to the offices they held; among these were the steward Robert de Waterville, the dispenser William of Hastings, and several butlers and receivers of money in the chamber.[36] One who could also be included in this group is Henry fitz Gerold, who succeeded his brother Warin as a chamberlain of the treasury in 1158; although Warin's extensive holdings in former royal demesne, plus much of the escheated honour of Eudo *Dapifer*, duly passed to him, he seems to have remained at the treasury and never to have enjoyed his brother's familiarity with the king.[37] Ability and congeniality, not landed wealth and inherited titles, determined the choice of these men for the roles they discharged.

Yet if hereditary claims and baronial status could not of themselves secure a regular administrative post, they were no bar to such an appointment either. 'The king . . . had such a high opinion' of the magnate Robert earl of Leicester, according to the *Dialogus de Scaccario*, 'that he appointed him justiciar, head not only of the exchequer but of the whole kingdom.'[38] In the context of the first decade of the reign, this description of the earl's pre-eminence is a little misleading, since the chief justiciarship was still in a formative stage: not only was the office shared with Richard de Lucy, but Henry normally looked to a member of his family to represent him when he was out of the kingdom, and there were others besides the earl with authority to issue writs for the disbursement of the king's money.[39] Even so, he was remembered for his sound judgement, diligence and strong-mindedness.[40] Other magnates high in the new king's favour were Nigel bishop of Ely, who was brought in to restore the efficiency of the exchequer and secured his former office of treasurer for his own son Richard,[41] and Reginald earl of Cornwall, who initially took

[35] Davis, *Stephen*, 67 n. 8; *RRAN*, III, nos. 64–5, 115–16, 372, 492, 495–6, 632, 702, 837; *RAH*, I, nos. 6, 11, 16, 27–8, 53, 56–8, 70–1, 74, 78, 85–6, 93, 95, 116, 126–8, 144, 159, 163, 166, 191, 198–9, etc.; *PR2H*, 14, 16–18, 20, 25, 27, 31, 33–4, 37, 41, 55–6, 59, etc.

[36] Robert de Waterville: *RRAN*, III, no. 438; *Historia et Cartularium Sancti Petri Gloucestriae*, II, 106; *Reg. Ant.*, I, no. 169; *PR2H*, 45, 50, etc. William of Hastings: *Itinerary*, 44, 63, 91, 112, etc.; *RAH*, I, nos. 165, 420, 432, etc.; *PR8H*, 67. Robert, Michael, Lucas, Richard *pincerna*: *PR2H*, 25, 44, 61; *RBE*, I, 291; *Itinerary*, 30, 75, 88. Stephen de Tours, another Stephen and his son Ralf (receivers in the chamber): *PR2H*, 27; *PR3H*, 87, 90; *PR4H*, 125, 127, 129, 136, 146, 153, 155, etc.; *RAH Intro.*, 459–60; Richardson, 'Chamber under Henry II', esp. 597–8. (Some other receivers did have alternative work, Ralf Waspail as a money lender and Geoffrey Monk as a larderer: *PR2H*, 27, 29; *PR3H*, 89; *PR4H*, 120, 125, 131, 138, 155, 162–3, etc.)

[37] *PR2H*, 34–6; *PR3H*, 80–1; *PR4H*, 123–4, 179; *RBE*, I, 354–6; *RAH*, I, nos. 126, 234; *Itinerary*, 39, 60–1, 68, 70, etc.; for the honour of Eudo *Dapifer*, see *HKF*, III, 164–295.   [38] *Dialogus*, 58.

[39] West, *Justiciarship*, 31–45; Bates, 'Origins of justiciarship', 10–11; Crouch, *Beaumont Twins*, 89–96.

[40] *Dialogus*, 57–8.

[41] *Ibid.*, xiv–xv, 50; *Liber Eliensis*, ed. E. O. Blake (Camden Society, 1962), 372; cf. lviii, n. 1, for a

precedence over the earl of Leicester in witness lists to royal charters.[42] Beyond these, William Malet, tenant-in-chief of twenty-five knights' fees in 1166, frequently attested for the king with his father's title of steward.[43] Robert de Dunstanville, possibly another steward, certainly a trusted *curialis*, was another substantial baron.[44] John fitz Gilbert seems to have given active service to Henry II in his hereditary office of marshal, as he had done to Henry I, Stephen and the empress in turn.[45] The hereditary constable Henry of Essex was also frequently in the king's company until July 1157; it was then that he fled from the ambush in North Wales and – to judge from charter attestations – was rarely seen at court thereafter.[46] A rather different case is that of William II Mauduit, chamberlain to Henry I in succession to his brother; although both the empress and – in 1153, prior to his accession – Henry II had acknowledged his tenure of this office, it was in a distinct chamberlainship of the treasury, granted separately in 1153, that both he and his son William III discharged regular duties for the king.[47] There is a measure of flexibility

defence of the substance of this passage against criticism of erroneous detail in H. G. Richardson, 'Richard fitz Neal and the Dialogus de Scaccario', *EHR*, 43 (1928), 161–71 (at 163–6).

[42] For early charters showing precedence to Earl Reginald, see *RAH*, I, nos. 50, 59, 93; *CCR*, III, 247–8; IV, 346–7; V, 455; *Itinerary*, 34; *Acta*, nos. 123, 235, 304; but cf. e.g. *RAH*, I, no. 6; *Itinerary*, 13, 39. For the earls working together, see *Becket Materials*, I, 16, 39; II, 392–3, 397–8; IV, 34, 50–1.

[43] Above, n. 26; *RBE*, I, 227–8; *PR2H*, 16, 31, 33, 59, etc.; *Baronies*, 38–9.

[44] *RAH*, I, no. 166 (also *CCR*, I, 31), where 'R. dapifero de Dunstanvilla' is among the witnesses. It is possible that the 'dapifero' was intended for the previous witness Manasser Bisset, who appears without any style; on the other hand, in the lists of witnesses to the Constitutions of Clarendon (*Becket Materials*, IV, 207–8 and V, 72–3), Robert de Dunstanville is included immediately after Manasser Bisset, William Malet and William de Courcy who were all entitled to the style *dapifer* although here only Manasser was so described. For other attestations, see *RRAN*, III, nos. 64–5, 111, 126, 128, etc. and *RAH*, I, nos. 6, 16, 26–8, 56–9, 64, 65, 70, etc.; cf. *PR2H*, 12, 55, 59; *Baronies*, 28.

[45] *Dialogus*, 134; *RRAN*, II, xvii; *RRAN*, III, xx, xxxii, xxxviii; *Itinerary*, 4, 9, 15, 68, 91; *Book of Seals*, no. 280; *PR2H*, 34, 37, 47, 51, etc.; *RBE*, I, 207, 300, 304, 309, 347).

[46] *RRAN*, II, xv; *RRAN*, III, xix–xx; *RAH*, I, nos. 6–9, 16, 26–8, 74; *Itinerary*, 2, 5, 11, 13, 15, 16, 26, 27; *CCR*, III, 418–19. There can be little doubt of the esteem in which Henry of Essex was held in the first two-and-a-half years of the reign. In a charter addressed by Henry II to Richard bishop of London and the justice and ministers of Essex, we read 'Sciatis me pro amore H. de Essexa constabuli concessisse Petro capellano suo et Willelmo de Wudeham servienti suo xxx ta. acras terre de Wudeham de feodo comitis de Ferreriis' etc., with Henry of Essex, constable, as sole witness. (P.R.O. C. 47/12/4, formerly Cartae Antiquae Roll OO, memb. 6, no. 26). For charters witnessed by him which may postdate 1157, see *Itinerary*, 31, 33, 38, 52, and *Cartae Antiquae Rolls 1–10*, ed. L. Landon (P. R. Society, 1939), no. 97. Henry of Essex 'junior' who attested *RAH*, I, no. 78 at Argentan, was presumably his son; a Henry of Essex also witnessed *ibid.*, I, no. 227, at Chinon in 1162.

[47] *PR 31 Hen. I*, 134; *RRAN*, II, xiv and nos. 1698, 1719; *RRAN*, III, xix, xxxi, xxxvii and nos. 581–2; *PR2H*, 23, 41–2, 55, etc.; *RBE*, I, 313–14; H. G. Richardson, 'Note on the officers of the exchequer and the transport of treasure' appended to 'William of Ely, the king's treasurer (?1195–1215)', *TRHS*, 4th ser., 15 (1932), 68–79; E. Mason, 'The Mauduits and their chamberlainship of the exchequer', *BIHR*, 49 (1976), 1–23 (esp. 1–4). Neither William II nor William III is readily to be found in the king's company, and the occasional references to the chamber in the pipe rolls make no mention of them.

apparent here, a readiness to utilise hereditary office-holders and those of considerable landed wealth where, when and for as long as they could be of advantage to the king. A good illustration of this is to be found in the careers of Humphrey II de Bohun and his son Humphrey III, who were both substantial tenants-in-chief:[48] some regard was had to their hereditary titles, but whether or not they fulfilled the duties associated with them depended on personal capacity. Humphrey II had bought a stewardship about 1130. He witnessed with that style for Stephen in 1136, for Henry in 1153, and had a grant of the office from the empress. After Henry II's accession he attested some early royal charters as a steward, but appears soon to have been dropped from routine service, forfeiting the *terrae datae* he had enjoyed since the beginning of the reign.[49] Humphrey III succeeded him about 1165. He does not occur as a steward, but from at least 1173 when he fought against the earl of Leicester at Fornham was actively employed as a constable instead.[50] The title was inherited through his mother from Miles of Gloucester, and the Bohun family went on to retain the constableship, not the stewardship, as their hereditary office.[51]

Sensitivity to hereditary claims, combined with a readiness to dispense with the services of those who did not suit his purpose, informed Henry II's dealings with his local government officials as well. Given the autonomy which many earls had come to enjoy during Stephen's reign,[52] it was clearly imperative that if Henry II was to exercise effective control of local government in the shires he had either to curb their powers or extinguish their earldoms altogether. J. H. Round was able to demonstrate that there was no general resumption after Henry's accession of comital titles granted in the previous reign,[53] but the king did seize opportunities to rid himself of some of them. The earldom of Northumberland, held by William the Lion since 1152, was surrendered as part of the settlement imposed upon the Scots in 1157, while the earldom of Buckingham was extinguished by the death without issue of Walter Giffard in 1164.[54] Waleran of Meulan, identified by Henry as a pro-

---

[48] *RBE*, I, 242–4; *Baronies*, 91.

[49] *RRAN*, III, nos. 111, 180, 193, 271, 902; *Itinerary*, 7, 29–30, 35; *CCR*, V, 268. His only tax remission was for *donum* in Wiltshire in 1156, and the loss of *terrae datae* in the same shire during 1158 may indicate a fall from royal favour (*PR2H*, 59; *PR4H*, 116, 119). On the other hand, he was one of those present at the promulgation of the Constitutions of Clarendon in 1164 (*Becket Materials*, IV, 207; V, 72).

[50] *PR11H*, 57; *Gesta Regis*, I, 61. The earliest reference to him as constable in the pipe rolls occurs at *PR20H*, 51. Attestations of royal charters as constable include *RAH*, I, nos. 413–14; *ibid.*, II, nos. 544, 551, 602, 604–5, 608; *Acta*, nos. 69, 81, 110, 216, 264.   [51] *CP*, VI, 457–77.

[52] White, 'Continuity', esp. 133–5.   [53] Round, *Geoffrey de Mandeville*, 267–77.

[54] *RT*, 192; Newburgh, I, 105–6; *CP*, II, 387; IX, 707; R. G. Ellis, *Earldoms in Fee* (London, 1963), 103.

Capetian enemy by 1152, and William of Aumale, who resisted the young king in 1155, continued to hold their Norman *comtés* but did not occur as earls of Worcester and York in Henry's reign: it is clear that royal recognition of their titles was withheld, although whether there were formal surrenders – as suggested by G. H. White – is debatable.[55] Elsewhere, Richard fitz Gilbert almost certainly lost the earldom of Pembroke: he was later known as earl of Strigoil, but was not given a comital title in any of Henry II's charters.[56] The earldom of Lincoln had lapsed by about 1161 through the deaths of the rival claimants Gilbert de Gant and William de Roumare, the title being denied to their heirs.[57] And although Roger earl of Hereford received a charter from Henry II soon after his accession conceding 'in feudo et hereditate sibi et heredibus suis' the third penny of pleas of the county of Hereford 'unde feci eum comitem', with the third penny of the revenues of the borough as well, neither the comital title nor the third pennies passed to any of Roger's younger brothers following his retirement and death during the course of 1155.[58]

Apart from that for the earl of Hereford, the terms of four grants of earldoms have survived from the period 1154–8, in favour of William II d'Aubigny (Arundel or Sussex), Aubrey III de Vere (Oxford), Hugh Bigod (Norfolk) and Geoffrey III de Mandeville (Essex).[59] The only specific privilege common to all these grants was the third penny of pleas of the shire, and since it also appears in Henry II's pipe rolls against several other earls, it may safely be assumed to have been a normal perquisite allowed by the king.[60] What is clear, however, is that – even where a

[55] White, 'King Stephen's earldoms'; cf. Dalton, *Conquest, Anarchy and Lordship*, 155–6; Crouch, *Beaumont Twins*, 74–6. No 'third pennies' were allowed to earls of Worcester or York in Henry II's pipe rolls.

[56] RT, 270; *Gesta Regis*, I, 51, 125, 161; *ibid.*, II, 73; Diceto, I, 330, 375, 407; *RAH*, I, nos. 319, 433; II, nos. 745, 753; *Book of Seals*, no. 40. Cf. Ellis, *Earldoms in Fee*, 183, n. 7; Warren, *Henry II*, 193; M. T. Flanagan, 'Strongbow, Henry II and the Anglo-Norman intervention in Ireland', in J. Gillingham and J. C. Holt, eds., *War and Government in the Middle Ages*, (Woodbridge, 1986), 62–77 (at 64).

[57] Davis, *Stephen*, 134–5; *CP*, VII, 669–75. Both Gilbert II de Gant (d. 1155–6) and William de Roumare (d. *c.*1161) appear to have used the title earl of Lincoln after Henry II's accession: *Reg. Ant.*, I, no. 126; *Rufford Charters*, ed. C. J. Holdsworth (Thoroton Society Record Ser., XXIX–XXXIV, 1972–81), I, lxxii, and II, no. 662 (cf. no. 667); *EYC*, II, nos. 1157, 1164; M. Abbott, 'The Gant Family in England, 1066–1191' (unpubl. PhD, University of Cambridge, 1973), 46.

[58] *Rotuli Chartarum in Turri Londinensi asservati*, ed. T. D. Hardy (Record Commission, 1837), 53; 'Charters of Hereford', 9, 10, 41–51; cf. *RRAN*, III, no. 393. *RBE*, II, 650, shows a 'third penny' allowance for three quarters of the year ending Michaelmas 1155; the sum is given as £124 0s. 9d, but scrutiny of other figures in the account suggests that £24 0s. 9d. was intended. For discussion of the relations between Henry II and Roger earl of Hereford in 1155, see Crouch, 'The march and the Welsh kings', 284–6; cf. below, n. 233.

[59] *CCR*, IV, 257; *Cartae Antiquae Rolls 11–20*, ed. J. C. Davies (P.R. Society, 1960), 157–8; Round, *Geoffrey de Mandeville*, 235–6; *Book of Seals*, no. 40.

[60] The earls of Devon, Essex, Gloucester, Hertford (Clare), Norfolk, Sussex (Arundel) and Wiltshire

formal grant is not extant – most of the earldoms which survived to the accession of Henry II did continue thereafter. Of the seven titles in existence at Stephen's accession, only that of Buckingham was allowed to lapse, when Walter Giffard died childless in 1164.[61] The earls of Derby, Hertford, Richmond and Sussex retained titles bestowed by Stephen, and all passed them to their heirs during the course of Henry II's reign.[62] So did the earls of Devon and Wiltshire, who had been promoted by the empress.[63] Two others, Reginald earl of Cornwall and Hugh Bigod earl of Norfolk, both retained their titles until death in the 1170s.[64] As we have seen, Aubrey III de Vere, who had deserted to Stephen after the empress had made him earl of Oxford, and Geoffrey III de Mandeville, whose father had received the earldom of Essex from both protagonists in turn, were also allowed their titles, and these were both inherited in due course.[65] Simon III de Senlis, who had succeeded his father in August 1153, seems to have been regarded as earl of Northampton before the dignity was granted with the honour and earldom of Huntingdon to Malcolm IV of Scotland in the summer of 1157; thereafter he continued to be styled *comes* (without a shire) until the honour, with the joint earldom, were restored to him in 1174.[66]

All these, however, were essentially courtesy titles, for outside Cheshire and (until Earl Reginald's death in 1175) Cornwall, the earls' control of local government was soon broken.[67] Royal writs directed to

appear consistently in Henry II's pipe rolls as in receipt of third pennies of pleas of the shire (earliest refs.: *PR2H*, 49; *PR3H*, 72–5, 77, 79). The earls of Derby, Huntingdon, Oxford, Pembroke, Richmond, Surrey and Warwick are not so mentioned in the pipe rolls, but silence is not conclusive. The earl of Oxford had specifically been granted the third penny by the king, (*Book of Seals*, no. 40), while the pipe roll for 1181 includes an account of £28 for the third penny of Leicestershire for the past seven years, the earl having refused to accept it without the increment customarily enjoyed by his predecessors under Henry I (*PR27H*, 79): neither the 1130 pipe roll, nor previous rolls of Henry II, had mentioned this earl's third penny. Elsewhere, the earl of Huntingdon was entitled to the third penny of Bedford borough, as his predecessor had been under Henry I, and the earl of Derby may have had the third penny of Derby borough, at least early in Henry II's reign (Fowler, 'Shire of Bedford and earldom of Huntingdon', 29–34; *Cartulary of Darley*, 1, xlv-xlix). On this subject in general, see also Round, *Geoffrey de Mandeville*, 287–96 (where earls' rights to third pennies without specific royal grants are questioned) and P. Latimer, 'The Earls in Henry II's Reign' (unpubl. PhD, University of Sheffield, 1982), 121–58.

[61] *CP*, II, 387.

[62] *Ibid.*, I, 233–5; IV, 191–3, 498–501; X, 788–94. Robert II de Ferrers succeeded in 1139 to the title granted to his father in the previous year; his own death and succession by his son William probably occurred early in Henry II's reign, but possibly at the end of Stephen's.

[63] *Ibid.*, IV, 312–13; IX, 375–7.

[64] *Ibid.*, III, 429; IX, 584–7; evidence relating to the creation of these earldoms is summarised in Davis, *Stephen*, 136, 138–9.

[65] *Ibid.*, V, 116–8; X, 199–208. *RRAN*, III, no. 43, suggests that the empress had recognised Geoffrey III as earl of Essex, but see Holt, '1153', 298–300 and n. 27; in his case, succession passed to a brother.

[66] *CP*, VI, 645; IX, 664 note (c); K. J. Stringer, 'A Cistercian archive: the earliest charters of Sawtry Abbey', *Journal of Society of Archivists*, 6 (1980), 325–34; Holt, '1153', 305–6.

[67] *VCH Cheshire*, II (1979), 1–8; A. T. Thacker, 'Introduction', in *Earldom of Chester*, 7–21; D. B.

specific shires in the early years of Henry II's reign were almost invariably addressed to the sheriff, and sometimes to the bishop, a justice and local officials in general.[68] Writs addressed to earls were exceptional – a signal from the outset of the reign that the king would brook no intermediary between himself and his ministers in the shires. One such writ, of 1155x58, announcing that the king had taken Romsey Abbey under his protection and ordering that it be quit of certain payments, was addressed to Earl Patrick and the ministers of Wiltshire; but Patrick was doubtless the addressee because he remained in the exchequer's eyes as sheriff of Wiltshire – an office his father and grandfather had held – until 1160.[69] Another was addressed to William [the Lion] earl of Northumberland, and all barons, sheriffs and faithful men of Northumberland, announcing the grant of the wood of Harwood to James fitz Gilbert of Newcastle; this obviously predates the Scots' surrender of Northumberland in 1157, and is scarcely representative of practice elsewhere in England.[70] In other writs, earls were addressed, not as heads of shire administrations but in their capacities as lords. A writ in which William de Roumare was described as earl of Lincoln concerned Asgarby, given by his father Roger fitz Gerold to the cathedral church of Lincoln.[71] Hugh earl of Chester and his mother Countess Matilda were ordered to hold a recognition into whether Arnulf fitz Peter had lost his land in Honington (Lincolnshire) in the court of Henry I: but this was because Hugh's predecessors, Countess Lucy and Earl Ranulf II, had granted the land to the nuns of Stixwould.[72] In short, Henry II pursued a deliberate policy towards his earls, that of divorcing them as far as possible from any role in the government of their shires. He applied this policy more consistently than Henry I – and his chancery – had done.[73] The contrast with Stephen's reign might seem obvious, but in fact – with very few

---

Crouch, 'The administration of the Norman earldom', *ibid.*, 69–95; *Pleas before the King and his Justices*, ed. Stenton, II, 117–18; *Cartulary of Launceston*, xx.

[68] E.g. *Royal Writs*, nos. 18, 90 (both 1155: to sheriff); 93 (1154x61: to sheriff); 96 (1155x66: to sheriff); 98 (1166: to sheriff and ministers); 118 (1163x73: to sheriff and ministers); 152 (1155: to justice, sheriff and bailiffs); 154 (c.1163x66: to sheriff); 155 (1163x1172/73: to sheriff and bailiffs); 156 (1154x79: to sheriff); 168 (1155x62: to archbishop, justices, barons, sheriffs and ministers); 170 (1158 or 1163: to bishop, sheriffs, ministers); 172 (1155x64: to archbishop, justice and sheriff); 175 (1154x70: to sheriff); 194 (1155x58: to sheriff); 195 (1155x58: to justice, sheriff, ministers and bailiffs).

[69] *CCR*, II, 104; *PR6H*, 16, cf. *PR7H*, 8; *CP*, XI, 373–9.

[70] B. L. Campbell ch. ii, 2 (extracts in L. Delisle, 'Notes sur les chartes originales de Henri II', *Bibliothèque de l'Ecole des Chartes*, LXVIII, 1907, p. 277, no. 12). The attestation by Herbert bishop of Avranches at Westminster suggests that it may have been issued at the assemblies of December 1154 or Lent 1155; the scribe may not have served Henry II after 1155 (Bishop, *Scriptores Regis*, plate xxiv). [71] *Reg. Ant.*, I, nos. 56, 126.

[72] *Hist. MSS Comm. Eleventh Report, Appendix, part vii* (London, 1889), 59; *Charters of Chester*, nos. 19, 20. [73] Davis, *Stephen*, 127.

exceptions, notably Huntingdonshire–Northamptonshire – the king's government in the shires had been conducted with little reference to earls after 1141.[74] Henry II was thus continuing, with far greater success, the reduction in the earls' local authority which his predecessor had eventually attempted.

It is true that a few earls were able to retain significant local administrative positions for a while. Apart from Earl Patrick, we find that Hugh Bigod in Norfolk and Suffolk accounted for the sheriff's farm in 1154–5, and that Richard de Redvers, who succeeded his father Baldwin as earl of Devon in 1155, did so for the next two years.[75] The 1156 pipe roll shows that Patrick had a subordinate sheriff who would have carried out the routine work and who accordingly had a remission of taxes; the other earls doubtless employed deputy-sheriffs as well.[76] But these arrangements did not last long. With the flexibility characteristic of his handling of several household servants, the king's policy seems to have been to give his ablest earls important alternative tasks: the appointments of the earl of Leicester as chief justiciar, the earl of Arundel repeatedly as an ambassador, the earl of Wiltshire as military commander in Poitou, the earl of Essex as an itinerant justice, the earl of Hertford as a commissioner for the 'Inquest of Sheriffs', all illustrate this point.[77] Many of the earls were also frequent visitors to court, in attendance on great occasions,[78] and several enjoyed remissions of taxes.[79] Given these compensations, they acquiesced in the removal of their power in the shires. In the *Dialogus de Scaccario*, the only reference to the earl is as the person who receives the third penny of pleas of the shire.[80] So Robert de Torigni was misleading, or misinformed, in giving the impression that at Henry II's accession, the 'pseudo-comites' were removed.[81] In reality, most earldoms continued, but in terms of local authority the titles lacked the

[74] White, 'Continuity', 133.
[75] *RBE*, II, 651–3; *PR2H*, 46; *PR3H*, 74; cf. *PR4H*, 157–8, where Richard de Redvers accounts only for old farms.
[76] Richard the sheriff was pardoned danegeld and *donum* in Wiltshire in 1156; he was probably the man who accounted for the sheriff's farm in his own right after 1160. Other deputies to figure in the 1156 pipe roll were the sheriffs Alan and Maurice in Gloucestershire and Herefordshire respectively, although Walter of Hereford who accounted for the sheriffs' farms here was not an earl (*PR2H*, 50–1, 59–60).
[77] Boussard, *Le Gouvernement*, 356 and n. 2; *CP*, I, 235; V, 117; VI, 500; VII, 529; XI, 376.
[78] E.g. the Winchester council of Michaelmas 1155 which considered an invasion of Ireland, the Clarendon council of January 1164 which produced the 'Constitutions', and the coronation of the king's son Henry the Younger in June 1170 (*Itinerary*, 12–3, 67–8, 138; Gervase, I, 219).
[79] E.g. the earl of Leicester (*PR2H*, 16, 20, 23, etc.; *PR8H*, 2, 8, 14, etc.); the earl of Cornwall (*PR2H*, 41, 47, 51, etc.; *PR4H*, 117, 144, 170; *PR8H*, 14, 16, 24); the earl of Oxford (*PR2H*, 16); the earl of Gloucester (*PR4H*, 122, 140, 150, etc.); the earl of Wiltshire (*PR4H*, 168, 182; *PR8H*, 14, 72); the earl of Hertford (*PR4H*, 142, 162, 181–2); the earl of Buckingham (*PR8H*, 27, 42, 44, etc.).
[80] *Dialogus*, 64.   [81] RT, 183.

substance they had enjoyed in Stephen's reign. In a sense, it was not Stephen's earls but those of Henry II who should have been dubbed the 'fiscal earls'.[82]

As with the earls, so with the sheriffs: we need to consider first the legacy from previous reigns. Henry I's general, but not invariable, policy had been to instal sheriffs drawn from families of modest wealth and standing, rather than the barons, often the leading tenants-in-chief in their shires, upon whom his father had frequently relied. There are dangers in too rigid classification, since some individuals can be fitted into more than one category, but if the year 1128–9 is allowed to serve as representative of the last phase of the reign, we can say that, in broad terms, at least half a dozen sheriffs were enjoying close links with the royal *curia*, four had strong hereditary claims to their offices, seven could be considered prominent barons in their regions and a further ten might best be described as modest local landholders; at least one of these had experience in baronial administration. The king's preference for indigenous first-generation sheriffs is clear enough, but hereditary sheriffs on the one hand, and those with duties in the royal household on the other, might also be appointed as occasion required.[83]

Under Stephen, several shrievalties had fallen once again to barons with hereditary claims, some of whom had been promised that they would render the same farms as their forebears.[84] Even Henry II had been obliged at the outset of his reign to grant the shrievalty of Gloucestershire to Roger earl of Hereford for the same farm that his father Miles had rendered under Henry I.[85] Whether any others struck similar bargains is

---

[82] Round, *Geoffrey de Mandeville*, 267–77.

[83] Green, *Sheriffs*, 13–18; Green, *Henry I*, 194–214. (cf. W. A. Morris, *The Medieval English Sheriff to 1300*, Manchester, 1927, 41–52, 75–87; F. Barlow, *William Rufus*, London, 1983, 187–8). The year 1128–9 is chosen for analysis because of the exceptional circumstances of 1129–30, when the *curiales* Richard Basset and Aubrey II de Vere held office in eleven shires. Evidence for tenure of the shrievalty is not clear cut in every case, nor are the categories mutually exclusive (e.g. in the cases of *curiales* who had risen to positions of considerable landed wealth). Here and below, nn. 116–17, a holding equivalent to at least five knights' fees is taken to distinguish a baron from more modest landholders. For details and references, see Green, *Henry I*, 194–214, 228–81 and *Sheriffs*, 25–90. *Curiales*: Rayner of Bath, Walter de Beauchamp, Geoffrey de Clinton, Miles of Gloucester, Payn fitz John, Robert d'Oilli, William de Pont de l'Arche. Hereditary claimants: Walter de Beauchamp, Bertram de Bulmer, Fulk nephew of Gilbert the knight, Robert d'Oilli, plus (possibly) Odard of Bamburgh (for Northumberland). Barons: Walter de Beauchamp, Geoffrey de Clinton, Miles of Gloucester, Payn fitz John, Meinfelin, Robert d'Oilli, William de Pont de l'Arche. Lesser landholders: Odard of Bamburgh, Bertram de Bulmer, William of Eynesford, Geoffrey de Furneaux, Fulk nephew of Gilbert the knight, Hildret, Hugh of Leicester (steward to Matilda of Senlis), Osbert Salvain, Robert fitz Walter, Warin. The analysis omits Fulk fitz Walter (London–Middlesex), Hugh de Warelville (Sussex) and Anselm *vicomte* of Rouen (Berkshire).

[84] *RRAN*, III, nos. 68, 275.

[85] *Rotuli Chartarum*, 53: 'concessi . . . vicecomitatum Glocestrescire per eandem firmam quam reddere solebat comes Milo pater ejus tempore Henrici Regis avi mei'.

unknown: if they did, the arrangements did not persist, since none of the farms in Henry II's pipe rolls match those of 1130.[86] Be that as it may, the replacement of this type of sheriff – barons who were established figures in their shires, second- or third-generation in office – had to be handled delicately, and took several years to accomplish. Roger of Hereford's brother Walter was sheriff of Gloucestershire until Michaelmas 1157, of Herefordshire until Michaelmas 1159. Henry d'Oilli, son of the 1130 sheriff of Oxfordshire, held that post from Michaelmas 1155 to the close of 1160. The hereditary sheriffs of Shropshire and Staffordshire, William fitz Alan and Robert of Stafford, continued until 1159 and 1160 respectively. William de Beauchamp had Gloucestershire from 1157 to 1163, Herefordshire from 1160 to 1170, and Worcestershire from 1155 to 1170.[87]

Leading *curiales* also figured among Henry's early appointments. Richard de Lucy appears as sheriff of Essex and Hertfordshire until Michaelmas 1157; Richard de Camville held Berkshire, Henry of Essex Buckinghamshire–Bedfordshire, both from 1155 to 1157; Richard du Hommet accounted in 1157 for Sussex, where Hilary bishop of Chichester is also found as sheriff in 1155 and from 1160 to 1162.[88] But this seems to have been regarded only as a temporary expedient, and in the period before 1170 – a convenient break for the purposes of this discussion – most appointments went to lords of varying degrees of wealth who had close associations with their shires. Several were prominent local barons whose families are not known to have held the shrievalty before. Gilbert de Pinkeny (sheriff of Berkshire from 1157 to 1160), Hamo Peche (Cambridgeshire–Huntingdonshire, 1163 to 1166), Robert de Beauchamp and Gerbert de Percy (successive sheriffs of Dorset, 1161 to 1166), Hugh of Dover (Kent, 1161 to 1168), William de Vesci (Northumberland, 1157 to 1170), Manasser Arsic (Oxfordshire, 1160 to 1163) and Geoffrey de Vere (Shropshire, 1163 to 1170) were all substantial tenants-in-chief in the shires to which they were appointed.[89] Wealthy under-tenants included Philip of Kyme, sheriff of Lincolnshire from 1167 to

---

[86] See appendix I for sheriffs' farms totals. A possible exception is the farm of Northamptonshire, which stood at £249 2s. 1d. by weight (*ad pensum*) in 1130, and £250 2s. 2d. 'blanch' in 1156, but the total settled at a different figure thereafter.

[87] William de Beauchamp's last accounts for Worcestershire and Herefordshire were for the year ending at Michaelmas 1169, but he probably continued in office until his death in the following year; he was also sheriff of Warwickshire for the second half of 1158–59 ('Annales de Wigornia' in *Annales Monastici*, IV, 382; *Cartulary of Worcester*, xxvii; *The Beauchamp Cartulary: Charters 1100–1268*, ed. E. Mason, P. R. Society, 1980, xxiv–xxv; J. Boorman, 'The Sheriffs of Henry II and their role in Civil Litigation', unpubl. PhD, University of Reading, 1989 [cited below as Boorman, 'Sheriffs . . . Litigation'], 520–8).

[88] For references to individual sheriffs, here and below, see the transcript of the 1155 pipe roll in *RBE*, II, 648–58, and otherwise the relevant roll from 1156 (*PR2H*) onwards.

[89] *Baronies*, 94, 19, 48, 51, 72, 103, 36, 113.

1170, who held some thirteen fees of various lords and William de
Boterel, sheriff of Devon between 1157 and 1160, with twelve fees of the
earl of Cornwall and one of the bishop of Exeter.[90]

Even so, it is fair to say that the majority of Henry II's early sheriffs
were of the type his grandfather had evidently preferred: local landholders
of modest means, possessors of only a few knights' fees, usually as
undertenants. Several of them had gained experience in baronial service.
We have seen already that a number of comital stewards had been
installed in shrievalties by the end of Stephen's reign, only to be required
to answer to the king in 1155.[91] Although most of this group were quickly
removed from office, Henry II clearly saw the benefits of appointing men
of their type. Simon fitz Peter, sheriff of Northamptonshire for most of
the period between 1155 and 1170, had been a steward to Simon II de
Senlis; Hugh Gubiun, who replaced him from 1161 to 1163, may also
have been one of Earl Simon's officials.[92] Turstin, succeeded in Hampshire by his son Richard in 1159–60, had been a clerk to William de Pont
de l'Arche.[93] Ralf Picot, who retained his shrievalty of Kent from
Stephen's reign until the close of 1160, served Archbishop Theobald as
constable.[94] Among the sheriffs of Lincolnshire, Walter de Amundeville
(1157–63) is known to have been a steward to the bishop,[95] Alured of
Pointon (1166–7) a steward to Maurice de Craon,[96] William de Insula
(1165–6) a constable to Simon II de Senlis,[97] Philip of Kyme a steward to
his son Simon III and also to Gilbert de Gant.[98] Oger *Dapifer*, sheriff of
Norfolk–Suffolk from 1164 to 1170, held one knight's fee *de novo* of
Richard de Lucy; his name suggests service in Richard's household. Of

[90] *RBE*, I, 248, 262, 375, 377, 381–3, 390, 416; Stenton, *English Feudalism*, 94, n. 2; *HKF*, II, 118–25;
cf. *Charters of Redvers*, 188, for further evidence of William de Boterel's association with Reginald
earl of Cornwall.　　[91] Above, ch. 2.

[92] Copies of charters issued by Simon II de Senlis and witnessed by Simon fitz Peter as *dapifer* are
found in the cartulary of St Andrews's Priory, Northampton (B.L. Royal MS. 11 B. ix, fos. 7v.–8,
12v.–13). Hugh Gubiun was also a frequent witness to charters of Simon II de Senlis, e.g. *ibid.*, fos.
7–9v., 12v.–13, but is not found with an official title and was consistently placed below Simon fitz
Peter when both attested. Cf. Fowler, 'Shire of Bedford and earldom of Huntingdon', 29, 32.

[93] *RRAN*, II, no. 1872; cf. III, no. 897.

[94] Saltman, *Theobald*, nos. 55, 161, and p. 542; cf. *RRAN*, III, no. 145.

[95] *Reg. Ant.*, II, nos. 576, 611; IV, nos. 1192, 1292; *RBE*, I, 374, 345, 390 for holdings of fees *de veteri* of
the bishop of Lincoln, Geoffrey III de Mandeville and Richard de la Haye in 1166; cf. C. T. Clay,
'The family of Amundeville', *Reports and Papers of the Lincolnshire Architectural and Archaeological
Society*, 1948, 112, 114.

[96] Peterborough Dean and Chapter MS. 23 ('Goxhill Leger'), fo. 31v. for grant of stewardship; cf.
fos. 33v., 43v. for grants of land formerly Roger the steward's; *RBE*, I, 385 for holdings of fees *de
veteri* and *de novo* of Maurice de Craon in 1166.

[97] B.L. Add. charter 6037 for William de Insula's attestation as constable of a charter of Simon II de
Senlis in favour of St James's Priory, Northampton.

[98] *Rufford Charters*, I, lix; II, nos. 667, 669–70, 684, 733, 756–7, 764–5; *EYC*, II, nos. 1185, 1219;
Abbott, 'Gant Family', 170–1, 277, 279, 281, 286, 288, 328, 333, 335–6, 341, 368; *Lawsuits*, II, no.
527, and (for fees held in 1166) above, n. 90.

all these, only Simon fitz Peter and – through the chief justiciar – Oger *Dapifer* had previous close links with the royal *curia*.[99]

Two who may be treated within this group of moderate landholders, William de Chesney and Bertram de Bulmer, were sons of sheriffs appointed by Henry I. William de Chesney occurs in 1166 as holding three knights' fees in chief and another four in mesne. He was in office in Norfolk and Suffolk from 1157 to 1163, but had already been sheriff of Norfolk late in Stephen's reign, in succession to his brother John who had died about 1146: Henry II apparently made him buy back the shrievalty, since a *gersuma* of 200 silver marks appears against his name in the 1159 pipe roll.[100] Bertram de Bulmer's estates, totalling about three knights' fees, were all held in chief. He had been sheriff of Yorkshire in 1130 and served Henry II in that capacity from 1155 to 1163, but had almost certainly lost the office under Stephen.[101] Many other sheriffs' careers are obscure, although it is likely that at least some had experience as stewards or other officers in the households of those from whom they held their lands. Payn of Hemingford, possibly the tenant of one-tenth of a fee of Simon de Beauchamp, Adam of Catmore, holder of half a fee of William de Ferrers, Maurice de Tiretot and Hugh de Ralega, who both held a few fees of various lords,[102] were among those who remained in office longest in the period to 1170: Payn had already been sheriff of Huntingdonshire, and possibly also of Cambridgeshire, during Stephen's reign, and Maurice de Tiretot of Essex in the 1140s or early 1150s.[103] Of the remainder, Geoffrey fitz Ralf and Richard fitz Osbert (Buckinghamshire–Bedfordshire), Robert fitz Bernard (Devon), Richard de Raddon, Warner de

[99] Oger *Dapifer* (for whose holding in 1166 see *RBE*, I, 352) also had custody of the honour of Eye during his term as sheriff; he was appointed by Richard de Lucy to hear the Anstey case early in 1163, only for it then to be summoned before the king at Woodstock (*Lawsuits*, II, no. 408e). Simon fitz Peter witnessed several royal charters (e.g. *Itinerary*, 33, 63; *CCR*, III, 112, 396–7) served as a royal justice in 1163 (*Lawsuits*, II, no. 411) and was present at the Clarendon council in January 1164 (*Becket Materials*, IV, 208; V, 73).

[100] *PR5H*, 11; *Life and Miracles of St William of Norwich by Thomas of Monmouth*, ed. A. Jessopp and M. R. James (Cambridge, 1896), 111–12, 128, 172; *RRAN*, III, nos. 401, 618; Green, *Sheriffs*, 61–2. William de Chesney appears in the 1166 *cartae baronum* under that name and also as William of Norwich, but must not be confused with the Midlands landholder also known as William de Chesney, the man who blackmailed his nephew Gilbert Foliot (GF, *Letters*, no. 20). The East Anglian William de Chesney had inherited a knight's fee in Mor and Filby (Norfolk), held of the king in chief, and also received Blythburgh (Suffolk) from Henry II as one knight's fee (*RBE*, I, 402, where the *carta* is in the name of his father Robert fitz Walter); in addition, he was tenant of four fees *de veteri*, one each held of the bishop of Ely, the honour of St Edmund, the honour of Clare and Roger of Kentwell (*ibid.*, I, 365, 393, 404, 410).

[101] *RBE*, I, 428–9 (return made on behalf of Bertram's son William); W. Farrer, 'The sheriffs of Lincolnshire and Yorkshire, 1066–1130', *EHR*, 30 (1915), 285; *EYC*, II, 127–8; Green, *Sheriffs*, 90; Dalton, *Conquest, Anarchy and Lordship*, 153, n. 38.

[102] *RBE*, I, 231, 253, 259, 321, 337, 339, 347. Payn of Hemingford was sheriff of Cambridgeshire–Huntingdonshire 1155–63, Adam of Catmore of Berkshire 1161–9 and of Oxfordshire 1164–9, Maurice de Tiretot of Essex–Hertfordshire 1157–60 and 1161–3, and Hugh de Ralega of Devon 1160–7.   [103] Green, *Sheriffs*, 29, 40, 49.

Lusurs and Robert Pucherel (Dorset and Somerset), Otvel de Bovilla and Stephen de Beauchamp (Essex), William Pipard (Gloucestershire), Peter of Goxhill (Lincolnshire), William de *Novavilla* (Norfolk), Robert fitz Ranulf (Nottinghamshire–Derbyshire), William de Fraisnet (Suffolk), Hervey of Stratton (Staffordshire), Ralf Basset (Warwickshire–Leicestershire), Robert fitz Geoffrey (Warwickshire), and Miles de Dantesey (Wiltshire) can all be found against a few knights' fees in the *cartae baronum*, mostly in their shrieval counties; only Warner de Lusurs was recorded as a tenant-in-chief.[104] None can be placed among Henry II's *curiales*, although Warner de Lusurs had been a frequent witness for Stephen, especially late in the reign.[105]

The upheaval after Easter 1170, when only six sheriffs appear to have retained their posts,[106] had been anticipated about Michaelmas 1155 when at least fourteen new appointments were made,[107] and about Michaelmas 1163 when there were a further fifteen.[108] It is clear that in the early months of the reign, the king had to use the local administrators available, including two clerks, Hilary bishop of Chichester in Sussex and William Cumin – possibly already archdeacon – in Worcestershire:[109] the exchequer of Michaelmas 1155 gave the opportunity for more considered appointments. The dismissals of 1163 arose out of a drive to improve the efficiency of sheriffs, following the king's return to England in January. It

---

[104] *RBE*, I, 321 (Geoffrey fitz Ralf); 345, 365, 396, 425 (Richard fitz Osbert); 228, 252 (Robert fitz Bernard); 219, 248, 265 (Richard de Raddon); 246 (Warner de Lusurs: one fee held in chief in Wiltshire); 221, 223 (Robert Pucherel); 345, 353 (Otvel de Bovilla); 299, 314, 403 (Stephen de Beauchamp); 309 (William Pipard); 376, 387 (Peter of Goxhill); 348, 396 (William de *Novavilla*); 344 (Robert fitz Ranulf); 395 (William de Fraisnet); 266 (Hervey of Stratton); 330–31 (Ralf Basset); 263, 274, 341 (Robert fitz Geoffrey); 241, 310 (Miles de Dantesey).

[105] Forty known charters of Stephen are attested by him, including seven of the period 1153–4 (*RRAN*, III, nos. 28, 129, 251, 519, 583, 696, 896).

[106] These were Robert fitz Troite in Carlisle, Robert fitz Bernard in Devon, Hervey of Stratton in Staffordshire, Gervase of Cornhill in Surrey, Richard of Wilton in Wiltshire and Gilbert Pipard in Gloucestershire (cf. *Gesta Regis*, II, lxvii–lxviii, and I, 4–5, where we are told that nearly all the sheriffs were dismissed but that some were later reinstated).

[107] New sheriffs were evidently appointed about Michaelmas 1155 to Berkshire, Gloucestershire, Herefordshire, Hertfordshire, Leicestershire, London–Middlesex, Norfolk, Northamptonshire, Nottinghamshire–Derbyshire, Oxfordshire, Somerset, Suffolk, Sussex and Worcestershire; the sheriffs who accounted for the farms in 1155 were replaced. There may also have been new appointments to Buckinghamshire–Bedfordshire, Hampshire and Warwickshire, for which there were no accounts in the *Red Book* transcript of the 1155 pipe roll.

[108] New sheriffs appear to have been installed about Michaelmas 1163 for Buckinghamshire–Bedfordshire, Cambridgeshire–Huntingdonshire, Dorset, Essex–Hertfordshire, Gloucestershire, Norfolk–Suffolk, Northamptonshire, Lincolnshire, Oxfordshire, Somerset, Surrey, Sussex, Warwickshire, Wiltshire and Yorkshire. On these changes in personnel, cf. Boorman, 'Sheriffs of Henry II', esp. 257–68, and for comparable purges during Richard I's sojourns in England in 1189 and 1194, see R. R. Heiser, 'Richard I and his appointments to English shrievalties', *EHR*, 112 (1997), 1–19.

[109] William Cumin had been archdeacon of Worcester before his excommunication in 1143, and had certainly recovered the benefice by 1157 (Saltman, *Theobald*, no. 270; GF, *Letters*, 539–40; J. le Neve, *Fasti Ecclesiae Anglicanae, 1066–1300*, II: *Monastic Cathedrals*, ed. D. E. Greenway (London, 1971), 105.

is worth adding, however, that unsatisfactory sheriffs were liable to be disciplined or removed, wherever the king was at the time. Walter of Hereford lost his hereditary shrievalty in Gloucestershire after Michaelmas 1157, when he apparently owed £67 15s. 9d. 'blanch' old and new farm.[110] Henry d'Oilli, hereditary sheriff of Oxfordshire, left office about Michaelmas 1160 evidently having incurred debts of over £62 'blanch'.[111] Robert fitz Hugh owed a total of £95 3s. 2d. 'blanch' on the farms of Leicestershire and Warwickshire at Michaelmas 1158, and does not appear as sheriff thereafter; he seems to have been arrested in the following year.[112] None of these debts recur in subsequent pipe rolls. Several other sheriffs were amerced for unspecified reasons. Henry of Oxford accounted for 100 silver marks in 1159, Bertram de Bulmer for £200 in 1160 and Robert of Stafford, William de Boterel, Gilbert de Pinkeny, William de Chesney, Ralf Picot, Richard fitz Turstin, Simon fitz Peter, Warner de Lusurs, Richard *Clericus* and Robert fitz Troite for sums ranging from 20 marks to £200 in 1161, although by no means all that was due was eventually paid.[113] Five of these sheriffs were among the eleven replaced in office during the course of 1160 and 1161, in what may have been another deliberate purge.[114] Further amercements were imposed in 1161 upon six sheriffs for delays in making their accounts at the exchequer, although none appears to have been dismissed in consequence.[115]

It is instructive to take a snapshot of the overall composition of the shrievalty once the initial difficulties of the new reign were past, in order to make comparison with that of Henry I's reign. While accepting the limitations of attempts at classification, it seems fair to say that, by 1159–60, there was little reliance on *curiales* but that hereditary sheriffs still

---

[110] Walter of Hereford owed £30 'blanch' old farm and £37 15s. 9d.'blanch' new farm in 1157 (*PR3H*, 100). The sum of £7 15s. 9d. 'blanch' was paid off by his successor in the following year (*PR4H*, 167) leaving two £30 debts; these were duly noted, but they did not figure in any subsequent pipe rolls. On the terms 'blanch' and *numero*, and also on old and new farms, see below, chapter 4.

[111] *PR6H*, 8–9: £62 10s. 10d. 'blanch' on his shire farm with a further £10 under *Nova Placita et Novae Conventiones*.

[112] *PR4H*, 183–4; he did not account for the farms in 1159, though his successors, William de Beauchamp in Warwickshire and Robert fitz Hardulf in Leicestershire, did so for half the year. The former's account includes an allowance of £35 0s. 9d. *numero* 'pro Captura Roberti filii Hugonis de Warewichscira' (*PR5H*, 25).

[113] *PR5H*, 35; *PR6H*, 15; *PR7H*, 7, 9, 11, 29, 32, 41, 50, 56, 63. The 1162 pipe roll records that Gilbert de Pinkeny's amercement was postponed by royal writ until the king should come to England (*PR8H*, 40); for other delays and non-payments, see Boorman, 'Sheriffs of Henry II', 263–5. Henry of Oxford was sheriff of Oxfordshire before Michaelmas 1155 (Green, *Sheriffs*, 70).

[114] Boorman, 'Sheriffs of Henry II', 260–5.

[115] The sheriff of Norfolk–Suffolk was amerced £10, the sheriff of Essex–Hertfordshire £7 10s., those of Northumberland, Oxfordshire, Staffordshire and Yorkshire each £5 (*PR7H*, 7, 24, 27, 37, 42, 67); cf. *Dialogus*, 79–80.

had a role to play; only two sheriffs can be placed in the first category, seven in the second. Fourteen may be regarded as modest landholders, mostly undertenants including some former honorial officials, while a further seven were of more substantial wealth.[116] By 1164–5, the personnel had largely changed, but sheriffs with modest local origins dominated the picture to an even greater extent; *curiales* and hereditary sheriffs had become exceptional, although there was still room for a few men of considerable regional wealth.[117] This is broadly in line with the position identified in 1128–9, except that Henry II had carried even further his grandfather's preference for first-generation sheriffs of moderate means. While Henry I had recognised the value in places of appointing *curiales* and hereditary claimants, Henry II usually removed them as soon as he reasonably could.

The 'Inquest of Sheriffs' of 1170 brought a further upheaval in personnel, although, as Julia Boorman has pointed out, the extent to which it marked a shift in favour of appointing *curiales* familiar to the royal household has been exaggerated.[118] Behind this enquiry lay a change in the government's priorities with the passing of the years: it was no longer enough for a sheriff to be efficient in levying the king's dues, he now had to appear incorruptible as well.[119] Although we have had occasion to note sheriffs dismissed after falling into debt, it is fair to say that, in Henry II's

---

[116] *Curiales*: Henry d'Oilli, Simon fitz Peter. Hereditary claimants: William de Beauchamp (for Worcestershire), Bertram de Bulmer, William de Chesney, Henry d'Oilli, Earl Patrick, Robert of Stafford, Richard fitz Turstin. Barons: William de Beauchamp, Henry d'Oilli, Earl Patrick, Gilbert de Pinkeny, Robert of Stafford, William de Vesci and (as a substantial undertenant) William de Botcrel. Lesser landholders, household officials, etc.: Walter de Amundeville (steward to bishop of Lincoln), Ralf Basset, Bertram de Bulmer, William de Chesney, Ranulf fitz Ingelran, Warner de Lusurs, Maurice (Herefordshire), Pagan, Simon fitz Peter (steward to Simon II de Senlis), Ralf Picot (constable to Archbishop of Canterbury), Richard de Raddon, Guy le Strange, Richard fitz Turstin, Maurice de Tiretot. Simon fitz Peter was entered against only two half-fees under Bedfordshire and Northamptonshire in the 1166 *cartae*, although a man of the same name held $8\frac{1}{2}$ fees under Somerset and a further fifth of one fee under Wiltshire (*RBE*, I, 224, 241, 322, 334).

[117] *Curialis*: Simon fitz Peter (although Ranulf de Glanville, sheriff of Yorkshire, had a distinguished career ahead of him). Hereditary claimants: William Basset, William de Beauchamp, Richard fitz Turstin. Barons: William de Beauchamp, Hamo Peche, Gerbert de Percy, William de Vesci. Lesser landholders, household officials, etc.: William Basset, Reiner fitz Berengar, Adam of Catmore, Alexander the Clerk, Gervase of Cornhill, Oger *Dapifer*, Nicholas the Dean, Hugh of Dover, Ranulf de Glanville, Roger Hay, Ranulf fitz Ingelran, William fitz Isabel, Hugh de Lalega, Richard fitz Osbert, Simon fitz Peter, William Pipard, Hugh de Ralega, Guy le Strange, Richard of Wilton, Peter of Goxhill (although the last-named might be classified as a baron through his tenure of $5\frac{1}{2}$ fees as an undertenant in *RBE*, I, 376, 387). On the circumstances of sheriffs named here and in the previous note, see the biographical details in Boorman 'Sheriffs . . . Litigation', 460–978.

[118] *Gesta Regis*, II, lxviii; *Select Charters*, 175; Boussard, *Le Gouvernement*, 453, n. 2; cf. Boorman, 'Sheriffs of Henry II', 269–74 and for a fuller discussion, Boorman, 'Sheriffs . . . Litigation', 98–119.

[119] See esp. caps. i, vi, xi of the Inquest of Sheriffs: *Select Charters*, 175–8; Gervase, I, 217–19.

early years as king, most of them successfully met their obligations as accountants for their farms. It is exceptional to find arrears of over £200 'blanch', which some had incurred by 1130, and nearly all the amounts left owing – rarely in excess of £20 'blanch' – were balanced in the following year.[120] In the first decade of the reign, when the finances were being restored through the regular render from all over the country of the farms and taxes due to the king, sheriffs were needed who would at least collect the sums required, whatever profit they might make for themselves. But the judicial measures of the 1160s afforded new opportunities for bribery and embezzlement, which hampered sheriffs' effectiveness and reduced the treasury's receipts. The wide variation in the thoroughness with which the Assize of Clarendon was enforced – from Yorkshire, whence Ranulf de Glanville accounted for the chattels of some 130 felons and fugitives in 1166, to Hampshire where only four criminals are recorded in that year, and Worcestershire where we are told of only one [121] – strongly suggests that some sheriffs had been ready to release the accused 'pro praemio vel promissione vel amore'.[122] The remedy chosen was to remove most of the local landholders from office, although this did not necessarily mean an end to their careers in the king's service, for some reappeared in an administrative capacity in subsequent years; moreover, the retention of one financier, Gervase of Cornhill, and the appointment of another, Robert fitz Sawin, [123] shows that the king was still prepared to use sheriffs for whom the office must have been seen partly as a means to a healthy personal profit.

This survey of Henry II's early sheriffs prompts two final comments on the king's handling of his administrators in general. First, although there was a natural tendency at the very beginning of the reign to take account of allegiance in the civil war, this never became a major issue. In his initial

---

[120] An exceptional case among Henry II's early sheriffs was that of William de Chesney, who left a debt of £319 9s. 8d. 'blanch' farm of Norfolk–Suffolk, plus an increment of £150 *numero* when he left office at Michaelmas 1163 (*PR9H*, 29). This may, however, be linked to repayment of the King's creditors (Boorman, 'Sheriffs ... Litigation, 575–6). Other debts above £20 'blanch' are found in Yorkshire (carried forward from 1155 to 1156), Wiltshire (1156–7), and Gloucestershire (1163–4), but all these were paid off in the ensuing year (*PR2H*, 26, 57; *PR3H*, 77; *PR9H*, 8; *PR10H*, 5).   [121] *PR12H*, 43–5, 82, 104.

[122] Above, n. 119 (cap. vi); cf. Richardson and Sayles, *Governance*, 201, and J. C. Holt, 'The assizes of Henry II: the texts', in D. A. Bullough and R. L. Storey, eds., *The Study of Medieval Records: Essays in Honour of Kathleen Major* (Oxford, 1971), esp. 106.

[123] On Gervase of Cornhill see Round, *Geoffrey de Mandeville*, 304–12; Richardson, *Jewry*, 59, nn. 1, 3; Boorman, 'Sheriffs ... Litigation', 115–19, 582–4. Evidence of his property dealings occur in *RRAN*, III, nos. 243, 244; Saltman, *Theobald*, no. 268; *Book of Seals*, nos, 84, 105. He accounted as sheriff of Surrey until 1182 and was succeeeded by his son (*PR28H*, 155; *PR29H*, 83; *PR30H*, 152). On Robert fitz Sawin, see Richardson, *Jewry*, 53–6; Boorman, 'Sheriffs ... Litigation', 878–80. He held the borough of Northampton at farm from 1155–6 onwards (*PR2H*, 42; *PR3H*, 106, etc.).

choice of *curiales* to advise him, Henry relied, understandably, on those he knew from the past through their commitment to his cause. Stephen's steward William Martel did not find a place in Henry's household and also lost the shrievalty of Surrey; it may have been past support for the previous king that led to the dismissals of the sheriffs of Hertfordshire and Somerset as well.[124] But there were important exceptions, for Richard de Lucy, Richard de Camville and Henry of Essex, who found places in the king's household or exchequer, had all been loyal to Stephen. So had Ralf Picot, Maurice de Tiretot and William de Chesney, who served him as sheriffs for several years.[125] Men of ability were welcome, from whatever source they came, and those with administrative experience under Stephen clearly had much to contribute to the restoration of effective royal government over the kingdom as a whole.

The second point is that, as the king surrounded himself with *curiales* who owed their substance not to inheritance but to patronage, as earldoms were reduced to honorific titles and shrievalties passed to landholders of modest means, it is possible to discern a shift away from dependence upon the magnates. No one took over Nigel bishop of Ely's functions at the exchequer, after his retirement about 1164, nor did another magnate succeed Robert earl of Leicester as chief justiciar on his death in 1168; Richard de Lucy became sole justiciar instead. Yet here again there are exceptions which must be acknowledged. William de Beauchamp, tenant-in-chief for the service of seven knights in 1166, retained his hereditary shrievalty of Worcestershire until 1170, and his administrative responsibilities were actually increased by his appointment to Gloucestershire in 1157 and to Herefordshire in 1160. Earls, or other local barons, were allowed to remain as sheriffs of Devon, Gloucestershire, Herefordshire, Shropshire, Staffordshire and Wiltshire at the beginning of the reign, and although none were in office after 1160, we find that in Kent in 1161, and in Cambridgeshire–Huntingdonshire in 1163, local barons came to replace sheriffs of long experience but humbler status.[126] A few prominent figures, such as William Malet, continued to perform regular duties in the royal household, and several earls were assigned from time to time to prestigious tasks. Use magnates of ability where appropriate, to enhance but not obstruct the king's authority;

---

[124] Guy fitz Tesc' (removed from Hertfordshire after Easter 1155) had campaigned with Stephen's army: *RRAN*, III, nos. 456, 874. Richard de Montacute (dismissed from Somerset about Michaelmas 1155) was grandson to a butler to the counts of Mortain and may have served in the household of Stephen or his queen (*HKF*, I, 199; *RRAN*, III, nos. 23, 503, 655, 991). William Martel accounted for Surrey in 1155 but Payn did so on his behalf at Michaelmas 1156 and in his own right thereafter.   [125] Green, *Sheriffs*, 40, 51, 62, 77.

[126] Kent, 1161: replacement of Ralf Picot by Hugh of Dover. Cambridgeshire–Huntingdonshire 1163: replacement of Payn of Hemingford by Hamo Peche.

allow hereditary titles which predated Stephen to persist, but ensure that they carried no real power; cast the net widely in seeking loyal and efficient administrators, demonstrate the rewards to be acquired, but drop those found wanting: these were the keys to the successful deployment of royal servants early in Henry II's reign.

BARONIAL ESTATES

According to R. H. C. Davis in 1964, 'what happened in Stephen's reign' was that 'the barons were reacting . . . against the notion that their lands were merely tenements which they held at the king's pleasure'. 'That was what the barons fought for in Stephen's reign, and that is what they won.' This view, which sees the hereditary principle for crown and lay baronies – hitherto tenuous – firmly established as a result both of the 1153 peace settlement and of measures subsequently taken by Henry II, rarely finds support today.[127] Through the work of several scholars, notably Sir James Holt and John Hudson, a presumption within Anglo-Norman society in favour of security of tenure and hereditary succession has been shown to be well established by the 1120s. By then, succession by heirs had come to be regarded as normal by the king and his tenants and would, as a rule, be upheld if there was litigation.[128] The use of 'inheritance language' in royal and private charters recording the grant of land to a vassal – such as the phrase *in feodo et hereditate* – was one indication of widespread acceptance that property would pass down the generations, and such language clearly became more frequent from Henry I's reign onwards.[129] Thus, when Henry II ascended the throne, hereditability was already an abstract right

---

[127] R. H. C. Davis, 'What happened in Stephen's reign', *History*, 49 (1964), 1–12 (quotation at 12). Recent support for Davis's interpretation may be found in K. S. B. Keats-Rohan, 'The Bretons and Normans of England 1066–1154: the family, the fief and the feudal monarchy', *Nottingham Medieval Studies*, 36 (1992), 42–78 (esp. 64–5).

[128] J. G. H. Hudson, 'Life-grants of land and the development of inheritance in Anglo-Norman England', *ANS*, 12 (1990), 67–80; Hudson, *Land, Law and Lordship*, esp. 15–153; J. C. Holt, 'Politics and property in early medieval England', *Past and Present*, 57 (1972), 3–52, and *ibid.*, 65 (1974), 127–35; Holt, 'Feudal society and the family in early medieval England', *TRHS*, 5th ser., 32–5 (1982–5), esp. II, 'Notions of patrimony', 33 (1983), 193–220, and III, 'Patronage and politics', 34 (1984), 1–26; P. R. Hyams, 'Warranty and good lordship in twelfth century England', *Law and History Review*, 5 (1987), 437–503; also, J. Biancalana, 'For want of justice: legal reforms of Henry II', *Columbia Law Review*, 88 (1988), 433–536, Dalton, *Conquest, Anarchy and Lordship*, 257–97, and S. Reynolds, *Fiefs and Vassals* (Oxford, 1994), 353–4; cf. E. J. King, 'The tenurial crisis of the early twelfth century', *Past and Present*, 65 (1974), 110–17, and S. D. White, 'Succession to fiefs in early medieval England', *Past and Present*, 65 (1974), 118–27.

[129] For examples of 'inheritance language', see e.g. Stenton, *English Feudalism*, no. 29; *Book of Seals*, no. 528; *RRAN*, II, no. clxxx, p. 355; *RRAN*, III, nos. 180, 273–6, 307, 319, 634–5. The subject is discussed (with reference to a much wider range of examples) in Hudson, *Land, Law and Lordship*, 77–85, and is considered from a political perspective in Green, *Aristocracy of Norman England*, 259–64, 324, 335–42.

as far as secular barons and their tenants were concerned, a right which had sometimes been infringed amid the turmoil of Stephen's reign but one which any monarch intent on restoring order was bound to respect.

Despite this, there were obviously some circumstances in which Henry II would intervene to disrupt the tenurial stability of barons and their heirs. Outright forfeiture was a rarity, but not so rare that tenants-in-chief could discount it as a possibility.[130] In 1155, William Peverel was deprived of his honour of the Peak, ostensibly for procuring the death of Ranulf II earl of Chester through poison;[131] his demesnes in Nottinghamshire and Derbyshire subsequently remained in crown hands, although the valuable demesne manor of Higham (Northamptonshire) was granted out again, initially to the earl of Derby.[132] In 1163 the constable Henry of Essex was accused before the king of cowardice, in having dropped the standard and fled during the invasion of North Wales six years previously; his accuser, Robert de Montfort, represented the line disinherited by Henry I in 1107. Robert defeated Henry of Essex in trial by battle but did not in fact receive his adversary's lands, mainly in Suffolk and Essex, which were retained by the crown.[133] In 1172, Adam II de Port was exiled and deprived of his barony of Kington (Herefordshire), allegedly for treason in plotting the king's death; in this case, the lands were soon alienated, the king's steward William fitz Adelin being in possession two years later.[134] And in 1174, William the Lion and his brother David of Scots forfeited the Midlands honour of Huntingdon following their involvement in the rebellion of Henry the Younger, the honour passing instead to Simon III de Senlis.[135] Yet Henry II was remarkably lenient to others who might be deemed to have merited forfeiture, including many of the rebels of 1173–4. Richard fitz Nigel in the *Dialogus de Scaccario* said as much: 'few of them lost their property, none their civil rights or life or limb . . . he preferred to spare his conquered foes rather than punish them, in order that they might, however unwillingly, watch his kingdom grow'.[136] The usual practice with defeated rebels, applied in the case of Hugh Mortimer as early as July 1155, was to confiscate castles, but not lands.[137] The principle was enshrined in the peace terms at the end of Henry the Younger's rebellion in autumn 1174: participants were to be restored to the lands they held

---

[130] Cf. Lally, 'Secular patronage', esp. 160, where the emphasis is upon the very occasional recourse to forfeiture.   [131] RT, 183; Gervase, I, 161.

[132] PR2H, 40; PR3H, 91; PR4H, 154, etc.; HKF, I, 201–4, 242–5; *Baronies*, 136.

[133] RT, 218; Gervase, I, 165; *Cronica Jocelini de Brakelonda*, ed. H. E. Butler (London, 1949), 68–71; *Baronies*, 120–1, 139; Davis, *Stephen*, 152.

[134] *Gesta Regis*, I, 35; *Baronies*, 57. On the king's rights to the lands of criminous tenants-in-chief, see *Dialogus*, 97.   [135] *Gesta Regis*, I, 71; *Baronies*, 118; Stringer, *Earl David of Huntingdon*, 28.

[136] *Dialogus*, 76–7.   [137] RT, 185.

fifteen days before the outbreak of war, but only those on the king's side were to have their castles as well.[138] Detailed studies of the honours of leading rebels do indeed suggest that – with the exception of William the Lion in the English Midlands – they regained their holdings virtually intact.[139] Henry II seems to have adopted a similar approach on the continent, towards recalcitrant vassals such as William Talvas in Normandy and Guiomar de Leon in Brittany: they were deprived of their castles but appear to have retained their lands. The disinheritance said to have been suffered by the *vicomte* of Thouars in 1158 was exceptional.[140]

However, to obtain a more complete picture of Henry II's attitude to baronial inheritances, some other cases should be considered. Eye and Lancaster, honours held by King Stephen before his accession to the throne, were withheld by the crown after the death of Stephen's son William in 1159; they did not pass with William's sister and heiress Mary to her husband Matthew (son of the count of Flanders) when they married in the following year.[141] Most of Reginald earl of Cornwall's honour was taken into the king's hands when he died in 1175, only small portions being allowed to pass to his daughters as co-heiresses.[142] William III d'Aubigny duly inherited Buckenham (Norfolk) from his father in 1176, but had to wait until 1190 to gain his mother's honour of Arundel, which Henry I had given her as dower.[143] Fulk II Paynel proffered 1,000 marks for Bampton (Devon) in 1180, claiming the estate as his inheritance following the death of his mother, but after he had fled the realm five years later it was retained by the crown until 1199.[144] Death did not provide the only occasion for the confiscation of estates. Richard fitz Gilbert's holdings in England and Normandy were taken into temporary royal custody during the campaign in Ireland in 1171. As a result of his minority, Adam II de Brus lost Danby, possibly the *caput* of his Yorkshire honour, first to William of Aumale then to the king, although in 1184 he received three other manors as compensation.[145] These examples are sufficient to show that the king reserved the ultimate right to control

---

[138] *Gesta Regis*, I, 77; *RAH*, II, no.468.

[139] Thus, *Charters of Mowbray*, xxx–xxxi. Hugh earl of Chester and Hamo de Mascy seem to have lost isolated holdings in southern England, but to have been restored in full to their extensive north Midlands estates (*HKF*, II, 288–93).

[140] RT, 227, 232; 'Annales de St Aubin', in *Recueil d'Annales Angevines et Vendomoises*, ed. L. Halphen (Paris, 1903), 15. It is worth noting, however, that the inference to be drawn from RT, 209, is that Waleran of Meulan lost only his castles in 1161; other evidence shows him to have lost his lands as well, albeit temporarily (Crouch, *Beaumont Twins*, 77–8).

[141] RT, 207; *Baronies*, 43, 126–7. The crown's resumption of Lancaster may have been delayed until the remarriage of William's widow in 1164.

[142] RT, 268; cf. Ellis, *Earldoms in Fee*, 114 and n. 6.   [143] *HKF*, III, 5–12; *Baronies*, 2, 70.

[144] *EYC*, VI, 51–2; *Baronies*, 5.

[145] RT, 252; Newburgh, I, 168–9; *EYC*, II, 12–13; Dalton, *Conquest, Anarchy and Lordship*, 166, 176–7.

tenure and succession. The lands of Stephen's son William and of Reg-inald earl of Cornwall were withheld by the king to prevent their passing in marriage to a potentially 'overmighty subject'. The seizure of Richard fitz Gilbert's lands helped to ensure that he would surrender his castles and maritime towns in Ireland, and acknowledge the king's suzerainty over his other conquests there.[146] Such interventions made a lot of political sense, but they serve to warn us against exaggerating Henry II's respect for the security of baronial tenure and succession, and also against the temptation to draw too sharp a contrast with the approach adopted by his predecessors.

It is not difficult to list the barons who had their English honours confiscated by the four Norman kings. Prominent among them are Roger de Breteuil in 1075, Robert de Mowbray and Roger de Lacy in 1095, Robert de Belleme, Roger de Poitou and Ivo de Grandmesnil in 1102, William of Mortain and Robert de Stuteville in 1106, Robert de Montfort in 1107, William Malet about 1110, Geoffrey Baynard in 1110, Robert de Lacy in 1114x18, Baldwin de Redvers in 1136, Robert earl of Gloucester in 1138.[147] But nearly all these cases followed armed opposi-tion to the king: the 'revolt of the earls' under William the Conqueror, the rebellions of 1095 and 1101, the battle of Tinchebrai in 1106, the manoeuvrings of the empress's supporters early in Stephen's reign. Less obviously explicable are the forfeitures of the second decade of Henry I's reign, but here the reasons probably lie in the conspiracies and conflicts in Normandy involving the king of France, the count of Anjou and William Clito.[148] If so, these confiscations were for equally 'good reason' as those of Henry II. Conversely, both William Rufus and Henry I fully recog-nised, as Henry II did in his time, the political value in sometimes allowing defeated rebels to retain their estates. This happened after each of the rebellions in, 1088, 1095, 1101 and, 1123–4, and Orderic Vitalis neatly summarised governmental thinking. William Rufus was aware of the dangers of too widespread retribution against his opponents in 1095 'for fear of fomenting their discontent still more, and goading them to another unlawful insurrection against the state, which could only cause general distress and great harm and loss'. Henry I was prepared to be

[146] G. H. Orpen, *Ireland under the Normans* (Oxford, 1911–20), I, 247–51; Warren, *Henry II*, 200.
[147] An indication of the property forfeited is given in *Baronies*, 110, 146, 95, 2, 126, 61, 43, 60, 136, 129, 138, 137, 6 (although in the last two cases, the confiscation was of limited effect because of civil war). Cf. Davis, *Stephen*, 15, and on the general context, M. Strickland, 'Against the lord's anointed: aspects of warfare and baronial rebellion in England and Normandy, 1075–1265', in Garnett and Hudson, *Law and Government*, 56–79.
[148] On the conflicts of 1111–13 and 1116–19, and the diplomacy which surrounded them, see e.g. C. W. Hollister, 'War and diplomacy in the Anglo-Norman world: the reign of Henry I', *ANS*, 6 (1983), 72–88; Green, *Henry I*, 15–17.

reconciled with – among others – William of Warenne in 1103 and William de Roumare in 1127: the former 'received the patrimony he had forfeited for his folly' and 'duly chastened, served the king faithfully . . . and throve as one of his closest friends and counsellors' while the latter, profiting from Henry's 'shrewd graciousness . . . was honourably reconciled with the king, and from that time became his close companion and friend'.[149] Yet there was also a readiness to intervene on the death of a tenant-in-chief, if political advantage would thereby be served. On the death in 1118 of Gilbert de l'Aigle, who had been given William of Mortain's forfeited barony of Pevensey, Henry I initially withheld it from Gilbert's son Richer, a recent rebel in Normandy; but after reconciliation, Richer received the estate after all. Following the death of Richard earl of Chester in the White Ship disaster of 1120, his cousin Ranulf Meschin was obliged to surrender his lands based on Carlisle (granted to him by the king earlier in the reign) and Bolingbroke (held in right of his wife Lucy) before being allowed to succeed to the honour and earldom of Chester.[150] All three of the holdings concerned – Pevensey, Carlisle, Bolingbroke – were acquisitions at the time of their reversion to the crown, not inheritances from a previous generation, and there were sound reasons for Henry I's retention of them. At Pevensey, he was withholding a potential inheritance from a declared enemy until he came to terms; in the cases of Carlisle and Bolingbroke, he was ensuring that too large a territory did not come into the hands of a single baron. Although the circumstances were far from identical, there were similarities in Henry II's treatment of Matthew of Flanders in 1160 and of Fulk II Paynel twenty years later.

In the light of all this, it is clearly unjustified to paint too black and white a picture: to depict tenure and succession as vulnerable to the manipulative Henry I, only to be protected – in fact and in law – under his grandson Henry II. Security of tenure, and hereditary succession, were already well established for lay fiefs by the early twelfth century, and both kings generally acknowledged baronial aspirations to pass on their inheritances intact.[151] On the other hand, both might interfere, to punish

---

[149] OV, IV, 284–5; VI, 14–5, 378–81. On this point generally, see various articles by C. W. Hollister, 'Henry I and Robert Malet', 'Magnates and *curiales* in early Norman England', 'The taming of a turbulent earl: Henry I and William de Warenne' and 'Henry I and the Anglo-Norman magnates', reprinted as ch. 5, 7, 8 and 10 of his *Monarchy, Magnates and Institutions*.

[150] *Baronies*, 18, 136; Holt, 'Politics and property', 51–2; Green, *Henry I*, 179–80; Hudson, *Land, Law and Lordship*, 115, 127. As pointed out in H.A. Cronne, 'Ranulf de Gernons, earl of Chester, 1129–1153', *TRHS*, 4th ser., 20 (1937), 105, it is not certain that Carlisle passed to the crown at the time of Ranulf Meschin's elevation to the earldom, but this is the most likely occasion. For the distinction between inheritance and acquisition, see esp. Holt, 'Politics and property', 12–20 and Hudson, *Land, Law and Lordship*, esp. 10–11, 209–10.

[151] Calculations from the data in *Baronies* suggest that of the 180 baronies in existence during Henry

rebels, to prevent a politically dangerous succession, or to profit from their position as overlords. Although 'the right of children to succeed by inheritance' had come by the 1170s to mean that reliefs were regarded by the exchequer as obligatory payments,[152] from the outset of his reign Henry II charged sums which were comparable in scale to the highest new reliefs of 1130.[153] Some of the fines he levied when inheritances were subject to partition seem especially harsh.[154] Both kings used wardship and marriage as sources of income and as means to reward royal officials and favourites.[155] The *Rotuli de Dominabus,* for example, makes it clear that by 1185 Henry II was frequently selling in marriage both heirs and heiresses who were in his wardship, several of the king's servants being able to secure the marriage of relatives to the wards they had in custody.[156]

If Stephen has so far been neglected in this discussion, it is because the turmoil of his reign made a consistent policy on tenure and succession impossible to sustain. There was no intention at his accession to disinherit Henry I's 'new men' in favour of his own: although he was soon obliged

---

I's reign, only sixteen were forfeited to the crown, with a further four escheating; thirteen of the forfeits and three of the escheats were subsequently regranted to new tenants. Twenty-five baronies were new creations from royal demesne following grants by Henry I, another twenty-four transferred to a different family through female succession and marriage, and the remainder were either held by the same man throughout the reign or passed to a son or other male relative. For comparison with the experiences under William II and Henry II, see Barlow, *William Rufus,* 171, Warren, *Henry II,* 364–8, and Lally, 'Secular patronage', esp. 159–62.

[152] *Dialogus,* 121.

[153] Thus, Robert de Helion, 100 silver marks for ten knights' fees (*PR2H,* 17; *Baronies,* 121); Robert de Valognes, 200 silver marks for just over thirty fees (*PR6H,* 11; *Baronies,* 12); William de Wormegay, £100 for fifteen fees (*PR6H,* 6; *Baronies,* 101). Cf. Ralf Hanselin, 200 silver marks for twenty-five fees, and Geoffrey Talbot 200 silver marks for twenty fees (*PR 31 Hen. I,* 9, 67; *Baronies,* 76, 114). *Dialogus,* 96, says that there was no fixed scale of reliefs due from tenants-in-chief, but that tenants of baronies temporarily in the king's custody paid £5 per knight's fee; there is evidence that this rule was being applied as early as 1165 (I. J. Sanders, *Feudal Military Service in England,* Oxford, 1956, 98, citing *PR11H,* 55 and *PR12H,* 15, 50–1).

[154] In 1158, Robert de Ros was charged 1,000 silver marks for approximately eight knights' fees, William de Bussy and Geoffrey de Trailly each 100 silver marks for shares in five fees; they were succeeding to portions of the honour of Walter Espec as the sons of his three sisters (*PR4H,* 140, 146; *Baronies,* 53, 133). In the same year, William de Braose was also charged 1,000 silver marks for his share of the honour of Barnstaple, where he subsequently answered for twenty-eight fees (*PR4H,* 183; *Baronies,* 105). In 1157, Geldwin fitz Savaric and Savaric his brother, vassals in Sussex of William d'Aubigny earl of Arundel, were each charged 100 silver marks, presumably for Henry II's confirmation of their agreement to divide the inheritance (*PR3H,* 80; *Book of Seals,* no. 434, with comment pp. 304–5).

[155] Southern, 'Place of Henry I'; Green, *Henry I,* esp. 176–9; Lally, 'Secular patronage', esp. 163–7.

[156] *Rotuli de Dominabus,* ed. J. H. Round (P.R. Society, 1913), xxiii–xxiv. In the first eleven years of the reign, the only recorded payments for wardships both concerned nephews (Engelard, *PR3H,* 89; *PR4H,* 170; William de Neufmarché, *PR7H,* 37; *PR8H,* 51; *PR9H,* 58; *PR10H,* 12; *PR11H,* 47; *PR12H,* 37; *PR13H,* 79). However, Henry II is known to have used his custody of William II de Roumare and Bertram de Verdun in this period to reward his *curiales* Richard de Camville and Richard du Hommet respectively (*PR7H,* 16; *Monasticon,* v, 662, no. 2).

to respond to open defiance, such as that of Baldwin de Redvers in 1136, he began with a respect for the pattern of baronial landholding bequeathed by his predecessor, and acknowledged his vassals' aspirations by granting or confirming several estates 'hereditarily'.[157] Like Henry I and Henry II, he used the opportunities for patronage presented by the succession of a minor or a female.[158] However, he was driven by the pressures of war – by the need to punish opponents and reward supporters – to become embroiled in a series of forfeitures and regrants: to deprive Henry of Scots of Huntingdon and give it to Simon II de Senlis, for example, to pass Belvoir from William d'Aubigny *Brito* to Ranulf II earl of Chester, to transfer Pevensey from Richer de l'Aigle first to Gilbert earl of Pembroke then to his own son William.[159] Alongside cases of forcible encroachment and violent seizure of land, these provided the claims and counter claims which outlasted the civil war. At least some of these disputes had to be resolved, if there was to be lasting political stability.

The 1153 peace settlement seems to have promised the restoration of inheritances, while signalling that acquisitions since the death of Henry I might be revoked.[160] Accordingly, security of tenure, and the presumption that the heir to a holding would normally succeed to it, were reaffirmed, but with the proviso that transfers of property other than by inheritance under Stephen, however authorised, were of doubtful validity. Stephen's reign was effectively categorised as an aberration, a *tempus guerrae* which must not be allowed to upset established patterns of tenure and inheritance; in the aftermath of war, the lawful landholders of Henry I's reign (normally those who held at the end of the reign, in 1135), or the heirs to estates held at that time, were to be reinstated. Such formal provision for the restoration of lawful heirs, undermining the authority of grants made in the recent past, was not without precedent: at the council of Lisieux in October 1106, following his acquisition of Normandy in the previous month, Henry I had passed decrees which in their concern for general pacification, and for the re-creation of a tenurial pattern which belonged to a previous reign, bear remarkable similarities to the terms of the 1153 settlement:

[157] Stephen's readiness to acknowledge acquisitions by his predecessor's favourites is implied by *Gesta Steph.*, 22–4; cf. P. Dalton, 'Eustace fitz John and the politics of Anglo-Norman England: the rise and survival of a twelfth-century royal servant', *Speculum* 71 (1996), 358–83 (esp. 366). It is clear that Stephen was confirming lands held in Henry I's time, or on the day of his death, from the outset of his own reign (e.g. *RRAN*, III, nos. 255–6, 386–7, 433, 832, 906). For grants or confirmations 'hereditarily', see e.g. *ibid.*, III, nos. 174–8, 276, 308, 319, 390, 493–4; Hudson, *Land, Law and Lordship*, 81.   [158] *RRAN*, III, nos., 201, 579.

[159] *Ibid.*, III, nos. 178, 272; *Baronies*, 118, 136; Hudson, *Land, Law and Lordship*, 117.

[160] Above, n. 6. Sir James Holt points out that an inheritance during Stephen's reign was also liable to be revoked, if it related to land acquired by the family since Henry I's death.

He decreed by royal authority that peace should be firmly established throughout Normandy, that all robbery and plundering should be wholly suppressed,
that all churches should hold their possessions as they had held them on the day
his father died, and that all lawful heirs should likewise hold their inheritances.
He took into his own hand all his father's demesnes, and by judgement of wise
counsellors decreed that all the gifts his brother had foolishly made to ungrateful
men, and all the concessions he had made through weakness, should be null and
void.[161]

But as with Henry I so with Henry II, to express such sentiments in the
immediate aftermath of war was not the same as to give them practical
expression. We have seen that – like his predecessors – Henry II, while
normally respectful of tenurial and hereditary security, was prepared to
override it if occasion demanded. It was inevitable that, when it came to
implementing the provisions for the restoration of pre-war landholders,
principle would be tempered by political reality.

One honour which was successfully reconstituted much as it had stood
in 1135 was that of the earl of Chester. The death of Ranulf II on 16 or 17
December 1153, leaving a minor whose lands were taken into the king's
custody, has long been recognised as a stroke of fortune which released
Henry II from a string of heavy commitments, enabling the baronial fiefs
granted to him, by Stephen in 1146 and by Henry in 1153, to be restored
almost entirely to the heirs of those who had held them in 1135. There
were minor exceptions, but in general it is clear that the holdings enjoyed
by Ranulf in 1135, and inherited by him earlier in Henry I's reign, duly
passed to his son Hugh de Kyvelioc, while those acquired under Stephen
– at the expense of William d'Aubigny *Brito*, Erneis de Burun, Ranulf de
Bayeux and others – did not. Earl Hugh's holdings were augmented by
part of the dower retained by his grandmother Countess Lucy until her
death around 1138. On the other hand, territories given up by Ranulf
Meschin about 1120 – Carlisle and another part of Lucy's inheritance –
were not granted to Hugh. Carlisle was recovered by Henry II from the
Scots in 1157, while this portion of Lucy's lands, including Bolingbroke
with its soke, remained with William de Roumare who had received it
from Henry I sometime after its surrender. Essentially, the honour of
Chester was restored to its position in 1135, and was preserved as such to
be passed to Earl Hugh virtually intact when he attained his majority in
1168. Losses before the end of Henry I's reign were not recovered, and
gains made since were not retained.[162]

---

[161] OV, VI, 92–5.
[162] *RRAN*, III, nos. 178–80; White, 'Stephen, Henry and Ranulf'; Dalton, '*In neutro latere*'.
Exceptions include the loss by the earls of Chester of Chipping Campden (Gloucs.) and of the

In this case, the king's custody of the honour during the heir's minority facilitated the redistribution of estates in favour of pre-war holders. Elsewhere, claimants might have to wait some years for their rivals to die, before they were restored.[163] As outlined above, the barony of Pevensey, forfeited by William count of Mortain in 1106, had passed under Henry I to Gilbert de l'Aigle and eventually to his son Richer; under Stephen it came in turn to Gilbert earl of Pembroke (died 1148) and the king's son William (died 1159), but Henry II ultimately restored it to Richer de l'Aigle about 1165.[164] William Trussebut did not regain Warter, as heir to the pre-1135 holder Geoffrey fitz Payn, until after the death of William de Roumare about 1161.[165] Yet there were occasions when Henry was not prepared to wait. The political imperative of reaching an accommodation with the Scots, and the incentive of establishing suzerainty over their king, may well have lain behind the decision to deprive Simon III de Senlis of the Midlands honour of Huntingdon, soon after Henry's accession. Simon had succeeded on the death of his father in August 1153, but he was apparently 'landless' by 1155x56 and in 1157 Henry granted his honour to Malcolm IV king of Scots, grandson of David I who had held it in 1135.[166]

Another honour which repays careful study is that of Miles of Gloucester. After the death of Miles's son Roger towards the end of 1155, Henry II recovered the borough of Gloucester, together with former royal demesne in Herefordshire given to Miles by the empress in 1141. Some royal manors in Gloucestershire passed to Roger's brother Walter, but these were also resumed in 1159–60.[167] These are straightforward examples of acquisitions made since 1135 at the king's expense, including those which had passed on to Roger as heir, being duly recovered by the crown. But Henry II resisted any temptation to diminish the rest of the honour, despite the opportunities presented by the deaths not only of

castle of Mountsorrel (Leics.): *HKF*, II, 53; Stenton, *English Feudalism*, 286–8; *Gesta Regis*, I, 73, 134. However, holdings in Marston and Warkworth (Northants.), lost under Stephen, were recovered: *RRAN*, III, no. 492; *Reg. Ant.*, I, no. 149; cf. *HKF*, II, 214–15.

[163] R. C. Palmer, 'The origins of property in England', *Law and History Review*, 3 (1985), 1–50, esp. 8–13, argues that it was the intention of the 1153 peace settlement that existing tenants should continue to have seisin of lands acquired in the war for the rest of their lives. This is effectively answered in Biancalana, 'For want of justice', 467–70; Hyams, 'Warranty', 497–503; Holt, '1153', esp. 293, 312.

[164] *Baronies*, 136; Richer's opposition to Henry in Normandy in 1152 (RT, 170) may explain the delay in restoring the honour to him after William's death.

[165] *Baronies*, 150; E. J. King, 'The parish of Warter and the castle of Galchlin', *Yorks. Archaeological Journal*, 52 (1980), 49–58.

[166] RT, 172, 189, 192; HH, 768; *HKF*, II, 296–8; Stringer, 'A Cistercian Archive', 329, n. 23 (for evidence that Simon III did briefly have seisin of the honour after his father's death); Stringer, *Earl David of Huntingdon*, 19.

[167] RT, 185; *RBE*, II, 650; *PR2H*, 49–50; *PR3H*, 93, 99–100, etc.; *PR6H*, 28; *RRAN*, III, no. 393.

Roger in 1155, but also of the three younger brothers, Walter, Henry and Mahel, who succeeded him over the following decade. The estates Miles had held in 1135 – by inheritance from his father Walter and by acquisition through his wife Sybil, daughter of Bernard de Neufmarché – seem to have been preserved intact; they can be traced in the hands of Miles's sons early in Henry II's reign and went on to form the honour which was divided between his daughters after 1165.[168] A subsequent acquisition, Abergavenny, which Miles received as a vassal of Brian fitz Count for the service of three knights about 1141, was also passed on to his successors, held of the king in chief following Brian's death without issue late in Stephen's reign.[169] By the close of the 1130s – probably before Henry I's death – Miles also held a few manors around Leominster, formerly in the possession of Hugh de Lacy. These also remained in the hands of his descendants, their retention by his family being of particular interest since most of Hugh de Lacy's honour, based on Weobley (Herefordshire), had passed by 1135 with his daughter Sybil to her husband, the *curialis* Payn fitz John. However, Payn was killed in 1137 and Miles's son Roger soon afterwards married Cecily, daughter to Payn and Sybil, thereby acquiring a claim to all or most of the Lacy honour of Weobley.[170] There followed bitter rivalry for this inheritance with Gilbert de Lacy, probably a nephew of Hugh de Lacy, which helped to fuel the civil war on the southern Welsh marches.[171] In Henry II's reign, however, the different portions of the Lacy honour were kept apart. The claims by Roger and his family to Weobley, arising from his marriage after 1135, were not acknowledged: Gilbert de Lacy enjoyed most of the honour and duly passed it to his son Robert about 1160. However, the manors around Leominster, which had come by a different route to Miles – probably before 1135 – seem to have remained with his family and were certainly never recovered by the Lacies. [172]

All the cases considered so far – Chester, Huntingdon, Pevensey, the Miles of Gloucester estates – suggest that Henry II's general intention was to restore the rightful heirs to holdings enjoyed at his grandfather's death. This was consistent with the stance taken in his coronation charter – which ignored Stephen but promised the full restoration of gifts, liberties and free customs conceded by Henry I [173] – and with the phraseology of

---

[168] D. Walker, 'Miles of Gloucester, earl of Hereford', *Trans. Bristol and Gloucs. Archaeological Society*, 57 (1958), 66–84; and '"Honours" of the earls of Hereford'.   [169] *RRAN*, III, no. 394; *Baronies*, 7.

[170] *Herefordshire Domesday*, ed. V. H. Galbraith and J. Tait (P.R. Society, 1950), 79; Wightman, *Lacy Family*, 81–2; *Gesta Steph.*, xxix, 24.

[171] Davis, 'Treaty between William earl of Gloucester and Roger earl of Hereford', esp. 144.

[172] Wightman, *Lacy Family*, 181–2, 188–9; Crouch, 'The march and the Welsh kings', 285.

[173] *Select Charters*, 157–8; Holt, '1153', 303.

his writs and charters generally. In response to lively demand in the first few years of the reign – as 'prudent landlords . . . joined the queue for confirmations . . . after the years of civil strife', any number of royal charters ordered that lands and privileges be enjoyed 'as in the time of King Henry', those with greater precision specifying 'the day when King Henry my grandfather was alive and dead'.[174] Yet in the case of Weobley, Gilbert de Lacy succeeded to an inheritance held by Payn fitz John in 1135; under a strict application of principle, it would have been confirmed by Henry II to Payn's daughter and heiress Cecily and passed with her to successive husbands. Gilbert de Lacy seems to have had a strong claim, but Henry I had preferred Payn fitz John: what probably weighed most heavily with Henry II was not the respective merits of the hereditary claims but the fact that Gilbert had obtained possession of much of the honour under Stephen, and it was pointless to deprive him in the interests of Cecily who was already a prized heiress.[175] Such pragmatism was to be evident in several local settlements in the years which followed the civil war.

As we have seen in the previous chapter, Stephen's approach to the resolution of tenurial disputes in the last months of his life seems to have been based primarily upon judicious compromise,[176] and this solution – rather than a rigid insistence upon the restoration in full of pre-war holders – obviously commended itself on many occasions to Henry II. The efforts made by Stephen to reconcile the Paynels and the Gants in Yorkshire appear to have been continued after his death, when the lands were divided between Robert de Gant and his wife's half-brothers Hugh and Fulk Paynel.[177] Henry was certainly involved – unlawfully and without judgment it was subsequently claimed – in the settlement early in his reign between Roald fitz Harscod and Richard de Rollos, whereby each was to hold half of the Constable's fee of the honour of Richmond; it is not clear whether the situation of 1135 was reconstituted as a result.[178] On the other hand, a settlement of 1154x58 between Roger de Mowbray, whose father Nigel d'Aubigny had received estates in Yorkshire forfeited by Robert de Stuteville in 1106, and Robert's grandson who had contested the holdings during the war, seems to have been reached

[174] Hyams, 'Charter as a source', 179; *RAH*, I, nos. 5, 30, 43, 54, 69, 99, 127, 133, etc.; *Royal Writs*, I, nos. 21, 22, 48, 153, 170, 172, etc. For orders that a sworn inquest be held to determine the position in Henry I's reign, see e.g. *RAH*, I, nos. 21, 22; *Royal Writs*, nos. 96, 195; *CCR*, IV, 141.
[175] After Roger's death, Cecily married William de Poitou and then Walter de Mayenne; she died without issue in 1207 (*Baronies*, 144). The rival claims of Gilbert and Cecily are discussed in Wightman, *Lacy Family*, 185; cf. *Gesta Steph.*, xxix.
[176] E.g. over Drax (Davis, *Stephen*, 122; White, 'End of Stephen's reign', 20) and over Brockenhurst (*RRAN*, III, nos, 129–31; Hudson, *Land, Law and Lordship*, 150, n. 149).   [177] *EYC*, VI, 33.
[178] *Curia R.R.*, v, 147–8; *EYC*, v, 89–92, 96, 98. Despite Holt, '1153', 310, the evidence presented in *EYC*, v, 89 and n. 4 does not prove conclusively that the estate was already shared in 1135.

without the intervention of the king, who did not confirm the arrangement; Roger bought Robert off with the grant of Kirby Moorside as a fee of ten knights, 'for his homage and the renunciation of his claim' to the honour as a whole.[179]

There are other cases in which it is clear that families failed to regain estates held at the end of Henry I's reign. The honour of Bourn, which William Peverel of Dover had enjoyed before his death on crusade in 1147x48, is known to have been divided between his four sisters, but his other demesnes, which lay in Kent, were resumed by Stephen and would continue in crown hands through successive reigns.[180] If later pleading before the king's justices is to be believed, a knight's fee acquired by Henry of Essex from the Raimes family 'by force and unjustly' during the civil war was never regained by the former holders, since Henry II subsequently granted it to one of Henry of Essex's vassals.[181] The *cartae baronum* of 1166 brought forward several complaints of losses in the war which had not yet been redressed. A Suffolk tenant-in-chief, William Blund, stated that his barony had had twelve knights' fees at Henry I's death; 'tempore Guerrae' his father Gilbert had been disseised of five of these fees, three in Wiltshire now in the king's hands, the others under the lordship of Earl Aubrey (de Vere) and Henry fitz Gerold. Reginald earl of Cornwall was alleged to have disseised Mabel de Bec 'tempore Guerrae' of 30 librates of land in Norfolk. Under Gloucestershire, Payn de Muntdublel claimed that Earl Patrick (of Wiltshire) had taken one of the fees held of him 'per gwerram', while Robert fitz Harding – to whom Henry as duke had granted the honour of Berkeley – complained that the previous holder Roger de Berkeley was not doing service for portions he had kept. Ecclesiastical lords made a series of similar allegations.[182]

So the intention of the Winchester peace settlement of 1153 – that the disinherited should be restored to the rightful holdings of Henry I's time – was only partly fulfilled, however loosely we interpret *tempore Henrici regis*. It was useful politically to present transfers of property under Stephen as lacking validity, and to emphasise a return to the *status quo* of Henry I's reign whenever writs and charters gave an opportunity to do so, but in certain cases it was even more expedient to leave well alone. If we turn to the resumption of royal demesne, we find much the same thing:

---

[179] *Charters of Mowbray*, xxviii; *EYC*, IX, 5, 75, 83 and no. 42 (from Howden, IV, 117–18); *Baronies*, 37.

[180] *Baronies*, 19, 151; Stephen's tenure is implied by the account of the honour as an escheat in *RBE*, II, 649.

[181] *Rotuli Curiae Regis*, ed. F. Palgrave (Record Commission, 1835), I, 93, with discussion in Biancalana, 'For want of justice', 469, n. 169.

[182] *RBE*, I, 408–9, 401, 298. There is further discussion of disputes cited in the *cartae baronum* below, ch. 5.

Henry's general policy was to recover what had been lost by the crown in the previous reign, but it was a matter for delicate judgement how far to apply this in particular cases. When it came to weighing political gain against financial loss, even the alienations of Stephen's reign might be better left to continue.

LAY HOLDINGS AND THE ROYAL DEMESNE

Henry II's coronation oath may well have included an undertaking to defend the lands, dignities and liberties of the crown, and to recover those dispersed, dilapidated and lost.[183] His coronation charter confirmed in general terms the grants made by Henry I, but the resumption of royal demesne lost since his death was treated as a matter of urgency. Robert de Torigni and William of Newburgh both place it among the reforms in progress during 1155; it is probably to this date that we should attribute the enquiry into the former extent of royal demesne, ordered by the king to be conducted by sworn inquest throughout the country.[184] William of Newburgh's picture of barons producing charters of Stephen, but losing their manors all the same, is supported by a recognition in the king's court in 1212. The jurors had been summoned to state whether Henry II had given Wendover to Hugh de Gournay before granting it to Faramus de Boulogne; they declared that Hugh had received the manor from Stephen and that, although he had sought a renewal of the grant, Henry had deprived him.[185] But it was not only Stephen's grants which were disregarded. There are no allowances for *terrae datae* in Henry II's early pipe rolls to show that William de Beauchamp was holding the 60 librates of land, or William Mauduit the 100 librates, which the empress and Henry had given them; this particular gift was omitted from Henry's subsequent charter for William Mauduit's son.[186] Despite the grant of Melksham by the empress in 1144, Humphrey II de Bohun lost the manor in 1158.[187]

Most of the evidence for the resumption of royal demesne is to be

---

[183] H. G. Richardson, 'The coronation in medieval England', *Traditio*, 16 (1960), 111–202 (esp. 159–61, 166–9); H. G. Richardson and G. O. Sayles, *Law and Legislation from Aethelberht to Magna Carta* (Edinburgh, 1966), 56–9; cf. Warren, *Henry II*, 217–20.

[184] RT, 183; Newburgh, I, 103; *Gesta Abbatum Sancti Albani*, I, 123. The accounts for assarts which appeared in the 1155 pipe roll may also have resulted from this enquiry (*RBE*, I, 648–58; cf. E. M. Amt, 'The forest regard of 1155', *Haskins Society Journal*, 2 (1990), 189–95, and *Accession*, 168–73).

[185] *Curia R.R.*, VI, 272–3. The statement was not free from error. The jurors said that Hugh had been allowed to retain the manor until after the Toulouse campaign (1159); however, *PR2H*, 24 and *PR4H*, 139, show that he had been deprived before Michaelmas 1156, and that Faramus had obtained possession by Michaelmas 1158.

[186] *RRAN*, III, nos. 68, 582; Richardson and Sayles, *Governance*, 435–6; cf.Mason, 'The Mauduits and their chamberlainship'.   [187] *RRAN*, III, no. 111; *PR4H*, 116, 119.

found in the pipe rolls, including the transcript of the 1155 roll in the *Red Book of the Exchequer*. We learn of the recovery of certain manors lost by the crown under Stephen when, having been omitted from the pipe rolls hitherto, they came to be accounted for separately outside the sheriffs' farms: Wargrave (Berkshire) possibly following Henry bishop of Winchester's flight from England in 1155, Warter (Yorkshire) regained as a purpresture from William of Aumale in 1165, Little Framlingham, Dunningworth and other Suffolk manors which reverted to the crown on the death of Hugh Bigod in 1177.[188] Much more can be gleaned, however, from the lists of *terrae datae,* recording allowances credited to sheriffs for manors no longer contributing to the farms.[189] Unfortunately, the transcript of the 1155 pipe roll gives a very inadequate picture of these allowances: the accounts recorded for six shires covered half the year or less, and farms do not appear to have been rendered for five others until the following year.[190] Former royal manors would almost certainly have been resumed within these shires before the period of account, but of this there is no record. Nevertheless, study of the transcript shows that there were several *terrae datae* noted in the 1155 roll which did not appear again; on the face of it, they seem to represent manors recovered for the crown during the course of the year.

In Staffordshire, the sheriff was allowed £61 14s. 0d. 'in terris quas barones tenuerunt': they were specified as Robert Marmion, Gervase Paynel, Robert de Mohaut and the monks of Radmore. Geoffrey Marmion, a cousin of Robert, appeared against another allowance. In Northamptonshire, the *terrae datae* included lands held by Earl Simon, Richard du Hommet, William of Aumale, William and John Mauduit and William de Tinchebrai. Under Surrey, we find the earl of Warenne (Stephen's son William), Walter Croc, William de Braose and Gilbert de Tany, under Dorset Earl Patrick, and under Essex Osmund Peisson, Reginald fitz Urse and Hubert de St Clare.[191] The allowances for Earl Simon and Richard du Hommet were stated to be for a quarter of the

---

[188] On Wargrave: *RRAN*, III, nos. 948–9; *Facsimiles of Charters in the British Museum*, no. 38; *PR2H*, 19; *PR3H*, 71–2; *PR4H*, 152, etc. On Warter: King, 'The parish of Warter', 49–58; Dalton, *Conquest, Anarchy and Lordship*, 158–9; *PR11H*, 51–2. On the Suffolk manors: *PR23H*, 136–7; *PR24H*, 26–7, *PR25H*, 9, etc.

[189] Although most *terrae datae* were allowed for within the sheriffs' farms of their counties, such allowances sometimes appeared in the accounts for manors or honours farmed separately: e.g. in *PR4H*, 154 (land of William Peverel), 156 (Trentham), 176 (Meon), 180 (land of the bishop of Bayeux).

[190] For information on the farms of individual shires in 1154–5, see appendix I. The sheriff of London answered for half the year, but there are insufficient details in *RBE*, II, 658 for inclusion in that table.

[191] *RBE*, II, 651–2, 654–5, 657. On those who held Staffordshire *terrae datae*, cf. Eyton, 'Staffordshire pipe rolls', 18–19.

year, those for the earl of Warenne and Reginald fitz Urse for half the year; the remainder were apparently for a full twelve months.

One must beware of intepreting all these items in the same way. In Northamptonshire, the allowance for a quarter of the year for Earl Simon strongly suggests that the land had been resumed by the crown soon after Henry's coronation, which fell about three months into the financial year. But the next allowance recorded, also for a quarter of the year but to Henry II's trusted counsellor Richard du Hommet, may represent land temporarily granted to his custody; this could be true of a few other items, against the names of men whose careers are less well known. None the less, most of these allowances imply the retention of royal demesne which had been acquired during the war; since they did not recur in the following year, we must presume that the lands were recovered for the crown before Michaelmas 1155 or shortly afterwards. It is instructive that supporters of both sides appear among the names. Robert Marmion's father had been loyal to Stephen and had died fighting against the earl of Chester in 1144.[192] William of Aumale, though he had witnessed the charter announcing the peace settlement, had to be brought to submission by force in the early months of 1155. On the other hand, Patrick earl of Wiltshire was a longstanding supporter of the Angevins, and Gervase Paynel had campaigned with Henry in 1153.[193] William de Braose had attested Stephen's charters for Lewes Priory in or after 1148, but was a brother-in-law of Roger earl of Hereford, from whom he eventually inherited Brecon and Abergavenny.[194]

These were immediate measures, accomplished before the end of Henry's first visit as king, in January 1156. Most of the lands were resumed while their holders were alive; apart from Earl Simon, only Hubert de St Clare is known to have died about this time.[195] The lists of *terrae datae* in the next two pipe rolls suggest that there were no further resumptions from the lay barons until after Henry's return to the country in April 1157. It was then that manors in Kent were recovered from William of Ypres; they had continued to be entered as *terrae datae*, even though William had almost certainly left the kingdom early in 1155.[196]

---

[192] HH, 744; WN, 70–3; R. H. C. Davis, 'An unknown Coventry charter', *EHR*, 86 (1971), 533–45; Davis, *Stephen*, 161–5; *RRAN*, III, no. 577.

[193] Davis, *Stephen*, 136–7; *RRAN*, III, nos. 492, 962. [194] *Ibid.*, III, nos. 448–50; *Baronies*, 7.

[195] According to a continuation of Ralf Niger's *Chronicon II*, Hubert de St Clare was slain at the siege of Bridgnorth by an arrow which would otherwise have hit the king (*Chronicles of Ralf Niger*, ed. R. Anstruther, Caxton Society, 1851, 170). It is not certain that the 'Earl Simon' of the 1155 transcript is a reference to Simon II de Senlis (died August 1153), since it may possibly refer to his son Simon III: cf. *CP*, VI, 645 and note (i), and above, n. 166.

[196] The pipe rolls of 1155, 1156 and 1157 show that William of Ypres had held *terrae datae* in Canterbury, Milton, Dartford, Eynesford, Boxley and Hoo; in the 1157 pipe roll the allowances were for half the year only, and they did not recur (*RBE*, II, 648–9; *PR2H*, 65; *PR3H*, 101–2).

Probably in May 1157, Stephen's son William was deprived of his castles in England and Normandy, of his holding in the honour of Pevensey, of lands in Norfolk given by his father, and of former royal demesne in Surrey worth £95 *numero* to the sheriff's farm; he was left with all that Stephen had held at Henry I's death, together with the honour of Warenne in right of his wife.[197] Around this time also, Hugh Bigod surrendered his castles [198] and John fitz Gilbert the marshal lost Marlborough, presumably with the castle which he had held for the Angevins in the war.[199] During the course of 1158, probably shortly before Henry II's next departure overseas in August, two other former Angevin supporters, Hubert de Vaux and Humphrey II de Bohun, were deprived of manors they had retained in Wiltshire; Hubert de Vaux had probably already been compensated with a grant of two knights' fees which had fallen to the king in Cumbria.[200]

These early resumptions of royal demesne, involving some of the most prominent survivors from the civil war and presumably authorised by the king during his two sojourns in England, in 1155 and 1157–8, were clearly seen as political priorities. Once Henry had left England in August 1158, the recovery of former royal manors proceeded more slowly, the policy becoming one of patiently awaiting opportunities. But enough has been said to demonstrate that Henry saw no difference in principle between acquisitions made by supporters and opponents in the civil war: between Stephen's grants to lay barons out of the royal demesne, and gains authorised (or acquiesced in) by the empress or himself before his coronation. All represented alienations of royal estates since the reign of Henry I and, accordingly, were liable to be revoked. Yet he was understandably reluctant to antagonise some prominent Angevin supporters. Reginald earl of Cornwall was allowed to retain former royal manors in Somerset, Dorset and Devon, in addition to those he held in Cornwall, until his

---

The evidence for the timing of William's departure is discussed in JS, *Letters*, I, 258–60. His later career is covered in detail in Amt, *Accession*, 89–91.

[197] RT, 192–3; PR3H, 94; Warren, *Henry II*, 67, n. 5.

[198] RT, 193. Hugh had recovered his castles at Framlingham and Bungay by 1173, possibly as a result of his fine with the king at Nottingham, first recorded in the 1165 pipe roll (PR11H, 7; R.A.Brown, 'Framlingham castle and Bigod', *Proceedings of the Suffolk Institute of Archaeology and Natural History*, 25 (1952), 127–48.

[199] John Marshal was recorded against *terra data* in Marlborough in 1156 and 1157; we lack details of the allowances in 1155 (PR2H, 57; PR3H, 77). Alan de Neville was named as holder of Marlborough in subsequent years (PR4H, 116, etc.). For John's activities as castellan of Marlborough, see *Gesta Steph.*, 106, 168, 218; *Hist. Nov.*, 44; JW, 62–3.

[200] PR2H, 57; PR3H, 77–8; PR4H, 116, 119, where the sheriff's account for the three Wiltshire manors for one quarter of the year suggests a summer confiscation; *The Barony of Gilsland*, ed. T. H. R. Graham (Cumberland and Westmorland Antiquarian and Archaeological Society, 1934), I; P.R.O. C52/28 (formerly Cartae Antiquae Roll DD), memb. I, no. 7, assigned to January 1159 in *Itinerary*, 33.

death in 1175 when most of his honour escheated to the crown.[201] Although he had been deprived of Marlborough in 1157, John Marshal continued to hold two other former royal manors in Wiltshire until he died in the mid-1160s; Henry II then 'restored and confirmed' one of John's sons in the office of marshal, and in the holdings on both sides of the Channel 'which he ought to hold' but the allowances for *terrae datae* came to an end.[202] Other former royal manors in Wiltshire, acquired in the war by Earl Patrick and Robert de Dunstanville, were retained until their deaths, and – in these cases – passed on to heirs.[203] Bedminster (Somerset) and Alveston (Gloucestershire), which Henry had conceded to Robert fitz Harding and Fulk fitz Warin from the royal demesne before his accession as king, were also eventually inherited.[204] Several of these longstanding *terrae datae* carried additional rights of hundredal jurisdiction, and their continued alienation perpetuated the devolution of royal authority to which attention has been drawn in the previous chapter.[205] Earl Reginald's effective control of the whole of Cornwall, for which he did not account at the exchequer before his death, and his retention of hundredal manors in the other west-country shires, made him an alternative power in the region throughout the first half of Henry II's reign. Wiltshire was another shire in which several manors had been alienated along with the profits from hundredal jurisdiction; they remained for many years in the hands not only of leading figures such as Earl Patrick but also of lesser men such as Ralf de St Jerman and Jordan of Samford.[206] Not all the beneficiaries were former Angevin loyalists. Stephen's *curialis* Richard de Camville, who clearly made his peace with Henry before his accession, was allowed to keep the manor of Sutton (Northamptonshire) with its hundredal profits, and it was eventually inherited by his

---

[201] Payments on lands formerly held by him are first recorded in *PR22H*, 141, 151, 153. See also *terrae datae* against his name in Devon, Dorset and Somerset, *RBE*, II, 657; *PR2H*, 30, 32, 46; *PR3H*, 74, 98–9, and so on until his death.

[202] One of the manors, Wexcombe, was entered in the 1165 pipe roll as land 'quem Johannes marescallus habuit'; the other was recorded in the same roll as having passed to Robert fitz Peter (*PR11H*, 56).

[203] *PR13H*, 126, 169; *PR14H*, 157, 125. The holders of Wiltshire *terrae datae* are not named individually in the transcript of the 1155 pipe roll, but the total allowed for there, £457 'blanch', is similar to the total of £439 10s. od. 'blanch' in 1156, and suggests that the alienations dated back to Stephen's reign (*RBE*, II, 649; *PR2H*, 57).

[204] *PR16H*, 111, 74; *PR17H*, 11, 84; *RRAN*, III, nos. 1000, 320; *Fouke le Fitz Warin*, 22; Amt, *Accession*, 40 and n. 64.

[205] On the significance of allowances 'blanch' as indicative of rights of hundredal jurisdiction, see *Dialogus*, 85–6; Yoshitake, 'Exchequer in the reign of Stephen', esp. 953; H. M. Cam, *Liberties and Communities in Medieval England* (London, 1963), 69–70. Cf. King, 'Anarchy of King Stephen's reign'; P. Dalton, 'William earl of York and royal authority in Yorkshire in the reign of Stephen', *Haskins Society Journal*, 2 (1990), 155–65 (at 160–2).

[206] Ralf held in Kington and Jordan in Chelworth (*PR2H*, 57; *PR3H*, 78, etc.).

son.[207] Even powerful opponents might be appeased: in Yorkshire, William of Aumale, whose accumulation of jurisdictional powers led him to be regarded as 'more truly the king beyond the Humber than King Stephen' was left in control of the hundredal manor of Driffield, which only disappeared from the *terrae datae* on his death in 1179.[208]

For Henry II, it was a matter of assessing each case individually and of grasping opportunities when they arose. Manors valued at over £400 per annum, in Lincolnshire, Nottinghamshire, Oxfordshire and Suffolk, were recovered from Thierry count of Flanders during 1160, an arrangement probably connected with the marriage of his younger son Matthew to Stephen's daughter Mary about May of that year.[209] Often, as we have seen, the king intervened when a landholder died, as Stephen himself appears to have done following the death of Simon II de Senlis in August 1153.[210] We lack evidence of Stephen's response to the even more significant death of Ranulf II earl of Chester in December of that year, but there can be no doubt that the succession of a minor, Hugh de Kyvelioc, facilitated the recovery of Ranulf's wartime acquisitions from the royal demesne, which were all in crown hands under Henry II. To what extent Ranulf had been able to make good some of the grants he had received, both from Stephen and from Henry as duke, must be a matter for conjecture, but it is clear that the boroughs of Stafford, Nottingham and Derby, the king's demesne in Staffordshire and Grimsby, the wapentake of Oswaldebeck and the manors of Torksey, Mansfield, Rothley and Stoneleigh, were all restored to the crown early in Henry II's reign, if not before.[211] The only resumption for which there is any evidence of delay is that of Rothley; at Michaelmas 1156 the sheriff

---

[207] *RBE*, II, 655; *PR2H*, 40; *PR21H*, 39; *PR22H*, 46, etc.

[208] Newburgh, I, 103; Dalton, 'William earl of York', 164; the last allowance as *terra data* was in *PR25H*, 16. Other longstanding *terrae datae* apparently deriving from alienations of royal demesne during Stephen's reign were Penkridge (Staffordshire) to Walter Hose, eventually resumed (presumably on death) in 1172 (*RBE*, II, 652; *PR2H*, 29; *PR18H*, 103), and Caerleon (Gloucestershire), initially held by the Welsh prince Maelgwn ap Owain, then by his son from 1158 onwards (*PR2H*, 49; *PR3H*, 100; *PR4H*, 167, etc.).

[209] *RT*, 207. The *terrae datae* were entered as £200 'blanch' in Kirton, £60 *numero* in Dunham, £76 'blanch' in Bampton plus a further 100s., and £65 *numero* in Exning. Kirton had been granted by Stephen to William de Roumare (*RRAN*, III, no. 494) but was recorded against the count of Flanders in the 1155 pipe roll (*RBE*, II, 656); Dunham and Bampton are shown in Count Thierry's possession in 1156, and Exning in 1158, the first year that full details of *terrae datae* in Suffolk appear (*PR2H*, 24, 36, 38; *PR3H*, 82–3, 89; *PR4H*, 125, 136, 149, 152, etc.). The allowances ceased at Michaelmas 1160, but were renewed in 1167–8 in favour of Thierry's son Matthew count of Boulogne, after he had threatened an invasion of the kingdom. The manors were recovered during 1173, when Matthew lost his life while supporting Henry the Younger's rebellion (*PR6H*, 1, 8, 43, 45; *PR14H*, 14, 60, 95, 205; *PR19H*, 116, 133, 167, 172; Gervase, I, 246; Round, *Peerage and Family History*, 174–6).

[210] Above, ch. 2, and White, 'End of Stephen's reign', 18.

[211] White, 'Stephen, Henry and Ranulf', esp. 556–7, 559.

of Leicestershire had an allowance of £21 'blanch' for the sokemen of Rothley, but we are told that 'henceforth they will render their farm'.[212] Had Earl Ranulf survived into Henry II's reign, it is difficult to believe that many of these properties would have been recovered during his lifetime.

The resumption of royal manors is of course only part of the story, for in his early years Henry II himself made considerable use of his demesne for the purpose of patronage; indeed, it is sometimes impossible to tell in whose reign an alienation first occurred. In the 1156 pipe roll, for example, *terrae datae* against the names of Robert fitz Hugh in Clayworth (Nottinghamshire) and of Ralf of Hastings in Witham (Somerset), both eventually inherited, might have originated under Stephen but could also have arisen from new grants made by the incoming king.[213] Alienations certainly attributable to Henry II include those to his brother William in eastern England from 1155 onwards, all resumed on the beneficiary's death,[214] and various grants to royal servants ranging from the steward Manasser Bisset [215] and chamberlain Warin fitz Gerold [216] to the king's goldsmith and falconers, a cook and a smith.[217] Other lands were possibly given as compensation to those who had lost territory in settlements with their rivals: further evidence that, like Stephen, Henry was sometimes prepared to compromise to bring disputes to a close. Lambourn (Berkshire), which Josce de Dinan was holding by 1156, may have been granted in place of lands around Ludlow which he had held against Stephen but had now had to yield to Gilbert de Lacy.[218] Blythburgh (Suffolk) had been given by Stephen to John de Chesney who had died about 1146, but first occurs as *terra data* against his brother William de Chesney for three-quarters of the year 1157–8;[219] the manor may have been granted to William in recompense for Acle (Norfolk) which he had received from Stephen but which Henry had given to Hugh Bigod in

<hr>

[212] *PR2H*, 45.

[213] *Ibid.*, 30, 38. The 1155 transcript does not include details of *terrae datae* for these shires (*RBE*, II, 653–4).

[214] *Ibid.*, II, 650, 654; *PR2H*, 17; *PR3H*, 72, 76, 101–2; *PR4H*, 125, 132, 180, etc. to *PR10H*, 33, 35, 36–8, 40.   [215] In Rockbourne (Hampshire): *PR2H*, 54; *PR3H*, 105, etc.

[216] In Sparsholt (Berkshire): *PR2H*, 34; *PR3H*, 80. It passed to his brother Henry fitz Gerold thereafter (*PR4H*, 123, etc.). The king's constable, Richard du Hommet, had *terrae datae* in Doddington (Northamptonshire) and Stamford (Lincolnshire) recorded against his name in *PR2H*, 24, 41; *PR3H*, 83, 103, etc. The 1155 pipe roll suggests that, while the grant in Northamptonshire probably postdated Henry II's accession, the alienation in Stamford (for which there was a full year's allowance) may well have preceded it (*RBE*, II, 655–6).

[217] Simon the cook in Warwickshire: *PR2H*, 44; *PR3H*, 86, etc. Solomon the goldsmith in Cambridgeshire: *PR4H*, 165; *PR5H*, 53, etc. Turgis and Henry, falconers, in Lincolnshire: *PR5H*, 64; *PR6H*, 45, etc. Cobb the smith in Hampshire: *PR5H*, 45; *PR6H*, 47, etc.

[218] *PR2H*, 34; *Fouke le Fitz Warin*, 21; Eyton, *Antiquities of Shropshire*, v, 248; Wightman, *Lacy Family*, 188.   [219] *RRAN*, III, no. 174; *Life and Miracles of St William of Norwich*, 111–12; *PR4H*, 125.

1155.[220] William de Chesney's tenure of Blythburgh duly passed to his heir,[221] but the allowance for Lambourn ceased with Josce de Dinan's death; however, his son-in-law Hugh de Plugenoi had an interest here some years later.[222]

By using the royal demesne not only to reward servants but also to solve awkward tenurial conflicts, Henry was inevitably depleting his resources, but it has been demonstrated that such initial generosity did not persist, and that the king looked elsewhere for sources of patronage once the earliest phase of the reign had passed. Indeed, by balancing resumptions of alienated demesne with new grants, Henry managed to ensure that the total amount of *terrae datae* was very similar in value at the end of his reign to what it had been at the beginning: around £3,000 in both 1156 and 1188.[223] The lists of *terrae datae* in the pipe roll accounts of sheriffs' farms hardly lengthened at all after 1160; where manors within the farms were still used for patronage, normal practice was to regrant those which had been recovered from a previous holder.[224] Moreover, most of Henry II's new grants from the royal demesne were made without accompanying hundredal jurisdiction, exceptions tending to be marks of special favour such as those to the queen in Devon, his brother William in Kent, Norfolk and Suffolk, and the Templars in Kent and Lincolnshire.[225] To this extent, Henry II was treated somewhat unfairly by Giraldus Cambrensis when he was criticised alongside Stephen as a

---

[220] *RRAN*, III, no. 176; *Cartae Antiquae Rolls 11–20*, no. 553.

[221] *PR20H*, 36; *PR21H*, 107 (Hugh de Cressy, son-in-law to William de Chesney); *Baronies*, 16.

[222] Although an allowance for Lambourn continued to be made out of the sheriff's farm, Josce de Dinan was not named as the holder after 1160 (*PR6H*, 21; cf. *PR7H*, 52). From 1160–1, the sheriff rendered a separate account for part of the manor; this is specified as 'that part which Josce de Dinan held' in the rolls of 1163 and subsequent years (*PR7H*, 52–3; *PR8H*, 43; *PR9H*, 51; *PR10H*, 42–3, etc.). Hugh de Plugenoi married one of Josce's daughters, Sybil, and confirmed his grant in Lambourn to the monks of Gloucester (*Historia et Cartularium Sancti Petri Gloucestriae*, I, 95, 367–8).

[223] Lally, 'Secular patronage', 159–84, and on the subject generally, T. Keefe, *Feudal Assessments and the Political Community under Henry II and his Sons* (Berkeley, 1983), 90–145; cf. Amt, *Accession*, 149–68, 194–7, where detailed calculations do show some increase in the early years of the reign (to almost £4,000 by 1159).

[224] E.g. Marlborough (Wiltshire) from John Marshal to Alan de Neville in 1157–8; Fordham (Cambridgeshire) from Ralf of Hastings to Lecelina de Trailly in 1162–63; Cawston (Norfolk) from the king's brother William to William fitz Ernulf in 1164–5; Boarstall (Buckinghamshire) from Adam the clerk to William de Rochell in 1166–7 (*PR3H*, 77; *PR4H*, 116; *PR8H*, 45; *PR9H*, 62; *PR10H*, 33; *PR11H*, 3–4; *PR12H*, 11; *PR13H*, 102). Cf. Lally, 'Secular patronage', 184.

[225] E.g. in 1162 pipe roll, £80 'blanch' unspecified to the queen; £52 'blanch' in Aylsham, £46 'blanch' in Hintlesham 'with the hundred and half' of Samford, £24 'blanch' in Cawston, £94 12s. 'blanch' in Dartford, all to William the king's brother; £6 'blanch' in Deal, £13 'blanch' in Stroud, £11 'blanch' in Eccles, all to the Templars (*PR8H*, 4, 62, 53, 17). Several of these can be found in earlier pipe rolls as well. It should be stressed, however, that a few lesser figures did receive 'blanch' allowances for *terrae datae*, e.g. Ralf Picot in Kent and Hugh Tirel in Hampshire (*PR3H*, 101, 105; *PR4H*, 171, 180, etc.).

king too lavish in his alienation of royal demesne.[226]

It is clear from the preceding review of *terrae datae* that Henry II adopted a flexible approach to the question of whether, and when, to recover them for the crown. The basic position was that manors lost to the crown under Stephen – by whosesoever authority – were vulnerable to resumption at any time, but the practical expression of this policy varied from one case to another. We may suspect that many lords, recognising the implications of the 1153 peace settlement, tried to obtain confirmations from Henry II of former royal demesne acquired since Henry I's death, and that those who duly retained *terrae datae* for several years were the successful ones; any fines they paid were probably received direct by the chamber.[227] But even grants made by Henry as king were liable to be revoked, if they concerned property alienated in the previous reign. Before his retirement to Gloucester Abbey where he died towards the end of 1155, Roger earl of Hereford won generous concessions which largely renewed grants made by the empress to his father Earl Miles. Henry II's charter announced that he had 'restored' all the fiefs of Roger's father, and of his maternal grandfather Bernard de Neufmarché; he had 'given' five named manors in Gloucestershire and another three in Herefordshire, with the forest of Treville and the hays of Hereford; he had 'given' the castle of Hereford, the third penny of rents of the borough, and the third penny of pleas of Herefordshire, with the earldom; he had 'given' the service of Robert de Candos and Hugh fitz William; and he had 'conceded' all the offices and holdings which Roger's father had had under Henry I, with custody of the castle of Gloucester and the shrievalty of Gloucestershire by the same farm that Miles had rendered in Henry I's time. All this was granted to Roger and his heirs, to hold of Henry and his heirs.[228] Yet much of it did not survive Roger's death a few months later. There is no evidence that his younger brothers Walter, Henry and Mahel, who succeeded to the honour in turn, held the castles of Hereford and Gloucester;[229] none of them received the third penny of pleas, as earls of Herefordshire, nor did they inherit former royal manors in that shire. The early pipe rolls record

---

[226] Giraldus, VIII, 316.

[227] Cf. Holt, '1153', 304–5. A fine proffered by Hugh Bigod in 1176 to retain manors from the royal demesne (*PR22H*, 70) has no parallel in the early pipe rolls of the reign.

[228] *Rotuli Chartarum*, 53. Cf. *RRAN*, III, no. 393, the empress's charter in favour of Roger's father Earl Miles; however, St Briavel's castle and the forest of Dean, which she had also given to Miles (*ibid.*, III, no. 391), were specifically excluded from the grants announced in Henry's charter. For the date of Roger's death, see 'Charters of Hereford', 9.

[229] *Ibid.*, 13–75, leaves no doubt that Earls Miles and Roger claimed authority over the city of Gloucester (no. 58), where they had their own reeve and where Miles took steps to improve the castle (nos. 5, 39); Roger also had the burgage rents in Hereford (no. 43). There are no similar references in the charters of Roger's successors.

payments due for the hays and for the forest of Treville;[230] although in the 1155 roll there was an allowance for *terra data* to Earl Roger which would correspond to the three Herefordshire manors, this item did not recur in subsequent rolls.[231] Walter of Hereford was sheriff of Gloucestershire until the end of 1159, and was entered in successive pipe rolls against *terrae datae* in three of the five Gloucestershire manors given to Roger; then – presumably on his own death – they in turn were resumed by the crown.[232] It should be added that friction between Roger earl of Hereford and the young Henry II early in 1155 clouds the picture; it is not certain whether Henry's generous charter was issued before the dispute – in which case some of the concessions may have been withdrawn when king and earl were reconciled in spring 1155 – or whether the grants were part of a *conventio* bringing conflict to an end: were, in effect, the price Henry had to pay to appease Roger and break up a dangerous alliance of marcher barons.[233] But in any event, it is clear that the king was prepared to rescind the terms of his own charter, at the earliest opportunity.

Hugh Bigod was another to receive a royal charter during 1155. This announced that Henry had 'made' Hugh earl of Norfolk, had 'conceded' a stewardship to him, and had 'recognised his right' to four manors in the Norfolk royal demesne which we may presume he had gained control of during the war; all would be held by Hugh and by his heirs.[234] But Hugh would take a leading part in the rebellion of 1173–4, and in the 1176 pipe roll he is found accounting for a fine of £466 13s. 4d. to cover old debts and 'that he might hold the lands he has from the king's demesne for life'.[235] On his death in 1177, the four manors were recovered for the crown; only in 1181–2, after he had been pardoned a further fine of 500 silver marks, did his son Roger come to possess them.[236] Certain other manors, in both Norfolk and Suffolk, were not restored to Roger; Hugh had retained them from the royal demesne to the time of his death, but may well not have had a relevant charter from the king.[237]

Here again, rebellion is a complicating factor, and could be held to

---

[230] *PR2H*, 52; *PR3H*, 93; *PR4H*, 144; *PR5H*, 50, etc. These record an accumulating debt on the 'hays' and from 1158–9 on the forest of Treville; payment is first recorded in *PR7H*, 20.

[231] *RBE*, II, 650; in 1156 the sheriff's account of 'old farm' included a debt of £52 10s. 0d. for demesnes given to Roger earl of Hereford, a sum pardoned in the following year (*PR2H*, 50; *PR3H*, 93).

[232] *PR2H*, 49; *PR3H*, 100; *PR4H*, 167–8; *PR5H*, 27; *PR6H*, 28, where the allowance was for only a quarter of the year.

[233] RT, 184; Gervase, I, 161–2; *CP*, VI, 454; Crouch, 'The march and the Welsh kings', 284–6.

[234] *Cartae Antiquae Rolls 11–20*, no. 553. Evidence that Hugh Bigod had had a previous grant of the manors, from Henry as duke, is considered in Richardson, 'Coronation in medieval England', 157–8.   [235] *Gesta Regis*, I, 45, 48, 60–1, 68, 73; *PR22H*, 70.

[236] *PR23H*, 124–5; *PR24H*, 21; *PR28H*, 64–5.   [237] Above, n. 188.

justify the forfeiture of lands despite their previous grant on hereditary terms. But nothing similar is known of Richard Talbot, who received a royal charter concerning Lenton (Herefordshire) in 1156x58; again, Henry II had 'given' the land to the grantee and his heirs, although Richard was certainly holding it during 1155 and doubtless during the latter part of Stephen's reign as well.[238] Richard died in 1175, when the manor was resumed by the crown; two years later, it was in the hands of Turstin fitz Simon.[239] Not until after the king's death did Richard's son Gilbert come into possession, following the proffer of a 200 marks fine for having the manor, first recorded in 1190.[240]

In Normandy, we find that Henry tackled the resumption of ducal demesne from the lay barons in a similar way. The attempt was made to revive the position of his grandfather's time, but with due regard to individual circumstances. Accordingly, as in the kingdom so in the duchy, Hugh de Kyvelioc earl of Chester was apparently restored to the holdings his father had enjoyed in 1135, but did not receive the various properties in Vire, Barfleur, Breuil, *Alebec*, or the Avranchin promised by Henry in 1153.[241] In other cases, the process was a slow one, for as in England Henry was prepared to wait for opportunities to arise. He took advantage of the death of Juhel de Mayenne at the end of 1161 to demand that his son surrender three border castles ceded by Geoffrey Plantagenet at the outset of the civil war. But several other barons must have retained their acquisitions from the war throughout the 1160s: Henry was said to have almost doubled his revenues in Normandy as a result of the inquests of 1171 into the lands his grandfather had been seised of at his death and which his barons had occupied since.[242]

ECCLESIASTICAL HOLDINGS AND THE ROYAL DEMESNE

Analysis of the treatment of the Church shows similar policies at work. Henry II confirmed his grandfather's charters [243] and also grants made by lords from their own lands since 1135; any previous confirmations by Stephen were consistently ignored.[244] He also gave his own alms: the

---

[238] *RAH*, I, no. 78. *Terrae datae* for the full period of the Herefordshire account are recorded against Richard Talbot and Hugh de Longchamp in the transcript of the 1155 pipe roll; these correspond to the *terrae datae* in Linton and Wilton entered against their names in subsequent pipe rolls (*RBE*, II, 650; *PR2H*, 51; *PR3H*, 93, etc.).   [239] *PR21H*, 85; *PR22H*, 41.

[240] *Cartae Antiquae Rolls 11–20*, no. 583; *PR 2 Ric. I*, 48; *PR 5 Ric. I*, 86–7; *PR 6 Ric. I*, 136, etc. (there are no accounts for the farm of Herefordshire in *PR 3&4 Ric. I*).

[241] White, 'Stephen, Henry and Ranulf', 561.   [242] *RT*, 128, 211–12, 251.

[243] E.g. *RAH*, I, nos. 18, 28, 33, 74; *Reg. Ant.*, I, nos. 158–60, 163, 165, 169–71.

[244] E.g. *EYC*, III, no. 1387 (for Meaux Abbey, ignoring *RRAN*, III, no. 583); *Cartularium Monasterii Sancti Johannis Baptiste de Colecestria*, ed. S. A. Moore (Roxburghe Club, London, 1897), I, 14–17 (for Colchester Abbey, ignoring *RRAN*, III, nos. 213, 215); *Cartulary of Missenden Abbey*, ed. J. G.

Templars, the hospital at Shrewsbury, the canons of Merton and the nuns of Fontevrault were all beneficiaries in the first decade of the reign.[245] But many of the gifts out of the royal demesne or revenues which had originated under his predecessor were withdrawn – many, but not all, because no principle was so absolute that it could not be overridden in practice.

We might expect that Stephen's own grants to religious houses would quickly be resumed, and this was usually the case. His donation to the abbey of St Denys, Southampton, of 20 solidates from his demesne, quit of all payments, was omitted from Henry II's subsequent charter for the canons, although Henry I's gifts were confirmed.[246] King's Ripton (Huntingdonshire), held by the monks of Ramsey at fee farm by grant of Henry I, was given in alms by Stephen but reverted to fee farm after his death; Henry II repeated the terms of his grandfather's charter.[247] Gifts in favour of the bishop and church of Lincoln were not renewed; the canons did not retain the tithe of the farm of the city, and Bishop Robert had to pay a £10 farm for the wapentake of Well (*alias* Stow) as his predecessors had done under Henry I.[248] If we search Henry II's pipe rolls, we find no allowances for the royal demesne in Stamford given in alms to the priories of Belvoir and St Mary's, Stamford, nor for the annual payments out of specified farms, conceded to Beverley Minster, Clerkenwell Priory, and St Peter's Hospital, York.[249] At the outset of his reign, Henry apparently renewed Stephen's grants of Wargrave (Berkshire) and East Meon (Hampshire) to the bishop and church of Winchester, but the manors were being treated as royal demesne by 1156.[250] On the other hand, by no means all such gifts were rescinded. Leaving aside those known to have been confirmed by the empress or by Henry as duke, we note gifts to Waverley and St Edmunds Abbeys. Neatham, given to

---

Jenkins (Bucks. Archaeological Society Records Branch, 1939–62) I, no. 6 (for Missenden Abbey, ignoring *RRAN*, III, no. 585).

[245] Templars (Kingswood, Strood, Dartford, plus a silver mark from each shire): *Records of the Templars in England in the Twelfth Century*, ed. B. A. Lees (British Academy, London, 1935), 140–2, 174; *PR2H*, 2, 6, 8, etc.; *PR3H*, 72–4, etc.; *PR5H*, 58 for first allowance for Strood; Shrewsbury hospital (30s. from the farm of Shropshire): *CCR*, III, 292; *PR2H*, 43; *PR3H*, 88, etc.; Merton (Ewell): *Cartae Antiquae Rolls 11–20*, no. 620; *PR4H*, 161–2; *PR5H*, 55, etc. Fontevrault (Leighton and Radnage): *RAH*, I, nos. 238–9; *PR10H*, 30; *PR11H*, 22, etc.

[246] *RRAN*, III, no. 827; *CCR*, III, 337.

[247] *Cartularium Monasterii de Rameseia*, ed. W. H. Hart and P. A. Lyons (RS, 1884–94), II, 82 (cf. the note to Henry's charter, *ibid.*, I, 84); *RRAN*, III, no. 667. Cf. *VCH Huntingdonshire*, II, 207.

[248] *RRAN*, III, nos. 469, 477–8; *Reg. Ant.*, I, no. 5; *PR 31 Hen. I*, 109; *PR2H*, 25; *PR3H*, 85, etc.

[249] *RRAN*, III, nos. 87, 835, 102, 202, 993.

[250] *Ibid.*, III, nos. 947–9; *Facsimiles of Charters in British Museum*, no. 38 (Henry II's charter, assigned to December 1154 shortly after his coronation, but without seal or seal tag). There is no mention of these manors in the transcript of the 1155 pipe roll, but for both of them a full year's farm was accounted for at Michaelmas 1156 (*PR2H*, 19, 62).

Waverley by Stephen early in his reign, continued to be allowed as *terra data* although briefly resumed by the crown in 1239;[251] the grant to St Edmunds of royal demesne in Beccles was renewed by Henry II 'for as long as it pleases me', but this, too, was still appearing in the pipe rolls in Henry III's time.[252]

The earls of Chester and Derby were among the barons whose grants to religious houses at the king's expense were resumed. Ranulf II gave two carucates in Rothley (Leicestershire) to Leicester Abbey; Rothley was one of the manors granted to him by Stephen, but it was recovered in full by Henry II. Robert de Ferrers gave tithe of his revenues in Derby to the canons of St Helen's there, having evidently gained control of the borough under Stephen: it was not one of his holdings under Henry I or Henry II. Both gifts were omitted from subsequent confirmation charters.[253] However, another donation by Earl Ranulf from royal demesne acquired in the war, that of 100 solidates of land in Trentham to restore the religious foundation there, was duly confirmed by Henry II. The king took the priory under his special protection, and although the manor of Trentham was recovered from the earls of Chester and appeared as royal demesne in the pipe rolls, the allowance of 100s. was regularly entered therein.[254]

Henry was also variable in his attitude to his own charters as duke. There is no sign in the pipe rolls of the grants worth £10 from the farm of Bedford, with the promise of more after he had come to the throne, which he had made to the canons there in the summer of 1153.[255] Nor does Aylworth (Gloucestershire), which he had granted to the canons of Bristol in 1153x54, appear to have remained with them after his accession.[256] The monks of Bermondsey do not seem to have had the rents from the farms of Southwark and Dartford which Stephen and William of Ypres had assigned to them, and which Henry had also given in 1153 or 1154; he had promised a royal confirmation if he won the kingdom, but

---

[251] *RRAN*, III, no. 921; *PR2H*, 54; *PR3H*, 105; *PR4H*, 171; *PR5H*, 45, etc., and *PR 14 Hen. III*, 184; *PR 26 Hen. III*, 258. On the resumption and regrant of Neatham in 1239, see 'Annales de Waverleia' in *Annales Monastici*, ed. H.R. Luard (RS, 1864–9), II, 321.

[252] *RRAN*, III, no. 767; *Feudal Documents from the Abbey of Bury St Edmunds*, ed. D. C. Douglas (British Academy, London, 1932), no. 85; *PR2H*, 8; *PR3H*, 76; *PR4H*, 125, etc. and *PR 14 Hen. III*, 337; *PR 26 Hen. III*, 189.

[253] *RRAN*, III, nos. 178, 436 (following the identification of *Roleia* in J. G. Nichols, *History and Antiquities of the County of Leicester*, London, 1795–1815, III (ii), 942); *Monasticon*, VI (i), 466–7; *Cartulary of Darley*, I, xlvii–xlix, and II, 572–3, 579, 595–9; White, 'Stephen, Henry and Ranulf', 556.

[254] *PR3H*, 92; *PR4H*, 156, etc.; 'Chartulary of Trentham', 296–7; *Charters of Chester*, no. 118. The allowance was entered in the pipe rolls against John, chaplain to the earl of Chester, who was first prior of the refounded house at Trentham.

[255] *RRAN*, III, no.81; cf. Richardson and Sayles, *Governance*, 254 and n. 7.

[256] *RRAN*, III, nos. 128, 997.

there is no mention of this in the annals of Bermondsey, and the pipe rolls do not record allowances for the payments.[257] Yet among Roger earl of Hereford's grants for the foundation of Flaxley Abbey had been his holding in Dimmock, one of the king's manors in Gloucestershire where he (or his father) had evidently gained control during the war. Henry confirmed Roger's gift as his own alms in 1153x54, and some time after his accession repeated the confirmation, referring to the land as 'all my demesne of Dimmock'; an allowance was duly recorded in the pipe rolls from 1160.[258] An exceptional case was Stephen's foundation, the abbey of Faversham, where he, his queen and his eldest son Eustace all lay buried. This had been given special protection under the peace settlement, when Henry had explicitly confirmed its possessions. As king, he duly honoured this obligation, repeating his confirmation so that the relevant *terra data* duly appeared in the pipe rolls from 1155 onwards.[259]

The young king showed greater respect towards his mother's grants in alms. Great Barrington (Gloucestershire), which she had given to Llanthony Priory, and Blewbury (Berkshire), her gift to Reading Abbey, were both allowed for in the pipe rolls.[260] The grants she had made to Bordesley Abbey, in Bidford (Warwickshire), Tardebigg (Staffordshire) and Holloway (Worcestershire), were renewed by Henry II and similarly recorded as *terrae datae*.[261] She allowed the canons of Oseney to have remission of the 5s $5\frac{3}{4}$d. landgavel in Oxford borough which Stephen had first given them, and relieved them of a further annual payment of 4s 0d.:[262] it was the full exemption of 9s $5\frac{3}{4}$d. which Henry II granted, and which (as 9s $5\frac{1}{2}$d.) was allowed by his exchequer.[263] Similarly, her remission of 17s $7\frac{1}{2}$d. rent to the canons of St Frideswide's, Oxford, was renewed by her son and acknowledged by the exchequer; in this case, Stephen's earlier remission of 20s $0\frac{3}{4}$d. was ignored.[264] Other grants first made by Stephen, in Walcot (Shropshire) to Haughmond Abbey, and in Walton (Oxfordshire) to Godstow Abbey, were renewed by the empress, and so by Henry as king, and accordingly entered among the *terrae datae* in

---

257 *Ibid.*, III, nos. 91, 98, 90; cf. 'Annales de Bermundeseia', in *Annales Monastici*, III, 434, 440–2.

258 *RRAN*, III, no. 321; *Monasticon*, V, 590; *PR6H*, 28; *PR7H*, 21–2, etc.

259 *Monasticon*, IV, 573 (confirming, among others, *RRAN*, III, nos. 300–2); *RBE*, II, 648; *PR2H*, 65; *PR3H*, 101, etc. Henry's protection for Faversham is specified in *RRAN*, III, no. 272.

260 *Ibid.*, III, nos. 497, 703. Stephen, Eustace and Henry also conceded Blewbury (*ibid.*, III, nos. 694–694a, 704). For the allowances, see *PR2H*, 34–5; *PR3H*, 80–1, etc.

261 *RRAN*, III, nos. 115–16; the properties had already been granted by the abbey's founder Waleran of Meulan and (in the case of Bidford) by King Stephen (*Monasticon*, V, 410; *RRAN*, III, no. 114; *RAH*, I, no. 117; *PR2H*, 29, 44, 62; *PR3H*, 86, 92, 97, etc.)

262 *RRAN*, III, nos. 626, 628–9.

263 *Cartulary of Oseney*, IV, no. 53; *PR2H*, 35; *PR3H* , 82, etc.

264 *RRAN*, III, nos. 643–4; *Cartulary of the Monastery of St Frideswide*, ed. S. R. Wigram (Oxford Historical Society, 1895–6), I, no. 26; *PR2H*, 36; *PR3H*, 82, etc.

the pipe rolls.[265] One of her gifts in alms, at Radmore in Cannock Chase for the foundation of a community there, was resumed by Henry II but only because the monks had requested a new site, which he gave them at Stoneleigh (Warwickshire).[266] All this accords with the picture of Henry II, respectful of his mother's pious generosity, presented by Robert de Torigni in describing the distribution of alms following her death in 1167.[267] Yet at about this time, the king also resumed Aston (part of Wellington, Shropshire), which she had given to the monks of Shrewsbury in 1141; it was not restored until early in Richard I's reign.[268] Her gift to Eynsham Abbey of the church of Combe (Oxfordshire) does not seem to have obtained his confirmation.[269]

Doubtless many of the religious houses whose grants were renewed by Henry II had been fined heavily for the concession – the fines, like those from lay barons who retained *terrae datae*, presumably going into the chamber and so finding no place in the pipe rolls. But although the new king's readiness to consider cases individually must have given some hope to those who had acquired royal lands under Stephen, the clear thrust of Henry's policy was to recover what had been lost in his predecessor's reign. It has been suggested that Nigel bishop of Ely, who in accordance with canon law had promised at his consecration not to alienate the possessions of his church, encouraged the application of this 'doctrine of inalienability' to the royal demesne. As a former treasurer to Henry I, brought in by the new king to supervise the restoration of the exchequer, Bishop Nigel would have been well aware of the financial importance of resuming royal demesne lost under Stephen, and hence of the need to reject charters recording such grants.[270] This remains unproven, but some support for the idea can be found in the pipe rolls, if we may detect Nigel's hand in the decision to include alienated royal manors as *terrae*

[265] *RRAN*, III, nos. 376–8, 368, 370–1; 'Extracts from the Cartulary of Haghmon Abbey', ed. W. A. Leighton, *Transactions of the Shropshire Archaeological Society*, 1st ser., I (1878), 180; *English Register of Godstow Nunnery*, ed. A. Clark (Early English Text Society, 1911), 654–6; *PR2H*, 43, 36; *PR3H*, 88, 82, etc. (On the correspondence of the allowance in Headington and the grant in Walton, cf. *VCH Oxfordshire*, V, 3.)

[266] *RRAN*, III, no. 839 (cf. Stephen's grant, *ibid.*, III, no. 838); *Stoneleigh Leger Book*, ed. R. H. Hilton (Dugdale Society, 1960), xii–xvi, 15–16.   [267] RT, 232–3; cf. Chibnall, *Matilda*, 177–90.

[268] *RRAN*, III, no. 820; Eyton, *Antiquities of Shropshire*, IX, 58–9; the allowance for *terra data*, from *PR2H*, 43 to *PR12H*, 59, was underlined for deletion in *PR13H*, 39, and did not recur in later pipe rolls of this reign.

[269] *RRAN*, III, no. 296; the grant was omitted from Henry II's general confirmation to Eynsham (*RAH*, i, no. 198) and also from archiepiscopal confirmations of 1179x82 and 1193x1200 (*Cartulary of the Abbey of Eynsham*, ed. H. E. Salter, Oxford Historical Society, 1906–8, I, nos. 42, 44).

[270] Richardson, 'Coronation in medieval England', 151–61; cf. M. G. Cheney, 'Inalienability in mid-twelfth century England: enforcement and consequences', *Proceedings of the Sixth International Congress of Medieval Canon Law*, ed. S. Kuttner and K. Pennington (Vatican City, 1985), 467–78.

datae in the annual accounts of sheriffs' farms. Very few such items appeared in the 1130 pipe roll, probably because of a recent reconstitution of the farms, and it would have been possible for Henry II's exchequer to handle these accounts without detailing these alienations, either by reducing the farms totals by the appropriate amounts, or by consolidating the allowances instead of naming individual manors.[271] Under Henry II, however, the enrolling of *terrae datae* helped to make a political point, one repeatedly enforced in the case of those which had originated in his predecessor's reign. The entries perpetuated the notion that the lands were the king's, and as such were his to resume when he chose to do so.

CONCLUSION

The Battle Abbey chronicle shows us Henry II scrutinising the charters of his grandfather, and of earlier kings, and regarding them as binding upon him. When Gilbert de Balliol, defendant in a plea concerning land in Barnhorn (Sussex), challenged the authenticity of a charter bearing Henry I's seal, the king is alleged to have replied: 'By God's eyes, if you could prove this charter false, you would make me a profit of a thousand pounds in England.'[272] But as long as his grandfather's charter was accepted as genuine, he was obliged to fulfil its provisions. Significantly, we do not read of charters of Stephen, the empress or Henry as duke being presented during any of the cases in which Battle was involved at this time;[273] their charters would not have helped to establish the abbey's rights.

Despite this episode, we ought not to exaggerate the extent to which Henry II was tied by the precedents of his grandfather's day. We have seen that, in his deployment of administrative personnel, he did not follow Henry I's model exactly: the appointment of joint chief justiciars and the virtual extinction of hereditary and curial sheriffs were two obvious points of departure. Nor was it possible, in practice, to restore every estate to the pre-war holders or their heirs. But in general he acknowledged the force of opinion among his vassals in favour of long-term security of tenure – hereditability in the case of lay fiefs, inalienability for ecclesiastical holdings – and normally protected tenures already established before Henry I died. His sensitivity to hereditary claims

---

[271] See above, n. 188, for examples of royal demesne manors reckoned outside the sheriffs' farms, on the alienation of which the pipe rolls were silent until their eventual resumption by the crown.

[272] *Chronicle of Battle Abbey*, 216–17.

[273] *Ibid.*, 154–250 (e.g. 178, the reference to charters only of William I, William II, Henry I and Henry II in the dispute with the bishop of Chichester).

emerges, also, in his treatment of office-holders, for he usually allowed succession to titles if they had originated before 1135, even if the duties which went with them were sometimes performed by others. But for lands and offices acquired under Stephen, there was no guarantee of security: as William of Newburgh put it, summarising Henry's approach at the outset of his reign, 'the charters of an intruder ought not to prejudice the rights of a legitimate ruler',[274] and even those of his mother and of himself as duke were not always respected. Just as Eleanor of Aquitaine had felt free after her divorce to revoke a gift she had made jointly with King Louis VII,[275] so Henry regarded it as his prerogative to withdraw concessions made while Stephen was king.

One final point is worth consideration. After his accession, whenever he renewed grants in England made by his mother the empress, Henry normally 'gave' the lands as if for the first time.[276] But on the rare occasions when he repeated grants made by Stephen, he deliberately avoided the phraseology of new donations and was prepared to acknowledge his predecessor as 'rex'.[277] In other words, when Henry chose to allow Stephen's gifts to endure, he accepted their provenance and did not pretend that the donor had never been king. Stephen had usurped the throne and had presided over a *tempus guerrae*, but he had been anointed and crowned and Henry had eventually done him homage. To have

---

[274] Newburgh, I, 103: 'chartae invasoris juri legitimi principis praejudicium facere minime debuerunt'. Cf. (for Normandy), *RAH*, I, no. 8 (1155x56) a grant by the king of a demesne manor of Henry I to the canons of St Mary, Rouen, whereby anyone who held therein other than by gift of Henry I or by his writ was to be disseised.

[275] *Ibid.*, I, no. 23* (dated 27 May 1152).

[276] Thus, *Cartulary of Oseney*, IV, no. 53 ('Sciatis me dedisse et concessisse') renewing the empress's *RRAN*, III, no. 629; *Rotuli Chartarum*, 53 ('dedi et concessi') renewing the grants made to Miles earl of Hereford in *RRAN*, III, no. 393. Cf. *RAH*, I, no. 117, in which Henry renews his mother's charter, ostensibly founding Bordesley Abbey (*RRAN*, III, no. 116), by claiming that both he and the empress were founders: 'Sciatis dominam et matrem meam Matilldem imperatricem et me fundasse abbatiam de Bordeslegha'. (The true founder was Waleran of Meulan: Crouch, *Beaumont Twins*, 200–1; above, n. 261.) But note *RAH*, I, no. 134 ('Sciatis me concessisse et confirmasse') confirming the empress's gift of a rent in Normandy to the monks of St André-en-Gouffern near Falaise. Henry might also use the language of a new gift when repeating his own donations as duke: in his royal charter for Flaxley Abbey (*Monasticon*, V, 590), grants specified in his ducal charter (*RRAN*, III, no. 321) are preceded by the phrases 'Sciatis me dedisse et confirmasse' and 'preterea dedi et confirmavi'; but cf. Richardson and Sayles, *Governance*, 434–6, where some of the lands 'restored and conceded' to William Mauduit in 1153 (also *RRAN*, III, no. 582) are 'conceded and confirmed' to his son ('Sciatis me concessisse et confirmasse').

[277] Thus, *Feudal Documents of Bury St Edmunds*, no. 85 ('Sciatis me concessisse . . . quicquid habebam in manerio de Beccles quamdiu michi placuerit'), renewing Stephen's *RRAN*, III, no. 767; *Monasticon*, IV, 573, ('Sciatis me concessisse et confirmasse . . . abbatiam de Faveresham, quam rex Stephanus fundavit . . . concedo etiam . . . manerium de Faversham') renewing *RRAN*, III, no. 300; *Facsimiles of Charters in the British Museum*, no. 38 ('Sciatis me concessisse . . . manerium de Meonis . . . et manerium de Weregrava') renewing *RRAN*, III, nos. 947–9. See also *RAH*, I, nos. 325, 444; II, no. 502, cf. no. 682. On the use of language for grants, regrants and confirmations generally, see Hudson, *Land, Law and Lordship*, 72–7.

suggested, retrospectively, that England had been ruled for nineteen years by a mere count of Mortain would have undermined the dignity of kingship which it was Henry's consistent purpose to maintain.

Chapter 4

FINANCIAL RECOVERY

INTRODUCTION

Although some royal revenues had continued to be levied during Stephen's reign – not always for the king – and although significant steps had been taken to recover income due to the crown in the months following the peace settlement, there was much to be done at Henry II's accession in the field of financial administration if the position in the closing years of Henry I was to be restored. The total raised for the king in the financial year 1129–30, according to the incomplete evidence of the pipe roll for that year, has been calculated at over £24,000; on the same basis, the income in 1155–6 has been put at only £13,000, although it had climbed to £19,000 by 1158–9 only to fall thereafter.[1] There are several *caveats* to be entered against these figures, but their overall message is clear. A king who began his reign in debt and put a high priority on the assertion of his political rights – by military force where necessary – desperately needed to increase his income. Greater efficiency in the administration responsible for bringing in money and handling accounts was also essential. Accordingly, the financial dimension to the restoration of orderly royal government was of major concern to the king and his advisers. Here as elsewhere, the pace of reform was at least partly linked to Henry's itinerary, urgent measures during his first visit to England as king giving way to a period of consolidation before further changes were introduced following his return in 1163. The details can be teased out from the pipe rolls, the annual exchequer accounts. Their survival as a continuous series from the second year of the reign means that Henry II's

---

[1] Green, *Henry I*, 225; Amt, *Accession*, 194–6. Totals are achieved by counting sums entered for advance expenditure as well as those for payments in; the former represent money which did not reach the treasury or chamber but was successfully raised none the less. Although Amt's figures for 1155–9 have now superseded those in J. H. Ramsay, *A History of the Revenues of the Kings of England, 1066–1399* (Oxford, 1925), the latter should be consulted (I, 75–83) for reduced income in the financial years ending 1160–4.

financial administration can be studied in more detail than that of any of his predecessors. The limitations of the pipe rolls as evidence must, of course, be recognised: they 'are not concerned with the whole of the revenue and they record the expenditure of but a fraction of the king's resources',[2] while giving tantalising glimpses of procedures – for collection and accounting, for the granting of allowances and the testing of coin – about which much remains uncertain. But they have much to reveal in response to patient analysis, and the bulk of this chapter depends heavily upon them.

TREASURY, CHAMBER AND EXCHEQUER

The system of financial administration inherited by Henry II was, in essence, that which had functioned during the later years of Henry I's reign, and which Stephen had done his best to maintain: a royal treasury at Winchester, payments to which were accounted for at the exchequer, and an itinerant chamber accompanying the king, drawing on the treasury at need but also receiving revenues direct. The exchequer continued to meet twice yearly, at Easter and Michaelmas, but whereas these sessions had normally been held at Winchester under Henry I, the usual location was now Westminster; alternatives included Worcester (Easter 1158), Oxford (Easter 1162) and Northampton (Michaelmas 1164). As explained in the *Dialogus de Scaccario*, there were two parts to the exchequer: the lower (or exchequer of receipt) which handled money paid in, acting in effect as an outpost of the treasury, and the upper where accounts were transacted and the 'highest skill' was demanded.[3] The chamber kept its own rolls[4] but these have not survived, and references to its activities in the exchequer's accounts are very limited. But the work of the chamber is only one among many problems of interpretation facing those interested in Henry II's financial administration.

There can be no doubt that the young king relied upon his chamber, not only to deal with the expenditure of the royal household, but also as an important department of receipt: in the financial year ending at Michaelmas 1158 alone, at least six different men were employed to handle money paid into the chamber.[5] Among the sources of income for

---

[2] Richardson and Sayles, *Governance*, 216; cf. 170–1. Cautionary words on the calculation of figures from the pipe rolls appear in Green, *Henry I*, 220–2 and Amt, *Accession*, 189.

[3] Green, *Henry I*, 30–3, 38–50, and 'Financing Stephen's war', esp. 110–11; *De Necessaris Observantiis Scaccarii Dialogus*, ed. A. Hughes, C. G. Crump and C. Johnson (Oxford, 1902), 44; *PR4H*, 175; *PR8H*, 26; *PR10H*, 26; *Dialogus*, 6–10.   [4] For reference to a *rotulus camerae*, see *PR11H*, 4.

[5] Stephen de Tours, Ralf Waspail, Ralf fitz Stephen, Geoffrey Monk, Warin fitz Gerold, Henry fitz Gerold (*PR4H*, 120, 125, 127, 129, 131, 136, 146, 153, 155, 160, 167–8, 170, 175, 179–80). See also ch. 3, n. 36.

which the chamber apparently had particular responsibility were payments for office. Several of these are recorded in the 1130 pipe roll as
having been made to the treasury (and therefore accounted for at the
exchequer),[6] but they must normally have been handled by the chamber
in our period. Only three such items occur in Henry II's first eleven pipe
rolls, and the account for one of them records that the money had already
been received in the chamber.[7] There is no mention in the pipe rolls of
the sums which, according to other sources, were paid for the offices of
chancellor and treasurer.[8] Several reliefs and various other fines and
amercements, as well as farms and taxes due from sheriffs, are also noted as
having been paid in part to the chamber;[9] we cannot know how many
accounts had been settled there in full, and so had not come before the
exchequer at all. It is tempting to invoke the chamber whenever the pipe
rolls are silent about renders presumed to have been made – such as
annual farms of mints and seigniorage fees from moneyers[10] – but we are
on firmer ground when the rolls make specific reference to such payments. Thus, the *vicomtesse* of Rouen, who according to the 1165 pipe
roll owed £1,423 9s. 2d. 'blanch' old farm of Southampton, was to
answer for it in the chamber and no more was to be exacted from her 'per
Rotulos de Scaccario'.[11] Accounts for the honour of Henry of Essex were
made to the chamber from 1166–7, but to the exchequer from 1178–9.[12]
Exchequer and chamber were complementary: the king might order
renders formerly made to one to go to the other instead. On the whole,
the decision seems to have been based on administrative convenience,
but it is possible that in a few cases – such as that of the *vicomtesse* of Rouen
– Henry wanted some personal involvement, through his chamber, in
pressurising a recalcitrant debtor.[13]

[6] Thus, *PR 31 Hen. I*, 4 (Henry de Lamara, felter), 18 (Humphrey de Bohun, steward; John Marshal,
father's office; Adam de Port, steward; William fitz Herbert de St Valery, father's office), 24
(Bertram de Bulmer, father's office); 31 (Serlo de Burg, son Osbert's office), etc.

[7] Aubrey III de Vere was charged 500 silver marks for having the chamberlainship which his father
had had (*RBE*, II, 651); Nicholas fitz Floh' owed two gold rings for his office; Robert de Chalz
accounted for 20 silver marks for a forest office, but was acquitted because payment had already
been made in the king's chamber to Warin fitz Gerold (*PR3H*, 75, 91). Nicholas fitz Floh's
payment occurs at *PR4H*, 159.

[8] For the allegation that Becket obtained the chancellorship 'multis marcharum milibus', see GF,
Letters, no. 170. *Liber Eliensis*, 372, says that Bishop Nigel bought the treasurership for his son for
£400.

[9] *PR2H*, 27, 29, 60, 65; *PR3H*, 87, 90–1; *PR4H*: above, note 5; *PR5H*, 42, 63; *PR10H*, 5, 19, 20, 31;
PR11H, 6, 7, 19, 31, 40, 42, 53, 105, 110. On the absence of these items from the pipe rolls of
1160–3, presumably because of the king's sojourn in France, cf. Richardson, 'Chamber under
Henry II', 602.   [10] Nightingale, 'King's profit', esp. 67; cf. Amt, *Accession*, 155.   [11] *PR11H*, 45.

[12] *PR13H*, 158; *PR14H*, 46; *PR15H*, 129, etc. to *PR24H*, 47; thereafter, *PR25H*, 129; *PR27H*, 107;
PR28H, 103, etc.

[13] Thus J. E. A. Jolliffe, 'The *Camera Regis* under Henry II', *EHR*, 68 (1953), 1–21. This article was
rightly criticised on a number of points by Richardson in 'Chamber under Henry II'. However,

Few comparisons can be made with the use of the chamber as an office of receipt in the two preceding reigns. The 1130 pipe roll includes only one reference to a payment to the chamber, despite the fact that Henry I had been in England during the preceding year.[14] Even this evidence is lacking for Stephen, but in circumstances where immediate payment had been demanded by the king, the chamber must have been called upon. Thus, the contributions raised from the people of Beverley and York in 1149, and the fines to ensure freedom of election by the monks of St Augustine's, Canterbury, and the chapter of London in 1151, had probably been paid into the chamber.[15] The chamber would also have handled loans made to Stephen by English and – almost certainly – Flemish financiers:[16] a role it clearly continued to play under Henry II. During the first decade of his reign, Henry borrowed extensively from William Cade and other Christian money lenders, some of whom were allowed to hold boroughs at farm.[17] Several had doubtless helped to finance his campaign in 1153, and they continued to fulfil a need until about 1164, after which the king appears to have borrowed less heavily and to have relied almost entirely on Jews.[18] However, we only learn of these loans through the pipe rolls when a crown debtor had been ordered by the king's writ to repay a creditor direct, and so had an allowance at the exchequer. In this as in other respects, the routine operations of the chamber are hidden from us.

In such circumstances, this chapter must follow the bias of the available sources and deal primarily with the exchequer. Accordingly, it is con-

---

Henry's personal interest in chasing up debts is attested by the accounts rendered to him in person (albeit probably in the exchequer, not the chamber) at *PR9H*, 13, 14, 21, 28, 48, 51, etc. Jolliffe certainly exaggerated the role of the chamber in enforcing payments from those who defied the exchequer but this does not preclude its occasional use for this purpose, whenever the king chose to take matters into his own hands. Cf. *PR11H*, 53, where Philip of Kyme accounts for the farm of Tickhill for three years together, his only recorded payment on this account being into the chamber. Although Richardson attempts to draw parallels between the position of the *vicomtesse* of Rouen as a farmer of Southampton and that of her fellow money-lender William Cade as farmer of Dover ('Chamber under Henry II', 607–9), the pipe rolls strongly suggest that whereas Cade repeatedly accounted for his farm to the satisfaction of the exchequer, the *vicomtesse* did not. Cf. Amt, *Accession*, 96–9.

[14] *PR 31 Hen. I*, 134. Henry I left for Normandy shortly before Michaelmas 1130 but he had been in England since July 1129 (W. Farrer, *Outline Itinerary of Henry I*, Oxford, 1919, 127–33; *RRAN*, II, xxx–xxxi; Green, *Henry I*, 31).   [15] JH, 323–4; *Historia Pontificalis*, 86, 88.

[16] Cronne, *Reign of Stephen*, 233–6; Green, 'Financing Stephen's war', esp. 105–6.

[17] On the activities of William Cade, William Trentegeruns, Robert fitz Sawin and Ralf Waspail, see H. G. Richardson, *The English Jewry under Angevin Kings* (London, 1960), 50–6 and Amt, *Accession*, 94–103. Payments *in soltis,* possibly covering repayments to moneylenders, also appear against the names of Reiner fitz Berengar (*PR2H*, 17, 18, 27; cf. W. Page, *London: its Origin and Early Development* (London, 1923), 244–8), William de Haie (*PR2H*, 9, 68), Geoffrey fitz Durand (*PR3H*, 85) and several others.

[18] Richardson, *Jewry*, 50–1, 56–66. For payments *in soltis* to Jews, see *PR5H*, 1; *PR8H*, 18, 24, 41, 61, 62, 69; *PR9H*, 61; *PR10H*, 31; *PR11H*, 35; *PR12H*, *passim*, etc.

cerned almost entirely with the king's receipts rather than with his expenditure, and in particular with those items which before the judicial eyres of 1166 onwards were by far the greatest sources of revenue to the treasury, namely farms and taxes. It is appropriate first of all, however, to examine the pipe rolls themselves as evidence of the condition of the financial administration early in Henry II's reign. This was the period when Nigel bishop of Ely had responsibility for ensuring that exchequer procedures were conducted according to form, and that its records were compiled accurately and consistently; his evident retirement about 1164 may indicate that his restorative work was deemed complete.[19] One obvious way to judge his achievement is to compare the physical appearance of Henry II's early pipe rolls with that of the 1130 roll, which though it covers a time of upheaval in the financial administration[20] does at least reveal many of the methods of Henry I's late exchequer. The original 1130 roll[21] gives an impression of care and confidence in the entering of accounts. We see the items arranged neatly one beneath another and 'Et Quietus Est' written with a flourish over on the far right-hand side against those which are closed. It is easy to run the eye down and pick off the items not so acquitted, and so due for account again. Mistakes such as gaps left unfilled, or entries begun and then abandoned, are uncommon. Henry II's early pipe rolls[22] do not compare favourably, for many of these irregularities can be found. But they do show the same layout, with several of the membranes carefully ruled across and down to help the scribes to maintain the standard pattern. If we look further, to the principles governing the order in which items are entered, we again find that, despite some errors of detail, the outward signs of carelessness or confusion, the exchequer had its model and followed it closely.

In accounts of sheriffs' farms, and of those escheated honours, boroughs and royal manors which were treated separately, items appear in strict sequence: sheriff's name, amount paid into the treasury, fixed allowances in alms or stipends, *terrae datae*, and finally a statement of quittance or of the amount left owing or in surplus. This is the order observed in the 1130 pipe roll and it can be found consistently in the

---

[19] *Dialogus*, 50; *Liber Eliensis*, 283–385 (esp. on his retirement and death, 384–5). For his authorisation of expenditure, see *PR2H*, 4, 65, and for his role in determining liabilities, *Cartularium de Rameseia*, I, 255. His last datable attestation of a royal charter was in 1164 (*RAH*, I, 238) and according to Gervase, I, 185, he was stricken with paralysis towards the end of that year.

[20] *Dialogus*, xxxix; Green, *Henry I*, 65, 91–2.

[21] P.R.O. E 372/1, on which see Green, 'Earliest surviving pipe roll', but cf. Green, *Henry I*, 51–5, 220–5.

[22] Those examined in the original: 2 Henry II (P.R.O. E 372/2), 3 Henry II (E 372/3), 4 Henry II (E 372/4), 5 Henry II (E 372/5), 6 Henry II (E 372/6), 8 Henry II (E 372/8), 9 Henry II (E 372/9), although E 372/8 is considered to be a chancellor's roll in *PR8H*, ix–x.

accounts of Henry II's farms. Only when it came to placing allowances for casual disbursements by the sheriff – such as payments *in soltis* (normally meaning the repayment of debts), to restock the royal demesne, to maintain prisoners or to entertain the royal household – did the exchequer lack a standard practice. The procedure had varied in 1130[23] and it was not until 1163 that the rule later set out in the *Dialogus* – that they should go in last of all, immediately before the statement of quittance or balance – was finally adopted.[24] The rules given in the *Dialogus* for the placing of old farm accounts were also being observed strictly, both in 1130 and from 1156 onwards.[25]

G. J. Turner, in his pioneer study of the sheriff's farm, drew attention to arithmetical errors and to the careless omission of the 'blanch' or *numero* qualification in some of the earliest pipe rolls.[26] It is hard to distinguish clerical errors from arithmetical ones[27] but ambiguous figures continued to appear in the accounts of farms for several years. Thus, in 1156, the entries for ten sheriffs' farms lacked the qualification 'blanch' or *numero* on sums paid into the treasury, left owing or in surplus;[28] there was a similar number in 1157,[29] and though some improvement may be observed thereafter,[30] it was not until 1163 that every one of the figures

---

[23] Thus, in the account of the farm of Gloucestershire, an allowance for the transport of wine (relating only to the current year) was placed after one for land (presumably a recurrent item), and immediately before the statement of debt left owing, in accordance with the *Dialogus* sequence; the Staffordshire and Berkshire farm accounts had allowances 'in Corredio Regis' and for restocking in similar positions. But occasional allowances were placed before those for land in farm accounts for Wiltshire–Dorset and Yorkshire (*PR 31 Hen. I*, 77, 72–3, 122, 12, 24).

[24] *Dialogus*, 29–30; see, for example, the variable placing of casual disbursements in relation to the fixed allowance to Roger the goldsmith in the farm of Berkhamstead, *PR4H*, 152; *PR5H*, 7.

[25] *Dialogus*, 92.

[26] G. J. Turner, 'The sheriff's farm', *TRHS*, new ser., 12 (1898), 117–49. The terms 'blanch' and *numero* are considered below, p. 147.

[27] The illustration Turner chose of an error in arithmetic – the account of the farm of Faringdon in 1156 – was unfortunate. In both the original pipe roll and the printed version (*PR2H*, 35) the addition is correct. There is an apparent error at the end of the *terrae datae* for Oxfordshire (*PR2H*, 36) where the printed version gives £127 as the sum of individual allowances 'blanch' when they actually add up to £126, but the original is correct for we find the total recorded there as 'cxxvj li.'. There are, however, some identifiable errors within the danegeld accounts, where the sums of figures pardoned, e.g. for Essex and Northamptonshire in 1156 (*PR2H*, 17, 41) and for Warwickshire and Oxfordshire in 1162 (*PR8H*, 2, 27–8), do not match the stated totals. Cf. the examples given for farms in Amt, *Accession*, 151, n. 9. In both the danegeld and the farms' accounts, however, it remains uncertain whether the mistakes lie in addition or in copying.

[28] Norfolk (into treasury), Surrey (into treasury and surplus). Huntingdonshire, Staffordshire (into treasury), Berkshire (owing), Northamptonshire (into treasury), Devon, Herefordshire (owing), Worcestershire, Kent (into treasury): *PR2H*, 6, 10, 13, 29, 34, 40, 46, 50, 62, 64.

[29] Hertfordshire, Norfolk old farm (into treasury), Norfolk–Suffolk (surplus), Lincolnshire old farm (into treasury), Yorkshire (surplus), Huntingdonshire, Cambridgeshire (owing), Dorset (into treasury), Northamptonshire, Hampshire (owing): *PR3H*, 73, 75–6, 83, 86, 95–6, 99, 103, 105.

[30] Thus, 1158: Norfolk–Suffolk (surplus), Suffolk old farm (owing), Buckinghamshire–Bedfordshire (into treasury), Northamptonshire old farm (into treasury), Dorset (into treasury), Kent, Leicestershire (into treasury): *PR4H*, 125–6, 139, 141, 156, 179, 183.

entered as paid, owing or in surplus carried the specification. We find some further disorder in the treatment of 'new pleas and new agreements', the accounts (other than farms) which were coming forward for the first time in the current year. In the 1130 pipe roll these are entered among each shire's accounts according to type: all the judicial amercements within the shire are entered together, all the fines and all the taxes likewise.[31] Such an arrangement is to be found only spasmodically in Henry II's first eleven pipe rolls. The exchequer still handled each shire's business separately, but once the farms had been dealt with, plus arrears carried forward from previous years, it showed little concern to sort 'new' items into categories: indeed, many of these accounts, though apparently for fines or amercements, mention only the sums to be answered for, not the reasons why. There was also slackness in the use of the heading 'Nova Placita et Novae Conventiones' to introduce these items: although in fairly general use by 1158,[32] it was only from 1166, when there were many new accounts arising from the judicial eyre to be dealt with, that it came to be entered with absolute consistency. From this time, also, we find far more of the fines and amercements carrying brief explanations and being arranged in distinct groups according to purpose.[33]

These early pipe rolls suggest that the exchequer had grown unaccustomed to handling fines and amercements in any quantity in the 1140s and early 1150s. But – as discussed in an earlier chapter[34] – a tradition of dealing with sheriffs' farms had doubtless persisted, even if only a few had been accounted for regularly. In terms of personnel, there can have been little continuity among the barons of the exchequer from one reign to the next. The composition of the court was more flexible than the careful description in the *Dialogus* would suggest,[35] but of the barons who may have been summoned to Henry II's early exchequer probably only Richard de Lucy and Henry of Essex had had experience there in Stephen's closing years.[36] Bishop Nigel himself had been reconciled to

[31] E.g. Warwickshire: five amercements, a fine, sheriff's render of danegeld, aid and farms of certain manors. Gloucestershire: a fine, two amercements, sheriff's render of danegeld, aids and some old pennies. Staffordshire: four amercements, two fines, sheriff's render of danegeld and aids (*PR 31 Hen. I*, 107–8, 79–80, 75–6).

[32] It is absent altogether from *PR2H*, but by *PR4H* is missing only from London, Middlesex, Carlisle, Norfolk–Suffolk, Herefordshire, Dorset, Shropshire and Northumberland.

[33] E.g. *PR12H*, 95–9. Among the *Nova Placita et Novae Conventiones* of Devon three accounts from claimants to land are followed by a plea of the forest, three unspecified items (probably also forest *placita*), another fine for land and the account of chattels arising from the enforcement of the Assize of Clarendon. Under Dorset–Somerset, the *Nova Placita et Novae Conventiones* contain a series of amercements and other payments arising out of lawsuits, again ending with the account of chattels.

[34] Above, ch. 2; cf. White, 'Continuity', 139–42.

[35] *Dialogus*, 13–35; cf. Richardson and Sayles, *Governance*, 245–60; Green, *Henry I*, 38–50.

[36] Henry of Essex, constable, witnessed a writ of Henry II 'apud Westmonasterium ad Scaccarium' ordering that certain land held by the abbess of Romsey should geld for $1\frac{1}{2}$ hides (*CCR*, II, 103).

Stephen from the mid-1140s onwards and had attested some late charters, including one ordering quittance from geld,[37] but this does not amount to evidence that he had been present at exchequer sessions towards the end of Stephen's reign. On the other hand, some of the subordinate staff – the calculator and the various clerks who served the treasurer, chancellor, chamberlains and constable[38] – may possibly have had a grounding in Stephen's administration on which Bishop Nigel could build when seeking to restore the exchequer's former efficiency. Yet how fair was Richard fitz Nigel in claiming that, the *scientia* of the exchequer having 'almost perished' during the civil war, his father 'revived its form in all its details'?[39] There is enough evidence of continuing exchequer activity under Stephen[40] to call the first assertion into question, although if *scientia* is taken to mean the confident transaction of business according to established routine, the uncertainties apparent in Henry II's early pipe rolls suggest that he did have a point. As for his second claim, there was certainly an element of exaggeration, for 'all its details' had not yet been revived by the time of Bishop Nigel's retirement about 1164. The heading for 'Nova Placita et Novae Conventiones' was still liable to be omitted, and fines and amercements were not yet divided into recognisable categories. Only in 1163 had the 'blanch' and *numero* qualification come to be inserted with complete consistency against sums paid, owing or in surplus. That said, the bishop did have to guide the exchequer at an unusually difficult time, and the detailed studies which follow of the handling of farms and taxes reveal some of the complexities of his task.

SHERIFFS' FARMS

The sheriffs' (or shire) farms were fixed sums accounted for annually, covering the king's income from all or most of the royal demesne in each shire. The total amount due for each sheriff's farm was not entered in the pipe rolls until 1197. The totals were, however, kept on an 'exactory roll' or 'roll of farms' which the treasurer consulted at the termination of each sheriff's account. If the total recorded therein matched the sums which had been accounted for in payments and allowances, the sheriff was

---

[37] *RRAN*, III, nos. 171, 183, 267, 301–2, 358, 760; *Liber Eliensis*, 333–4.

[38] *Dialogus*, 22, 24–5, 29, 33–5.

[39] *Ibid.*, 50; cf. Warren, *Governance*, 99, and esp. J. G. H. Hudson, 'Administration, family and perceptions of the past in late twelfth-century England: Richard fitz Nigel and the Dialogue of the Exchequer', in P. Magdalino, ed., *The Perception of the Past in Twelfth-Century Europe* (London, 1992), 75–98. For Bishop Nigel's career and eventual retirement, see above, n. 19.

[40] Yoshitake, 'Exchequer in the reign of Stephen'; White, 'Continuity', esp. 121–2, 129, 139–42; cf. Green, 'Financing Stephen's war', esp. 110–13.

pronounced quit. If he had fallen short, he was entered as owing the appropriate amount.[41] In practice, during Henry II's early years as king – as indeed throughout the reign – nearly all the sheriffs met the sums required in full or paid off the debts in the following year, so preventing the accumulation of substantial arrears. To cite one typical example, Ralf Picot as sheriff of Kent carried forward a debt of £8 14s. 2d. 'blanch' in 1154–5 and in the following year discharged this as 'old farm', only to leave a further debt of £11 7s. 6d. 'blanch'. In 1156–7 he duly paid this off as 'old farm' but still ended £14 17s. 4½d. 'blanch' in arrears for the current year. Having made this good in 1157–8, he finished that year with a 12s. 3d. 'blanch' surplus. This was duly credited to him in the accounts for 1158–9, when he left a debt of 4s. 9d. 'blanch' and £16 4s. 0d. *numero*. These sums duly appeared as 'old farm' in 1159–60, when he closed his account of 'new farm' quit. His final account of the Kent farm was for the first quarter of 1160–1 and again he ended quit.[42]

Against this, the incidence of sheriffs leaving office with very heavy debts on their farms was exceptional. Walter of Hereford lost his hereditary shrievalty in Gloucestershire after Michaelmas 1157, owing £30 'blanch' old farm and £37 15s. 9d. 'blanch' new farm; his successor paid off £7 15s. 9d. 'blanch' in the following year, but there is no record in the pipe rolls thereafter of the two outstanding debts of £30 'blanch', which have the appearance of a disputed increment.[43] Henry d'Oilli, hereditary sheriff of Oxfordshire, left office late in 1160 with a recorded debt of £12 10s. 10d. 'blanch' which failed to recur in subsequent pipe rolls.[44] Robert fitz Hugh owed a total of £95 3s. 2d. 'blanch' on the farms of Leicestershire and Warwickshire at Michaelmas 1158, and was apparently arrested the following year: these debts, likewise, were not mentioned in the pipe rolls again.[45] Unusual though such cases were, actual defaults by sheriffs may have been rather more frequent, since the exchequer sometimes acquitted those who had accounted for lower farms than were customarily due. No accounts were rendered for the farms of London–Middlesex and Buckinghamshire–Bedfordshire at Michaelmas 1157: the 'old farms' answered for in the following year were much lower than the usual

---

[41] *Dialogus*, 65, 125–6.

[42] *PR2H*, 64–5; *PR3H*, 101–2; *PR4H*, 179–80; *PR5H*, 57–8; *PR6H*, 53–4; *PR7H*, 61–2. Even here, however, some lapses in accounting are apparent. The sum of £16 14s. 0d. *numero* due as 'old farm' in 1159–60 was carried forward to await the king's decision on his return to England, but was not referred to in the pipe rolls again. An odd halfpenny also seems to have been written off in the carrying forward of old farm from 1156–7 to 1157–8.   [43] *PR3H*, 100; *PR4H*, 167.

[44] *PR6H*, 8.

[45] *PR4H*, 183–4; he did not account for the farms of these shires in 1159, although his successors, William de Beauchamp in Warwickshire and Robert fitz Hardulf in Leicestershire, did so for only half the year. William de Beauchamp's account includes an allowance of £35 0s. 9d. *numero* 'pro Captura Roberti filii Hugonis de Warewichscira', *PR5H*, 25.

totals.[46] In these cases, the fluctuations in the sums accounted for are spectacular, but it is not difficult to point to other, less dramatic, examples. If we calculate the sheriffs' farms from successive pipe rolls, we find that it is only from 1165 that – with rare exceptions – the totals remain stable down to the last penny. Before then, especially before 1163, they are liable to fluctuate from year to year, often by a few shillings or pence, sometimes by several pounds. Although it has been claimed that imprecision in exchequer accounting means that 'differences of less than a pound or two need not . . . concern us unduly',[47] the fact that the farms did eventually stabilise with absolute consistency from one year to the next implies that even minor deviations are significant: they suggest that, early in the reign, problems of procedure, or enforcement, had not yet been fully overcome. Details of sheriffs' farms for the period 1155–65 (plus those for 1130 and for 1197, when totals first appeared in the pipe rolls), are given in appendix I. Reference should be made to these pages during the discussion which follows.

G. J. Turner, who calculated several of these farms totals over a century ago, suspected that clerical errors were responsible for some of the apparent fluctuations: a point reinforced by Emilie Amt in her more recent discussion of this issue.[48] It was easy enough – even if reprehensible in an exchequer clerk – to write the wrong number of digits when dealing with figures such as 'xj', 'xij' and 'xiij' and we may guess that totals such as those for Dorset and Gloucestershire in 1158, Berkshire in 1160 and Wiltshire in 1162 were freaks caused in this way.[49] We can be almost certain of one such error among the *terrae datae* of Gloucestershire: Hugh de Gundeville's sister appeared against 25s. od. 'blanch' in 1162, but against only 15s. od. 'blanch' in every other year from 1156 to the end of the century. Another apparent mistake, also in the Gloucestershire accounts, concerns *terra data* to the canons of Ste Barbe. The sheriff was normally credited with £30 'blanch' for their tenure of Beckford, but according to the printed version of the pipe roll was allowed only 30s. od. in 1159. Here, the editor has gone astray, for the original roll shows £30.[50] In both cases, the data for Gloucestershire in appendix I is based

---

[46] *PR4H*, 111–12 (old farm of London, totalling £463 9s. 1od. 'blanch'), 138 (old farm of Buckinghamshire–Bedfordshire, £52 11s. 2d. 'blanch'); cf. the details of sheriffs' farms in appendix I.

[47] Amt, *Accession*, 151.   [48] *Ibid.*; Turner, 'Sheriff's farm', 125.

[49] Dorset: £119 10s. od. (1158) against 'standard' of £120 0s. od. Gloucestershire: £372 12s. 6d. (1158) against 'standard' of £372 13s. 6d. Berkshire: £542 8s. 2d. (1160) against 'standard' of £541 8s. 4d. Wiltshire: £542 8s. 1od.(1162) against 'standard' of £542 9s. 1od. (all blanch).

[50] 1162: *PR8H*, 59; the original (P.R.O. E 372/8, memb. 2 dorso) also gives 'xxv s.' although if this was a chancellor's roll a copying error may be responsible. 1159: *PR5H*, 27; cf. P.R.O. E 372/5, memb. 2, where the allowance is for 'xxx lj', although the 'lj' is difficult to make out.

upon the 'corrected' figures; all the other information is derived from the printed data.

It is of course possible that in some cases where 'bad debts' were apparently left by departing sheriffs, or where farms totals seem to have been lower than usual, unrecorded payments had been made into the chamber. This may help to explain the low totals for Buckingham-shire–Bedfordshire, Huntingdonshire, Kent and London in 1157, and for Kent again in 1161.[51] On the other hand, the exchequer was supposed to record such payments and did so in several sheriffs' farm accounts;[52] accordingly it has been possible to include these sums, whenever mentioned, in the calculations of totals. If this argument has some validity, it points, at best, to slackness and inconsistency in exchequer procedure. Other explanations which have been offered for the instability of the totals do not take us very far: there was no consistent link, for example, between fluctuations in the farms and either the appointment of new sheriffs or the separate accounting of individual manors.[53] A further suggestion is that 'the sum of the farms remained uncertain because of the gradual restoration of the estates devastated in the years of the anarchy'.[54] This was probably true of Norfolk–Suffolk, where the sheriff accounted for only half the year in 1156–7, and where the farms totals were markedly low before 1158; it had evidently not been possible to compile a full list of *terrae datae* before 1157–8, and allowances for 'waste' continued until 1159.[55] But if this held good as a general hypothesis, we would

[51] For the farms of Buckinghamshire–Bedfordshire and London, see above, n. 46. The farm of Huntingdonshire in 1157 was roughly half that of the years immediately before and afterwards. In Kent in 1157 and 1161 the sum 'blanch' was at the standard figure but the increment *numero* was significantly lower than usual. Cf. appendix I.

[52] E.g. *PR2H*, 29 (Staffordshire), 65 (Kent); *PR3H*, 90 (Nottinghamshire–Derbyshire); *PR4H*, 125 (Norfolk–Suffolk), 136 (Lincolnshire), 146 (Yorkshire), 155 (Worcestershire), 167 (Gloucester-shire), 170 (Shropshire), 180 (Kent).

[53] On changes of sheriff, see Boussard, *Le Gouvernement*, 445–7; but between 1156 and 1165, the only shires in which a change of sheriff coincided with a significant adjustment to the farm were Devon (1158), Norfolk–Suffolk (1163) and Warwickshire–Leicestershire (1158, 1164). In Devon, the farm was reduced from over £336 to the 'standard' of £312 7s. 0d. (both 'blanch'). In Norfolk–Suffolk, the increment was raised from £50 to £100 *numero*. In Warwickshire–Leicester-shire, a £40 *numero* increment was withdrawn in 1158 but reimposed in 1164. On changes in the treatment of certain manors, see Turner, 'Sheriff's farm', 131–2; Amt, *Accession*, 153–4. Bayford (Hertfordshire), Whatborough (Leicestershire) and Halesowen (Worcestershire) were dealt with separately in 1155 (*RBE*, II, 651, 655–6) but then apparently absorbed into the relevant sheriffs' farms which all show an increase in 1156. Against this, however, Darlton (Nottinghamshire) was accounted for separately from 1155–6 to 1160–1, and Petherton (Somerset) in 1157 and from 1161 onwards, without there being any effect upon the sheriffs' farms (*PR2H*, 39; *PR3H*, 90, 98; *PR4H*, 153; *PR5H*, 51; *PR6H*, 43; *PR7H*, 30, 49, etc.). [54] *Dialogus*, xlviii.

[55] *PR3H*, 76. The farm of Suffolk was also rendered for only half the year in 1155 (*RBE*, II, 652). *Terrae datae* here are much fuller in *PR4H*, 125, than in previous years and include for the first time the manors conceded to Hugh Bigod in 1155 (*Cartae Antiquae Rolls 11–20*, 157–8). For 'waste', see *PR3H*, 76; *PR4H*, 125; *PR5H*, 8.

expect to see a gradual increase in several sheriffs' farms, and to observe the greatest uncertainty in those parts of the country which suffered most severely in the previous reign. Neither expectation is fulfilled. The most stable totals come not only from Kent and Sussex but also from Berkshire and Wiltshire, in the disputed south of England between the heartlands of royalist and Angevin support, and in Nottinghamshire–Derbyshire for which there is abundant pipe roll evidence of 'waste'.[56] And there is scarcely room for any general increase in the farms, for apart from the sheriffs of Norfolk–Suffolk only two, those for Herefordshire and for Hertfordshire, accounted in 1156 for markedly lower totals than the sums consistently achieved a decade later.

It is clear that as early as 1156 the exchequer knew what the totals of most of the sheriffs' farms should be. Of the twenty-eight new sheriffs' farms recorded in the pipe-roll of that year, six (those of Berkshire, Dorset, Gloucestershire, Hampshire, Sussex and Worcestershire) matched the 'standard totals' of Richard I's reign exactly, while two (London and Nottinghamshire–Derbyshire) returned totals which were standard in subsequent years but were eventually changed. Another six (Buckinghamshire–Bedfordshire, Lincolnshire, Shropshire, Somerset, Staffordshire and Wiltshire) were only odd shillings or pence out. In a further two (Oxfordshire and Warwickshire) the figures involved bear sufficient similarities to those of later 'standard totals' to suggest that there may have been scribal errors. This covers about three-fifths of all sheriffs' farms. Of the remaining twelve, Herefordshire, though returning a lower figure in 1156, had been accounted for on the basis of a 'standard total' in the previous year. Leicestershire would achieve its standard in 1157, Kent and Yorkshire in 1158, Devon, Essex and Hertfordshire in 1159. The sheriff of Norfolk–Suffolk answered for fairly consistent farms from 1159–60 to 1162–3, after which a further increment was imposed and the totals ceased to fluctuate. Cambridgeshire, Huntingdonshire and Surrey, accounted for together by that time, achieved a total in 1161 equivalent to the sums which would be answered for separately a few years later. Northamptonshire returned 'standard totals' from 1163. Of the two shires for which no accounts were rendered until 1158, Carlisle's farm had settled at a standard figure by 1159 although Northumberland's did not do so until 1164.

Turner thought that most of the sheriffs' farms totals had been fixed before Henry II's accession, and several of the figures involved in the

---

[56] G. J. White, 'Were the Midlands "wasted" during Stephen's reign?', *Midland History*, 10 (1985), 26–46. Herefordshire: £159 2s. 3d. 'blanch' in 1156 against 'standard' of £164 16s. 5d. 'blanch'. Hertfordshire: cannot be determined precisely because accounted for with Essex, but estimated as £100 'blanch' in 1156 against 'standard' of £140.

accounts of farms at Michaelmas 1155 support the contention that the totals would already have been known to Stephen's exchequer. Five of those rendered for the full year Michaelmas 1154 to Michaelmas 1155 – Berkshire, Dorset, Staffordshire, Surrey and Wiltshire – were for sums recognisably close to subsequent 'standard totals'. In the cases of Herefordshire and Sussex, although the accounts were for only three-quarters of the year (as from Christmas 1154, so after Henry II's accession), the full year's equivalent totals matched later standards exactly. And although Rutland has been omitted from this discussion because not constituted as a shire at this time, here too a 'standard farm' was demanded for the full year 1154–5.[57]

If most of the sheriffs' farms totals of Henry II's early reign were indeed inherited from his predecessor, we are bound to ask when they were fixed. The evidence is slight, but points to a date late in the reign of Henry I. The *Herefordshire Domesday*, a book probably compiled early in Henry II's reign for use at the exchequer, includes a list of manors which contributed to the farm of the shire 'tempore regis Henrici' and adds a total which, at £164 16s. 4d., is precisely that found in 1155 and later.[58] In 1141 William de Beauchamp was granted the shrievalty of Worcestershire for the farm rendered by his father Walter, who had died sometime between 1130 and 1133;[59] he accounted for a standard total from 1156, and his full year's farm for 1155 might also be considered reasonably close to this total. It is unfortunate that the absence of accounts for Herefordshire and Worcestershire in Henry I's sole surviving pipe roll makes it impossible to compare their farms totals under Henry II with those pertaining in 1130. Where such comparisons can be made, however, it is clear that the totals were not identical but markedly different: even in Gloucestershire, where the shrievalty was granted to Earl Roger in 1155 for the farm his father Miles had rendered under Henry I,[60] the farm total both in that year and subsequently was appreciably higher than it had been in 1130. As Judith Green has stressed, the 1130 pipe roll records a year of exceptional administrative measures, with no less than eleven shires in the hands of Richard Basset and Aubrey de Vere who accounted for their shires *ad pensum*.[61] One possibility is that there was a fresh

---

[57] Turner, 'Sheriff's farm', 133. £10 *numero* was demanded from Rutland every year from 1154–5, although initially as an old debt (*PR2H*, 42); on its status, see *VCH Rutland*, I, 165–71. It is fair to add that comparisons of the *Red Book of the Exchequer* transcript with the pipe rolls of 2 Henry II onwards suggest that the information given for the year 1154–5 in *RBE*, II, 648–58, may be significantly flawed in places (Amt, *Accession*, 122–3); if so, there may have been more sheriffs' farms totals close to later 'standards' than is apparent here.

[58] *Herefordshire Domesday*, ed. V. H. Galbraith and J. Tait (P.R. Society, 1950), 75.

[59] *RRAN*, III, no. 68; Green, *Henry I*, 233.   [60] *Rotuli Chartarum*, 53.

[61] Green, *Henry I*, 62–5.

assessment of the farms soon after their tenure of office was over, during Henry I's last visit to England between August 1131 and August 1133, and that these were the totals, now reckoned 'blanch' in most cases, which were passed on through Stephen's reign to Henry II's. But this is to build one speculation upon another. The essential point here is that, however many problems were encountered in collecting the sums due, Henry II's exchequer possessed established totals for the sheriffs' farms from very early in the reign, most of them previously determined.

In the mid- to late 1150s, the exchequer may have been more confident of the sheriffs' farms totals than it was of the identity of the manors which should contribute as royal demesne. We know from the *Gesta Abbatum* of St Albans that Henry issued an edict soon after his accession, ordering that former royal manors were to be determined by sworn inquest and restored to the crown.[62] Such a process would undoubtedly have helped to settle which manors were covered by the appropriate sheriff's farm, but there is no proof that totals were adjusted in consequence. Some correspondence can be found between shires known from the 1156 pipe roll to have been visited by barons of the exchequer, and those achieving 'standard totals' for their farms in the same year. The farms of Dorset, Essex, Hampshire, Lincolnshire. Somerset, Sussex and Wiltshire all came very close to such standards in 1156, and all received visits from Robert earl of Leicester, Thomas Becket or Henry of Essex during the year; however, Dorset and Wiltshire had already come very close to these totals in the previous year, while Kent – which was also visited – did not settle on a 'standard total' until 1158.[63] One of the references to such a visit relates to the levy of an assize, the others concern the imposition of *placita*, but the accounts are so few in number that they clearly did not arise from a wide-ranging judicial eyre. It is likely that the barons of the exchequer occasionally heard pleas, but that their principal tasks were the imposition of taxes and the conduct of sworn inquests into the extent of royal demesne.

Of course, the task of determining the royal demesne was far from complete by Michaelmas 1156. We learn of inquests sometime between 1156 and 1158 into property in Derby and Pickering,[64] and in 1164 there was evidently another general enquiry, which led to the first accounts of purprestures in the following year. The lists of purprestures – representing portions of royal demesne which had been recovered after encroachment – were longest in 1165 for Yorkshire, Norfolk–Suffolk, Surrey and Oxfordshire: the sheriffs' farms for these shires had already been fixed

[62] *Gesta Abbatum Sancti Albani*, I, 123.
[63] *PR2H*, 17, 26, 31–2, 54, 57, 60–1, 65.   [64] *Cartulary of Darley*, I, 71–2; *EYC*, I, nos. 401–3.

without them, and these additional manors now represented extra income for the crown.[65] The enquiry seems to have preoccupied several exchequer officials, for the 1164 pipe roll is the briefest of those to have survived, and includes no new accounts apart from recurrent farms and cesses.[66]

It is worth adding that some boroughs and manors which appear from the 1130 pipe roll to have been included within the sheriffs' farms were treated separately under Henry II. This is true, for example, of Berkhamstead (Hertfordshire) and Bray (Berkshire), accounted for from 1155–6, and of Odcombe (Somerset) which first appeared in the pipe roll of 1157. Presumably all had passed from Stephen's control during the civil war, only now to be recovered as royal demesne. There is firmer evidence of this in the cases of Faringdon (Berkshire), where a castle had been held for the Angevins until 1144, of Colchester, where the castle had been promised by the empress to Aubrey III de Vere, and of Northampton, whose revenues had been diverted to Simon II de Senlis. Northampton was dealt with separately from the first year of the reign, the others from 1156. None appear to have been accounted for outside the sheriffs' farms in 1130.[67] Since there seem to have been no corresponding reductions in the sheriffs' farms totals under Henry II, it must be presumed that this was another way in which the crown was seeking to increase the yield from the royal demesne.

Prominent within the accounts of·farms under Henry II were the allowances *in terris datis,* for lands alienated from the royal demesne. There were a few such allowances in the 1130 pipe roll, under Essex–Hertfordshire, Kent, Norfolk–Suffolk, Windsor and Carlisle, yet other portions of former royal demesne, known on charter evidence to have been granted away by William II and Henry I, were not entered as such. The most likely explanation is that the *terrae datae* of 1130 represented recent alienations made since the farms had been reconstituted, probably

---

[65] *PR11H*, 51, 10, 111–12, 72, with recurring sums (including references to restocking of manors) in subsequent rolls.

[66] All accounts in *PR10H* of fines, amercements and taxes had already appeared in *PR9H*. It may be significant, given the officials' preoccupation with this enquiry, that the Michaelmas 1164 exchequer met at Northampton: apparently the first Michaelmas session of the reign to be held outside Westminster (*PR10H*, 26; cf. H. G. Richardson in *Memoranda Roll 1 John*, P.R. Society, 1943, xii, n. 7).

[67] Berkhamstead, Bray, Odcombe: *PR2H*, 19, 21; *PR3H*, 72, 98; *PR4H*, 121, 152; *PR5H*, 7, 22, 38, etc. and on Berkhamstead cf. *VCH Hertfordshire*, II, 165; *Baronies*, 14. Faringdon, Colchester, Northampton: HH, 746; *RRAN*, III, nos. 634–5; *VCH Northants.*, III, 3–4; *RBE*, II, 655; *PR2H*, 21, 35, 42; *PR3H*, 81, 106; *PR4H*, 124, 135, 143; *PR5H*, 7, 20, 36–7, etc. Dr Judith Green has suggested to me that Berkhamstead may have been accounted for outside the sheriff's farm as early as 1130, as one of the unspecified manors against the name of Geoffrey the chancellor at *PR 31 Hen. I*, 139–40.

Financial recovery

during an earlier financial reorganisation.[68] Only one of these *terrae datae*
reappeared in the pipe rolls of Henry II: Garsilius de Buignun was entered
against £20 *numero* in Diss (Norfolk) in the rolls of both 1130 and 1158,
and was replaced by Richard de Lucy thereafter.[69] This was an exceptional case; it may well be that all the other *terrae datae* in Henry II's
pipe-rolls arose from grants made since his grandfather's death. Several
can be traced to charters of Stephen, the empress or Henry as duke,[70] but
none to those of previous kings; charters issued since 1135 which merely
confirmed gifts by Henry I did not result in *terrae datae* either. But the
inclusion of these items in respect of at least some of the alienations of
Stephen's reign demonstrates that, in practice, it was not possible to
reconstitute the royal demesne precisely as it had stood 'on the day King
Henry was alive and dead'.

The exchequer's procedures for handling manors resumed by the
crown varied according to circumstance. We have seen that some former
royal manors apparently lost in the war, such as Faringdon and Odcombe,
were dealt with separately when they were recovered. They had no part
in the accounts of sheriffs' farms, so had not been entered as *terrae datae*
while they remained out of the kings' hands. Likewise Wargrave, evidently granted to the bishop and church of Winchester both by Stephen
and (soon after his accession) by Henry II, did not appear among the *terrae
datae* of Berkshire in 1155.[71] The manor was subsequently resumed by the
crown, probably soon after Bishop Henry's departure from the kingdom,
and was accounted for outside the sheriffs' farm by Richard de Lucy from
1156, for £52 in the first year, for £80 *numero* thereafter.[72] Similarly,
certain manors which Hugh Bigod had apparently encroached upon in
Norfolk and Suffolk were not enrolled as *terrae datae* in successive accounts of sheriffs' farms: we read of them only when they were taken into
the king's hands and treated as escheats, following Hugh's death in 1177.[73]

Such cases demonstrate flexibility in procedure, faced with the realities

[68] *Ibid.*, 52 (church of Séez), 63 (Robert de Crevequer), 90 ('Garsirius delbuinnum', presumably
Garsirius de Buignun), 127 (William fitz Walter), 140 (Richard the knight); Green, *Henry I*, 64–6.
[69] *PR4H*, 125; *PR5H*, 8; *PR6H*, 1, etc.
[70] E.g. Faversham (Kent), granted for the foundation of the abbey by Stephen (*RRAN*, III, nos. 300,
302; cf. *RBE*, II, 648; *PR2H*, 65, etc.); Aston (Shropshire), given by the empress to Shrewsbury
Abbey but resumed *c.*1167 (*RRAN*, III, no. 820; cf. *PR2H*, 43; *PR3H*, 88; *PR13H*, 59); Bedminster
(Somerset), confirmed by Duke Henry to Robert fitz Harding after it had originally been granted
from the royal demesne by Robert earl of Gloucester (*RRAN*, III, no. 1000; cf. *PR2H*, 30; *PR3H*,
98, etc.). Cf. above, ch. 3, nn. 204, 259, 268. A fuller discussion of *terrae datae* appears in Amt,
Accession, 156–68.
[71] Above, ch. 3, n. 250. The details of alienated lands in Berkshire do not appear in the transcript of
the 1155 pipe roll (*RBE*, II, 657–8) but the total for *terrae datae* there, £431 5s. 7d. 'blanch' (albeit
including 'waste') is very close to the corresponding total in 1156.
[72] *PR2H*, 19 (where there is no qualification for 'blanch' or *numero*); *PR3H*, 71–2; *PR4H*, 152;
PR5H, 38, etc.   [73] *PR23H*, 136–7; *PR24H*, 26–7; *PR25H*, 9, etc.

of reconstituting the royal demesne. Entries under Wiltshire from 1157 and under Oxfordshire from 1158 illustrate further problems, for here there were doubts over whether holdings in Marlborough and Benson should contribute to their respective shire farms, or be treated as *terrae datae*. No payments were made for them by the sheriffs, but the accumulating debts 'pro calumpnia' were recorded year after year pending a decision.[74] This suggests a confused territorial position, but it also shows that the exchequer was diligent in recording its difficulties and knew precisely what the total to be accounted for should be. The uncertainty over whether amounts should be paid or pardoned had no bearing on the full totals for which the two sheriffs had to answer, totals already settled for these shires by 1156 or 1157.

To summarise the main points from this discussion of sheriffs' farms, we may picture an exchequer giving the highest priority to their regular render from virtually the whole of the country, but doing so in difficult circumstances. There was initial uncertainty over which manors should contribute as royal demesne, changes in the personnel of the shrievalty meant that not all arrears could be recovered, and some unfamiliarity with clerical procedures led to irregularities in the entering of accounts. Even so, there was clearly a model to follow in the recording of sheriffs' farms in the pipe rolls and the majority of the farms totals themselves appear to have been known to the exchequer from the outset of the reign. This reinforces the point made in chapter 2 that there had been continuity in procedure under Stephen, from whose reign an 'exactory roll' had almost certainly been handed down,[75] even if farms had actually been rendered from only a small part of the country.

Yet while the exchequer strove to balance its accounts, what measures were taken to safeguard the value of money paid into the treasury? During 1158, Henry II introduced a new coinage, pennies of the cross-and-crosslets ('Tealby') type bearing his own inscription, and seems to have used the occasion to install new moneyers in a reduced number of mints: several accounts for moneyers in the pipe rolls of 1158 and 1159 appear to cover payments by those leaving office. Before 1158, pennies of Stephen's type 7, produced at mints over most of England and generally considered to be the product of the currency reform agreed by Stephen and Henry as part of the peace settlement, would have circulated widely. After 1158, the new currency came instead to be 'alone received and

---

[74] For Marlborough, where Earl Patrick claimed to hold 18 librates 'blanch', see *PR3H*, 78; *PR4H*, 116; *PR5H*, 39, etc. The allowances persisted after Patrick's death in 1168 and were still being made – with the debts continuing to accumulate – in the next reign (e.g. *PR 2 Ric. I*, 118). The allowances for 25 librates in Benson (*PR4H*, 150; *PR5H*, 33–4; *PR6H*, 8, etc.) continued until *PR15H*, 83; arrears were pardoned to the sheriff of Oxfordshire two years later (*PR17H*, 132).

[75] *Dialogus*, 65, 125.

accepted in the kingdom' until a further recoinage in 1180.[76] Detailed procedures for the weighing and testing of these coins in order to protect the king's income were described in the *Dialogus*, but – despite references to fraudulent moneyers in the 1156 pipe roll[77] – there is room for debate over how quickly these processes were introduced.

The farms of Carlisle, Northumberland, Rutland, Shropshire and Sussex were accounted for *numero* – that is, 'by tale' or at the face value of the coins – throughout Henry II's reign. All the other shire farms were reckoned 'blanch' – that is, in blanched silver – most from 1155, the remainder from 1156, although those of Buckinghamshire–Bedfordshire, Kent, London, Norfolk–Suffolk, Nottinghamshire–Derbyshire and Warwickshire–Leicestershire included round sums *numero* which presumably had been added as increments. According to the *Dialogus*, all payments into the lower exchequer (the exchequer of receipt) were tested for weight. One of the knights of the chamberlains weighed a sample against the exchequer pound. If he had to put more than 20s. 6d. into the scale, the whole payment was rejected. There was, however, an additional process, known as the assay, for payments on account of 'blanch farm'. A sample 20 shillings was 'blanched' by melting in the furnace, and the ingot was then weighed against the exchequer pound, note being taken of the number of pence which had to be added to balance the scales. The same number of pennies was deducted from every other pound paid in by the sheriff on account of his farm, in order to obtain a 'blanch' equivalent. So for every sum entered in the pipe rolls as paid into the treasury 'blanch', the sheriff had had to add a 'combustion' of so many pennies per pound to cover the difference between the face value of the coins and their value in assayed silver.[78]

The *Dialogus* ascribes the introduction of the assay to Roger bishop of Salisbury, who after several years' experience at the exchequer was concerned about the standard of the coinage. However, the process was by no means fully established in 1130, when thirteen sheriffs' farms were accounted for by weight (*ad pensum*) and none was entirely reckoned 'blanch'.[79] Indeed, the mere recording of accounts as 'blanch' does not prove that payments had been subject to the assay: some of the items

---

[76] Diceto, I, 297; cf. Howden, I, 215 (although he misdates the recoinage to 1156); Nightingale, 'King's profit', 61–75; Amt, *Accession*, 128–32, with references 130, n. 97. The treasury accepted a payment by the sheriff of Devon in 'old money', alongside another one in 'new money', as late as 1164–65 (*PR11H*, 82). [77] *PR2H*, 4, 45.

[78] *Dialogus*, xxxvii–xli, 11, 36–43; cf. 9–10, where there is an interpolation suggesting that in Henry I's reign, and also in Henry II's, the sheriffs of Northumberland and Carlisle were allowed to pay in any good coin available. The pipe rolls confirm that the sheriffs of both accounted for their farms *numero*, not in blanched silver. See also Green, *Henry I*, 63 and n. 49; Amt, *Accession*, 129–30.

[79] Cf. the details on sheriffs' farms in appendix I.

entered as 'blanch' in the 1130 pipe roll have been shown to be sums on which a standard addition of a shilling in the pound was charged, a system described in the *Dialogus* as one of payments *ad scalam*.[80] If the assay had not had a long history under Henry I, and if we may safely assume that – amid the numismatic confusion of the civil war – it had lapsed under Stephen, we are bound to wonder how quickly it could have been reintroduced within Henry II's exchequer, despite the careful recording in the pipe rolls of sheriffs' farm accounts as 'blanch' from the beginning of the reign. The first direct evidence of the process in operation comes from 1163, when a schedule of combustions was attached to the chancellor's copy of the pipe roll for that year.[81] The schedule listed all the shires whose farms were accounted for 'blanch', with the extra sums which the sheriffs had paid, and it suggests considerable variation in the quality of coin paid in. The sheriff of Norfolk–Suffolk added only 10 pence to a sum of £7 19s. 8d. 'blanch' paid into the treasury, little more than a penny in the pound. On the other hand, his colleague in Essex–Hertfordshire was charged a combustion of £4 5s. 11d. on a sum paid into the treasury of £130 9s. 1d. 'blanch', equivalent to 8 pence in the pound. In Worcestershire, the combustion was about 4 pence in the pound, in Devon 5 pence. Similar schedules are to be found with either the pipe roll or the chancellor's roll in most subsequent years, and continue to show wide variations in the combustions paid: from 2 pence to 11 pence in the pound in 1165, for example, and from 4 pence to 19 pence in 1173.[82]

Such discrepancies are absent from Henry II's pipe rolls before 1163. Here, the relationship between sums 'blanch' and *numero* is remarkably stable at one shilling in the pound. In 1157, Richard de Lucy accounted for £40 10s. 10d. 'blanch' old farm of Essex; £40 10s. 10d. *numero* was allowed as the third penny to the earl, and 40s. 6d. paid into the treasury 'for combustion': a phrase which implies familiarity with the concept of the assay, but not necessarily with the practice.[83] In 1158, in an account of the old farm of East Meon (Hampshire), Richard du Hommet paid into the treasury 18s. 3d. *numero* 'for the blanching of £18 5s. 6d.' which he had paid *in soltis* (repayment of debt) to the *vicomtesse* of Rouen.[84] In the same year, Richard de Lucy accounted for the farm of Bray (Berkshire),

---

[80] *Dialogus*, 41–2; J. H. Round, *The Commune of London* (London, 1899), 85–93.
[81] PR9H, 74–5
[82] The 1165 schedule is in PR11H, 1–2. Ratios have been calculated by comparing recorded combustions with sums paid into the treasury in the relevant sheriffs' farms accounts, e.g. the Essex–Hertfordshire combustion of 1163 was 1,031 pence on a payment of just over £130, approximately 8 pence for every pound. For the 1173 ratios, see *Dialogus*, xl–xli, and on the chancellor's roll, *ibid.*, 17, 19 and PR8H, ix–x.
[83] PR3H, 72. A variation, equally contrived, occurs *ibid.*, 73, where in an account of £19 15s. 9d. 'blanch', Richard de Lucy is allowed £20 *numero* as the earl's third penny but pays in the odd 15s. 9d. for combustion.   [84] PR4H, 176.

paid in £33 *numero* for £30 'blanch' and was allowed a further £30 in gifts: a difference of £3, that is 60 shillings, on a total of £60. Twelve months later, the farm of Bray was entered as owing, but from 1160 onwards he was repeatedly shown as having received £60 *numero* in gifts but with 60 shillings paid into the treasury 'for blanching'.[85] The recurrence of the shilling-in-the-pound ratio has been taken to indicate the consistent fineness of the coinage in Henry II's early years as king,[86] but given the wide variations in combustions after 1163 this view is untenable. The explanation is surely that, despite the references to 'blanching' and 'combustion' in the pipe rolls, the exchequer was contenting itself in the early part of the reign with standard additional payments of the type otherwise described as *ad scalam*. The shilling-in-the-pound ratio was certainly applied without reference to the assay in the case of allowances out, as the *Dialogus de Scaccario* makes clear and as virtually all the instances in pipe rolls from 1156 onwards demonstrate: thus, in both 1156 and 1157, the sheriff of Northamptonshire was pronounced quit of the £15 'blanch' farm of the manor of Kingsthorpe through an allowance for expenses of £15 15s. *numero*, while in 1160 the sheriff of Berkshire was allowed £40 'blanch' from the farm of Faringdon for repaying £42 *numero* to the moneylender William Cade.[87] There is no reason why the formula could not also have been applied to payments into the treasury, in a period before the exchequer felt ready to reintroduce the assay: a process so complex that even Richard fitz Nigel confessed his lack of proper understanding. In the immediate aftermath of a civil war during which the coinage had been in chaos, it would also have been helpful to sheriffs to know the fixed amount to be added to every pound of 'blanch farm' paid in, rather than to have to face the uncertainties of the assay. But by 1163 the new coinage of 1158 would have been in wide circulation and it would have been appropriate to introduce measures to safeguard its quality. Moreover, 1163 does appear to have been a year of significant reform, when concerted efforts were made to improve the efficiency of the financial administration. Making no allowance for possible clerical error and taking the figures exactly as reported in the pipe rolls, we find that twenty-one out of the twenty-six new shire farms rendered in 1163 matched (to within one penny) what we may regard as 'standard totals', compared to only seven in the previous year. The king took a direct interest in the accounts, insisting that all renders for old sheriffs' farms,

---

[85] *PR4H*, 152; *PR5H*, 38; *PR6H*, 22; *PR7H*, 52, etc. Another interesting example is at *PR2H*, 56, where Earl Patrick is found discharging a debt of £3 12s. 3d. 'blanch' on the Wiltshire farm of 1153–4 by payment of £3 16s. od. *numero*; the difference of 3s. 9d. appears to be based upon the shilling-in-the-pound ratio, if the payment is treated as £3¾.

[86] Boussard, *Le Gouvernement*, 447–8 and 448, nn. 1, 2. [87] *PR2H*, 42; *PR3H*, 104; *PR6H*, 21.

and those for some other arrears, be made to him in person, possibly at an Easter session of the exchequer.[88] The first known combustion schedule appears, and in contrast to the consistent 'blanch'–*numero* ratio of previous years, it shows wide variations in the additional sums required. Although the evidence is circumstantial, it does suggest that this would have been the year of the reintroduction of the assay, at least in the form described in the *Dialogus*.

TAXATION

The subject of taxation poses its own problems of interpretation. There is no doubt that, with a relatively small income from fines and amercements, Henry II relied heavily on taxes during the first eleven years of the reign.[89] In that time, he raised two danegelds, three common assizes, a series of levies on knights' fees, and various aids (*auxilia*) and 'gifts' (*dona*) from boroughs. He also taxed the Jews, who are known to have paid *dona* in 1155–6 and 1158–9 and may have had to make several other contributions about which the pipe rolls are silent.[90] It is unlikely that the taxable capacity of the Jews had escaped the attention of Henry I, and he had certainly had recourse to all the other levies, but for much of his reign danegelds and borough aids had probably been annual taxes while the others had been occasional imposts. Henry II spread the burden, the increased emphasis upon tenants' obligations through assessments on knights' fees foreshadowing the importance placed upon this form of taxation in the last quarter of the twelfth century.[91]

[88] *PR9H*, 13–14, 21, 24, 28, 48, 51–2, 54–5, 61, 67–70. It is not certain that these accounts were handled at an exchequer (cf. Jolliffe, '*Camera Regis* under Henry II', 15–16) but the entries make no reference to the chamber and there is nothing in the king's known itinerary to prevent his attendance at Westminster at either Easter or Michaelmas 1163 (*Itinerary*, 61–4).

[89] Amt, *Accession*, 190–7; Ramsay, *Revenues*, I, 66–85. These figures may be compared with the data from the 1130 pipe roll in Green, *Henry I*, 220–5. Henry II's income from fines and amercements increased with the heightened activities of royal justices from 1163, but before then appears not to have exceeded £400 per annum, compared to about £6,000 in 1130. Taxation yielded just over £3,000 in 1130 but this figure was exceeded in 1156, 1159 and 1162. (All figures relate to sums paid in, plus allowances for advance expenditure, including those carried forward from previous years. For fines and amercements, all items in Green's table iii under Pleas and Agreements are counted and all in Amt's table 8 under pleas, murder fines and reliefs; for taxation, all in Green's table iii from cornage to *dona regis* and all in Amt's table 8 under danegeld, *auxilia/dona* and scutage.)

[90] On taxation of Jews, see *PR2H*, 8, 15, 36; *PR5H*, 3, 12, 17, 24, 28, 35, 46, 53, 65; Richardson, *Jewry*, 161–2. As for the levies on knights' fees, in addition to those discussed in the next paragraph there may have been one in 1156–7, most of the proceeds of which went to the chamber. The abbot of Abbotsbury (Somerset), besides paying 10s. owing from the previous year's *scutagium*, accounted for 2 silver marks 'de Exercitu Walie' (*PR3H*, 99). The 1157 pipe roll does not appear to have any other accounts of this levy, which must have been raised in connection with the campaign in North Wales in the summer of that year.

[91] Green, *Henry I*, esp. 69, 76; Keefe, *Feudal Assessments*, 191–201; Reynolds, *Fiefs and Vassals*, 362–6.

Among the levies upon knights' fees in this period, the term *scutagium* ('scutage') was applied to only two. The first, a levy of £1 on knights' fees held of abbots and bishops, came in 1155–6, a year when Henry had to campaign in Anjou against his brother Geoffrey.[92] The levies on fees for the Toulouse campaign of 1159 were entered as *dona*; on this occasion, the rate was two marks per fee, but several bishops and abbots, including abbots who did not owe knight-service, had to pay additional sums.[93] Two years later, there was a tax of one or two marks per knight's fee, for which accounts were entered 'de militibus'. Henry's manoeuvres in the Vexin[94] may have justified the levy, but it seems clear that he was prepared to raise taxes on knights' fees whether or not there was a major campaign to be undertaken. Accordingly, there was a further levy of one mark per fee – this time described as a scutage – in 1161–2, although certain shires were excluded.[95] In the following year, an *assisa militum* was imposed upon Staffordshire, Worcestershire, Gloucestershire and Herefordshire against the expenses of a brief campaign in south Wales.[96] In 1165, another expedition against the Welsh prompted the levy of a mark per knight's fee, commonly described as 'de Exercitu' or 'de Exercitu Walie'.[97] There seems no obvious reason, either in the rate charged or in the ostensible purpose of the levy, why one of these taxes on fees bore a different name from another. They all had the merit of being relatively simple to assess, and the king's enthusiasm for them seems evident from the tax three years later – occasioned by his daughter Matilda's marriage – which utilised the returns of knights' fees furnished in the *cartae baronum* of 1166.[98]

All the shires from which accounts were rendered were liable to the common assize or *donum comitatus* in 1156. All except Cambridgeshire, Dorset, Hertfordshire, Huntingdonshire, Norfolk and Suffolk contributed to a similar levy two years later. The *donum comitatus* allowed some

---

[92] JS, *Letters*, I, no. 13, p. 21, and generally on the scutages of Henry II's early reign, C. W. Hollister, 'The significance of scutage rates in eleventh and twelfth century England', *EHR*, 75 (1960), 577–88.

[93] E.g. St Albans (100 marks *donum*, plus 12 marks *donum* of knights); Peterborough (100 marks *donum*, plus £80 *donum* of knights); Gloucester (£80 *donum*); Ramsey (£10 *donum*); Thorney (20 marks *donum*); *PR5H*, 6, 17, 28, 46, 53. [94] RT, 210–11.

[95] None was collected from Carlisle, Gloucestershire, Oxfordshire, Shropshire or Staffordshire.

[96] *PR9H*, 9; £95 9s. 10d. was accounted for, of which £70 9s. 1d. had been spent on knights and sergeants in the army of Wales. Ramsay, *Revenues*, I, 81, took certain accounts, usually in marks, from ten shires in 1163 to represent a 'petty scutage', but these are interpreted in ch. 5, below, as amercements arising from visits by itinerant justices.

[97] E.g. *PR11H*, 7–8, 13–14, 33, 52, 61, 70, 79–80, 87–8, 92–3, 96–7. Several boroughs made similar payments, in the cases of Yarmouth, York and Northampton expressly 'de Exercitu' or 'de Exercitu Walie' (*ibid.*, 9, 49, 96). For the possibility of two levies on knights' fees in this year, see *ibid.*, 25, 52, 62, and Hollister, 'Significance of scutage rates', 580.

[98] *PR14H*, 3–4, 10–11, 13, 20–3, etc.

flexibility within the taxation system. Maitland first suggested that it was 'so constructed as to redress in a rude fashion the antiquated scheme of the danegeld' and pointed to the contrast between Wiltshire, which was heavily assessed to geld but paid comparatively little *donum*, and Kent and Devon where the reverse was the case. This did not of course apply everywhere: as Maitland's table shows, relatively poor shires such as Herefordshire, Worcestershire and Shropshire were lightly burdened by danegeld and *donum*, while richer Norfolk, Suffolk and Essex paid heavily to both.[99] But the *donum* allowed the exchequer to take some account of current regional conditions, and had the advantage of being straightforward to assess. Richard fitz Nigel explained that itinerant justices imposed a total sum on each shire, and it was then left to the landholders to apportion liability among themselves according to their holdings in hides.[100] The shire totals were normally in round numbers of marks – for example 70 in Oxfordshire, 80 in Nottinghamshire–Derbyshire in 1155–6, compared to 100 and 140 respectively two years later – although this was sometimes obscured in 1155–6 by the inclusion of accounts for *placita* and *murdrum*-fines. The levies may well be connected with the visits to several shires by the earl of Leicester, Becket the chancellor and Henry of Essex, evidently in 1155–6, and by Becket again in 1157–8, which are known from occasional accounts of *placita* against their names.[101] Yet it is clear from the pipe rolls that the usefulness of this tax was eroded by the number of exemptions granted. The *Dialogus* mentions quittance from the tax only for those who sat at the exchequer, who were exempt both on their demesnes and on fees held of them.[102] In practice, however, it was also pardoned to several religious houses and government officials, and far more of these pardons figured in the lists of 1158 than had done in 1156. As a result, in 1155–6, about a quarter of the total liability to *donum* was pardoned, in 1157–8 about two-fifths.[103] Exemption on this scale seems to have persuaded Henry II's exchequer to

---

[99] F. W. Maitland, *Domesday Book and Beyond* (Cambridge, 1897), 545–6; cf. Green, *Henry I*, 76.

[100] *Dialogus*, 47–8; see also J. Tait, 'Common assizes in the pipe rolls and Dialogus de Scaccario', *EHR*, 53 (1952), 669–75.

[101] *PR2H*, 17, 26, 31–2, 54, 57, 60–1, 65; *PR4H*, 114, 164. For examples of additional items obscuring the totals for the *donum* alone, see *PR2H*, 5 (Middlesex), 34 (Berkshire), 49 (Gloucestershire), 67 (Kent). [102] *Dialogus*, 48.

[103] My own calculations are that the total liability to the *donum comitatus* in both 1156 and 1158 was about £2,000. Of this, approximately £1,584 was paid (including *in soltis*), £497 pardoned in 1156; about £1,122 was paid, £782 pardoned in 1158. These figures differ somewhat from those in Amt, *Accession*, 192–3, but *dona* and *auxilia* are there treated together. The reduced income from the *donum comitatus* was characteristic of almost the whole country: Essex was the only shire to yield more revenue in 1158 (£50 9s.5d.) than in 1156 (£47 2s. 0d.) from the same total liability (200 silver marks). Among other shires, Yorkshire – assessed for 500 silver marks in both years – paid £308 13s. 4d. in 1156 but only £197 10s. 7d. in 1158, while Surrey paid exactly half its total liability of 80 silver marks in 1156, but a mere £9 from the same total in 1158.

abandon the tax as a major source of revenue. In 1155–6 it had been most useful as a means of discharging debts incurred in advance, and a few similar payments were made out of the 1157–8 collections.[104] But the only other occasion when a common assize was levied in the early years of the reign was in 1159–60, when it was paid by eight shires, chiefly in the west of England, again with heavy remissions. There is some correspondence with the shires which apparently received a judicial visitation from William fitz John about that time.[105]

Boroughs, besides contributing aids (*auxilia*) to accompany the danegelds of 1156 and 1162, rendered several arbitrary *dona* in this period. Many had to pay in 1159 and 1161, a few in 1158 or 1160. No individual borough, however, was called upon every year, and although the amounts of *dona* normally exceeded those for aids, most boroughs paid less under this system than they would have done under Henry I's practice of levying an annual aid. On the other hand, a few rich boroughs had to make massive contributions. London answered for *dona* of £1,043 in 1159 and 1,000 marks in 1161, compared with an *auxilium* of £120 in 1156. Norwich, assessed for *auxilium* at 50 marks in 1156 and at £30 in 1162, paid a total of about £800 in *dona* in 1158, 1159 and 1161. York contributed an aid of £40 in 1156, but the *dona* charged in 1158, 1159 and 1161 totalled over 1,000 marks and when danegeld was levied again in 1162 it had to pay not the customary aid but a further sum of £650.[106] It seems clear that the exchequer was using the *donum* imposed on boroughs in the same way as the common assize imposed on counties, freeing itself from old, unrealistic assessments to aid, in order to tap such urban wealth as it could. By contrast, Derby and Nottingham, pardoned half their jointly assessed *auxilium* of £15 as 'waste' in 1156, each paid only one *donum* of 10 and 20 silver marks respectively in the next five years, before

---

[104] *PR2H*, 7 (Norfolk), 10 (Suffolk), 12 (Surrey), 16 (Cambridgeshire), 18 (Essex), 20 (Hertfordshire), 23 (Buckinghamshire–Bedfordshire), 27 (Yorkshire), 34 (Berkshire), 38 (Oxfordshire), 46 (Leicestershire), 47 (Devon), 49 (Gloucestershire), 51 (Herefordshire), 63 (Worcestershire), 67 (Kent); cf. *PR4H*, 133 (Essex), 137 (Lincolnshire), 147 (Yorkshire), 182 (Sussex).

[105] The eight shires were Devon, Dorset, Herefordshire, Oxfordshire, Shropshire, Somerset, Staffordshire and Wiltshire (*PR6H*, 51–2, 41–2, 30, 9, 26, 58–9, 6–7, 18), plus Gloucestershire and Worcestershire where payment was postponed (*ibid.*, 29, 24). There are accounts of *placita* imposed by William fitz John under Devon, Gloucestershire, Herefordshire and Somerset, *ibid.*, 51, 59, 28, 31, although in the first two shires they had evidently arisen in the previous year (cf. *PR5H*, 27, 42); he seems also to have visited Yorkshire in 1158–9 (D. M. Stenton, *English Justice between the Norman Conquest and the Great Charter*, London, 1965, 69).

[106] Examples of *dona* in 1159 and 1161: Bedford 40 silver marks twice, Bridgnorth 10 and 5 silver marks, Cambridge £20 twice (*PR5H*, 19, 63, 53; *PR7H*, 12, 39, 45). In 1158: Carlisle £20, Newcastle 20 silver marks (*PR4H*, 119, 177). In 1160: Bridgnorth 12 silver marks, Hereford £20 (*PR6H*, 27, 30). London: *PR2H*, 4–5; *PR5H*, 2; *PR7H*, 18; *PR8H*, 67–8 (damaged). Norwich: *PR2H*, 8; *PR4H*, 129; *PR5H*, 12; *PR7H*, 4; *PR8H*, 65. York: *PR2H*, 27; *PR4H*, 147; *PR5H*, 31; *PR7H*, 37; *PR8H*, 51.

being charged another £15 aid in 1162. Rochester was allowed £3 6s. 8d. out of £10 as 'waste' in 1156, and was pardoned £5 out of £10 'for poverty' in 1162; it only had to answer for two £5 *dona* in the intervening period. The 'waste' at Winchcombe in 1156 was £4 8s. 0d. out of £5; no further levies were made until the aid of 1162.[107]

Among all Henry II's sources of revenue in the early years of his reign, most attention has been paid to the danegeld, largely because the items for 'waste' in the 1156 accounts have been scrutinised for evidence of conditions under Stephen. The association of danegeld entries for 'waste' with physical devastation in the civil war goes back to the early eighteenth century and was presented most systematically by H. W. C. Davis in his highly influential article of 1903: 'the figures for the danegeld in each shire give a test by which to compare the sufferings of the various shires'.[108] Although some doubt was subsequently expressed,[109] these arguments were not seriously challenged until the 1980s, when three scholars suggested (with varying degrees of emphasis) that administrative problems in the collection of danegeld would have been at least a partial explanation for sums being written off as 'waste'.[110] Since then, Davis's traditional interpretation has been defended by Emilie Amt: 'the waste entries should . . . be taken seriously as evidence for conditions during Stephen's reign, and for the scale of the economic problems – rather than administrative or political ones – faced by the government of Henry II'.[111] Amt's arguments have themselves been challenged in defence of the 'administrative' explanation,[112] and there is no reason to go over the ground in detail again. Here it is sufficient to draw some conclusions arising from the debate.

The first point to stress is that, whatever economic or administrative dislocation there may have been, the 1156 danegeld yielded almost as much revenue as that of 1130: £2,391 compared to £2,460 if all available

---

[107] Derby and Nottingham: *PR2H*, 39; *PR5H*, 52; *PR8H*, 33. Rochester: *PR2H*, 67; *PR5H*, 59; *PR7H*, 63; *PR8H*, 55. Winchcombe: *PR2H*, 50; *PR8H*, 61. On contributions made by the boroughs in this period, see S. K. Mitchell, *Taxation in Medieval England* (New Haven, 1951), 265–6 and esp. C. Stephenson, 'The aids of English boroughs', *EHR*, 34 (1919), 457–75, which includes a table showing that the assessments to aids in 1156 and 1162 were normally the same as in 1130.

[108] Madox, *History and Antiquities of the Exchequer*, 479–80; Davis, 'Anarchy of Stephen's reign'.

[109] Poole, *Domesday Book to Magna Carta*, 151–3; cf. K. R. Potter in *Hist. Nov.*, xxv, n. 1.

[110] J. A. Green, 'The last century of danegeld', *EHR*, 96 (1981), 241–58 (at 252); King, 'Anarchy of King Stephen's reign', 143–6; White, 'Were the Midlands "wasted"?'

[111] E. Amt, 'The meaning of waste in the early pipe rolls of Henry II', *Economic History Review*, 44 (1991), 240–8 (quotation at 248); Amt, *Accession*, 133–43. Support for this interpretation appears in e.g. Hollister, 'The aristocracy', 52–4, and Bradbury, *Stephen and Matilda*, 184, although here it is suggested that famine and pestilence, as well as warfare, may have been contributory factors.

[112] G. J. White, 'Damage and "waste" in Yorkshire and the north Midlands in the reign of Stephen', in Appleby and Dalton, eds., *Government, Religion and Society*, 63–76.

figures are counted, or £1,773 against £1,964 if calculations are restricted to shires which can be directly compared. The 1162 collection was more lucrative than either: £3,153 from all available totals or £2,185 from comparable shires.[113] This meant that danegeld was appreciably more beneficial to the treasury than any of the other taxes levied in the first eight years of the reign; for example, the *dona* (or 'assizes') collected from the shires brought in little more than £1,500 in 1156 and £1,100 in 1158,[114] while the various aids and scutages yielded considerably less. Danegeld was therefore well worth the trouble of collecting early in Henry II's reign, even if 24 per cent of the total liability was written off as 'waste'. What mattered most to the exchequer was not how much was pardoned or otherwise uncollected, but how much was actually brought in. Yorkshire managed to pay 75 per cent of its total danegeld in 1156, with only 7 per cent declared as 'waste', despite there being abundant chronicle and charter evidence of fighting and physical damage during the civil war.[115] Yet in the same year, Buckinghamshire and Bedfordshire, shires which had certainly seen some conflict but had not been at its heart, contributed only 38 per cent of their joint liability; the figure for 'waste' here was – at £107 14s. 3d. – the highest in the country and represented 34 per cent of the total due.[116] The crucial point here is not how much physical damage there had been in these regions, but how realistic the tax assessments were in current circumstances. Yorkshire was the biggest shire by area in the kingdom but was relatively lightly burdened by danegeld: its total liability of £165 9s. 5d. was close to the average for all shires, large and small. It therefore retained the means to contribute most of the danegeld due, despite the sufferings of the civil war. By contrast, Buckinghamshire and Bedfordshire had (together) the second highest danegeld liability in the country: it needed less damage here to make inroads into the capacity to pay.[117] To this extent, there is much to be said in favour of Amt's point that the allowances for 'waste' represented a recognition by the exchequer 'that the condition of the country, at least in some regions, would not bear the weight of all the taxes being demanded'.[118]

It must be acknowledged, however, that the administrative difficulties

---

[113] Figures are based on my own calculations, as in 'Were the Midlands "wasted"?', 43–4.

[114] Above, n. 103.

[115] Yorkshire's total liability to danegeld, according to the figures in the 1156 pipe roll, was £165 9s. 5d., of which £124 10s. 10d. was paid into the treasury and £11 1s. 8d. entered as 'waste' (*PR2H*, 27; White, 'Damage and "waste"', esp. 64–5; Dalton, *Conquest, Anarchy and Lordship*, 145–95). The figure for 'waste' excludes £2 for 'waste forest'.

[116] *PR2H*, 23; for fighting centred upon Bedford, mostly in the early and late stages of Stephen's reign, see *Gesta Steph.*, 46–50, 116, 184, 222, 234; HH, 710; JW, 45–6; OV, VI, 510.

[117] Totals are given in White, 'Were the Midlands "wasted"?', 45 and in Amt, *Accession*, 139.

[118] *Ibid.*, 141; cf. King, 'Economic development', 20.

faced by the exchequer in levying danegeld, especially in 1155–6, were formidable.[119] The tax had not been collected over the whole of the kingdom since 1139 at the latest and there seems little doubt that sheriffs, armed with outdated lists of hides and carucates, would have encountered a series of disputed tenures and contested claims to exemption. The last problem would have been exacerbated by the restrictive policy on the granting of official pardons, whereby several tenants-in-chief and religious houses, exempt in 1130, were now denied that privilege. It is true that in some cases of disputed liability accounts were postponed for further consideration, to be settled by payment or pardon in 1156–7, but this cannot be shown to have been generally applicable; indeed, several of the individuals treated in this way held other land which was dealt with differently. And the fact remains that many of the figures for 'waste' in the 1156 danegeld accounts are not of the same character as those elsewhere in the pipe rolls where remissions for poverty or damage are known to have been involved. In 1130, pardons for poverty had consistently been in round sums: £4 to two boroughs in Dorset, £5 to the burgesses of Hertford, both from the *auxilium*, and various amounts counted in silver marks or fractions thereof to individuals liable to *placita*. In 1156, the items for 'waste forest', which seemingly relate to physical damage, were in whole shillings: £1 16s. in Staffordshire, £2 in Yorkshire.[120] The same year's borough *auxilia* also carried remissions for 'waste' which were almost all in round figures, such as £6 (out of £12) at Cambridge, £3 (out of £5) at Hertford and £25 (out of £60) at Lincoln. All these sums read as if a central authority, the exchequer, had accepted a plea of poverty and had made an informed, but essentially arbitrary, decision on the amount to be written off, in pounds, shillings or marks. If economic dislocation had been the sole explanation for danegeld 'waste' in 1156, this is surely how the figures would have appeared. In fact, we have £77 16s. 7d. 'waste' in Berkshire, £38 12s. 1d. in Northamptonshire, £51 8s. 2d. in Leicestershire, £29 17s. 4d. in Hertfordshire, and so on. It is true that there are a few shires with fine round figures, notably Middlesex (£10) and Shropshire (£6), but the general impression is of sums which have resulted not from authoritative estimates of capacity to pay but from a concern to insert whatever was necessary to make up the account.[121]

[119] The arguments in this paragraph are set out more fully in White, 'Were the Midlands "wasted"?', and 'Damage and "waste"'.

[120] *PR 31 Hen. I*, 16, 18–19, 63; *PR2H*, 27, 30. On 'waste forest', see *Dialogus*, 60–1, where the reference appears to be to the destruction of woodland without grubbing up of stumps; this deprived the land of much of its value, since arable cultivation could not proceed.

[121] *PR2H*, 5, 16, 20, 27–8, 35, 41, 43, 45; full lists of remissions on *auxilium* and danegeld appear in White, 'Were the Midlands "wasted"?', 45–6. Amt, 'Meaning of waste', 244–5 and *Accession*, 137, criticises the suggestion made in my PhD thesis that sums for waste were inserted 'merely . . .

The position we are left with is that Henry II's exchequer, anxious to press on with a danegeld collection in 1155–6 despite the administrative problems which would inevitably arise, was prepared to exercise discretion in the handling of accounts. The total liabilities to danegeld were known for each shire – in most cases they were identical or close to those of 1130 – but the enforcement of payment from the individuals who were supposed to contribute to those totals was fraught with difficulty. Physical damage, economic distress, were undoubtedly among the reasons for sheriffs' failure to collect all that was due, especially in shires where the tax burden was relatively high, but there were a range of other factors as well. In some cases, disputed claims to exemption were dealt with by recourse to the items for 'owing', pending subsequent decisions, but there must have been so many unresolved issues arising from this levy that 'waste' became the most convenient means to close the accounts. Accordingly – in most shires' accounts if not in all – the figure needed to bridge the gap between what had been collected or could otherwise be formally accounted for, and what the total liability was known to be, was inserted under this heading. Richard fitz Nigel would no doubt have been disparaging had he written this up for the *Dialogus de Scaccario*, but in the circumstances of 1155–6 sheriffs and barons of the exchequer had accomplished all that could reasonably have been asked, in raising nearly as much danegeld as their predecessors had done in 1129–30.

CONCLUSION

Other items treated in Henry II's early pipe rolls require only brief discussion here. There were infrequent entries for fines and amercements down to 1162, the marked reduction in this source of revenue – in accounts for both current and previous years – representing a significant contrast between Henry II's early pipe rolls and that of 1130.[122] The sharp increase in these items apparent in the rolls of 1163 and 1165 – the result in part of the activities of justices in eyre – is discussed in the next chapter. The accounts of several sheriffs' farms were followed in the pipe rolls by those for cesses of woods[123] and for lands which had fallen to the king. The demesnes of Odo bishop of Bayeux were farmed throughout the

to fill up the account' ('The Restoration of Order in England, 1153–65', unpubl. PhD, University of Cambridge, 1974, 275). My phraseology might have been better, but this is essentially the position being defended here: I would contend that the sequence in which items are presented in the pipe rolls should not be taken to reflect the order in which sums were calculated. [122] Above, n. 89.

[123] *Dialogus*, 30–1, 103–4: e.g. Gloucestershire (forest of Dean), Oxfordshire (forest of Cornbury), Worcestershire (forests of Feckenham and Malvern).

reign, those of William Peverel of Nottingham from 1155–6.[124] Others –
entered as the lands of the earl of Chester, of Earl Ferrers, of Simon de
Beauchamp and of William fitz Alan [125] – were accounted for during the
minorities of heirs. A farm for the vacant bishopric of London was also
recorded for half the year ending at Michaelmas 1162 and Becket's exile
led to the appearance of accounts for the farm of the archbishopric of
Canterbury from 1165.[126] These were not, of course, the only lands
which passed to the king in this period. The profits of the vacant sees of
Exeter, Worcester and Coventry were believed in 1160 to have been
assigned to chancellor Becket;[127] he also had receipts from Eye, which
had escheated on the death of King Stephen's son William in 1159 but
was not accounted for at the exchequer until 1164.[128] This is further
testimony to the flexibility of the financial administration, and serves to
warn us again of the limitations of the pipe rolls as source material.

To summarise, it is clear that the first eight years of the reign were
important years of restoration, when most of the techniques in operation
at the exchequer at the end of Henry I's reign – in so far as they had lapsed
under Stephen – were revived. Mistakes by the scribes, notably the
occasional omission of the 'blanch' or *numero* qualification in the entries
of sheriffs' farms, hint at the shortcomings of an exchequer which now
had to grow accustomed to handling accounts from the kingdom as a
whole. Most of the sheriffs' farms totals were already established by 1156
or 1157, almost certainly by reference to information passed on from the
exchequers of Henry I and Stephen, but uncertainties persisted over
which manors should contribute to these farms, as royal demesne. Taxes
on knights' fees, and the arbitrary *dona* imposed on counties, boroughs
and Jews, provided important sources of revenue, but some reliance
continued to be placed on danegeld even though the exchequer's information was out of date and a host of exemptions could be claimed.
However, the exchequer was only part of a financial administration, the
ultimate purpose of which was to serve the political needs of the king, and
we know relatively little of the activities of his itinerant chamber.
Overall, it must be acknowledged that – despite the many irregularities highlighted in this chapter – Henry II was generally very
well served by his financial officials. Four different taxes were
levied in 1155–6 – danegeld, *auxilium, donum* and scutage; they
raised over £4,500 out of a total recorded income of some

---

[124] *RBE*, II, 648–9; *PR2H*, 40, 65; *PR3H*, 91, 102; *PR4H*, 154, 180; *PR5H*, 51–2, 58–9, etc.

[125] *PR2H*, 22; *PR4H*, 138, 186; *PR5H*, 22, 57, 63; *PR6H*, 7, 27, 39, 44;. *PR7H*, 29, 35, 39–40; *PR8H*,
15–16, 20–1; *PR9H*, 3–4, etc.

[126] *PR8H*, 73; *PR11H*, 108–9; *PR12H*, 114–15, etc.   [127] JS, *Letters*, I, no. 128, and p. 266, n. 1.

[128] *PR10H*, 34–5; cf. *PR9H*, 34, where Carham, a servant of the archbishop, is said to have paid £150
3s. 7d. into the treasury but to have made no account at the exchequer.

£13,000,[129] and if administrative problems with the most complicated tax, danegeld, had to be glossed over as 'waste', this was a small price to pay. The Toulouse campaign of 1159 prompted the levy of *dona*, mostly from boroughs and knights' fees, which raised about £8,000, nearly all paid in the first year of account.[130] In 1162, the second danegeld of the reign was collected without obvious administrative difficulty, and raised more than either of the other recorded levies in 1130 and 1156.[131]

Yet if the period 1155–62 represented a period of administrative recovery, the year 1163 was highly significant for the completion of the process. Obvious lapses in exchequer efficiency – significant scribal errors, major fluctuations in the totals for sheriffs' farms – became far less common after 1157, but they had continued none the less. In 1163, however, following his return from his lengthy sojourn in France, the king took personal cognisance of several accounts in arrears, there was greater standardisation in sheriff's farm totals, and a new precision became apparent in matters of clerical detail. From this year, also, we have the first clear evidence of the operation of the assay, through the survival of a combustion schedule. It is tempting to associate the improved efficiency with the arrival of the royal clerk Richard of Ilchester, for whom the king created a new seat at the exchequer between the president and the treasurer, and who kept his own record of proceedings: although he cannot be proved to have been in attendance before 1165, his appointment as archdeacon of Poitiers in 1163 may signal his promotion to become a baron of the exchequer.[132] Whatever the truth of this, it is clear that the advances of that year were subsequently maintained, as part of a general reform of the financial administration. At Woodstock in July 1163 the council debated Henry's proposal to add sheriff's aid to the royal revenues.[133] Evidently in the following year, 1164, there was a change in the king's borrowing policy, with more reliance on Jewish instead of Christian moneylenders.[134] In 1164 also came the general enquiry, apparently conducted by exchequer officials, which led to the first accounts of purprestures in 1165. These developments mark an important stage in the reign. The period had passed when Henry, preoccupied with military and diplomatic affairs, was obliged to leave the repair of the financial

---

[129] Amt, *Accession*, 192, 194 (the total income has been calculated by the addition of advance expenditure, £3,798, to receipts by treasury/chamber, £9,222; the total from taxation covers allowances *in soltis* in pipe roll accounts of the *donum comitatus*, as well as sums paid in as danegeld, *auxilia/dona* and scutage).   [130] *Ibid.*, 183, 194.

[131] White, 'Were the Midlands "wasted"?', 43–4.

[132] *Dialogus*, xxxiii–iv, 26–7; *PR11H*, 4; Duggan, 'Richard of Ilchester, royal servant and bishop'; Warren, *Henry II*, 311.

[133] *Becket Materials*, II, 373–4 (Edward Grim); IV, 23–4 ('Roger de Pontigny'); Green, 'Last century of danegeld', 255–8.

[134] Richardson, *Jewry*, 56–61; cf. for a detailed discussion of royal borrowing, Amt, *Accession*, 94–109.

machinery to others, and had to be content with the old sources of revenue. Now he was at liberty to devote considerable attention to the finances of the kingdom, and to devise new means of enhancing his income.

Some measure of what had been achieved by the king's financial officials in the first decade of the reign may be gleaned from the pipe roll of 1164–5, selected for scrutiny because it marks the end of the period covered in detail in this book.[135] In that year, the total recorded as paid into treasury or chamber (overwhelmingly the former) was a little over £17,000; to this should be added nearly £4,000 which was raised but repaid to those who had incurred advance expenditure on the king's behalf. The resultant total of £21,000 was the highest of the reign to date and was not far short of the £24,500 brought in for the king in 1129–30. To this extent, the task of restoring Henry II's financial position to that enjoyed by his grandfather could be said to have been accomplished with fair success. There was, however, a contrast in the proportions contributed by different sources of revenue. In 1130, farms and associated accounts had been responsible for 57 per cent of the total income, and fines, amercements and other profits of justice for 29 per cent, the remaining 14 per cent coming from taxes and various customary levies. In 1165, 61 per cent was raised from the farms category and 23 per cent from taxation; judicial and other payments contributed only 16 per cent. Even so, the last figure, which embraced a handful of reliefs but related mostly to *placita*, amercements and fines for the king's intervention in lawsuits, was in excess of £3,000 and represented a significant increase on the sums entered under these headings in earlier pipe rolls of the reign.[136] The growing importance of this category reflected the quickening pace of the king's judicial administration and it is to developments in this area that we now turn in the chapter which follows.

[135] Figures derived from the 1165 pipe roll appear in appendix II, with explanatory notes.

[136] For comparisons with other pipe rolls, see Green, *Henry I*, 225 (where amounts paid have been added to advance expenditure to give total receipts), Amt, *Accession*, 192–4 and Ramsay, *Revenues*, I, 64–86. For the purposes of calculation, Green's items for county farms, estates in hand, borough farms and forest revenues have been treated as farms and associated accounts; her sums for regalian rights have also been counted within this category, since these relate almost entirely to the vacant bishopric of Durham which was being farmed for the king at the time. My calculations from the 1165 pipe roll similarly treat the king's receipts from the archbishopric of Canterbury among the farms. Green's sums for cornage, danegeld, aids and *dona* have been counted as taxation, and all other items as fines and 'profits of justice', although some taxation is doubtless to be found among the miscellaneous and composite entries.

Chapter 5

THE ADMINISTRATION OF JUSTICE

INTRODUCTION

The early thirteenth-century story of Warin of Walcote, the 'honest itinerant knight' who fell into poverty after the death of Stephen because he could no longer rob as he had done,[1] may tell us more about later perceptions of the transition from one reign to another than about realities at the time, but the impression of changed circumstances is one borne out by contemporary observers. Henry of Huntingdon and the abbey chroniclers of Battle and Peterborough all claimed that the accession of Henry II brought an end to lawlessness and disorder.[2] Without a civil war, without a disputed succession to the throne, opportunities for violent self-help were much diminished: it was time for old disputes to be peaceably settled, or at least buried until the next conflagration. But if there was now a disposition to resolve conflicts by negotiation or litigation rather than by force, the task which faces historians in tracing the development of processes available for that purpose is by no means straightforward. The first decade of Henry II's reign has been placed by one respected commentator among 'the most obscure periods of English legal history'.[3] We have no legal treatises to bridge the gap between the *Leges Henrici Primi* and the *Tractatus de Legibus* which goes under the name of 'Glanvill'.[4] Henry II's early pipe rolls rarely give reasons for such fines and amercements as they recorded, so fail us in the search for clues to the nature and extent of judicial activity. Several chronicle accounts relate cases of immediate concern, but their stories must be read with an eye to bias, misunderstanding and omission. There are also references to the lawsuits of this period in contemporary royal writs and later *Curia Regis*

[1] *Rolls of the Justices in Eyre for Gloucs., Warwicks, [Salop]*, no. 390; Poole, *Domesday Book to Magna Carta*, 151–3.
[2] HH, 774–6; *Chronicle of Battle Abbey*, 212–13, 222–5; *ASC*, 202–3; cf. above, ch. 3, n. 7.
[3] P. A. Brand, 'New light on the Anstey case', *Essex Archaeology and History*, 16 (1983), 68–83 (at 68).
[4] *Leges Henrici Primi*, where a compilation date of 1116–18 is suggested, 34–7; *Tractatus*, apparently written between 1187 and 1189 (*ibid.*, xxx–xxxi).

Rolls, although the information they furnish can prompt more questions than answers. Yet if the evidence is difficult to interpret, it does at least survive in sufficient quantity to permit informed discussion.

In recent years, judicial developments prior to 1166 have attracted a good deal of attention from legal historians, but here the issues are approached primarily from a governmental perspective. The *Tractatus de Legibus* stressed at the outset how closely associated were a king's duties to maintain order and to uphold justice,[5] and in the aftermath of civil war it was obviously important that means were made available for the peaceable resolution of private disputes. But with so many competing priorities, there were bound to be limits to what could be accomplished through the direct involvement of the crown. Accordingly, this chapter will argue that, while demand for the king's intervention in lawsuits was buoyant from the outset of the reign, Henry's initial response was normally to encourage settlements which did not involve the royal courts: defined for present purposes as those conducted by himself or his justices. He looked instead to the traditional – especially seignorial – courts, albeit with frequent provision for a hearing before himself or his representatives in default of justice therein. Through issuing writs to initiate proceedings or to enforce their outcome, often with the sanction that cases might ultimately be removed to a royal court if not dealt with as he ordered, Henry was able to present himself as a 'lion of justice' in the tradition of his grandfather, without his courts becoming overburdened with business before they were ready to receive it. It should be stressed that shire courts and (unless in private hands) hundred courts were also customary elements in the provision of 'royal justice', and that early in Henry II's reign the former, especially, still played a significant role in civil litigation: but with hearings before sheriffs, often without accompanying royal justices, unless there was default. However, from 1163 – a year in which we have already seen important developments in financial administration – there are signs of a new approach, as efforts were made to ensure greater activity for the courts of the king and his justices. A concerted attempt to extend the scope of royal justice had begun.

DISPUTE AND SETTLEMENT WITHOUT RESORT TO THE KING

At the close of the war, religious houses faced a period of negotiation, and possible litigation, in order to recover their losses.[6] Some secured recom-

---

[5] *Ibid.,* 1–2.
[6] Cf. *Papsturkunden in England,* ed. Holtzmann, II, 272–3: a letter of Pope Adrian IV, dated 22 February 1156, ordering Nigel bishop of Ely to recover the possessions alienated from the see of Ely within three months on pain of suspension. Cf. above, ch. 3, n. 270.

pense for damage, others had alienated property restored.[7] Cases from the last years of Stephen's reign or the early part of Henry II's show the Church militant and triumphant in secular courts. Thus, Ranulf de Belmeis recognised in the shire court of Shropshire the right of the monks of Shrewsbury to the vill of Betton which he was holding unjustly; Geoffrey de Ivoi restored 'the land which in English is called Gare' (Oxfordshire) to the nuns of Godstow, after their right had been proved through a recognition of his hallmoot; Walchelin Maminot restored land in Leigh to Shrewsbury Abbey, after the men of Ellesmere had acknowledged before him and his knights – so in his honorial court – that his uncle William Peverel of Dover had taken the land unjustly.[8] The bases for some successful ecclesiastical claims were hardly secure. For example, Biddlesden Abbey (Buckinghamshire) was founded in 1147 by the earl of Leicester's steward Ernald de Bosco on land which a previous tenant Robert of Meppershall had forfeited to the earl for failure to do service. After a time, Robert of Meppershall intended to plead for the land, but the monks, advised by the earl of Leicester, bought him off and obtained his charter of confirmation for 10 marks.[9] Kirkstead Abbey was another to benefit from a disputed donation. In a charter dated 20 June 1158, Maurice de Craon announced the gift of 30 acres within his Lincolnshire lands in exchange for 25 which his kinsman William fitz Roger had claimed against him; but the 25 acres reclaimed by William were then given to the monks as his own alms, with the consent and in the presence of Maurice de Craon.[10] Another typical story is preserved in the Goxhill Leger, the fourteenth-century cartulary of the prominent Lincolnshire family. Peter of Goxhill had been disseised 'in time of dissension and war' by a knight, Josce, of part of his inheritance, and a messuage thereon had been sold to a canon of Lincoln. In time of peace, the canon acknowledged Peter's right and restored the messuage, whereupon Peter gave another in place of it, as his own alms.[11]

---

[7] On recompense for damage, see e.g. *Charters of Chester*, nos. 34, 115 (datable 1153); 'Staffordshire Chartulary, Series II', ed. R. W. Eyton, in *Staffs. Colls.*, II, 236 (early Henry II); R.A.Brown, 'Early charters of Sibton Abbey, Suffolk' in Barnes and Slade, *Medieval Miscellany*, 69–70 (datable 1161). On the restoration of alienated property, see e.g. *Historia et Cartularium Sancti Petri Gloucestriae*, II, no. 565, (dated 30 March 1154); *EYC*, II, nos. 880, 887–89 (1148x1166); *Cartulary of Darley*, II, 335–6 (before 1175); *Cartulary of Worcester*, nos. 212–13 (1148x63).

[8] *Lawsuits*, II, no. 387; I, nos. 332, 346.

[9] B. D. Hill, *English Cistercian Monasteries and their Patrons in the Twelfth Century* (Urbana, Illinois, 1968), 50–1; Crouch, *Beaumont Twins*, 80, 116, 204.

[10] B.L. Cotton MS.Vespasian E. xviii (Kirkstead Abbey cartulary), fos. 179–179v. The 25 acres claimed by William fitz Roger, and those he granted to the monks, lay in *Westcotemerse*. William fitz Roger's original charter has survived, and is printed as *Documents Illustrative of the Social and Economic History of the Danelaw*, ed. F. M. Stenton (British Academy, London, 1920), no. 157.

[11] Peterborough Dean and Chapter MS. 23, fos. 47v., 48. Peter of Goxhill founded Newhouse Abbey *c.*1143 and was sheriff of Lincolnshire from 1163 to 1166; he was dead by Michaelmas 1167

The Church emerges from all this as anything but the helpless victim of injustice, but – needless to add – it was not always so fortunate. Even when a settlement had been reached, there might be problems of enforcement: some time between 1152 and 1161 we find Archbishop Theobald, for example, instructing the bishops of London and Norwich to compel Richard de Calva and Geoffrey Tresgot to restore land in Norfolk to the abbot and monks of St Albans, land they were continuing to occupy despite their agreement before Theobald to vacate it.[12] Frequently, the agreements themselves – compromises as many twelfth-century settlements were – involved a short- or long-term loss of land. In Theobald's presence on 28 March 1155, Godfrey of South Malling renounced his claims in Patching and Wootton (Sussex) to Christ Church, Canterbury, but was allowed to retain Patching for life at an annual farm payable to the monks of £18.[13] Not later than 1167, in the presence of the dean of chapter of York, Jueta of Carlton released 'whatever right she had' ('quicquid juris habebat') in two bovates in Carlton (Yorkshire) to St Peter's, but they were restored to her for life at an annual rent of 3 shillings.[14] A charter of 1141x57 embodied an agreement whereby Robert de Montalt gave the church of St Mary, Bruera (Cheshire) to St Werburgh's Abbey, Chester; in return, the monks had to surrender their claim to the neighbouring vill of Lea-cum-Newbold, originally granted to them by Robert's cousin and predecessor William.[15] Late in Stephen's reign, or early in Henry II's, agreement was reached between Henry Tuschet and the canons of Darley, whereby Tuschet made grants, including 40 acres which the canons had previously bought from him and other land which they had already ditched and built upon; in return for this, the canons surrendered whatever his father had bequeathed to them, and abandoned their 'action' to secure the bequest. The charter suggests encroachment and harassment by Tuschet until the canons were driven to bargain.[16]

It is worth rehearsing these cases, all apparently belonging towards the

---

(*HKF*, II, 204; *PR10H*, 22; *PR11H*, 34; *PR12H*, 1; *PR13H*, 50; cf. above, ch. 3, n. 117). Other examples of religious houses benefiting from disputed donations during the war may be found in GF, *Letters*, 511 (Kingswood Abbey); Historical Manuscripts Commission *Tenth Report, Appendix, pt vi* (HMSO, London, 1887), 98–101; *Book of Seals*, p. 349 and nos. 507–8, 510, 512–13 (Bordesley Abbey).   [12] Saltman, *Theobald*, no. 20.   [13] *Ibid.*, 535–6.

[14] *EYC*, I, no. 159.

[15] Some years later, Robert's son Ralf made a further gift in recompense for offences by himself and his predecessors 'especially concerning Lea': *Chartulary or Register of the Abbey of St Werburgh Chester*, ed. J. Tait (Chetham Society, 1920–23), II, nos. 500, 527, with comment pp. 287–8.

[16] *Cartulary of Darley*, II, 499–500. Cf. the settlements, almost certainly involving compromise, between Fountains Abbey and the sons of Drogo the forester, and between Missenden Abbey and John Morel, finalised in the seignorial courts of Roger de Mowbray and Hugh de Bolbec respectively in the early years of Henry II's reign (*Lawsuits*, II, nos. 368, 391).

end of the civil war or soon after its close, most of them probably arising from episodes within it, because in none does Henry II, as duke or king, seem to have been closely involved. There are no extant royal writs ordering the restitution of land or initiating pleading thereon. None of the charters associated with the cases makes reference to such a writ. It is true that those who pleaded in shire courts were availing themselves of what had customarily been regarded as a forum for 'royal justice',[17] but otherwise this was litigation – or settlement without litigation – which ignored the crown: indeed, many of the agreements cannot be assigned for certain to one reign or the other, because the king and his justices were not called upon. Although the evidence is less abundant, it is clear that settlements between layman and layman might also be reached without recourse to the king at any stage. Roger de Mowbray's grant of ten knights' fees to Robert III de Stuteville, possibly in 1157, in order to settle their rival claims to the Mowbray barony, did not involve the crown until their descendants sought confirmation as part of a fresh agreement before King John in 1201.[18] It was in the shire court of Nottinghamshire–Derbyshire, in the presence of sheriff Ranulf (1155–65), that different branches of the d'Aincurt family resolved a dispute between them: Ralf fitz Roger d'Aincurt remitted his claim in Holmesfield (Derbyshire) while his lord Walter d'Aincurt and his son John reduced the service due from Ralf from four knights to three, the fourth having been in contention between them.[19] Sometime between 1158 and 1165, in the abbot of Reading's seignorial court, Roger of Letton recovered land at Hurstley (Herefordshire) formerly held by his grandfather; his tenure was to be for the same service as that rendered by the unsuccessful defendant Robert of Brobury.[20] The honorial court of Richmond, meeting at Boston, was the forum in which Nigel fitz Alexander recovered his father's holding in Fulbeck (Lincolnshire) from an intruder of Stephen's reign who was still in possession under Henry II.[21] And charters datable *c*.1162x66 refer to a case in which Ivo fitz Ulf deraigned land at Nettleham (Lincolnshire) against the heirs and wife of Godwin who had occupied it unjustly; the conclusion was reached in the seignorial court of Ivo's lord Robert II bishop of Lincoln.[22] There is no

---

[17] E.g. Stenton, *English Justice*, 79–82; Hudson, *English Common Law*, 34–7.
[18] *EYC*, IX, 1–6, 200–1 and no. 42; *Charters of Mowbray*, xxviii, 247; Holt, '1153', 303, 311.
[19] *Descriptive Catalogue of Derbyshire Charters*, ed. I. H. Jeayes (London, 1906), no. 1397.
[20] *Reading Abbey Cartularies*, I, no. 349 with notes p. 284.
[21] *Curia R. R.*, V, 181–2; *ibid.*, VI, 17–18; Holt, '1153', 303.
[22] *Reg. Ant.*, II, nos. 613–14; on the dates, cf. *ibid.*, VII, 203, n. 7. Two Derbyshire charters from early in Henry II's reign also show lords' courts securing vassals' family arrangements, without recourse to royal confirmations, although there is no reason to suppose formal litigation in these cases: *Cartulary of Darley*, II, 518–19; Stenton, *English Feudalism*, 51–3, 263–4; *Lawsuits*, II, no. 388.

mention in the accounts of any of these cases of Henry II sending an initiating writ or issuing a confirmatory charter.

Beyond this, a host of grievances went unredressed altogether, not least for the reason given by the monks of Pipewell in 1164: they were unable to go to court to recover a messuage and a few virgates of land on account of their poverty.[23] For example, lords conscious of dubious titles might seek to forestall impleading by enfeoffing vassals, adding provisions should rivals successfully press their claims.[24] Thus, about 1160 William Malbanc granted land in fee and inheritance to Hugh fitz Nicholas at Draycott, Cresswell, Newton and elsewhere in Nottinghamshire and Derbyshire, as three-quarters of a knight's fee; but if anyone deprived Hugh of his three carucates in Newton, he would keep the rest for the service of half a knight.[25] Elsewhere, there appear to have been accommodations to encroachments by vassals through the formal grant of land in return for service. Some time early in Henry's reign, Matthew of Benniworth made a grant in fee and inheritance to Richard of Halton, which included 18 acres of meadow in Halton Holgate (Lincolnshire) already enclosed by Richard.[26] The *carta* of Walter de Meduan in 1166, entered under Kent and listing several fractional and monetary new feoffments 'in the time of King Stephen . . . from which I have no service', may well indicate that he had enfeoffed those who had disseised him, only to find that they still failed to acknowledge the service due.[27]

Indeed, the *cartae baronum* provide ample evidence of discord between lords and their vassals: if 'many passages . . . sound like direct requests for help' from the king,[28] they also imply that, as yet, royal intervention had been either non-existent or ineffective. Reference to a dispute is not in itself proof that no court had met to settle the issue, but it does suggest the persistence of an unresolved conflict. Having already seen the variety of settlements achieved early in Henry II's reign without recourse to the king, we do well to remember that many disputes simmered on, suppressed as they might not have been during the civil war. Allegations of injustice, several blamed specifically upon the war, are heard in the *cartae baronum* from nearly every shire. The majority come from East Anglia and the West country, a fact which may serve as comment upon the efficacy of the judicial administration maintained by Stephen and the Angevin leaders even in those parts of the country where some governmental

---

[23] *Ibid.*, II, no. 422.
[24] On lords' obligation to offer vassals an exchange (*escambium*) in the event of loss, see Hyams, 'Warranty', esp. 465–6; Hudson, *Land, Law and Lordship*, 55–7.
[25] 'Staffordshire Chartulary, Series III', ed. G. Wrottesley, in *Staffs. Colls.*, III, 223–4.
[26] *Documents Illustrative of Danelaw*, no. 505; cf. no. 506 where Richard of Halton's son William quitclaims the land to Matthew of Benniworth.   [27] *RBE*, I, 196.
[28] Hudson, *Land, Law and Lordship*, 37.

continuity had been upheld.[29] Thus, in Devon, the abbot of Tavistock claimed that 'in tempore gwerrae' Richard of Coleville had 'extorted' one fee, Geoffrey of Leigh and William his son half a fee, of the demesnes restored to the church through the good offices of Henry I.[30] Under Wiltshire, the bishop of Salisbury reported that Walter Waleran was holding of him one fee in *Litelinge* but had failed to do half the service due upon it 'a tempore gwerrae'.[31] The bishops of Bath, Chichester, Ely, Exeter, Hereford, Norwich and Worcester,[32] the abbots of Abingdon, Cerne, St Edmunds, Glastonbury and Westminster,[33] all claimed to have been deprived of demesnes, or to be lords of fiefs on which service was being withheld, without expressly stating when the 'injustice' had begun. There was much confusion also among secular baronies, a recurring problem being that outlying fiefs had been lost. A Suffolk landholder, William Blund, complained that Gilbert his father had been disseised 'tempore Gwerrae' of five of his twelve fees, three of which (in Wiltshire) had passed to the king, the others to Earl Aubrey and Henry fitz Gerold.[34] Under Norfolk, Reginald earl of Cornwall was accused of having disseised Mabel de Bec 'tempore Gwerrae' of 30 librates in Cornwall.[35] The Essex baron William de Montfichet had allegedly lost one knight's fee in Farnham (Suffolk) during his minority 'in Gwerra', although in this case a plea had begun for its recovery from the current holder Roger *Anglicus*.[36]

Other disputes are known to have lingered on for decades, before eventually reaching a settlement in an honorial, shire or royal court. Some time after obtaining his Lincolnshire inheritance, about 1128, William de Roumare had granted to Robert *nepos comitisse* the land of Ivo and Colswain, Robert's uncles, for a quarter of a knight's fee, tenure confirmed by William II de Roumare in Henry II's reign. Robert, styling himself 'chamberlain of Pontefract', subenfeoffed William fitz Amfrey of Miningsby in the land, and it was not until after Ranulf III earl of Chester had succeeded to the Roumare honour of Bolingbroke (about 1198) that in a plea in the honorial court begun by writ of right, Alan of Hareby grandson of Ivo managed to recover the land from Robert the chamberlain his kinsman.[37] What appears to have happened is that – perhaps during a minority – the better right of the Hareby family to the inheritance of Ivo and Colswain had been passed over. Whatever the reasons for Alan of Hareby's delaying his plea until after the death of William III de Roumare, and seemingly until the very end of Robert the chamberlain's

---

[29] Above, ch. 2.   [30] *RBE*, I, 251.   [31] *Ibid.*, I, 237.
[32] *Ibid.*, I, 221–2, 200, 364, 249–50, 279, 392, 300.   [33] *Ibid.*, I, 306, 212, 394, 224, 188–9.
[34] *Ibid.*, I, 408–9.   [35] *Ibid.*, I, 401.   [36] *Ibid.*, I, 351; cf. above, ch. 3, n. 182.
[37] *Documents Illustrative of Danelaw*, nos. 507–11. Under the settlement, Robert surrendered the relevant charters to Alan; the tenant William of Miningsby agreed to quitclaim to Alan three of the seven bovates involved, retaining the rest to hold of him in fee and inheritance.

life, this is a striking demonstration of a grievance festering for fifty years or more.

Between 1170 and 1175, before William fitz Ralf sheriff of Nottinghamshire, Bernard abbot of Burton reached agreement with a tenant, Humphrey, over a rent of 8 shillings which had not been paid for the past thirteen years; it represented half the sum due to the abbot for tenure of Potlock (Derbyshire). Brought to plead on a royal writ, Humphrey acknowledged his default but claimed that he had been deprived of part of the vill, called 'the island', by the earl of Chester's officers at Repton since the beginning of Henry II's reign. The implication is that, although Ranulf II earl of Chester, close to death in 1153, had quitclaimed to the abbot of Burton the 'islands' of Willington and Potlock which his officers had occupied unjustly, at least part of Potlock had either been reclaimed or never restored, and that the wrong had gone unredressed for well over a decade.[38]

A final concord before the king's justices at Northampton on 7 July 1183[39] ended what appears to have been a dispute between Roger fitz William of Huntingfield and his kinsman and overlord Maurice de Craon, arising from the terms of an enfeoffment in Stephen's reign. According to charters of Maurice and his son Guy confirming the eventual settlement, Alan de Craon (father of Maurice) had granted to William fitz Roger (father of Roger of Huntingfield) the vill of Fishtoft, the fee of Frampton, and the services of Thomas of Moulton, Walter fitz Matfrid of Pinchbeck and Walter Maleg in Tytton.[40] No charter of Alan has been preserved, but three confirmations by King Stephen (in whose presence the enfeoffment was made) describe the gift as of 'land in Holland'.[41] Fishtoft, Frampton and the other portions were all in Holland, but they did not constitute the full Craon holding there, for they also held in Freiston and Whaplode.[42] It may be that the Huntingfields as feoffees had chosen to interpret the generalised reference to 'land in Holland' as including these additional portions, since there is a charter showing their tenure around Freiston in Henry II's reign.[43] However, under the terms of the 1183 concord, Roger fitz William duly quitclaimed Freiston and Whaplode in return for a reduction of service due from four knights to two and three-quarters.

All this must be taken into account when considering the role of royal

---

[38] 'Burton Chartulary', ed. G. Wrottesley, in *Staffs. Colls.*, v pt i, 39–40, 48; *Charters of Chester*, no. 115. For William fitz Ralf's shrievalty, see *PR16H*, 80; *PR21H*, 29; cf. *PR22H*, 86.

[39] *Final Concords of the County of Lincoln*, II, ed. C. W. Foster (Lincoln Record Society, 1920), 307–8.

[40] Lincolnshire Archives Office, 3 Ancaster 2/1 (Huntingfield cartulary), fos. 5–5v.

[41] *RRAN*, III, nos. 412–14.

[42] *Lincolnshire Domesday and Lindsey Survey*, ed. C. W. Foster and T. Longley (Lincoln Record Society, 1924), 179–85.   [43] *Documents Illustrative of Danelaw*, no. 157.

justice during Henry II's early years as king. These were years when religious communities were busy negotiating, in and out of court, for the restoration of property, but in several cases the crown apparently did not intervene. Disputes between lay landholders might also be resolved, normally in seignorial courts, without any reference to the crown, or might linger on for decades without coming to a settlement. Nor, in his early years as king, was Henry inclined to challenge the jurisdiction of ecclesiastical courts.[44] He sometimes issued licences before appeals were made to the pope, but the period of indecision between Victor IV and Alexander III in 1159 seems to have been the only time that he actively prevented them.[45] It is clear from the correspondence of Archbishop Theobald and of Gilbert Foliot as bishop of Hereford that cases of advowson and presentation to churches were heard by ecclesiastical courts, and that the Church asserted its jurisdiction over criminous clerks.[46] At the end of his life, Stephen clearly felt sufficiently secure to hear the charge of poisoning against Osbert archdeacon of York and had fixed 13 January 1155 as the date for the trial in his court; it was the new king Henry who, albeit most reluctantly, allowed jurisdiction to pass to the archbishop of Canterbury.[47] Far from upholding his own claims to do justice, Henry was prepared to concede that a favoured religious house need not be impleaded concerning its tenants outside its own seignorial court.[48] This readiness to leave traditional courts to settle matters themselves needs to be stressed. Although a good deal of evidence can be found to show the king's intervention in lawsuits, we do well to remember that there were also many cases which passed him by.

THE KING AND HIS JUSTICES: 1154–62

John Hudson has suggested that the promise in the 1153 peace treaty to restore the disinherited 'may well have encouraged unprecedented royal participation in land cases' including a demand for writs initiating pleading, once Henry II had come to the throne. Tenants' complaints against their lords would have been a particularly vigorous source of pressure upon the king and his advisers.[49] Demand for royal intervention there

---

[44] E.g. M. G. Cheney, 'The compromise of Avranches of 1172 and the spread of canon law in England', *EHR*, 56 (1941), 177–97; Saltman, *Theobald*, 153–64; Richardson and Sayles, *Governance*, 285–320; Warren, *Henry II*, 427–46.

[45] Saltman, *Theobald*, 543; Warren, *Henry II*, 438, 445–6; cf. JS, *Letters*, I, no. 116.

[46] *Ibid.*, I, nos. 2, 57, 78, 80, 89, 102, and cf. for the case of Osbert archdeacon of York (below, n. 47) nos. 16, 18, 25, 26, with comment pp. 261–2; GF, *Letters*, no. 117.

[47] Saltman, *Theobald*, 124–5; Richardson and Sayles, *Governance*, 288, 291–2.

[48] *Acta*, no. 187, for the canons of Holy Trinity, Aldgate (1155x62).

[49] Hudson, *Land, Law and Lordship*, 255; cf. Hyams, 'Warranty', 476–7.

certainly was, but it has been said often enough in the foregoing pages that for the first eight years of the reign – until his return to England in January 1163 – Henry had major political preoccupations which were bound to take precedence over the personal hearing of lawsuits or the devising of new arrangements for their delegation to others. The king – in person or through his justices – continued to hear some crown pleas, cases where his rights had been infringed and suits between tenants-in-chief or those who held of different lords. He also intervened when he chose to in any other cases of interest and might issue prohibitions on impleading except before himself or his justices. All this had been familiar under Henry I, had been maintained as far as possible by Stephen,[50] and remained common practice through Henry II's early years as king. Accordingly, several religious houses received royal writs soon after his accession forbidding that they be impleaded except in the king's court or by his order.[51] The monks of Furness, Malmesbury, Ramsey, Kirkstall, and St Evroult were among those who resolved disputes with tenants or local landholders in the presence of the king.[52] That notorious brigand Warin of Walcote was duly brought before the king at Northampton, where Henry 'that he might set an example to others to keep his peace, by the counsel of his barons' condemned him to the pillory where he died.[53] But all this was time consuming and some of the stories surrounding the king's dispensation of justice betray a hectic royal programme. The abbot of Battle's case against the bishop of Chichester came before Henry in 1157, as it had previously come before Stephen. The parties were summoned to St Edmunds at Whitsun, only for the king 'occupied with other affairs', to fix another day at Colchester. As a heated debate developed on the first day of pleading, the king intervened to cut it short and 'strode out to settle other business'.[54] Another of Battle's *causes célèbres*, the dispute with Gilbert de Balliol over land in Barnhorn (Sussex), which had originated in Henry I's reign, only reached Henry II at Clarendon – probably in the summer of 1158 – after persistent application by the

---

[50] Green, *Henry I*, 102–17; Hudson, *Land, Law and Lordship*, esp. 36–9, 133–9; White, 'Continuity', 119–21, 131–2, and above, ch. 2.

[51] *Royal Writs*, 216, n. 4; 217, n. 1 (several attributable to 1155x58); cf. *ibid.*, nos. 168–75, and *Acta*, nos. 152, 187, prohibitions of Henry II's early years on impleading in any court, but with reference to specific issues. The citizens of York paid 40 silver marks in 1156–7 that they be not impleaded outside their shire until the king should come: *PR3H*, 86.

[52] Furness, Malmesbury, Ramsey: *Lawsuits*, II, nos. 364, 382, 385. Kirkstall: 'Fundacio Abbathie de Kyrkestall', in *Thoresby Society: Miscellanea*, II (Thoresby Society, 1895), 173–80; *Coucher Book of the Cistercian Abbey of Kirkstall*, ed. W. T. Lancaster and W. P. Baildon (Thoresby Soc., 1904), no. 266. St Evroult: P.R.O. C52/21, formerly Cartae Antiquae Roll W, memb. 1, no. 5 (cf. *Itinerary*, 3). For lawsuits involving French religious houses, also settled before Henry early in his reign, see e.g. *RAH*, I, nos. 72, 129, 160.　[53] Above, n. 1; Hudson, *English Common Law*, 121, 139.

[54] *Lawsuits*, II, no. 360 (quotations pp. 310, 312); *Chronicle of Battle Abbey*, 174–208.

abbot. Although the house was a royal foundation and the abbot had excellent connections as brother of the chief justiciar Richard de Lucy, Henry's initial response was to order the case to be heard in the honorial court of John count of Eu, with the sheriff of Sussex named in the *nisi feceris* clause. None of this brought Gilbert to justice, but the abbot 'kept petitioning the king, both personally and through his friends' and despite the frustration of Henry's crossing and recrossing of the Channel 'at length got the case transferred to the royal court' where he was success-ful.[55] It was symptomatic of Henry's difficulties in finding time to attend to judicial business in person that, having summoned Archbishop Theobald to answer for a false sentence in a case involving the dean of Scarborough – again in the summer of 1158 – he was unable to proceed because the death of his brother Geoffrey called him overseas.[56]

If it was difficult to obtain a hearing before the peripatetic king, there was nevertheless considerable expectation that he would become in-volved in other ways. The demand for royal writs to expedite or enforce the settlement of disputes had certainly increased during Henry I's later years and had persisted under Stephen especially in the east and south-east of the country; the provision of a *nisi feceris* clause, so that the matter could be transferred to a sheriff or royal justice if the addressee failed to obey, had been fairly common but by no means the invariable practice.[57] Henry II faced similar pressure from the beginning of his reign, either to order a settlement or to confirm its terms. For example, those successful in pleadings held in shire,[58] hundred,[59] wapentake,[60] seignorial[61] and episco-pal courts,[62] even in the court of papal judges delegate,[63] obtained royal writs ordering that the judicial decisions be upheld; again, a *nisi feceris* clause was often added to provide for action by a royal justice if the writs were disobeyed.[64] One of these cases came to court on the strength of a royal writ,[65] but the others appear not to have done so, the king's first known intervention being his subsequent enforcement of the outcome.

Where the king was called upon not to enforce but to initiate the resolution of a civil dispute, and chose to do so, there were various formulae which might be employed in the ensuing writ. His normal response was to give an opportunity for there to be a local hearing before

---

[55] *Lawsuits*, II, no. 377 (quotations p. 338); *Chronicle of Battle Abbey*, 210–18.

[56] *Lawsuits*, II, no. 371.

[57] Above, n. 50. For examples of Henry I's and Stephen's writs which include a *nisi feceris* clause (or equivalent), see *Royal Writs*, nos. 12, 13, 33, 36–8, 40–3, 46, 80, 83, 86, 88, 107, 188, 191, 192. But these are interspersed in the collection with others of similar date and purpose which do not carry the clause.

[58] *Lawsuits*, II, nos. 352, 357, 370, 375b, 398.   [59] *Ibid.*, II, nos. 358, 372.

[60] *Ibid.*, II, no. 369.   [61] *Ibid.*, II, no. 373.   [62] *Ibid.*, II, nos. 383a, 383b.

[63] *Ibid.*, II, no. 402c.   [64] For the *nisi feceris* clause, see *ibid.*, II, nos. 358, 370, 383a, 383b, 398, 402c.

[65] *Ibid.*, II, no. 375a.

the appropriate lord or sheriff, although reference to the hearing is not always obvious. In 1155, for example, he commanded the sheriff of Lincolnshire to reseise the abbot of Ramsey of his land at Threckingham; sometime between 1155 and 1157 he ordered the sheriff of Norfolk to see that the abbot of St Benet's, Holme, held his land at Ranworth as on the day when Henry I was alive and dead; not later than 1158, he instructed Hamo Peche, Geoffrey of Watervill and Hugh of Dover to restore to the abbot and monks of Shrewsbury the land at Crugleton given by Hamo Peverel to whom they were heirs.[66] All these writs qualified the executive order with the word 'juste', and it was this which served as the invitation for a preliminary local hearing, to determine the justice of what was being commanded.[67] Moreover, like several of the writs already discussed, they included a *nisi feceris* clause providing for the king's justice to carry out the order if the addressee did not, but he was only to become involved in the event of such a default. Other royal writs were couched in terms which made preliminary hearings more explicit. Ralf de Hauvill and his wife were ordered justly to reseise the monks of Colchester if they had been unjustly and without judgment disseised of land at Takeley, otherwise (*nisi feceritis*) the sheriff of Essex would.[68] Geoffrey de Belfago was instructed to reseise the monks of Belvoir if they had been disseised unjustly and without judgment of a virgate at Horton (Gloucestershire), and Hugh (Bigod) earl of Norfolk was told to reseise them rightly if they had been disseised unjustly and without judgment of certain lands in Suffolk; both writs added *nisi feceris* clauses to the effect that a king's justice would step in if the addressees failed to comply.[69] All three writs cited here probably belong to the early years of Henry II's reign, although none can be dated with conviction. All three imply that the recipient had the opportunity to hold a plea in his court so as to determine the facts, and that the beneficiaries could then apply to a royal justice or sheriff in default of justice there. Alternative formulae open to the chancery ordered local hearings in even less ambiguous terms. By 1158 at the latest, the king ordered his justice and sheriff of Kent that if the nuns of Malling could

---

[66] *Royal Writs*, no. 90; *Lawsuits*, II, no. 366; B.L. Add. MS. 30311 (transcript of Shrewsbury Abbey cartulary), fo. 43: date of 1155x58 based on attestation by chancellor at Brampton, and on Geoffrey of Watervill's death in 1162 (cf. *Baronies*, 19).

[67] Cf. *Royal Writs*, 274–5; Biancalana, 'For want of justice', 443–4 and nn. 31–3; Hudson, *Land, Law and Lordship*, 133–4.

[68] *Cartularium Monasterii Sancti Johannis de Colecestria*, ed. S. A. Moore (Roxburgh Club, London, 1897), I, 42; Henry II is thought to have visited Worcester in 1158, 1179 and 1184, and possibly also in 1155 (*Itinerary*, 35, 229, 256, 11).

[69] 'Belvoir Chartulary', ed. J. H. Round, in *Historical Manuscripts Commission Report on MSS. of His Grace the Duke of Rutland*, IV (HMSO, London, 1905), 151, 158; in the cartulary copy, both writs were witnessed solely by Earl Reginald [of Cornwall: d. 1175] at Nottingham, so dating evidence is slight.

show by the testimony of lawful men that they had bought their land in Thorne in the time of Henry I, they should hold it in peace, so that he heard no further complaint thereon for lack of full right: a writ known to have led to a sworn recognition in favour of the nuns in the shire court of Kent.[70] Not later than 1162, he commanded his justices and sheriffs of Lincolnshire and Nottinghamshire to hold a sworn recognition into the customary jurisdiction of the bishops of Lincoln over illegal hunting in their warren.[71] And – apparently in 1158 – he sent a writ to John count of Eu instructing him to do full right to the abbot of Battle over his land at Barnhorn, otherwise the sheriff of Sussex would do so, in terms analogous to those of the writ of right as set out in the *Tractatus de Legibus*.[72]

The royal chancery of the late 1150s and early 1160s, like its predecessors under Henry I and Stephen, still lacked standardised wording for these writs,[73] but the key point is that there were many precedents from the two previous reigns for royal intervention to order the resolution of civil disputes before lords or sheriffs, and also for the use of the *nisi feceris* clause for reinforcement.[74] It is hard to believe that when he responded to plaintiffs' demands early in his reign for an expedition of justice on their behalf, Henry II saw himself as doing other than meeting the customary obligations upon a king, obligations duly undertaken by Stephen and – especially – by Henry I, the grandfather whose good times he had promised in his coronation charter to restore.[75] It is fair to say that the inclusion of a *nisi feceris* clause in judicial writs early in Henry II's reign seems to have been more consistent than hitherto, although still not to be found in every case.[76] Many of these clauses cited a royal justice either instead of, or in addition to, a sheriff; in this way, the king's direct involvement, through his justices, was increasingly envisaged. But – at this stage – such involvement was normally treated only as the 'back up', to be called upon in the event of failure elsewhere.

It is worth reiterating that in the first eight years of Henry II's reign – when he spent less than one-third of his time in England – the king's obligations to do justice were by no means easy to fulfil. Despite the pressure for his intervention, he was obviously far too busy to give ear to more than a tiny fraction of the litigation in person, and the routine

---

[70] *Lawsuits*, II, no. 375.   [71] *Ibid.*, II, no. 399.

[72] *Chronicle of Battle Abbey*, 212; *Lawsuits*, II, no. 377; *Tractatus*, 138.

[73] E.g. *Royal Writs*, nos. 3, 4, 7, 9, 10, 12–20, 36–8, 43, 44a, 47a, 48.

[74] Green, *Henry I*, 102–5; Biancalana, 'For want of justice', esp. 443–8; White, 'Continuity', 120–1; Hudson, *Land, Law and Lordship*, 131–9.   [75] *Select Charters*, 158.

[76] For examples of judicial writs early in Henry II's reign which lack a *nisi feceris* clause, see *Royal Writs*, nos. 47, 47a, 91, 115–17, 152, 154, 168, 170, 172, 195. *Ibid.*, nos. 92, 97, 121, 173 are early Henrician writs which cite the sheriff, not a royal justice, in this clause. There is a good discussion of the citation of sheriffs and justices in *nisi feceris* clauses in Boorman, 'Sheriffs . . . Litigation', 181–91.

deployment of royal justices to act on his behalf could not be achieved without a good deal of care and attention to their appointment and terms of reference. As discussed below, itinerant and local justices certainly figured in Henry II's early years as king, but scarcely in a systematic fashion. In these circumstances, seignorial courts – or in appropriate cases ecclesiastical, shire or hundred courts – frequently offered the best prospects for the peaceful resolution of disputes, until the king had the opportunity to turn his attention to the administration of justice in a more consistent manner. That opportunity was to come in the years immediately following his return to England in January 1163, but until then the king's interventions in lawsuits were primarily concerned to encourage their settlement in traditional courts: through initiating writs, through threats of transfer to his justices but only in cases of default, through subsequent enforcement of their decisions, and sometimes through legislation on their procedures. Henry's active interest in judicial affairs was apparent from the earliest years of the reign, but initially that concern had of necessity to be expressed largely outside the courts of the king and his justices.

We are often left with the impression that the young king, preoccupied with more pressing matters, was singularly reluctant to become personally involved in the resolution of civil disputes. One illustration of this is the case between the abbot of Abingdon and Turstin fitz Simon. Near the end of his reign, Stephen had responded to Turstin's complaint that he had been disseised by the abbot of a church and certain land in Berkshire by ordering first the abbot and then the sheriff to deal with the case; it was as a result of the hearing before the sheriff – 'depraved by love of money . . . and unjustly' in the abbey chronicler's version of events – that Turstin had been granted seisin of the property he sought. On Stephen's death, the monks took the issue to Henry II, but his initial reaction was not to treat the shire court's decision as a 'default of justice' which justified his taking over the case. Instead, he ordered a fresh hearing in the shire court. This evidently produced no result, because he ordered another one. Only after Turstin had avoided the shire court for over two years was the case eventually brought before royal justices, and settled to the Church's satisfaction, following a further approach by the abbot to the king.[77]

Another dispute which seems significant in this connection was that between Arnulf fitz Peter and the nuns of Stixwould, which dates probably to 1158. Henry II twice ordered this case to be settled in the seignorial court of Hugh earl of Chester and of his mother Countess

---

[77] *Lawsuits*, II, no. 363; cf. below, n. 141.

Matilda, even though the point at issue was the verdict reached by a royal court in the time of Henry I. There appears to have been no eagerness on the king's part to claim the jurisdiction which his grandfather had evidently exercised: 'my justice' figured only as a back up in the *nisi feceritis* clauses of the two writs. Even so, jurisdiction did eventually pass from the earl of Chester's court, for it was to the justice, sheriff and other officials of Lincolnshire that William de Roumare, the earl's uncle, later addressed his decisive testimony against Arnulf.[78]

Both these cases were resolved after initial delays, but some of Henry II's early interventions in judicial affairs might have little more effect than Stephen's. A prolonged dispute between the abbot of Burton and the family of Nicholas of Stafford over land at Cotes (Derbyshire), granted to Nicholas in the time of William Rufus by an abbot subsequently deposed, had brought from Henry I two writs, one ordering that Nicholas should plead in the sheriff's court, the other that he do so in the king's court; in both cases, the abbot was to have the land if Nicholas failed to appear. From King Stephen had come a writ addressed generally, ordering that the abbot should have Cotes in peace without molestation from Stephen de Beauchamp – successor to Nicholas – or anyone else. This had evidently made little impact, for Henry II is found addressing Robert de Perer, sheriff of Nottinghamshire and Derbyshire for the year ending Michaelmas 1155, ordering him justly to reseise the abbot and monks of Cotes, or else (*si non feceris*) the king's justice would. This in turn seems to have been ignored, for Henry also sent a writ to an unnamed sheriff of Nottinghamshire, directing him to do full right to the abbot of Burton as his other writ had ordered; again, the king's justice would do it, if he failed. What was the immediate outcome of Henry's writs we do not know, but abbot Bernard (1160–75) eventually moved a plea over Cotes in the king's court. The suit was continued by abbot Roger (1178–82), who secured from the dying Stephen de Beauchamp a quitclaim of Cotes 'quam injuste occupavi'.[79] In this case, the writs early in the reign addressed to the sheriffs may or may not have led to a temporary compromise, but they had certainly not settled the issue; nor is there any sign that the *nisi feceris* clauses had brought a royal justice into play. It was only when the matter was taken directly to the king's court, apparently in the 1170s, that a firm decision was reached.

In Staffordshire – probably in the reign of Henry I – William of Ridware, who evidently took his name from a virgate of land there held in 1086 by one Walter of Roger de Montgomery, acquired land in Edingale and by marriage another part of Ridware. King Stephen issued a

---

[78] *Ibid.*, II, no. 376.
[79] *Ibid.*, II, no. 517; *RRAN*, III, no. 136; *RBE*, II, 653; 'Burton Chartulary', 8–10.

writ ordering that he hold his land in Edingale and be justly reseised in it if he was unjustly disseised; Robert of Stafford confirmed his possession of the additional portion of Ridware in 1157x66. For his part, Henry II ordered the sheriff of Staffordshire that William should hold his land in Ridware well and in peace, and not be unjustly put in pleas or have new customs laid upon him; the writ was probably issued in response to the one mark on 'his land' for which William of Ridware is found accounting under Staffordshire in 1156. The wording of both royal writs, that of Stephen concerning Edingale, that of Henry II concerning Ridware, imply that William's tenure was insecure. Neither, as it turned out, ensured his right to hold the lands in the long term, for he was subsequently obliged to defend his claims to Ridware in Robert of Stafford's seignorial court and a later royal writ confirming him in the lands, datable 1166x74, shows that he had had to plead on them before the king's itinerant justices at Lichfield.[80]

In the last two cases, over Cotes and Ridware, the accession of Henry II appears to have had no immediate impact upon the efficacy of royal justice. Even the celebrated Anstey case, known in more detail than any other of the mid-twelfth century, demonstrates continuing frustration and delay, despite repeated attempts to involve the king. Maitland was impressed by the application to Henry at each routine stage: 'royal justice is still very royal indeed; though the king has left his justiciar in England, there is no one here who can issue what we might have supposed to be ordinary writs'. Professor van Caenegem included it among a list of cases showing the 'total control by the crown of the whole system of courts . . . the king opened and shut the gates to justice as he wished'.[81] Yet the attention Henry gave to this case was both haphazard and expensive. While it lingered in the archbishop of Canterbury's court, he issued writs in favour of both sides. He had to be followed to Toulouse, without any guarantee that he would give the suitor a hearing. Richard of Anstey's expenditure included a bribe to a royal servant to bring the case to Henry's notice, and even then a series of distractions delayed its eventual resolution in the presence of the king.[82] The case may be compared with that between the abbot of St Albans and Robert de Valognes over the wood of Northaw (Hertfordshire). Both parties approached Henry at Toulouse in 1159, and the abbot subsequently paid him a personal visit in Normandy. After initially issuing a writ protecting Robert's seisin, the king was reluctant to reopen the case, but eventually did so in return for

---

[80] *Lawsuits*, II, no. 459; 'Rydeware Chartulary', ed. G. Wrottesley, in *Staffs. Colls.*, XVI, 230–8, 274, 277–8, 280; 'Staffordshire Chartulary Series II', 240–4; *PR2H*, 29.

[81] F. Pollock and F. W. Maitland, *History of English Law before the Time of Edward I* (2nd edn, Cambridge, 1898), I, 159; *Royal Writs*, 221, 223.

[82] Barnes, 'Anstey case'; *Lawsuits*, II, no. 408; cf. above, n. 3.

the promise of £100; it was his writ to Robert earl of Leicester as chief justiciar, ordering that he determine proprietary right to the wood, which led to the abbot's final vindication.[83] The clear message of these cases is that it was the plaintiffs' determination, not the king's, which ensured that royal courts finally brought the disputes to a close: Henry II seems to have had no wish to be involved beyond the issue of writs to achieve settlements elsewhere.

That said, it would be wrong to portray Henry, even in the first years of the reign, as insensitive to the importance of swift and true justice. It was not a priority to bring litigation before the king and his justices, but he had a genuine concern to improve judicial procedures in other courts. For instance, he clearly disliked the abuses of local church courts. A letter of John of Salisbury, probably written in 1160 or 1161, tells of his ordering Bartholemew archdeacon of Exeter to investigate a case in which a citizen of London alleged that he had been despoiled by a dean; Archbishop Theobald had the king's command to do justice, if Bartholemew did not.[84] He was also prepared to intervene in cases of advowson, while leaving the hearings themselves to the ecclesiastical courts. Theobald admonished William bishop of Norwich, who 'under pretext of the king's command, and after the semblance of a trial' had attempted to transfer the advowson of a church at Ringstead (Norfolk) from Richard and Alexander of Drayton to Ralf Lestrange. The terms might indicate one of Henry's writs ordering the bishop to reseise Ralf 'if he had been unjustly disseised', but in any event Theobald now told the bishop to restore the church to Richard.[85]

The king also legislated, on these and other matters. As early as 1158, we find a burgess of Scarborough complaining to Henry that, contrary to a royal *constitutio*, the local dean had condemned his wife for adultery 'sine alio accusatore'; the dean had taken 22 shillings from him in consequence.[86] This has long been recognised as evidence of a measure preventing the condemnation of criminals on the basis of unsupported accusations – albeit confined to church courts – and hence of an early interest both in criminal procedures and in ecclesiastical jurisdiction, destined to bear fruit in the Assize and Constitutions of Clarendon.[87] Two of Archbishop Theobald's letters mention another royal *constitutio* or *edictum* apparently framed to protect advowsons against disseisin without judgment. One of 1156x61 says that 'contra constitutionem regis', Ernald of Devizes had ejected Earl

---

[83] *Ibid.*, II, no. 396.   [84] JS, *Letters*, I, no. 118.   [85] *Ibid.*, I, no. 78.
[86] *Becket Materials*, III, 44 (William fitz Stephen); *Lawsuits*, II, no. 371.
[87] Haskins, *Norman Institutions*, 330–2; N. D. Hurnard, 'The jury of presentment and the Assize of Clarendon', *EHR*, 56 (1941), 374–410 (at 395); R. C. van Caenegem, 'Public prosecution of crime in twelfth-century England', in C. N. L. Brooke *et al.*, eds., *Church and Government in the Middle Ages* (Cambridge, 1976), 41–76 (at 68–70).

Reginald's clerk Osbert from the church of Hinton; the king had sent a writ ordering Theobald to give the earl justice regarding the advowson, and to restore to Osbert the church of which he had been deprived 'since the king's departure and against his edict (contra ipsius edictum)'. Another, of 1160, relates how the abbess of Amesbury had 'post edictum domini regis . . . violenter et absque ordine iusticiario' ejected Jordan treasurer of the church of Salisbury from the church of Froyle (Hampshire); the queen had ordered that Jordan should hold the church as he had when the king went overseas, and Theobald had summoned the abbess to appear before him on a specified date.[88] Both letters imply that the constitution protected seisin of advowson and presentation at the king's last departure from England, and point to 1158, possibly immediately before his crossing to Normandy in August, as the likely date of its promulgation.[89] Its provisions evidently ensured that, if disseisin without judgment – without proper judicial process – occurred after that time, a royal writ could be obtained which would order reseisin before any further pleading could begin. By 1162, moreover, Henry had apparently introduced another decree – referred to as an 'assize' – forbidding free tenures in general from being disseised without judgment, framed in similar terms to that protecting advowsons; indeed, it is possible that the 'constitution' and the 'assize' were one and the same, advowson being merely the particular issue which arose in the cases cited above.[90] Yet further measures on seisin are known from royal writs in favour of the monks of St Mary's, Worcester,[91] St Swithin's, Winchester[92] and St Martin's, Dover,[93] who were not to be impleaded by Englishmen unable to show seisin in, or since, 1135 by themselves or their predecessors; the writ for Winchester, datable 1155x62, suggests that there had been a *statutum* in these terms.[94]

---

[88] JS, *Letters*, I, nos. 102, 115, cf. no. 114; *Lawsuits*, II, nos. 395, 386.

[89] Biancalana, 'For want of justice', 473–4.

[90] *Ibid.*, 474–5; cf. D. W. Sutherland, *The Assize of Novel Disseisin* (Oxford, 1973), 7–8. The earliest references to this assize are in writs in favour of St Benet's Abbey, Holme, datable between Becket's consecration as archbishop in June 1162 and the king's return to England at the beginning of 1163 (despite the dating offered in *Register of the Abbey of St Benet of Holme*, ed. J. R. West, Norfolk Record Society, 1932, I, nos. 39, 36, and *Royal Writs*, nos. 21, 22). There is further comment on these assizes (which in my opinion were probably separate from one another) in the conclusion to this chapter.

[91] *Cartulary of Worcester*, no. 44 (where a date of c.April–August 1158 is suggested since the attestation by Richard du Hommet at Evesham corresponds to others assigned to that period in *Itinerary*, 37).

[92] *Royal Writs*, no. 169 (witnessed by Thomas the chancellor, so 1155x62).

[93] *Ibid.*, no. 172 (witnessed by Earl Reginald at Dover, so not closely datable). On these writs, and especially on the *statutum*, cf. Hyams, 'Warranty', 499–500, and *Kings, Lords and Peasants in Medieval England* (Oxford, 1980), 252; Stenton, *English Justice*, 31–2; *Royal Writs*, 216–18. Although Hudson, *Land, Law and Lordship*, 256–7 n. 11, questions whether the *statutum* was limited to pleading by *Anglici*, the repeated reference to them in writs citing the legislation suggests that it was. Cf. *PR28H*, 45, and *PR31H*, 66, for a claim deriving from seisin by an *Anglicus* at Henry I's death as late as 1182.

Nor does this exhaust the evidence for royal enactments on judicial processes during Henry II's early years as king. By 1164, he had refined procedures whereby a plaintiff could complain of delays in his lord's court and have the case transferred to the court of his next highest lord.[95] The processes by which lords were to distrain their vassals may also have been the subject of legislation early in the reign.[96] But it is important to stress that all these ordinances or decrees, assizes, *statuta* or *constitutiones*, were designed to work within the existing judicial framework and to improve the operation of seignorial, communal or ecclesiastical courts. The constitution infringed by the dean of Scarborough protected defendants in the church courts against unsupported accusations. The writs for the monks of Worcester, Winchester and Dover forbade Englishmen without recent seisin to implead them in shire or seignorial courts. The provisions on advowson adumbrated the assize of *novel disseisin* in ordering the redress of disseisins committed since a specified date, as the assize on free tenures generally appears to have done, but the church's traditional jurisdiction was respected: there is no evidence at this stage of recognitions before royal justices to determine the facts. It is true that transfers to the courts of superior lords following delays lower down might ultimately lead to pleas before the king or his justices, as happened with John Marshal's complaint against Becket in 1164 which provides the first clear evidence of legislation on this matter.[97] It is also true that contempt of a royal constitution might result in a crown plea. Archbishop

---

[94] The precise phraseology of the writ for Winchester suggests that the *Anglicus* had to show seisin by himself or his ancestor on the day of Henry I's death or afterwards ('vel postea') and that for Worcester says virtually the same ('vel post'); on the other hand, the writ for Dover names only the day on which Henry I died. Hyams is probably right in suggesting that the *statutum* was introduced to forestall over-zealous claims by *Anglici* in the aftermath of the civil war, and that their humble status explains the exceptional respect shown to seisin under Stephen, which was not to be taken as a precedent. Even so, the reference back to seisin in the years *following* 1135 underlines the experimental nature of the king's judicial policy in the early phase of the reign.

[95] M. G. Cheney, 'The litigation between John Marshal and Archbishop Thomas Becket in 1164: a pointer to the origin of novel disseisin?' in J. A. Guy and H. G. Beale, eds., *Law and Social Change in British History* (London, 1984), 9–26; Cheney, 'A decree of Henry II on defect of justice', in D. E. Greenway, C. Holdsworth and J. Sayers, eds., *Tradition and Change: Essays in Honour of Marjorie Chibnall* (Cambridge, 1985), 183–93; Biancalana, 'For want of justice', 460–2; Hudson, *Land, Law and Lordship*, 139. Mary Cheney draws attention to precursors in Henry I's reign, from which it seems clear that Henry II's decree was reinforcing and defining an established procedure, rather than introducing a new one. On the other hand, the notification she cites from 1159 (now *Lawsuits*, II, no. 362), while it shows the prior of Spalding acting on a royal writ of right and inviting to his court the sheriff to whom judgment was liable to pass by default, makes no mention of the decree and does not prove it to have been operational by that time.

[96] *Reg. Ant.*, I, no. 313; Hudson, *Land, Law and Lordship*, 28.

[97] Cheney, 'Litigation' and 'Decree of Henry II' as above, n. 95. By the time of the *Tractatus de Legibus*, cases evidently passed under this procedure from a lord's court straight to the shire or king's court (*ibid.*, 139–41), but it seems clear that in 1164 they were normally supposed to go first to the court of a superior lord.

Theobald told the abbess of Amesbury that 'if our lady the queen corrects your breach of the king's edict by condign punishment, we shall ratify it'.[98] The dean of Scarborough who had allowed an unsupported accusation was duly brought before Henry, although in this case, in answer to Richard de Lucy's question of what penalty should be paid to the king, the treasurer of York argued that he had no claim from a clerk.[99] But royal involvement of this nature was not the main intention behind all this early legislation. The prospect of a crown plea, or of the transfer of a case all the way to the king as overlord, gave teeth to these constitutions, and may well have encouraged the peaceful resolution of disputes which might otherwise have led to violence. Their essential purpose, however, was not to draw cases to the royal courts, but to improve the working of justice outside them.

It has, of course, long been recognised that there were some parallels between Henry II's early legislation in England and in Normandy. The *Continuatio Beccensis* preserves a series of ordinances decreed by Henry at Falaise at Christmas 1159. No dean was to accuse anyone without the testimony of reputable witnesses. At the monthly sessions of the 'judices singularum provinciarum', nothing should be judged without the testimony of neighbours. No one was to be 'injured or prejudiced', peace was to be observed, convicted thieves punished, quiet enforced and churches were to enjoy their rightful possessions.[100] Among all this, it is quite possible that the first clause echoed the constitution in England infringed by the dean of Scarborough,[101] while the second ensured that local ducal justices would normally proceed by sworn recognitions, a method of proof frequently laid down by Henry for specific cases on both sides of the Channel.[102] Thus, the bishop of Lincoln's local rights and privileges were defined by a series of recognitions which he ordered early in the reign.[103] The sheriff of Derbyshire was instructed (probably in 1155) to let the monks of Burton have the customs they claimed in the shire, if they could prove them through lawful men of the 'province'.[104] Roger earl of Hereford was told to cause a recognition to be made by the men of the hundred, into whether Rudge belonged to the abbot of Gloucester or to Reginald de St Valery.[105] These have their parallels in the series of

[98] JS, *Letters*, I, no. 115; *Lawsuits*, II, no. 386.   [99] *Ibid.*, II, no. 371.   [100] RT, 327.

[101] Thus, Haskins, *Norman Institutions*, 332; Hurnard, 'Jury of presentment', 395.

[102] For Henry II's order of an enquiry by recognition into the extent of royal demesne throughout England, shortly after becoming king, see *Gesta Abbatum Sancti Albani*, I, 123; this was probably the method used for similar inquests pertaining to Normandy in 1163 and 1171 (RT, 217, 251) and to England in 1164 (enquiry into purprestures, above, ch. 4).

[103] *Reg. Ant.*, I, no. 175; *RAH*, I, nos. 142, 217–19, 380; *CCR*, IV, nos. 15, 21, 23. Cf. Haskins, *Norman Institutions*, 236–7.   [104] *Royal Writs*, no. 18, and 'Burton Chartulary', 11.

[105] This is the inference to be drawn from Earl Roger's reply in *Historia et Cartularium Sancti Petri Gloucestriae*, II, 98.

recognitions by lawful men concerning the demesnes, rights or appurten-
ances of the bishops of Bayeux and Coutances,[106] the dean and chapter of
Rouen, the abbey of St Stephen's, Caen, and the priory of St Ymer,[107]
apparently ordered by Geoffrey Plantagenet and Henry during the 1140s
and 1150s.

However, there is nothing in England before the assize *utrum* in 1164
which corresponds to the assize making provision for recognitions before
the duke's justices, the existence of which in Normandy seems evident by
1159.[108] Among the writs of Geoffrey Plantagenet and Henry II ordering
recognitions for the bishop of Bayeux are three which specify recognition
'according to my assize'; a confirmation by Geoffrey for the bishop of
Coutances also refers to a verdict sworn by six jurors 'per meum precep-
tum in assisia mea'.[109] Not later than 1159, William fitz Thetion de Fonte
demanded an assize in the king's court on his claim against the monks of
Caen to meadows at Bapaume.[110] In that year also, Osmund fitz Richard
proved his right to the presentation of the priest of Mesnil-Drey by the
oath of lawful men in the king's court at Gavray.[111] Although the assize
under which the recognitions for the bishops of Bayeux and Coutances
were conducted cannot be proved to be the same as that for which
William fitz Thetion applied, there is an indication here that as early as
Geoffrey Plantagenet's time a ducal ordinance had been promulgated
which in some way defined procedure by recognition. By 1159, claimants to meadow and to advowson in Normandy were availing themselves, one of an 'assize', the other of a recognition, in Henry II's courts,
without there being any suggestion that they were enjoying special
favour. As C. H. Haskins argued long ago, all this was indicative that in
the duchy sworn recognition by juries had become the normal procedure
in certain types of proprietary action governing land. He believed, quite
reasonably, that it had been introduced by an ordinance as a process
available before the duke's justices, and pointed out the lack of evidence
that, by the close of the 1150s, 'matters had reached this point on the
English side of the Channel'.[112]

Our conclusion must be that they had not. As far as England was
concerned, until 1163 Henry II had no wish to encourage pleading before

[106] *RRAN*, III, nos. 52–7, 61, 64–5, 245; *RAH*, I, nos. 14, 21, 22, 38.
[107] *RRAN*, III, nos. 726, 782; *RAH*, I, nos. 104, 153. [108] Haskins, *Norman Institutions*, 198–215.
[109] *RRAN*, III, nos. 54–5, 245; *RAH*, I, no. 21.
[110] Haskins, *Norman Institutions*, 216–17 and *RAH*, I, no. 153: a royal charter issued at Caen while
  Becket was chancellor, confirming the results of various recognitions held since Henry II's
  coronation. William fitz Thetion's case cannot be later than 1159 since it was heard 'coram
  Roberto', i.e. Robert de Neufbourg, chief justiciar of Normandy until shortly before his death in
  that year.
[111] Haskins, *Norman Institutions*, 218 and RT, 344–5 (from the cartulary of Mont St Michel).
[112] Haskins, *Norman Institutions*, 169, 219–20.

himself or his justices. Yet any king intent on upholding peace and restoring order had to concern himself with the efficient judicial settlement of property disputes. Accordingly, he legislated to improve procedures, frequently responded to requests to initiate proceedings and sometimes specified a recognition as the method of proof when doing so: but the focus of all this concern was upon communal, seignorial and ecclesiastical courts. As already stressed, the communal courts of shire and hundred had traditionally been regarded as within the framework of 'royal justice', but the king was certainly not attempting to increase the range of their work: in this phase of his reign, it is fair to describe him, with some conscientous effort, as seeking 'to make the old system work according to its own terms'.[113] Beyond this, the courts of the king and his justices heard cases of particular interest, including those involving tenants-in-chief, as they had done under his predecessors, but otherwise their involvement was envisaged only if there was default of justice elsewhere. In Normandy, where there was a resident duke for at least two-thirds of the time between April 1144 and January 1163, it was feasible to tackle disputed claims to land by actively involving the ducal justices and furnishing them with a procedure, the recognition, which was swift, attractive and routinely available. In England, such measures had to wait.

The king's justices themselves deserve rather more attention at this point, beginning with the two chief justiciars, Robert earl of Leicester and Richard de Lucy. Their appointments were probably made within a few months of Henry's accession, but there is no reason to see this move as intended to stimulate the activity of the royal courts. Although both heard lawsuits on the king's behalf early in the reign, this was an occasional task shared with others; their principal work, like that of

---

[113] Hudson, *English Common Law*, 139: a deliberate echo (cf. 20) of phrases used in S. F. C. Milsom, *The Legal Framework of English Feudalism* (Cambridge, 1976), 37, 186, despite a major difference in interpretation. Milsom's work, which sets procedural developments in the context of the king's alleged concern to compel seignorial courts to observe their own customs, is critical to consideration of the issues addressed here. In so far as Henry II is seen in the present chapter to have encouraged litigation in traditional courts, and to have sought to improve procedure therein, my interpretation is consonant with certain aspects of Milsom's thesis. The view advanced here, however, is that royal intervention in the affairs of lords and their vassals, already long-established by the mid-twelfth century, became much more frequent after 1163 as a result of measures deliberately introduced to enhance the role of royal justice. This interpretation is closer to that of Hudson and, especially, of P. A. Brand (e.g. *The Making of the Common Law* (London, 1992) 224). A more fundamental challenge to Milsom appears in Reynolds, *Fiefs and Vassals*, esp. 375–9, but this may underplay the significance of seignorial courts in early and mid twelfth-century England. For the involvement of hundred courts in land pleas, see e.g. *RRAN*, II, no. 1185 (for Henry I's reign), *ibid.*, III, no. 547 (Stephen's reign), *Lawsuits*, II, no. 348 (early Henry II).

Henry I's chief minister Roger bishop of Salisbury, was the handling of finances through the exchequer. Even the duties of regent in the king's absence were normally performed in this period not by a chief justiciar but by Queen Eleanor, although the earl of Leicester does appear in that capacity, albeit subordinate to Empress Matilda, during Eleanor's absence on the Toulouse campaign in 1159.[114] As for local and itinerant justices, they had clearly been essential to the activity of the king's courts in Henry I's time, while under Stephen there are indications of judicial eyres before 1139 and of the continued employment of local justices in the south-east later in the reign; Stephen had also installed the bishop of Lincoln as justice of Lincoln and Lincolnshire during the summer of 1154.[115] Itinerant justices had a significant part to play in Normandy, where in the years after the war they were active over a wide area in the service of Geoffrey Plantagenet and Henry in turn;[116] their duties included the conduct of inquests into the possessions of religious foundations [117] and the hearing of cases over rights to lands, tithes, a granary and presentation to churches.[118] But the evidence for England does not suggest comparable dependence upon their counterparts in the years immediately following Henry II's accession.

Our knowledge of itinerant justices in England at this time depends almost entirely upon the pipe rolls.[119] Thomas Becket, Henry of Essex, Robert earl of Leicester and Gregory of London are shown in the 1156

---

[114] West, *Justiciarship*, 31–45; cf. Green, *Henry I*, 38–50; Bates, 'Origins of the justiciarship', 10–11. For evidence of the two chief justiciars in connection with the exchequer, see e g *Dialogus*, 57–9; *Lawsuits*, II, no. 421a.

[115] *RRAN*, III, no. 490; Hollister, 'Rise of administrative kingship', in *Monarchy, Magnates and Institutions*, esp. 236–9; Green, *Henry I*, 107–10; Hudson, *English Common Law*, 31–4.

[116] Haskins, *Norman Institutions*, 148–50, 164–9.   [117] Above, nn. 106–7.

[118] *RAH*, I, no. 153; Haskins, *Norman Institutions*, 216–17, 323, 325–6. Although in England Henry II initially left cases of advowson and presentation to the church courts, in Normandy they were by custom a matter for the duke's court or that of the lord of the fief (*ibid.*, 171–3).

[119] There is very limited charter evidence, which unfortunately cannot be dated with certainty to the earliest phase of the reign. *Royal Writs*, no. 20, has 'justicia mea errans' in the *nisi feceris* clause; the original editor, Sir Frank Stenton, dated this to 1155x72 but suggested *c*.1165 because it appears to be an early imperfect form of the writ of right, arguments accepted by van Caenegem. Relevant also is B.L. Harl. MS. 2110 (Castle Acre Priory cartulary), fo. 77v. where there is the notification of an agreement between Richard of Fleet (Lincolnshire) and Walter clerk of Fleet over pasture in the vill, reached at Northampton on the feast of St John 'quando justicie regis ibi fuerunt'; the text goes on to say that in the same year Richard and Walter came to Earl Aubrey at Lincoln and swore to abide by the agreement. C. W. Foster, in a transcript of this cartulary (Lincolnshire Archives Office, Foster Library P. 10) suggested a date of 1160x63 but without reasons. Most of the witnesses are too obscure to permit close dating, but one, Ralf de Caen, attested as subdean charters of *c*.1160 (*Reg. Ant.*, I, nos. 287, 304). It is interesting to find Aubrey III de Vere, whose father had served Henry I and Stephen as a justice (*RRAN*, II, no.1608; III, nos. 82, 143, 883 and p. xxiii; cf. Green, *Henry I*, 276) possibly fulfilling a similar role under Henry II, for he seems to have figured little in public life after 1154.

pipe roll to have been on eyre, mostly in the south and east.[120] The earl of Leicester had also visited Shropshire by Michaelmas 1157 and twelve months later Becket had heard pleas in Huntingdonshire and Middlesex.[121] William fitz John passed through Yorkshire, Devon, Somerset, Gloucestershire and Herefordshire between 1158 and 1161.[122] But, as suggested in the previous chapter, the first three – chancellor, constable and chief justiciar respectively – probably had as the main purpose of their visits the imposition of taxes and the conduct of inquests into the extent of the royal demesne. For his part, William fitz John may well have helped in the assessment of the *donum* levied in selected shires during 1160.[123] In some shires, there is only one entry 'de placitis' against the name of the visiting justice; nowhere do we find more than six. *Murdrum* fines appear to have been imposed by Henry of Essex and possibly by Becket [124] but the other *placita*, entirely unspecified, were often heavy amercements of individuals and probably arose from cases heard by the royal officer as an incidental duty.[125] Not until 1163, it would appear, were officials sent out on eyre primarily to hear a series of pleas: a topic discussed in the next section of this chapter. Until then, the activity of itinerant justices in England seems to have been very limited indeed.

What can be said, then, of their local equivalents, the shire justices? William of Newburgh's statement that, at the outset of his reign, Henry II 'appointed in all the districts of his kingdom judges and legal officials, to coerce the boldness of the wicked and do justice to litigants, according to the merits of the cases'[126] has been widely interpreted as evidence that local shire justices had a significant part to play in the years

---

[120] Thomas Becket: *PR2H*, 17 (Essex), 26 (Lincolnshire), 65 (Kent) as chancellor. Henry of Essex: *ibid.*, 17 (Essex), 31 (Somerset), 32 (Dorset), 54 (Hampshire), 57 (Wiltshire), 61 (Sussex), 65 (Kent). Earl of Leicester: *ibid.*, 26 (Lincolnshire); cf. 22 (Buckinghamshire–Bedfordshire), where there is mention of pleas having been heard by an unnamed justice, possibly a reference to the earl of Leicester as chief justiciar. Gregory of London: *ibid.*, 11 (Surrey), 22 (Buckinghamshire–Bedfordshire). [121] *PR3H*, 89; *PR4H*, 114, 164.

[122] *PR6H*, 51, 59, 28, 31 (cf. *PR5H*, 27, 42); *PR7H*, 49. On Yorkshire, see *PR5H*, 31 (William Tisun's debt of 10 silver marks which appears in *PR9H*, 58, as an old plea of William fitz John) and *PR7H*, 36. On these early eyres generally, cf. Stenton, *English Justice*, 68–70.

[123] Above, ch. 4, n. 105. [124] *PR2H*, 31; *PR4H*, 164.

[125] See the *placita* imposed by Henry of Essex, e.g. under Hampshire Ralf Lechewai 100 silver marks, under Somerset Edward de Brentemareis 30 silver marks, under Wiltshire Roger Waspail 100s., under Sussex Aelard 60 silver marks, Ralf monk 10 silver marks, (*PR2H*, 54, 31, 57, 60–1). Cf. *ibid.*, 26 under Lincolnshire, an account by Robert fitz Gilbert of Tadwell of 5 silver marks of pleas of the chancellor and earl of Leicester. But at *PR4H*, 114 we find a communal amercement: the men of Laleham (Middlesex) accounted for 2 silver marks of pleas of the chancellor. It is possible that other *placita* were not recorded in the pipe rolls because full payments went to the chamber; however, the number is unlikely to be high, since the king was overseas for most of the year ending at Michaelmas 1156 and for the whole of the time that William fitz John was (apparently) on eyre. [126] Newburgh, I, 102.

before the introduction of regular judicial eyres.[127] However, the extent to which Henry I had relied on shire justices is by no means clear,[128] and evidence of their frequent and widespread employment by his grandson is scarcely convincing. The appearance of unnamed justices in the address clauses of writs ordering action on behalf of the beneficiary,[129] or in notifications of royal grants or confirmations,[130] tells us nothing about their duties, or even whether there were men actually in post: these are no more indicative of the appointment or activity of local justices than similarly phrased documents of Stephen had been.[131] There is good reason to believe that they had a role to play in criminal jurisdiction: the accounts of *placita* and *murdrum* fines in Henry II's early pipe rolls, where they are not linked to the name of a justice in eyre, may well indicate that local justices had heard crown pleas in the relevant shires,[132] and measures against crime between 1163 and 1166 – also treated in the next section – do appear to have relied upon them. But their role in civil litigation deserves reconsideration.

One point of possible significance is that the assize *utrum* of 1164 seems originally to have ignored local justices altogether. While the relevant writ in the *Tractatus de Legibus* assumes a hearing before itinerant justices,[133] the text of clause ix of the Constitutions of Clarendon says that the dispute should be settled before the king's chief justiciar.[134] If we move back to the preceding decade, we have the evidence of a string of royal writs ordering action in civil lawsuits, almost invariably addressed to a sheriff or to an alleged wrongdoer direct, but often with 'my justice' named in the *nisi feceris* clause as someone whose jurisdiction might be invoked if a writ was disobeyed. As discussed earlier, such arrangements appear to have been intended not to increase the activity of royal courts

---

[127] Stenton, 'England: Henry II', 584–5; H. A. Cronne, 'The office of local justiciar in England under the Norman kings', *University of Birmingham Historical Journal*, 6 (1957–8), 18–38; Richardson and Sayles, *Governance*, 194–6.

[128] Hollister, 'Rise of administrative kingship', in *Monarchy, Magnates and Institutions*, 238–9; Green, *Henry I*, 107–8.

[129] E.g. (among those from Henry II's reign not later than 1165, cited in Richardson and Sayles, *Governance*, 194, n. 4) CCR, IV, 290 (Berkshire); III, 382 (Hampshire); IV, 141 (Nottinghamshire–Derbyshire); V, 59 (Kent); IV, 110 (Lincolnshire); IV, 145–6 (Lincolnshire and Nottinghamshire); III, 67 (Norfolk); II, 171–2 (Northumberland); IV, 109 (Oxfordshire); V, 59–60 (Suffolk); IV, 440 (Sussex); V, 472 (Yorkshire).

[130] *Ibid.*, II, 295 (Buckinghamshire–Bedfordshire); III, 271 (Cornwall); III, 82 (Cumberland and Westmorland); II, 132 (Dorset); V, 57, 159–60 (Essex); V, 160 (Gloucestershire); II, 105 and III, 337 (Hampshire); IV, 83 (Herefordshire); IV, 107–8 (Huntingdonshire); III, 312 and IV, 106–7, 110, 145 (Lincolnshire); V, 160 (Norfolk); II, 171 and III, 393 (Northumberland); III, 292 (Shropshire); II, 347 (Staffordshire); V, 58 (Suffolk); IV, 183 (Surrey); I, 61 (Yorkshire).

[131] *RRAN*, III, xxvi; White, 'Continuity', 133.

[132] Richardson and Sayles, *Governance*, 195–6; D. M. Stenton, 'The development of the judiciary, 1100–1215', in *Pleas before the King or his Justices*, III, li. [133] *Tractatus*, 163–4.

[134] *Select Charters*, 165.

but genuinely to encourage the settlement of disputes elsewhere, resort to a royal justice being envisaged only as a precaution against default.[135] But in a clause such as 'et nisi feceris, justicia mea faciat fieri', which royal justice was intended? One answer might be the local justice of the shire,[136] but the clause could surely refer to anyone whom the king might appoint to hear a case. Naturally, references in *nisi feceris* clauses to a 'justicia de Lincolnesira', to 'justicia mea de Norfolca' and to 'iusticia regis de Londonia'[137] specified local justices, but the general 'justicia mea' was far more common. Fortunately, it is possible to test the outcome of this phraseology by reference to two cases known in some detail.

Attention has already been drawn to two writs which Henry II issued concerning the abbot of Burton's claim to land in Cotes (Derbyshire).[138] They are placed next to one another in the Burton cartulary, amidst an account of the prolonged series of disputes over this property. The second, but apparently earlier, writ is addressed 'Roberto de Piro Vicecomite' (presumably Robert de Perer, sheriff of Nottinghamshire and Derbyshire up to Michaelmas 1155) ordering that without delay and justly he reseise the abbot of Burton of his land of Cotes; unless he does it, 'my justice' will. The writ entered immediately before this one orders an unnamed sheriff of Nottinghamshire without delay to do full right to the abbot of Burton concerning his land of Cotes 'as I ordered by my other writ'; again, 'my justice' will do it if the sheriff does not.[139] Although the latter writ's attestation and place dating, by Richard du Hommet as constable at Westminster, are insufficient to prove that it belongs to the earliest years of the reign, the inference is that this was issued to the new sheriff on the failure of Robert de Perer to act on the 'other writ'. Although a justice had been mentioned in the *nisi feceris* clause, Henry II chose to address himself afresh to the incoming sheriff. There is nothing in this episode to suggest reliance upon a local justice in Nottinghamshire and Derbyshire in the early years of the reign. Indeed, another royal writ probably of 1155, again for Burton Abbey but on a different subject, is addressed to the sheriff of Derbyshire but names in the *nisi feceris* clause not a local justice but the chief justiciar the earl of Leicester.[140]

The Abingdon chronicler's story of the abbot's dispute with Turstin fitz Simon over property in Marcham, Middleton and Appleford (Berkshire)

[135] Above, nn. 66–76.
[136] Thus, Richardson and Sayles, *Governance*, 174, 194–5, from *Chronicon de Abingdon*, II, 223, 225, and *Historia et Cartularium Sancti Petri Gloucesteriae*, II, 98.
[137] *Royal Writs*, nos. 94, 127; *Cartularium de Colecestria*, I, 41 (witnessed by Henry of Essex as constable so presumably not later than 1157). Cf. *Historia et Cartularium Sancti Petri Gloucestriae*, II, no. 584, for reference by Roger earl of Hereford in the early months of Henry II's reign to 'the king's justice in the province' who might hear a plea in the shire court.   [138] Above, n. 79.
[139] 'Burton Chartulary', 9; *Lawsuits*, II, no. 517.
[140] *Royal Writs*, no. 18, from 'Burton Chartulary', ed. Wrottesley, 11.

sets other royal writs in their context. Henry sent two on this subject to successive sheriffs of Berkshire. Henry of Oxford (sheriff until Michaelmas 1155) was ordered, if the abbot was unjustly disseised, to reseise him without delay and make him hold in peace as in Henry I's time, otherwise 'my justice' would. Richard de Camville (sheriff for two years from Michaelmas 1155) also received a writ, in substantially similar terms, and again 'my justice' was to have it done if he failed to act. We are told that Turstin, 'conscious of his misdeed, cleverly evaded the meetings of the county for two years and more, under pretext of the king's service, or illness or some other cause', but no one seems to have contacted a local justice of Berkshire in order to expedite matters. Instead, the abbot went back to the king. Already, as he had for Burton Abbey, Henry had repeated his command to a second sheriff. Now, he 'summoned his justices, Gregory of London, William fitz John, Nigel de Broc and other wise men of his court' and 'ordered them to deal with the case of the abbot and of Turstin'.[141] In this story, the abbot does not seem to have interpreted the *nisi feceris* clause as a promise of intervention by a shire justice should the sheriff fail to act. He used the clause instead to obtain a hearing on reapplication to the king, before men named as justices for the occasion.

We know that royal justices named in *nisi feceris* clauses might eventually be called into play. For example, Robert de Valognes, seeking to recover the wood of Northaw from the abbot of St Albans, obtained from Henry II at Toulouse a writ forbidding the abbot to deprive him unjustly of what he held hereditarily, 'and unless you do it, Robert earl of Leicester shall'. When the abbot maintained that he had no hereditary right in the wood, Robert duly took the writ to the earl of Leicester, who summoned the parties to a royal court at Northampton and found in his favour.[142] We also know of royal officials being appointed *ad hoc* to hear particular cases, as Stephen had sent his steward William Martel to preside at an assembly of the shire courts of Norfolk and Suffolk about 1150.[143] Not later than 1159, an 'inquisicio . . . iussu regis Henrici' held in the house of Hugh dean of Derby was conducted by the sheriff and by local royal servants Froger archdeacon of Derby and Peter of Sandiacre: a jury of twenty-four composed of burgesses of Derby, priests, knights and a clerk, affirmed on oath that the church of St Peter's Derby was built on the patrimony of dean Hugh, to whom its advowson belonged.[144] In the

---

[141] *Chronicon de Abingdon*, II, 184–7; *Lawsuits*, II, no. 363.   [142] *Ibid.*, II, no. 396; cf. above, n. 83.
[143] *Ibid.*, I, no. 331.
[144] *Ibid.*, II, no. 365, with comment p. 329 n. 5; cf. *Cartulary of Darley*, I, 71–2 and F. M. Stenton, 'An early inquest relating to St Peter's Derby', *EHR*, 32 (1917), 47–8. Froger may be identified as the king's almoner, who in December 1159 was consecrated bishop of Séez; he accounted for the farm of part of William Peverel's honour in 1156 and 1157 (RT, 205; *PR2H*, 42; *PR3H*, 92). Peter

Anstey case, we see Richard de Lucy in the summer of 1163 appointing two of his own tenants, Oger *Dapifer* and Ralf *Brito*, both servants of the crown in other capacities, to do justice to Richard of Anstey without delay.[145] To set against these recorded examples of the intervention of royal justices, there appear to be none surviving from the early years of Henry II's reign in which the vague 'justicia mea' in a *nisi feceris* clause led to the transfer of a case to a local justice of the shire.[146]

The pipe rolls also have little to say about local justices. In 1157 under Somerset, the bishop of Bath accounted for £100 'pro placito Johannis de Chent',[147] while the previous year's roll seems to indicate work by the justices of Lincolnshire and London. The sheriff of Lincolnshire accounted for 10 marks on pleas of the bishop of Lincoln in Holland, the bishop having received from Stephen in the summer of 1154 a grant of 'the king's justice of Lincoln and Lincolnshire'.[148] Under London and Middlesex, Robert de Ponte owed 20s. 0d. on pleas of Guy fitz Tesc', a debt not paid off until 1158.[149] Yet there appears to have been no confirmation by Henry II of the bishop of Lincoln's justiciarship, and he may soon have resigned.[150] Moreover, since Guy fitz Tesc' had campaigned with Stephen's army and had suffered his own brushes with the law,[151] the 'iusticia regis de Londonia' referred to by Queen Eleanor in a writ datable 1156x57 [152] may have been not Guy but Gregory of London, the man who accounted for the farm of London for the second half of 1154–5, was on eyre before Michaelmas 1156 and would later hear the abbot of Abingdon's case against Turstin fitz Simon.[153] It may well be that

of Sandiacre was pardoned *donum* in Nottinghamshire–Derbyshire in 1158, presumably as a royal servant (*PR4H*, 153); his family is known to have held Sandiacre as a serjeanty through the office of falconer, although there is no firm evidence of this before 1198 (*Cartulary of Darley*, I, xxx).

[145] *Lawsuits*, II, no. 408, p. 402; cf. Barnes, 'Anstey case', 13–14, for comment that Ralf *Brito* was apparently bailiff of the honour of Boulogne, and Oger *Dapifer* sheriff of Norfolk–Suffolk by 1164.

[146] Cf. for Henry I's reign a writ of the queen as regent, in 1111, addressing Nigel d'Aubigny local justice of Northumberland, after the sheriffs had failed to obey an earlier writ; however, the previous writ had specifically named Nigel in the *nisi feceris* clause (*RRAN*, II, nos. 993, 1001; *Royal Writs*, no. 143; Cronne, 'Office of local justiciar', 35).   [147] *PR3H*, 98.

[148] *PR2H*, 26; *RRAN*, III, no. 490.   [149] *PR2H*, 5; *PR4H*, 115.

[150] No confirmation of the office by Henry II survives either in *Reg. Ant.* or in the series of charters for the cathedral church of Lincoln preserved in *CCR*, IV. In a writ of 1155x58, Henry II addressed (among others) 'episcopo Lincolniensi et justic' de . . . Lincolnescira' (*Reg. Ant.*, I, no. 144). Writs addressing the shire justice and mentioning the bishop in the movent clause or notification include *ibid.*, I, nos. 108, 148, datable 1155x64 and 1155x58 respectively. A writ of Henry II in the Spalding Priory Register, B.L. Add. MS. 35296, fo. 88, is addressed to the bishop of Lincoln and ends 'et nisi feceris, justicia meus [*sic*] faciat', but the omission of witnesses prevents close dating.

[151] *RRAN*, III, nos. 456, 874, attestations for Stephen 'in obsidione' and 'in exercitu' respectively. Henry II, possibly in 1158, restored to Guy fitz Tesc' the land of which he had been disseised for manslaughter (*EYC*, I, no. 466).   [152] *Royal Writs*, no. 127.

[153] *RBE*, II, 658; *PR2H*, 11, 22; *Lawsuits*, II, no. 363.

these two accounts from Lincolnshire and London arose from pleas heard in Stephen's reign.

One other local justice merits some attention. In 1156 the burgesses of Cambridge owed 10 marks 'de placitis Henrici de Pomeria'.[154] In a writ of uncertain date within the first half of the reign, ordering that Robert bishop of Lincoln should have corn from his assarts, Henry II addressed 'H. de Pontn'' (otherwise unknown, and conjecturally a copyist's error for H. de Pomm') and his sheriff of Huntingdonshire.[155] Another royal writ, of May–July 1155, has the king ordering Henry de Pommeraye to maintain and protect the lands of St Andrew's, Northampton, 'que in tua potestate sunt'.[156] St Andrew's Priory held lands in Bedfordshire and Huntingdonshire as well as in Northamptonshire, [157] and while we cannot say whether Henry de Pommeraye's jurisdiction covered them all, this combination of evidence suggests that he had judicial authority over a *potestas* covering a group of adjacent shires, as had been the case with Aethelwig abbot of Evesham in the west Midlands in the Conqueror's time and Earl Geoffrey de Mandeville in London, Middlesex, Essex and Hertfordshire between 1141 and 1143.[158] It is a point of interest that Henry de Pommeraye, though a prominent tenant-in-chief in Devon, held little if any land in the area of his *potestas*.[159] The arrangements made for him do not appear to have been replicated elsewhere, but they are sufficient to demonstrate that there was no uniform pattern to the appointment of local justices early in Henry II's reign.

Lack of evidence prevents further treatment of these officials. We might expect them to have been appointed, on the whole, from the same class as many of Henry II's early sheriffs: holders of a few knights' fees, perhaps experienced in baronial service. But we have very few names, and Henry de Pommeraye, a wealthy baron with experience in the royal household,[160] would be an exception to this. Some shires may well have been without local justices, at least in the first few years of the reign, and almost everywhere they were destined to be superseded by justices in

---

[154] *PR2H*, 15.   [155] *Reg. Ant.*, I, no. 153.

[156] B.L. Royal MS. 11 B. ix, fo. 21v; B.L. Cotton MS. Vespasian E. xvii, fo. 19v. (witnessed by Robert de Dunstanville at Bridgnorth).   [157] *VCH Northants*, II, 102.

[158] Cronne, 'Office of local justiciar', 25–6; *RRAN*, III, nos. 275–6.

[159] His 1166 *carta*, entered under Devon, shows thirty fees; he also held one fee of Earl Reginald, one fee of Robert *filius Regis*, and one and a half fees of the bishop of Exeter, although service for the half-fee was denied (*RBE*, I, 249, 252, 260–2: cf. *Baronies*, 106). W. Farrer, *Feudal Cambridgeshire* (Cambridge, 1920), 137, notes a grant before 1201 to Henry de Pommeraye of part of 10 librates of land in Fordham, but there does not appear to be any earlier evidence that the family held in this shire.

[160] £40 10s. 6d. due on the old farm of Huntingdonshire was spent 'in Corredio Regine per Henricum de Pomerei' during 1157–58 (*PR4H*, 141–2), but his attestations of royal charters are few (*Itinerary*, 15, 22; *RAH*, I, no. 35). For his career in general, including previous service in the constable's department, see Green, *Henry I*, 266–7.

eyre making regular visitations from the late 1160s onwards.[161] There is no reason to doubt that, for as long as they continued, they retained special responsibility 'de placitis et forisfactis que pertinent ad coronam',[162] responsibilities which may temporarily have increased in certain shires following the criminal assizes of the mid-1160s to be discussed below.[163] But for civil suits, when occasion arose for royal justices to become involved, the king seems to have preferred *curiales* specifically appointed to each case. Given the dearth of references to local justices in chronicle and cartulary accounts of land pleas early in Henry II's reign – despite the appearance of royal justices in other guises – it is difficult to believe that they had a major part to play in the resolution of property disputes in the years immediately before their replacement by regular justices in eyre. If the king's courts had been central to the conduct of civil litigation between 1154 and 1162, the king's local justices would certainly have figured prominently. Their comparative obscurity reinforces the point that, in this period, the focus of civil litigation continued to lie elsewhere.

THE KING AND HIS JUSTICES: 1163–5

Henry II returned to England in January 1163, after four-and-a-half years away, fully aware of the importance of devoting close attention to the government of his kingdom. In judicial affairs, this meant a shift in policy, for there was now to be a sustained attempt to involve the royal courts directly. One obvious manifestation of this was the king's increased availability: for instance, tenants-in-chief, though they had customarily had access to the king's courts, now took advantage of Henry's greater accessibility, so that a series of disputes came to be settled in his presence during the course of the year. The bishop of Lincoln had started complaining to Henry about the abbot of St Albans's claims to exemption soon after the death of Pope Adrian IV in September 1159. There appears to have been no response from the king until 1162, when a royal writ ordered the earl of Leicester as chief justiciar to hear the case, but in March of the following year at Westminster Henry took personal cognisance of the affair – anxious that it should not pass to the jurisdiction of papal judges-delegate – and brought the parties to a compromise.[164] At Windsor on 6 April 1163, 'praesente domino Rege Henrico', Geoffrey III de Mandeville assigned an annual rent of 100 shillings to the monks of Ramsey in recompense for damage done by his

---

[161] R. F. Hunnisett, 'The origins of the office of coroner', *TRHS*, 5th ser., 8 (1958), 91; Richardson and Sayles, *Governance*, 196; Hudson, *English Common Law*, 128.
[162] Cronne, 'Office of local justiciar', 34.   [163] Below, nn. 183–8.   [164] *Lawsuits*, II, no. 405.

father.[165] Before the king at Windsor and Reading in March and April, Robert de Montfort accused Henry of Essex of treason and cowardice, and then defeated him in trial by battle.[166] But it was not only tenants-in-chief who sought Henry out: at Woodstock in July, as Richard of Anstey recorded with relief, 'we came before the king . . . and at last, by the grace of God and of the king, and by judgment of his court, my uncle's land was adjudged to me'.[167] Moreover, just as Anstey's fine of 100 silver marks, presumably to have his case heard in the king's court, [168] does not find notice in the pipe rolls until 1165, so many other accounts by ecclesiastics and laymen in that year, entered as Richard's was 'de misericordia',[169] may relate to fines to bring cases before the king or his justices anytime during the two preceding years.

It may also be significant that 1163 is the date of the first known final concord to be levied in a royal court, involving a compromise between Hamo fitz Herefrid and Ralf of Dene over land in Surrey. This was settled in the presence of the king, his brother William, the bishop of Chichester and others, on 23 May at Northampton, and its form is very similar to other early concords which survive from the 1170s and to the examples given in the *Tractatus*.[170] Another final concord, made before the king at Westminster between the abbot of St Benet's, Holme, and William and Henry de Neville, is known from the period 1163–6: Round suggested a date of March 1163, which would put it earlier than the Northampton example, but since we learn of it only from a royal charter of confirmation we cannot comment on its wording. Indeed, the resort to a subsequent charter suggests that procedure was still evolving, since by the second half of the reign it was accepted that the chirographs which each party received as a record of the concord rendered further confirmation unnecessary.[171] Be that as it may, we have further evidence here of Henry responding, through his courts, to demand for his intervention in lawsuits: it may indeed have been through the initiative of the king and his justices, following his return to England at the beginning of

---

[165] *Cartularium Monasterii de Rameseia*, ed. W. H. Hart and P. A. Lyons (RS, 1884–94), II, 196–7; cf. *Chronicon Abbatiae Rameseiensis*, 306.   [166] *Lawsuits*, II, no. 407; cf. RT, 218.

[167] *Lawsuits*, II, no. 408, p. 402.   [168] Barnes, 'Anstey case', 13, 22–3.

[169] PR11H, 18; cf. 7, 13, 17–18, 22, 35–7, 41–2, etc. C. R. Cheney, *From Becket to Langton: English Church Government, 1170–1213* (Manchester, 1956), 56, n. 3, suggests that the fine was Richard of Anstey's relief, but payment for a favour after it had been granted accords with *Dialogus*, 120. For queen's gold, which Richard of Anstey also had to pay, see *ibid.*, 122–3.

[170] *Curia R. R.*, X, 334; L. F. Salzmann, 'Early fines', *EHR*, 25 (1910), 708–10, which establishes the date, despite Hyams, 'Charter as a source', 185; cf. *Tractatus*, 94–7.

[171] *Register of the Abbey of St Benet of Holme*, ed. J. R. West (Norfolk Record Soc., 1932), II, no. 10; J. H. Round, *Feudal England* (London, 1895), 515, and generally 509–16; Round, 'The earliest fines', *EHR*, 12 (1897), 293–302; *Final Concords*, II, ed. Foster, ix–xli.

1163, that final concords in the royal courts first became available as one means to terminate tenurial disputes and record their outcome. [172]

This must, of course, remain a matter for speculation, but 1163 certainly witnessed increased judicial activity in other respects. The king's anger at the leniency shown towards criminous clerks, treated by Becket's biographers as preliminaries to the tragic conflict which ensued, should be seen in the context of a general concern to bring offenders to justice. The 'first estrangement' between king and archbishop, according to one manuscript of William fitz Stephen's *Vita Sancti Thomae*, arose from the case of a clerk in the Worcester area whom the king wanted to have 'examined by the judgment of a lay court' on a charge of seducing a girl and killing her father; Becket ensured that he remained in the bishop of Worcester's custody, 'so that he would not be given over to the king's justice'.[173] Henry also wished to have a clerk who had stolen a silver chalice committed to the secular justices, but the archbishop claimed jurisdiction and to appease the king ordered that he be branded.[174] From Herbert of Bosham we know in more detail of a priest accused by his neighbours of a homicide for which he was notorious. He claimed the privilege of his order and was brought before his diocesan, the bishop of Salisbury. The king's officials and his accusing neighbours urged that justice be done, but after the priest had failed to answer his accusers and to clear himself by compurgation, the bishop consulted Becket; the archbishop's instruction was that he be deprived of his benefice and committed to a monastery for the rest of his days. Herbert added that an archiepiscopal decree to this effect, providing for the punishment of criminous clerks 'without any mutilation or deformation of limbs' was promulgated throughout the province, though with provision for some variation in the sentence according to rank and offence.[175] Finally, the case of Philip de Brois, a canon of Bedford, can be pieced together from several accounts. The original charge of homicide against Philip had 'long been forgotten';[176] he had been tried before the bishop of Lincoln and had cleared himself by compurgation.[177] But while the king's itinerant justices were at Dunstable,[178] the justice Simon

---

[172] There is an isolated earlier example of a final concord from Henry I's reign: in 1131x32, the king confirmed a 'peace and final concord' between Kenilworth Priory and Hugh the king's watchman (*RRAN*, II, no. 1744; *Lawsuits*, II, no. 275, cf. no. 325). This casts some doubt on the novelty of final concords under Henry II, but no details of procedure are given and it may not have been agreed in a royal court. On the wider context, cf. King, 'Dispute settlement', 126–9.

[173] *Lawsuits*, II, no. 409.   [174] *Ibid.*, II, no. 410.   [175] *Ibid.*, II, no. 416.

[176] '[A]b olim consopita', given the more modest translation 'in the past' *ibid.*, II, no. 411, p. 406 (Edward Grim). On this and the preceding case, cf. F. Barlow, *Thomas Becket* (London, 1986), 92–3.

[177] *Ibid.*, II, no. 411, pp. 405 (Anonymous I), 406 (Edward Grim), 408 (Guernes de Pont-Sainte-Maxence), 410 (William of Canterbury).   [178] *Ibid.*, II, no. 411, p. 411 (William fitz Stephen).

fitz Peter [179] revived the charge, and the canon replied in insulting terms.[180] The king was informed and ordered that the canon be tried,[181] but Becket, refusing to allow a clerk to be judged in a secular court, claimed jurisdiction instead. The king sent bishops, clerks and laymen to the archbishop's court, where Philip argued that the homicide plea had already been settled, but admitted the insult. Judgment was given that he humble himself before Simon fitz Peter and be deprived of his prebend for two years; the king had wanted the death penalty, and let his outrage be known.[182] It would be good to have fuller details of the judicial procedures involved, but there is significant information here. The accusation by neighbours of a priest in Salisbury diocese whose homicide was notorious, and a retrial before the king's justices in Bedfordshire for a 'long-forgotten' offence, may well be indicative of a deliberate enquiry into crime through juries of presentment – perhaps dating back to the beginning of the reign – conducted either by local officials or by itinerant justices. The pipe roll of 1163, itself less explicit than we might wish, lends some weight to this suggestion.

Evidence of a fresh attack on crime is to be found in the first known accounts at the exchequer for the possessions of thieves and fugitives: the sheriffs answered for the profits arising from their sale. Under the term *pecunia*, they are found in 1163 under Berkshire, Northumberland, Somerset, Sussex and Yorkshire; [183] known thereafter as *catalla*, they were accounted for by the sheriffs of Northumberland and Yorkshire in 1164,[184] and by those of Devon, Norfolk–Suffolk, Staffordshire, Warwickshire–Leicestershire and (again) both Northumberland and Yorkshire in 1165.[185] Apart from isolated accounts, one by the sheriff of Hampshire in 1157, the other by the sheriff of Shropshire in 1160, of the *pecunia* of individuals whose faults are not stated,[186] there are no similar entries in the pipe rolls of 1130 or 1156–62, and it seems quite possible that their appearance in 1163 was the result of a fresh government initiative. The amounts involved are small, mostly relating to individual

---

[179] *Ibid.*, II, no. 411, pp. 405 (Anonymous I), 408 (Guernes de Pont-Sainte-Maxence), 411 (William of Canterbury). For Simon fitz Peter, see above, ch. 3, n. 92. The reference in Anonymous I to his being appointed 'as judge in the region of Bedford' might indicate a local justiciarship, but could also be interpreted to mean that he was a visiting itinerant justice.

[180] *Lawsuits*, II, no. 411, pp. 405 (Anonymous I), 407 (Edward Grim), 408 (Guernes de Pont-Sainte-Maxence), 409 (Herbert of Bosham), 410 (Ralf de Diceto), 411 (William of Canterbury, William fitz Stephen).

[181] *Ibid.*, II, no. 411, pp. 406 (Anonymous I), 407 (Edward Grim), 408 (Guernes de Pont-Sainte-Maxence).

[182] *Ibid.*, II, no. 411, pp. 406 (Anonymous I), 407 (Edward Grim), 409 (Guernes de Pont-Sainte-Maxence, Herbert of Bosham), 411 (William of Canterbury, William fitz Stephen).

[183] *PR9H*, 52, 44, 27, 14, 61.   [184] *PR10H*, 1, 12.   [185] *PR11H*, 82, 7, 76, 85, 30, 52.

[186] *PR3H*, 106; *PR6H*, 27.

offenders in each shire, but some of them are comparable with the returns of chattels in 1166 from those shires not visited by Richard de Lucy and Geoffrey III de Mandeville.[187] While there are no grounds for suggesting that an earlier version of the Assize of Clarendon lay behind the accounts of chattels in 1163–5, we should at least accept that this measure was introduced in the context of a drive against crime which had already begun.[188]

Meanwhile, we also learn from the pipe rolls of *placita* imposed by the king's justices during the course of that year: by Alan de Neville in Oxfordshire and by Richard de Lucy in Carlisle.[189] Moreover, these accounts are matched by a series under Buckinghamshire–Bedfordshire, Cambridgeshire–Huntingdonshire, Northamptonshire, Northumberland, Warwickshire–Leicestershire and Yorkshire in the same year;[190] all show small sums, usually in multiples of half a silver mark, against the names of individual persons or vills. There is no word in the pipe roll to say that these reflect the work of an itinerant justice, nor indeed to mark them off from other 'new pleas and new agreements' for that year. But they appear to form distinctive sequences, and bear striking similarity in content, and in the sums involved, to the accounts arising from Alan de Neville's forest eyre recorded in the 1167 pipe roll. Amercements in 1167 were usually charged to the defaulters, whereas the sheriff was normally entered as responsible for them in 1163, but there seem to be no other significant differences. A few of the *placita* entered under Oxfordshire in the 1163 pipe roll may be quoted as examples:[191]

The same sheriff renders account of 5s. for Robert Chevalchesal, of pleas of Alan de Neville. He has paid into the treasury, and he is quit.

The same sheriff renders account of 1 mark of Coggs. He has paid into the treasury, and he is quit.

---

[187] For example, the 49s. od. raised from chattels in Somerset, the 32s. 5d. in Berkshire and the 15s. 1d. in Northumberland, all entered in the 1163 pipe roll, may be set against the 1166 returns of 8s. 11d. in London–Middlesex, 16s. od. in Worcestershire and 42s. 4d. in Devon (*PR12H*, 132, 96, 82).

[188] Hurnard, 'Jury of presentment', 405, drew attention to a reference to an *alia assisa* at *PR12H*, 48; the most convincing interpretation of this item is that in Corner, 'Texts of Henry II's assizes', esp. 18–19, where it is seen as indicative of a 'Clarendon-like' assize, enforced by local officials, promulgated shortly before the more famous measure which brought in itinerant justices. It is most unlikely that this earlier assize led to accounts of chattels as early as 1163, since these make no mention of the distinctive 'judgment of water'. (Cf. *PR12H*, 5, 13, for the separate treatment of the chattels of criminals convicted other than by assize procedures.) On forfeiture of criminals' chattels generally, see *Dialogus*, 97–8, 101–3; Pollock and Maitland, *History of English Law*, I, 583.

[189] *PR9H*, 48, 10; under Carlisle, the first account 'de placitis Ric(ardi) de Luci' is followed by seventeen further entries 'de placitis eiusdem'.

[190] *Ibid.*, 15–20, 63–5, 36–42, 43–4, 31–3, 59–61.   [191] *Ibid.*, 48–9.

The same sheriff renders account of 1 mark of Stanton. He has paid into the treasury, and he is quit.

The same sheriff renders account of 1 mark of the Abbot of Eynsham. He has paid into the treasury, and he is quit.

These may be compared with the Oxfordshire items in the 1167 pipe roll, beneath the general heading 'De Placitis Alani de Nevilla': [192]

The abbot of Eynsham renders account of 1 mark. He has paid into the treasury, and he is quit.

Stanton, of the King, renders account of 1 mark. It has paid into the treasury, and it is quit.

Coggs, of Manasser Harsic, renders account of 10s. It has paid into the treasury, and it is quit.

Robert Chevalchesal renders account of $\frac{1}{2}$ mark. He has paid into the treasury, and he is quit.

It is unusual, in both the 1163 and the 1167 pipe rolls, for entries to specify offences, but occasionally we have direct evidence of a plea of the forest. One of Richard de Lucy's *placita* in Carlisle, in 1163, related to assarts, and items that year under Northamptonshire included the following: [193]

The same sheriff renders account of 10 marks for Ralf Brito, of waste forest. In pardon by the king's writ to the same Ralf, 10 marks, and he is quit.

The same sheriff renders account of 26s. 8d. of Waste of Geddington. In pardon by the king's writ to Ralf Medicus 26s. 8d., and he is quit.

The same sheriff renders account of 20s. of Assarts of Gretton. He has paid into the treasury, and he is quit.

Two of these names recur amongst Alan de Neville's *placita* in 1167: [194]

The same sheriff renders account of 40s. of Geddington, of Ralf Medicus. In pardon by the king's writ to the same Ralf 33s. 4d., and he owes $\frac{1}{2}$ mark.

The same sheriff renders account of 1 mark of Gretton, of the King. He has paid into the treasury, and he is quit.

The same sheriff renders account of 10s. for Wuluric of the same vill. In the treasury 7s. and he owes 4s. [*sic*]

---

[192] *PR13H*, 14–15. [193] *PR9H*, 10, 36–7.
[194] *PR13H*, 118 (the Northamptonshire items are unusual in that accounts are charged to the sheriff rather than to the individuals concerned). On the two eyres in Northamptonshire, cf. E. J. King, *Peterborough Abbey, 1066–1310* (Cambridge, 1973), 72.

It may well be that most of the new *placita* of 1163 arose from forest offences. However, there are indications of a wider brief in occasional amercements for defaults and a concealed *murdrum*,[195] and, accordingly, it seems fair to draw parallels with the amercements imposed on individuals and vills by Henry I's itinerant justices and by Richard de Lucy and Geoffrey III de Mandeville in 1166: most of the 1166 sums would again be only a few marks, though in Henry I's day they seem usually to have been heavier.[196] In short, we do appear to have here evidence of two judicial eyres, one possibly covering Carlisle, Northumberland and Yorkshire and involving Richard de Lucy, another through the Midlands featuring Alan de Neville. Again, there is much that is speculative here, but the pipe roll evidence of a Midlands eyre, including entries in Buckinghamshire and Bedfordshire, corresponds to a known visit to Dunstable (where Simon fitz Peter served as a justice) during the course of the year.

The judicial developments of 1164 constitute a more familiar story. At the Clarendon council in January – or more probably, in preparation for it – the king ordered 'the oldest and wisest of his magnates' to consult with clerks and write down the laws and customs of his grandfather's reign. The Constitutions of Clarendon were the outcome.[197] Here again, Henry II legislated on criminal trials in church courts. By clause vi, laymen could only be accused in the presence of a bishop, and by 'lawful accusers'; the sheriff would empanel a jury of twelve lawful men of the neighbourhood or vill to state the truth of the matter if individual accusers were not forthcoming. This may well have been a modification, perhaps a straightforward renewal, of the constitution infringed by the dean of Scarborough in 1158.[198] But unlike in his earlier legislation, the king was now manifestly seeking business for his own courts as well. Clause viii interposed them as courts of appeal from the archbishop, and appeals were not to proceed further (to the pope) without royal consent.[199] Furthermore, in clauses i, iii and ix, certain categories of pleas

---

[195] PR9H, 17 (defaults, Buckinghamshire–Bedfordshire), 50 (default, Oxfordshire), 65 (concealed *murdrum*, Cambridgeshire–Huntingdonshire)

[196] Compare, for example, the *Nova Placita* and *Novae Conventiones* entered under Lincolnshire in the pipe rolls of 1130 and 1166. PR 31 Hen. I, 114–21, has evidence of an eyre conducted by William d'Aubigny and Richard Basset. In a total of over sixty *placita*, only eight are of 40s. or less; those for breach of the peace vary between 5 and 20 silver marks. In PR12H, 7–10, among the accounts arising from the eyre of Earl Geoffrey and Richard de Lucy, sums of over 40s. are exceptional (although Ulkil of Croxton is shown owing 40s. for breach of the peace). Analysis yields similar results for Yorkshire and Essex (PR 31 Hen. I, 27–31, 55–8, and PR12H, 46–9, 128–9).

[197] Gervase, I, 178–80; *Becket Materials*, v, 71–9; *Select Charters*, 163–7.

[198] Hurnard, 'Jury of presentment', 395.

[199] Richardson and Sayles, *Governance*, 306–9, suggest that only less important cases, those begun in archdeacons' courts, were affected by this clause.

were reserved for the king's jurisdiction. By clause i, cases concerning advowson and presentation to churches – which, despite his demonstrable interest in the subject, Henry seems previously to have left almost entirely to the ecclesiastical courts – were now to be dealt with by his own. By clause iii, those accused of serious crime before a royal justice, who were able to prove benefit of clergy, would be tried in the presence of the king's officials in an ecclesiastical court, but if found guilty degraded and returned for sentence as laymen in the royal court.[200] This scheme seems to have operated up to a point during 1163 in the cases of Philip de Brois and the priest of Salisbury diocese, both of which had begun in secular courts only to be removed to church courts albeit with royal representatives in attendance: the crucial exception here had been that the clerks' ultimate sentences had been pronounced by the archbishop, not by the king's justices.[201] By clause ix, disputes over whether land was held in free alms or lay fee were also to be determined in a royal court, by recognition of twelve men before the king's chief justiciar, although Henry did not seek to deprive ecclesiastical or seignorial courts of their jurisdiction over the land, once its status had been settled.[202] A precedent for this measure had been Stephen's order that the men of Luton conduct a recognition into whether five hides appurtenant to the church of Luton were held in free alms or lay fee,[203] but this appears to have been an isolated instance of royal intervention on the subject, and Henry II is not known to have issued any similar instructions before 1164.

In acknowledging the Church's exclusive jurisdiction over land proved to be free alms, and its right to try criminous clerks, Henry seems to have claimed less for the crown than had been practised in his grandfather's time.[204] Otherwise, the assertion that he was reviving the jurisdiction of Henry I – a claim doubtless based on suitable cases recalled by his

---

[200] This is the interpretation of clause iii given in the chapter on 'Henry II and the criminous clerks', in F. W. Maitland, *Roman Canon Law in the Church of England* (London, 1898), 132–47. It has been generally accepted, e.g. Warren, *Henry II*, 481; *English Historical Documents, II, 1042–1189*, ed. D. C. Douglas and G. W. Greenaway (2nd edn, London, 1981), 768, n. 1; Barlow, *Thomas Becket*, 101. [201] Above, nn. 175–82.

[202] In some circumstances, however, the settlement by recognition of the land's tenurial status made further pleading unnecessary: *Royal Writs*, 326–7; Warren, *Henry II*, 342, n. 1.

[203] *Lawsuits*, I, no. 296.

[204] On jurisdiction over free alms (frankalmoign), see S. E. Thorne, 'The assize *utrum* and canon law in England', *Columbia Law Review*, 33 (1933), 428–36. On criminous clerks, see Z. N. Brooke, *The English Church and the Papacy* (Cambridge, 1931), 204–5; Barlow, *Thomas Becket*, 101–4. Cf. Richardson and Sayles, *Governance*, 304–6, where it is suggested that the custom of trying criminous clerks in the king's court had lapsed when, at the outset of his reign, Henry had allowed Archbishop Theobald to take cognisance of the murder case involving Osbert archdeacon of York. This interpretation is followed by W. L. Warren in *Henry II*, 463–4, although stress is laid here also on the growth of ecclesiastical jurisdiction over criminous clerks under Stephen. But for interpretations less favourable to Henry's case, see C. Duggan, 'The Becket dispute and the criminous clerks', *BIHR*, 35 (1962), 1–28; D. Knowles, *Thomas Becket* (London, 1970), 91.

investigators – has found general acceptance.[205] But clause ix did mark a significant advance, with recognitions on the specific issue of whether land was held in free alms or lay fee now to be generally available to litigants but only in the king's courts. It is by no means certain that clause ix embodies the assize *utrum* in the form in which it is known from the *Tractatus de Legibus*,[206] but it represents the first legislation of Henry II by which a certain category of civil pleas came before his courts in first instance.

Further provisions were soon to follow. At the council held at Clarendon early in 1166 were devised the Assize of Clarendon, probably an assize similar if not identical to that known as *novel disseisin*,[207] and possibly an assize of the forest as well.[208] It may also have been about this time that the exchequer began to hear civil suits unconnected with finance, so becoming, in effect, the king's court based at Westminster, and that arrangements for the prosecution of crown pleas by appeal underwent some reform.[209] Together with the eyre conducted during 1166 by

---

[205] E.g. Stenton, 'England: Henry II', 559–61; R. Foreville, *L'Eglise et la Royauté en Angleterre sous Henri II Plantagenêt, 1154–89* (Paris, 1943), 122–61; Richardson and Sayles, *Governance*, 285–320; Knowles, *Thomas Becket*, 88–92; Barlow, *Thomas Becket*, 102.

[206] W. L. Warren, 'Royal justice in England in the twelfth century', *History*, 52 (1967), 171–5; Hudson, *English Common Law*, 129. *Tractatus*, 163–4, says that a recognition shall be held if either party wants to settle the question in that manner, but the Constitutions of Clarendon suggest compulsion: 'if a dispute shall arise . . . it shall be determined by a recognition', etc.

[207] The date of an assize against disseisins seems apparent from the first accounts 'pro dissaisina super breve Regis' and 'pro dissaisina super assisam Regis' in the 1166 pipe roll (*PR12H*, 7, 10, 65). Despite van Caenegem in *Royal Writs*, 283–94 (cf. S. F. C. Milsom, 'Introduction' to Pollock and Maitland, *History of English Law* (2nd edn., reissued Cambridge, 1968), xxxviii–xliv; Milsom, *Historical Foundations of the Common Law* (London, 1969), 117; Warren, *Henry II*, 336–41), most modern commentators accept that the assize of *novel disseisin* originated in 1166, even if subsequently modified: Stenton, *English Justice*, 35–43; Sutherland, *Novel Disseisin*, 5–18; Cheney, 'Litigation', 21–3; Biancalana, 'For want of justice', 478–81; Hudson, *English Common Law*, 131.

[208] Richardson and Sayles, *Governance*, 444–7, where it is suggested as a preliminary to Alan de Neville's forest eyre of 1166–7.

[209] P. A. Brand, '"Multis vigiliis excogitatem et inventam": Henry II and the creation of the English common law', *Haskins Society Journal*, 2 (1990), 197–222 (esp. 206–9); M. H. Kerr, 'Angevin reform of the appeal of felony', *Law and History Review*, 13 (1995), 351–91. In discussing prosecution of crown pleas other than by presentment, Kerr argues (353–4) that 'Henry II modified the approver's appeal of felony for his own uses and between 1155–6 and 1165–6 recruited approvers on a case-by-case basis to appeal of offenses committed against the Crown. Between 1165–6 and *c.*1187, approvers were kept on retainer to prosecute'. Although good use is made of pipe roll evidence to support this case, the extent of change may be exaggerated. First, as Kerr points out,(355) there is a possible reference to such king's approvers in 1130 (*PR 31 Hen. I*, 1); lack of pipe rolls may also conceal their employment under Stephen. It could be, therefore, that – as in other areas of government during the early years of his reign – Henry II began by continuing, or reviving, an already established system. Secondly, the switch to 'crown approvers' on long retainers may be more apparent than real, partly explicable by changes in the style of pipe roll entries; anonymous approvers in early pipe rolls may also have been retained long term, as seems to have been the case with Humphrey Pincewerre who occurs at both *PR2H*, 4 and *PR4H*, 111, 113.

Richard de Lucy and Geoffrey III de Mandeville, these measures were of great significance for judicial development. But important steps had already been taken. Itinerant justices were active in the North and Midlands during 1163, with results similar in some respects to those of Alan de Neville's forest eyre of 1166–7. There appears to have been a drive against crime in 1163, resulting in some shires in the forfeiture of chattels to the king. Juries of presentment may have been employed against criminals, as they certainly were in church courts from 1164, probably earlier. On a specific issue, that of whether land was held as free alms or lay fee, procedure by recognition in the king's courts was made generally available to litigants in 1164. By that time, also, the earliest final concords in royal courts had appeared, and detailed procedures were in place whereby tenants could take cases to superior courts on complaint of delay by their immediate lords. And there had already been legislation on seisin, even before 1163. One ordinance, probably dating to 1158, had prohibited the disseisin without judgment of advowsons since the king's last departure overseas. Another – possibly the same – had given similar protection to all free tenures. Yet another appears to have forbidden Englishmen to plead for land unless they could show seisin at, or since, the death of Henry I by themselves or their *antecessores*.[210] All this is sufficient demonstration of royal interest in judicial procedure, in a variety of contexts, throughout the first decade of the reign: but it was in the months which followed Henry's return to the kingdom in January 1163 that concerted efforts began to be made to extend the scope and increase the activity of the king's own courts. Preparations were under way for the measures which would transform the administration of royal justice in the middle and later years of the reign.

CONCLUSION

Already by the death of Henry I, the 'feudal world' of England had been obliged to take account of regulation by the king, which had enforced the services due from vassals to their lords but had also tended towards the protection of tenants' rights in land, to security and inheritance.[211] Stephen – or the alternative Scots and Angevin rulers – had maintained as best they could a style of government familiar from the previous reign, and had attempted therefore to continue the practice of royal intervention in disputes over land and in the affairs of lords and vassals.[212] Accordingly, Henry II came to the throne as heir to a tradition of royal

---

[210] Cf. above, n. 94.
[211] Hudson, *Land, Law and Lordship*, 36–9, 59–61, 135–8; cf. e.g. Green, *Henry I*, 102–5; Dalton, *Conquest, Anarchy and Lordship*, 261–3.   [212] White, 'Continuity', 120–1, 132; above, ch. 2.

involvement, especially in the activities of seignorial courts, a tradition which had remained alive – in memory if not always in practice – through the years of civil war, and which imposed a weight of expectation upon him. He also took the throne having agreed with Stephen at Winchester in November 1153 that the disinherited should be restored *ad propria*, a task the old king had begun but in which he can hardly have made much headway before his death less than twelve months later.[213] Henry's response was to do as his predecessors had done: to deal with cases between tenants-in-chief and any of particular interest either in person or through his justices, but otherwise to rely heavily on the jurisdiction of others, which he would prompt and enforce as occasion required. To this extent, 'royal justice in the first decade of Henry II's reign is indistinguishable' from what had gone before.[214] But Henry did much more than this. He issued ordinances protecting seisin and prohibiting unsupported accusations, which – albeit focused on the work of courts other than the king's – demonstrate a concern for judicial process surpassing that of previous rulers. And when opportunity arose in the mid-1160s, he turned his attention to wide-ranging reform of royal justice. He spent all but three months out of thirty-eight between January 1163 and March 1166 on the English side of the Channel,[215] the political and military crises of his early reign behind him. This was the context in which the royal courts could be made more accessible, more attractive to litigants, and hence more active as agencies of governmental control.

This analysis, which summarises the arguments presented on the foregoing pages, owes much to scholars still active on both sides of the Atlantic. But there is room for further discussion here of some of the issues they raise. Much of what follows is controversial and is offered as a contribution to debate, but it seems consonant with the interpretation of Henry II's approach to the dispensation of justice presented in the foregoing pages. We may ask, first of all, about the significance to be attached to the writ of right, whereby (in the versions given in the *Tractatus de Legibus*) the king ordered a lord to do full right to a plaintiff who claimed to be his tenant, or else the case would pass to the sheriff. This writ, which certainly increased in popularity during the course of Henry's reign, has been seen as the means whereby the incoming king sought to restore the disinherited, as promised in 1153,[216] and also as the key to an understanding of the basis on which Henry claimed jurisdiction

---

[213] *Gesta Steph.*, 240; Holt, '1153', 297; White, 'End of Stephen's reign', 17–21, and 'Continuity', 138.   [214] Warren, *Henry II*, 324; cf. Hudson, *English Common Law*, 139.

[215] *Itinerary*, 58–92 (cf. Stenton, 'England: Henry II', 554, n. 1).

[216] Milsom, *Legal Framework*, 178–9, and *Historical Foundations*, 128–9; cf. Palmer, 'Origins of property', 11.

from seignorial courts, namely that there had been 'default of justice'
therein.[217] Both propositions have some validity, but their advocates have
overstated their case. Royal commands that wrongdoers do right to a
plaintiff, under threat of removal of the suit to another's jurisdiction,
were obviously one way in which disseisins committed during the civil
war could be reversed, but there are no grounds for making this the
driving force behind the writ of right: the writ was applicable to property
disputes whenever they arose, there being no emphasis in surviving
examples upon the upheavals of Stephen's reign.[218] The tenor of the writ,
which left jurisdiction in first instance to a seignorial court, but
threatened removal elsewhere in 'default of justice', was clearly appropriate to the circumstances of Henry II's early years, when the king found
demand for his intervention in civil lawsuits outstripping his capacity to
become involved in person or through his justices; but to suggest that,
almost from the outset of the reign, the king was concerned to assert the
jurisdiction of his courts, and saw this ostensible respect for seignorial
justice as a calculated means to that end, is to strain the evidence too far.[219]
A fairer interpretation is surely that, aware of the importance of there
being some sanction from the king to underpin the activities of seignorial
courts, provision was made for transfer elsewhere but only as a last resort.
A more certain method of claiming jurisdiction for the royal courts was to
issue a writ *praecipe*, whereby the king – via a sheriff – ordered a
wrongdoer to redress a grievance or come to his court to show why he
had not done so.[220] But although Stephen had issued a writ of 1140x54
which adumbrated this formula,[221] hardly any comparable examples
survive from the first years of Henry II's reign, and there is no firm basis
for the suggestion that the writ was developed at this time 'alongside the
writ of right' as part of a concerted policy.[222] Through the late 1150s and
1160s, it seems to have been issued only occasionally. Writs which left
jurisdiction in first instance to the traditional courts were clearly Henry
II's favoured device in the early years of his reign, because he had no wish

---

[217] Biancalana, 'For want of justice', 442–66, esp. 461.

[218] *Royal Writs*, nos. 19, 20; *Register of St Benet*, I, nos. 32–4; *Chronicle of Battle Abbey*, 212; cf.
Biancalana, 'For want of justice', 450–1; Brand, *Making of the Common Law*, 221. Although several
of these disputes arose during Stephen's reign, the writs did not labour the point.

[219] Biancalana, 'For want of justice', 442–66; for example, the arguments for significant developments in the formulae of writs of right (449–50), and the claim that plaintiffs 'frequently' had
difficulty invoking the help of superior lords named in *nisi feceris* clauses (463–4), are based on very
few cases.   [220] *Tractatus*, 5, 179–80; *Royal Writs*, 234–51.

[221] *RRAN*, III, no. 692; Chibnall, *Anglo-Norman England*, 178.

[222] Biancalana, 'For want of justice', 465 and n. 153. None of the writs of Henry II classified under
praecipe in *Royal Writs*, nos. 47–9, provide for immediate summons to a royal court if the defaulter
failed to act, in a manner similar to those given in *Tractatus*; however no. 127, issued by Queen
Eleanor in 1156–57, does so (cf. *Reading Abbey Cartularies*, I, no. 467).

at that stage to inundate the royal courts with a rush of business. Writs of right suited his purposes well.

The early development of the writ of right is itself problematical. The phrase *breve de recto* cannot be proved to have been in use before 1158, and first appeared in the pipe rolls during the 1170s.[223] On the other hand, there is no reason to suppose that contemporaries restricted the term to writs in the standard form set out in the 1180s in the *Tractatus,* invariably addressing a lord with the sheriff in the *nisi feceris* clause.[224] Accordingly, several writs issued by Henry I commanding a lord or sheriff to 'do right', sometimes with an alternative figure who was supposed to intervene if they did not, may in fact have been described as 'writs of right'.[225] Moreover, there are forty-four accounts *pro recto* (or similar) in the 1130 pipe roll, although not all arose in the same year; these have rightly been taken as indications of lively demand from plaintiffs for royal intervention in their lawsuits, intervention which in at least some cases probably led to the production of writs.[226]

It is worth emphasising, however, that – in contrast to the picture presented by the 1130 pipe roll – evidence from between 1135 and 1162 for the issue of what may be acknowledged as 'writs of right' is by no means abundant. The canons of St Frideswide's, Oxford, recovered a hide of land in the earl of Leicester's seignorial court about 1147, apparently after the case had begun on a writ of right, but since its text does not survive we do not know whether this later cartulary reference is to be trusted.[227] The writs classified by van Caenegem as nascent 'writs of right' include none at all from Stephen's reign and only two from the period 1155–62, one of which did not use the phrase 'do right' and might properly belong in a different category altogether.[228] There are a few other examples which may be assigned to Henry II's early years, including three in favour of St Benet's Abbey, Holme, but most of these cannot be securely dated.[229] Meanwhile, the pipe rolls of Henry II's first ten years have only six accounts *pro recto terre* or some variant thereof, and while it is

---

[223] *EYC*, iv(i), 37–8; *PR22H*, 85; *Royal Writs*, 206, 231; Stenton, *English Justice*, 28–9.

[224] *Tractatus*, 137–8.   [225] *Royal Writs*, nos. 12, 13, 139, 141, 143.

[226] *Ibid.*, 231–3; Green, *Henry I*, 102–3, and *Aristocracy of Norman England*, 201–2.

[227] *Lawsuits*, I, no. 316; cf. *Royal Writs*, 207. Crouch, *Beaumont Twins*, 161–2, dates this plea to Henry II's reign, apparently because of the reference to a writ of right, but a papal confirmation of the eventual settlement is dated 27 May 1147 (*Cartulary of St Frideswide*, II, no. 1122).

[228] *Royal Writs*, nos. 18, 19, the former recurring as no. 151.

[229] Above, n. 218. Of these, the two in *Royal Writs* are tentatively dated 1162 and 1165 respectively, while two in favour of St Benet's, Holme, may belong to 1163x66. *Lawsuits*, II, no. 362 rehearses a case of 1154x57 in the prior of Spalding's court begun by a royal writ of right. The Battle chronicler mentions what appears to be a writ of right in his account of the abbey's dispute over Barnhorn early in Henry II's reign, and may well have copied from a text held in the abbey, but given that he was writing a generation later it is possible that his wording is anachronistic.

almost certain that some relevant payments failed to be properly described, the stark contrast with much higher totals in subsequent rolls cannot be dismissed.[230] The upshot of all this is that those who would see the writ of right as central to Henry II's policies for judicial reform almost from the beginning of the reign – even to the point of suggesting that there was legislation to encourage its use [231] – are making too much of very limited evidence. Writs to 'do right' were one option available to Henry II as a means to initiate pleading without the royal courts becoming immediately involved. They were one of the devices Henry I had resorted to, and possibly Stephen as well, and as such they were a well-tried solution to the problems of meeting demands from plaintiffs in the pressurised circumstances of the early years of his reign. They were not the only possible response, and their principal role was not to increase the activity of the king's courts, although clearly that might be one consequence, given the provisions for removal of cases elsewhere in 'default of justice'. An earnest desire for royal intervention is evident from the sudden leap in accounts for writs of right entered in the 1165 pipe roll, a reflection of demand once the king was back in the country from January 1163:[232] they oscillated thereafter, in a manner which may also relate to the readiness with which he could be approached at any time.[233] It was in this context of buoyant demand from below that the king, having dealt with the political and military crises of the early phase of his reign, felt able from 1163 to introduce measures which were bound to enhance the jurisdiction of his courts.

As alternatives to writs of right, Henry I, Stephen and Henry II in his early years all had recourse to writs ordering that plaintiffs justly be reseised of property they had lost.[234] With their focus upon seisin and

---

[230] *Royal Writs*, 231–4; cf. 98–9 for Professor van Caenegem's own reservations on statistics derived from pipe rolls.

[231] *Tractatus*, 148, states that 'no one is bound to answer concerning any free tenement of his in the court of his lord, unless there is a writ from the lord king or his justice' (cf. the restatement of this rule from the plaintiff's viewpoint, *ibid.*, 137). Although Stenton, *English Justice*, 26–9, argues for the deliberate introduction of this rule early in Henry II's reign, 'whether . . . by a general ordinance or a series of instructions', *Tractatus*, 148, states that its origins were customary and this has been widely accepted (e.g. *Royal Writs*, 223–5; Biancalana, 'For want of justice', 467; Hudson, *Land, Law and Lordship*, 255–6, n. 6; Hudson, *English Common Law*, 192; cf. Milsom, *Legal Framework*. 57–9). For examples of freeholds impleaded in seignorial courts early in Henry II's reign, apparently without initiating royal writs, see above, nn. 20–2.

[232] *Royal Writs*, 231–3; above, n. 172, for an entry in the 1165 pipe roll relating to a fine apparently proffered in 1163.

[233] Henry II returned to England after a four-year absence in March 1170; in the pipe roll of that year there were thirty accounts apparently for writs of right, twice the total from the previous four years put together. A sojourn in England between June 1184 and April 1185 may also explain the second highest annual total of the reign, twenty-two, in the 1185 pipe roll (*Itinerary*, 92–135, 256–63; *Royal Writs*, 232–3).   [234] *Ibid.*, nos. 64–72, 74–7, 79–89.

disseisin, based upon facts surrounding possession and dispossession more readily ascertainable than those concerned with invisible 'right', such writs had long been seen as a means towards the swift resolution of disputes, and they must often have been preferred by plaintiffs to the prospect of delay and either compromise or trial by battle which might follow an order to 'do right'.[235] The reasons for the choice of writ – why one dispute called forth a writ of right but another an order to reseise – are not always clear,[236] but both were attractive, from Henry II's point of view, because they directed that issues be settled outside the king's courts, albeit with the latter available if orders were disobeyed. Nor was this the only respect in which Henry's early writs ordering reseisin 'show no advance on those of his Norman predecessors',[237] for such preliminary hearings as were envisaged in seignorial or communal courts were normally without prescription as to the mode of proof. Thus, Henry I had ordered the sheriff and (apparently) the local justice of Oxfordshire to ensure that the abbot of Abingdon held a hide of land in Fencote 'and if he has been diseised there, let him be reseised' and also recover any chattels taken away. Stephen had instructed Walter fitz Gilbert and his reeve of Maldon that 'if the canons of St Martin's London can show' that they had been 'unjustly and without judgment disseised . . . of their burgage land of Maldon', they were to 'cause them to be reseised as they were seised of it on the day when King Henry was alive and dead' with restoration of chattels; a *nisi feceris* clause was added, providing for the intervention if necessary of Richard de Lucy and the sheriff of Essex. In his turn, Henry II commanded Simon de Caus to let the monks of Spalding hold four bovates in Welton in peace, 'and if they are unjustly and without judgment disseised of any lands in the said vill . . . I order that you justly reseise them'; here the justice of Lincolnshire featured in the *nisi feceris* clause.[238] The writs of Stephen and Henry II both envisaged the prospect of a royal justice taking cognisance of the case – Richard de Lucy having been local justice of Essex [239] – but only if the initial orders were disobeyed: to this extent they were less assertive of royal jurisdiction than the writ of Henry I, which had evidently been directed in first instance to a (presumed) royal justice alongside a sheriff. This is not a point to be pressed: like his successors, Henry I had certainly addressed other writs to disseisors direct,[240] and it is possible that he had already done so, and been ignored, in this case. But it seems clear that, in the early years of Henry

[235] Sutherland, *Novel Disseisin*, 35–6; Hudson, *English Common Law*, 110–12.
[236] Biancalana, 'For want of justice', 444–5; cf. Green, *Henry I*, 103.
[237] Stenton, *English Justice*, 34.   [238] *Royal Writs*, nos. 76, 86, 94.
[239] *RRAN*, III, xxiv and nos. 546–7, 549, 559.   [240] *Royal Writs*, nos. 75, 80.

II's reign, while several ingredients later found in writs of *novel disseisin* were already familiar – the restoration of chattels, the reference back to seisin enjoyed at a given point in time, above all the allegation of disseisin 'unjustly and without judgment' to which the writ was responding – there was as yet no hint of a distinctive new procedure available only in the royal courts.

Even so, it would be wrong to suggest that there were no developments in this period which had a bearing upon the *novel disseisin* process. By the middle years of the twelfth century, laymen as well as ecclesiastics were being increasingly exposed to the distinction in Roman canonical law between *possessio* and *proprietas*, and it is hard to believe that these ideas had no influence upon those who subsequently framed Henry II's possessory assizes.[241] Writing about 1188, the author of the *Tractatus de Legibus* clearly recognised a difference between the two. In setting out the scheme of the book, he separated pleas which 'concern solely claims to the property (*super proprietate*) in the disputed subject-matter' from those 'in which the claim is based on possession (*super possessione*), and which are determined by recognitions'. When he eventually came to deal with the latter, he repeated the division as one between right and seisin: those pleas 'which are concerned with seisin (*super saisinis*) only' are 'by virtue of a constitution of the realm called an assize . . . for the most part settled by recognition'.[242] The author of the *Tractatus*, an experienced practitioner in the courts of Henry II, would not have seen *proprietas* and *possessio* in quite the same way as a diligent student of canon law,[243] but it was essential nevertheless to the efficient operation of Henry II's possessory assizes that some distinction between right and seisin be acknowledged. In practice, both represented entitlement to tenure. However, for the king's justices charged with applying the law, to determine right might involve complex issues with a long history, leading ultimately to settlement by the judgment of God through trial by battle (although, as the *Tractatus* explained, the magnanimous king did eventually provide an alternative through the Grand Assize).[244] On the other hand, questions of seisin and disseisin were seen as susceptible to resolution by reference to recent, well-known, facts: facts based on the evidence of manifest possession, but with some account taken also of whether such possession was 'just'. These were facts which a jury of recognition could declare, albeit

---

[241] M. G. Cheney, '*Possessio/proprietas* in ecclesiastical courts in mid-twelfth-century England', in Garnett and Hudson, *Law and Government*, 245–54.   [242] *Tractatus*, 4, 148.
[243] *Ibid.*, xxx–xxxiii; Sutherland, *Novel Disseisin*, 41–2; R. V. Turner, 'Who was the author of *Glanvill*? Reflections on the education of Henry II's common lawyers', *Law and History Review*, 8 (1990), 97–127.   [244] *Tractatus*, 26–8, 180–1.

with the possibility of there being subsequent pleading on the more difficult issue of right.[245]

The distinction so important to the later possessory assizes can occasionally be glimpsed in lawsuits early in the reign. Sometime between Henry's accession in 1154 and the death of Archbishop Theobald in April 1161, there was a case in the archbishop's seignorial court between one Peter and the canons of St Paul's, London, in which Peter sought seisin of land in Wimbledon and Barnes; his claim rested on his father's possession of the land on the day of Henry I's death and his mother's subsequent tenure until her own death. Peter's claim to seisin failed because he had nothing to show that the tenure was hereditary, but the court ruled that he could plead again on the question of right (*jus*) if he wished to do so. While Theobald's seignorial court might be expected to be more sensitive than most to the influence of canonical thought, it is surely significant that this case began on the strength of a royal command – presumably a writ which ordered that Peter be reseised 'if disseised unjustly and without judgment', but one which did not prohibit subsequent pleading on right.[246] Another relevant case is the canons of Lincoln's claim to land near the water of the city, which prompted a writ from Henry probably to be dated either 1158x63 or 1165. This ordered the sheriff to conduct a recognition by lawful men of the city into whether the canons were seised of the land at Henry I's death, and were subsequently disseised unjustly and without judgment. If so, they were to be reseised thereof, but further impleading (presumably on the issue of right) was still envisaged, since the king expressly prohibited this until his return to England.[247] The key feature of the possessory assizes was already in place: focus on disseisin would allow the swift resolution of disputes over property but would not debar a plea on the issue of right if this was pursued.

Henry's early legislation against unjust disseisin merits further scrutiny here, particularly with reference to the legacy of Stephen's reign. It is fair to suggest that, in general terms, the experience of violent self-help under Stephen prompted a concern to guard against such conduct in future, but

---

[245] Sutherland, *Novel Disseisin*, 36–42; cf. e.g. S. E. Thorne, 'Livery of seisin', *Law Quarterly Review*, 52 (1936), 345–64; N. D. Hurnard, 'Did Edward I reverse Henry II's policy upon seisin?', *EHR*, 69 (1954), 529–53; *Royal Writs*, 306–16; Warren, *Henry II*, 341; Milsom, *Historical Foundations*, 119–22; Hudson, *Land, Law and Lordship*, 267–8 and *English Common Law*, 88, 150.

[246] *Lawsuits*, II, no. 393; cf. Stenton, *English Justice*, 34; R. C. Palmer, 'The feudal framework of English law', *Michigan Law Review*, 79 (1981), 1130–64 (at 1148); Hudson, *Land, Law and Lordship*, 104, 135.

[247] *Royal Writs*, no. 96; cf. Stenton, *English Justice*, 34–5 (dated 1155x66 *ibid.* and in *Reg. Ant.*, I, no. 156, but limited by the place-date, Tinchebrai; on the other hand, the attestation by Manasser Bisset does not rule out a later date).

the measures taken to protect seisin during the late 1150s and 1160s were not framed specifically to help resolve disputes left by civil war. Consistently, it was seisin enjoyed at some date in Henry II's reign which was safeguarded and – where lost – was to be restored. The edict or constitution mentioned in Archbishop Theobald's letters suggests that advowsons were protected against disseisin without judgment after the king's departure for Normandy in August 1158; where this had occurred, as in the cases to which the letters refer, the disseisee was to be put back in, pending further pleading in an ecclesiastical court.[248] Evidence for the assize apparently covering disseisin of all free tenures is a little more complicated. Probably in the second half of 1162, Henry issued from Rouen two writs in favour of St Benet's Abbey, Holme. One ordered William bishop of Norwich to cause the parishioners of Waxham to come to their church which was of the abbot's fee as in Henry I's time, and to cause the abbot to have land unjustly occupied by Walter priest of Waxham in time of war. The other ordered the bishop to cause the abbot and monks to have tithes due from Ernald fitz Roger of Ingham, as from Ernald's predecessors in Henry I's reign. Both concluded with the phrase 'et non remaneat pro assisa mea', before adding, in the *nisi feceris* clause, that Thomas archbishop of Canterbury would do it if the bishop failed.[249] Another writ, issued from Poitiers, ordered Bartholemew bishop of Exeter without delay to cause a recognition to be held by the oath of lawful men of Treger hundred into land in Cornwall held by the canons of Plympton in the time of one of his predecessors Robert Warelwast (who had died in 1155). He was to ensure, justly and without delay, that the canons held whatever was so recognised, 'et non remaneat pro assisa mea vel exercitu meo'; Earl Reginald would do it if the bishop did not.[250] A further writ in the Spalding Priory register, unfortunately without witnesses or place-date, has the king ordering all who held of the prior and convent to render the services and allow them the demesne of Henry I's time, unless they could show quittance of service or a claim to the land

---

[248] Above, n. 88–9.

[249] *Register of St Benet*, I, nos. 39, 36; *Royal Writs*, nos. 21, 22. Van Caenegem followed the original editor's dating, 1162x66 and 1162x68. However, the writs were issued from Rouen and Henry II was in England from January 1163 to *c.*February 1165 and again from May 1165 until March 1166 (*Itinerary*, 58, 78–9, 92); Becket, named (as archbishop) in the *nisi feceris* clause of both writs, was in exile from November 1164. The writs may safely be assigned to the period between Becket's consecration as archbishop on 3 June 1162 and the king's return to England at the beginning of 1163.

[250] *Royal Writs*, no. 23. Bartholemew was consecrated bishop of Exeter soon after 18 April 1161 (Diceto, I, 304); Reginald earl of Cornwall died on 1 July 1175 (*CP*, III, 429). Robert Warelwast was bishop from 1138 until his death on 28 March 1155.

by charter or other reasonable proof in the prior's court: 'et non remaneat prope assisam meam vel exercitum'.[251]

The assize and the *exercitus* were matters which might obstruct the order but must not do so. The puzzling reference to the *exercitus* is of little help in dating the writs and should not be allowed to deflect us from the main argument: it may relate to some provision in the assize which protected the seisin of those providing knight-service for one of the king's military campaigns. Be that as it may, we have here four writs which envisaged the possible transfer of seisin – of land or tithes – from one party to the other, by order of the king and apparently against the terms of his assize. If we accept that the word 'juste' could serve as an invitation to a preliminary hearing,[252] all four envisaged a judicial enquiry in a local court, but the thrust of the writs was that the king expected the abbot of St Benet's, the canons of Plympton and the monks of Spalding to recover seisin of what they had lost. The three writs for which we have place-dates were all issued in France and could all have been sent in or about 1162: those for Holme almost certainly belong to that year, while the king probably visited Poitiers – source of the Plympton writ – in 1161 and may have been at Chinon (little over forty miles to the north) in June 1162.[253] There is good reason here to conclude that the assize referred to in the writs was one protecting free tenures against disseisin without judgment, since the king's last departure overseas in 1158. It may have been the same legislation as that referred to in the specific context of advowson in Theobald's letters, although this is unlikely since none of the writs makes express provision for pleading subsequent to the redress of disseisin, as was envisaged in the advowson disputes. Whether the same 'constitution' or a new one, it was offering general protection to seisin – presumably seisin enjoyed at the time of Henry's departure in 1158 – which the king had now been prevailed upon in these specific cases to override. The assize had almost certainly been introduced as 'a general peacekeeping measure' to prevent disputes left over from Stephen's reign breaking out into violent self-help once the king was out of the coun-

---

[251] B.L. Add. MS. 35296, fo. 88. The king ordered all tenants of Spalding Priory to do service as in Henry I's time unless they could show quittance by charter or other reasonable proof in the priory's court. 'Precipio etiam ut prefati prior et monachi sui habeant omnes terras de dominio suo quas ipsi vel predecessores sui habuerunt tempore predicti avi nostri, nisi monstrare poteritis per cartas prioris et conventus quod eas habere debeatis vel alicuius rationabiliter in eorum curia et non remaneat prope assisam meam vel exercitum' (no witnesses copied). This is a classic example of what Milsom has called a 'downward claim' whereby a lord sought to recover land or rights lost to his tenants (Milsom, *Legal Framework*, 88; Biancalana, 'For want of justice', 474).

[252] Above, n. 67.

[253] A. Richard, *Histoire des Comtes de Poitou, 778–1204* (Paris, 1903), II, 133–4; *RAH*, I, no. 227; *Itinerary*, 54, 57.

try.[254] But here we have the king, in or about 1162, intervening on behalf of the abbot of Holme and others, to annul the provisions of his own assize. Why? The probable answer is that, in practice, the assize was protecting seisins wrongfully acquired – mostly during the civil war although in the Plympton case possibly since 1155. The disseisors were benefiting from the fact they had still been in occupation (or still withholding tithes) at the time of the king's departure in August 1158, so Henry found himself obliged to step in to correct a manifest injustice. If this interpretation is valid, there was obviously a need for a less cumbersome solution to the problem of how to reverse unjust disseisins, especially where the issue at stake was an acquisition under Stephen.

Out of a recognition by Henry II and his advisers of the importance for peacekeeping of there being swift redress for unjust disseisins, out of their growing appreciation that, for these purposes, seisin could be treated separately from right, and out of a policy of extending the scope of royal justice in response to demand from below, were forged the assize of *novel disseisin*, available only in the courts of the king and his justices. Of the procedures envisaged under this assize in the *Tractatus de Legibus*, the use of the 'returnable writ' was a genuine innovation of Henry II's reign; this ensured that the sheriff would bring not only the interested parties before the king's justices on the appointed day, but also the document which authorised the action.[255] Otherwise, the assize represented a regularisation and routinisation of familiar features, to the implementation of which the sheriff's cooperation was essential: his responsibilities included the restoration of chattels and the summoning of a jury to view the property and make recognition before the king's justices of the facts as it knew them.[256] But the widespread availability of royal justices was crucial to the success of the measure, especially if disputes left over from the civil war were to be resolved. The stated intention of the assize was to reverse *novel* disseisins – those committed in the recent past, certainly no earlier than Henry II's accession and usually much nearer in time.[257] That being the case, there was a danger that it would work, perversely, to protect those who had acquired seisin in the turmoil of Stephen's reign and had remained in place thereafter, against those who sought to correct an injustice once Henry was king. This did not, in fact, happen because the royal justices who controlled proceedings could guard against the protection of seisins acquired *tempore guerrae*. Under the assize, the jury was

---

[254] Biancalana, 'For want of justice', 474–5 (although a later date for the Plympton writ is suggested there).   [255] Stenton, *English Justice*, 32.

[256] See *Royal Writs*, nos. 5, 26, 33, 37, 38, 61, 66, 74–6, 79, 82, 86, 106–17, 153–4 for examples of earlier writs ordering restoration of chattels (under various phrases) and *ibid.*, nos. 14, 96, 144, 148, 150 for writs ordering recognitions.

[257] *Tractatus*, 167; *Royal Writs*, 286; Sutherland, *Novel Disseisin*, 9–10 and n. 6.

obliged to declare not only whether there had been a disseisin without judgment within the time limit but also whether it had been done 'unjustly'; the justices could ensure a uniform interpretation that to disseise an intruder of Stephen's reign was in no way 'unjust'.[258] Frequent accessibility to the king's justices, accomplished through the revival of systematic judicial eyres, therefore became essential if the assize of *novel disseisin* was not only to serve as a swift and widespread remedy for civil disputes, but also if it was not to frustrate the resolution of conflicts which had arisen under Stephen. Accordingly, these eyres would become regular features from 1168 onwards, following previous visitations by Richard de Lucy and Geoffrey III de Mandeville two years earlier.[259]

We do not know how soon the assize of *novel disseisin* achieved the fully developed form shown in *Tractatus de Legibus*, but given the agonising which went into its preparation,[260] and given the opportunities for revision occasioned by frequent changes to the time limit, it is quite possible that it underwent some refinement after its first appearance. Nevertheless, the assize on disseisins which prompted pleas before the king's itinerant justices, first recorded in the 1166 pipe roll, can probably fairly be described as that of *novel disseisin*.[261] As such, it represented a major advance for the jurisdiction of the king's courts. Henry II's previous interventions on this subject, like those of his predecessors, had envisaged preliminary hearings on the justice of disseisin or reseisin in seignorial or other local courts: that responsibility now passed as a matter of routine to the courts of the king's justices, who applied fixed procedures and consistent interpretation of the law.

The 'routinisation' of royal justice has come to be seen in recent years as the critical advance in judicial administration under Henry II.[262] By the

---

[258] According to testimony given in 1219, Hervey *cum Barba* successfully recovered his holding in Suffolk in a royal court (apparently some time in Henry II's reign) on the grounds that he had been disseised 'occasione guerre' under Stephen (*Curia R.R.*, VIII, 19). See *Rolls of the Justices in Eyre for Gloucs., Warwicks, [Salop]*, nos. 1002, 1016, 1017 (all in 1221) for seisins acquired 'tempore guerre' during John's reign failing to enjoy protection in actions of *novel disseisin* (cf. Hurnard, 'Did Edward I reverse Henry II's policy?', 531 and n. 1). It is, however, worth noting the case cited in Stenton, *English Feudalism*, 82, 270, where the principle that seisin acquired violently under Stephen should not be protected is upheld by Richard de Clare earl of Hertford, rather than by the king's justices.

[259] Warren, *Henry II*, 285–7, and *Governance*, 111 (although contrasts with eyres of Henry I's reign are stressed).

[260] Bracton, *On the Laws and Customs of England*, ed. G. E. Woodbine and S. E. Thorne, III (Harvard, 1977), 25.

[261] Thus (with some variation, notably on the significance of precursors) Stenton, *English Justice*, 35–43; Sutherland, *Novel Disseisin*, esp. 5–18; J. Loengard, 'The assize of nuisance: origins of an action at common law', *Cambridge Law Journal*, 37 (1978), 144–66 (at 153–7); Cheney, 'Litigation' esp. 22–3; Biancalana, 'For want of justice', 473–81; Hudson, *English Common Law*, 131. Arguments for a later date for the assize appear in e.g. *Royal Writs*, 283–94, and Warren, *Henry II*, 336–41. [262] Hudson, *English Common Law*, 139–44.

1170s the country was growing accustomed to nationwide general eyres and the exchequer at Westminster was also being used regularly for civil litigation. The justices involved, here and on eyre, were expected not merely to preside over but also to judge the cases before them; according-ly, they developed into a professional 'core', committed to applying the king's 'common law' throughout the land.[263] Probably during the same decade, further possessory assizes – *mort d'ancestor, darrein presentment* – were introduced, as was the Grand Assize which sought to use juries of recognition to determine questions of right.[264] All this is sufficient to demonstrate that the notion of an 'Angevin Leap Forward' retains some validity, even though there are *caveats* to be entered. The crown had already become heavily involved in civil litigation, in particular in the relationship between lords and vassals, through the issue of writs to initiate or prohibit impleading as early as the reign of Henry I: to this extent, the 'feudal world' had already been accustomed to royal regula-tion long before Henry II's reforms. The demand for royal intervention had continued, even under Stephen, and had persisted through the early years of Henry II's reign despite the king's prolonged absences from the country. Although it is fair to assume that the king and his advisers welcomed the opportunity to assert royal authority through enhancing the activities of royal courts, it must be recognised that they were responding to demand from below, and were prepared to wait until more pressing political matters were behind them. It is also true that the subsequent impact of Henry II's judicial reforms should not be exag-gerated: though beneficial to freeholders in general, they were of limited applicability to the king's tenants-in-chief, and they certainly did not put an end to aggressive self-help in the transfer of land.[265] Yet when all this is acknowledged, it remains true that Henry II and his circle were successful in making royal justice significantly more accessible and more attractive, through devising processes available only in the king's courts, and through appointing teams of increasingly professional justices to conduct them. These measures can be seen, with hindsight, to have contributed to a 'transformation of government', to the routine, more penetrative, involvement of the crown in the affairs of ordinary people through most of the country.[266] The promulgation in 1166 of assizes against crime and disseisins, and the despatch of justices to put them into effect, mark that

---

[263] Brand, '"Multis vigiliis"', and on non-professional justices hitherto, 'The origins of the English legal profession', *Law and History Review*, 5 (1987), 31–50.
[264] *Tractatus*, 26–37, 149–63, 180–1; *Royal Writs*, 87–9, 316–35; Warren, *Henry II*, 341–8, 352–4; Hudson, *English Common Law*, 132–4.
[265] Hudson, *Land, Law and Lordship*, 280, and *English Common Law*, 209–12, 219.
[266] Warren, *Governance*, 105–6; cf. Hudson, *English Common Law*, 145–6.

year as a significant one for judicial reform, the momentum of which continued for the rest of the reign. But the first signs of positive action by Henry II to attract cases to his courts belong to 1163, when he spent a good deal of time hearing cases in person, when royal justices were active in several shires, and when there appears to have been a drive against crime in certain parts of the country, involving the forfeiture of chattels to the king. Early in the following year, procedure by recognition in the king's courts was made generally available to litigants on the specific issue of whether land was held in free alms or lay fee. These measures, which helped to fuel the king's conflict over rival jurisdictions with Archbishop Becket, signalled a change in policy.

It is of course quite possible that Henry II and his advisers intended from the outset of the reign to increase the activity of the royal courts as soon as opportunity allowed: indeed, a man such as the chief justiciar Richard de Lucy, who had intimate experience of the problems of government under Stephen, may well have been contemplating such reforms from the time of the 1153 peace settlement. The expansion of royal justice may have appealed to Henry from the beginning: he devoted most of his first decade as king to asserting royal authority by diplomatic and military means – on both sides of the Channel – and was surely not blind to the jurisdictional dimension to this task. But we can only judge policy by its manifestation, and what we see is a significant change between 1163 and 1166. Concerned as Henry II was to provide for the resolution of disputes and for the maintenance of peace, his courts were not at first equipped to deal with more than the relatively small number of cases in which the king had a special interest, or which might pass to them by default under the terms of a *nisi feceris* clause. Accordingly, his writs to lords and sheriffs should be read as they were written, as instructions to deal with the issues in their own courts: co-operation between royal and seignorial jurisdiction, portrayed by the *Tractatus de Legibus* towards the end of the reign,[267] was a necessity right from the beginning. But after a decade or so in which disputes arising during and after the civil war had been resolved – if resolved at all – largely in traditional courts, albeit with the king in the background to initiate or take over if called upon to do so, the time eventually came for royal justice to adopt a more assertive role.

[267] *Tractatus*, 112.

Chapter 6

CONCLUSION

Henry II made many enemies during his long and turbulent reign and William of Newburgh, writing from the perspective of the 1190s, acknowledged that 'in his own time he was hated by almost everyone'. But – like the grandfather he professed to emulate – Henry won rather more appreciation with the benefit of hindsight, and, as William of Newburgh went on to say, he 'is now declared to have been an excellent and profitable prince'.[1] In the political arena, he did of course accomplish a great deal. Although reverses in his last days against Philip Augustus and his own son Richard led him to die in misery and humiliation, bewailing his fate as a 'vanquished king',[2] his success in assembling and sustaining an Angevin empire embracing most of the British Isles and the western half of France, in defeating rebellion on several fronts in 1173–4, and in averting a disastrous rift with the papacy following the tragic conclusion to the Becket affair were all formidable achievements. In the administrative field, his reign witnessed a transformation in the activity and availability of the king's courts in England, which bore fruit not only in enhanced revenue but also in new perceptions of the pervasiveness of royal government over most of the kingdom.[3] But the focus of this book has been upon less dramatic events and, in relation to his government of England in the early phase of his reign, there remain three questions for further consideration here.

We may ask, first of all, the extent to which Henry II was personally responsible for such reforms as we have identified in this period. The *Tractatus de Legibus* praised the king primarily for his prowess in overcoming his enemies; impartial royal justice was accorded equal importance for the good governance of the realm, but there was no reference to Henry as the deviser of new procedures to facilitate this. He was commended

---

[1] Newburgh, I, 283 (transl., *English Historical Documents*, II, 403). [2] Giraldus, VIII, 297.
[3] E.g. Warren, *Governance*, 105–22; Hudson, *English Common Law*, 123–85.

213

instead for deferring to the judgment of the real heroes of the book, those king's justices 'most learned in the laws and customs' who 'excel all others in sobriety, wisdom and eloquence . . . most prompt and clear-sighted in deciding cases . . . and in settling disputes'.[4] William of Newburgh also depicted Henry II as 'most diligent in defending and promoting the peace of the realm' and in 'appointing judges and legal officials to . . . do justice to litigants'; he might apply a 'royal remedy' when pressurised by complaints, but he preferred to leave his men to get on with the job.[5] In other words, Henry was blessed with good administrators but deserved some credit as the one who appointed them. This accords with certain passages in the *Dialogus de Scaccario*. Although, like the author of the *Tractatus*, Richard fitz Nigel chose to focus on Henry's military triumphs, he did acknowledge the king's role in selecting the earl of Leicester as justiciar to preside at the exchequer, in inviting the bishop of Ely to restore procedures, and in finding seats at the table for Richard of Ilchester and Thomas Brown. It was also the king to whom were attributed the introduction of a decree on distraint and the decision to create six circuits for justices in eyre.[6] The picture is one of loyal, efficient administrators, who owed not only their appointments to Henry II but also the frames of reference within which they worked.

Although much in Henry II's personality was contradictory, his boundless energy, his impulsiveness and his commitment to enhancing the dignity of the crown are beyond doubt.[7] In his early years as king, he expressed all this through due regard for regal ceremony, through an insistence on the recovery of lost revenues and estates, through diplomacy and, when deemed appropriate, through military force against rebel barons and neighbouring princes. This left little opportunity for administrative reform, but it would seem quite in character that he would react vigorously when he learned of some manifest wrong: William of Newburgh said as much when referring to his interventions in response to complaints. We have no way of telling, but the decree to safeguard shipwrecked sailors, which he issued at the outset of the reign, has all the appearance of an outraged response to some atrocity he had seen or heard of.[8] Similarly, his constitution to prohibit unsupported accusations in ecclesiastical courts, in place by 1158,[9] was quite possibly born out of cases brought to the king's attention, and hence of his conviction that matters could not be left as they were. The fact that royal intervention in these

---

[4] *Tractatus*, 1–2.   [5] Newburgh, I, 102 (transl. from Gillingham 'Conquering kings', 170).
[6] *Dialogus*, 26–7, 35–6, 50, 58, 77, 112, 117.
[7] On Henry II's character, see Peter of Blois, *Opera Omnia*, ed. J. A. Giles (Oxford, 1846–47), I, 192–7 and *Becket Materials*, VII, 570–6; Map, *De Nugis Curialium*, 484–6; Giraldus, V, 302–6; cf. Warren, *Henry II*, 207–17.   [8] Newburgh, I, 102, 282.   [9] Above, ch. 5, nn. 86–7.

areas enhanced perceptions of the king as a 'fount of justice', and might
lead in certain circumstances to pleas being heard in his courts, chimed in
with his general concern to uphold the dignity of kingship, but – given
the image we have of Henry's relations with his officials, and given his
many preoccupations in this phase of the reign – it is likely that the king's
personal role was confined to ordering that 'something be done': the
detailed framing of legislation, as well as its implementation, was probably
left to others. Yet if further proof were needed of the king's importance as
the driving force behind reform, one has only to look at his itinerary, the
significance of which has been stressed repeatedly throughout this book.
The enquiry into ducal revenues in Normandy, the ordinance issued at
Falaise on church courts, and the re-enforcement of judicial decrees from
the council of Lillebonne all originated during the years when Henry
spent most of his time in the duchy, from autumn 1159 to the beginning
of 1163.[10] Significant financial and judicial reform in England had to
await his return thereafter.

Reference to administrative measures in Normandy leads us to the
second question: what impact did Henry's continental territories have
upon the manner in which he governed England in his first decade as
king? He is said to have been warned by his father, Geoffrey Plantagenet
count of Anjou, against transferring customs from one territory to another,[11] and, throughout his reign, he generally heeded this paternal
advice. There was no attempt, for example, to provide a uniform system
of local government in the continental lands; regional variations in law
and custom continued to be respected.[12] But he was sometimes prepared
to introduce similar measures on both sides of the Channel, and in the
later stages of the reign there are signs of greater readiness to legislate for
his empire as a whole. The ordinance promulgated at Falaise at Christmas
1159, requiring the testimony of neighbours in ecclesiastical courts,
anticipates clause vi of the Constitutions of Clarendon and may well have
been based upon the law broken by the dean of Scarborough in 1158. An
assize of Geoffrey Plantegenet as duke of Normandy, in some way
specifying procedure by recognition before his justices, adumbrates the
various possessory assizes which his son introduced in both kingdom and
duchy.[13] There were inquests into knights' fees, in England in 1166, in

[10] Above, ch. 1, n. 77.
[11] John of Marmoutier, 'Historia Gaufredi Ducis', in *Chroniques des comtes d'Anjou et des seigneurs d'Amboise*, ed. L. Halphen and R. Poupardin (Paris, 1913), 224.
[12] F. M. Powicke, *The Loss of Normandy* (2nd edn., Manchester, 1961), 19.
[13] Above, ch. 5, nn. 100, 108–11. For the possessory assizes in Normandy, see 'Le Tres Ancien Coutumier de Normandie', caps, 7, 16–9, 21, 23, 57 in *Coutumiers de Normandie*, ed. E.-J .Tardif (Société de l'Histoire de Normandie, 1881–1903), I, 7, 18–23, 46–8; cf. Haskins, *Norman Institutions*, 189.

Normandy about six years later.[14] In 1177 at Verneuil, Henry introduced legislation on debt, which was to apply in Normandy, Aquitaine, Anjou and Brittany. In 1180 at Le Mans, he issued an assize of arms which covered all his continental territories and formed the model for that applied the following year in England.[15] The 'Saladin tithe' of 1188 was levied throughout his empire.[16]

However, we cannot say that any of this was specifically Norman or Angevin in origin.[17] The jury of lawful men – a crucial element in many of these measures – would still have figured prominently, had Henry II ruled nowhere except England. We must look elsewhere for the relevance of the Angevin empire to the governance of the kingdom in the early phase of the reign. First, Henry's prolonged absence in France between August 1158 and January 1163 almost certainly delayed the introduction of administrative reforms in England. The key restorative measures had already been implemented during his first three years: foreign mercenaries had been expelled, castles surrendered or destroyed, royal demesne largely recovered, taxes levied over most of the country, a new coinage ordered. Had Henry II then remained in the kingdom, he might have moved on to procedural reform at the exchequer, to a concerted attack on crime, and to the introduction of processes available only in the royal courts, much sooner than he did. The attempt to recover ecclesiastical jurisdiction, which fuelled the quarrel with Becket, would possibly have been postponed in any case until the death of Archbishop Theobald, but measures akin to the Assize of Clarendon and the assize of *novel disseisin* might well have been in place by the early 1160s. The second point is that, despite arrangements for Henry to be represented by a regent while he was out of the kingdom – in practice the queen or the earl of Leicester during this phase of the reign[18] – his absence did breed a sense of insecurity. Archbishop Theobald, writing to the king in 1160, begged him to 'return to the people that is all your own', since 'during your absence there is no hope of quiet for our countrymen'.[19] The king and his advisers were well aware that frequent lengthy absences on his part increased the risk of violent self-help among disaffected landholders,

---

[14] For the Norman returns, see *RBE*, II, 624–45; cf. F. M. Powicke, 'The honour of Mortain in the Norman *Infeudationes Militum* of 1172', *EHR*, 26 (1911), 89–93.   [15] *Gesta Regis*, I, 194, 270.

[16] *Ibid.*, II, 30–3, 44; Gervase, I, 409, 422; Newburgh, I, 275. Mitchell, *Taxation in Medieval England*, 114–22, argues for similar levies on movables in England and France in 1166 and 1184 but in the light of Gervase, I, 198–9 and *Gesta Regis*, I, 311 it is by no means certain that England contributed on either occasion.

[17] Boussard, *Le Gouvernement*, 586–9, argues that several governmental techniques within the Angevin empire had Norman precedents, but this rests on doubtful claims, e.g. that the exchequer, the deployment of justices in eyre and the regular use of the sworn inquest can all be traced in Normandy earlier than in England.   [18] West, *Justiciarship*, 31–5.

[19] JS, *Letters*, I, no. 121.

and this may well have prompted their concern to offer protection to seisin, especially in the aftermath of civil war.[20] As early as 1158 there seems to have been a decree prohibiting disseisins without judgment since the king's last departure overseas, and although this was a crude measure – which may in some cases have protected wrongful acquisitions under Stephen – it did provide a basis for further legislation. The assize of *novel disseisin* was to be a much more subtle device, which opened the king's courts to a host of freeholders, but the repeated reference under this assize to the king's most recent voyage away, as the fixed point in time from which seisins were protected, testifies to enduring anxiety at the potential impact of his absence overseas.

The third question is the most important, given the focus of this book, and the answer may therefore serve as a fitting conclusion. If we consider England alone, and leave the Becket conflict aside, should the first eleven years of Henry II's reign be seen other than as a period of reconstruction after the chaos of Stephen's civil war? It has been the argument of this book that the breakdown in the king's administration under Stephen was far from complete, that he took steps to restore royal authority in the last months of his life, and that, accordingly, Henry II had some foundations on which to build in seeking to recover ground lost by the crown since 1135. The destruction of castles, the settlement of rival claims to estates, the recovery of royal demesne, the collection of sheriffs' farms where they had not previously been rendered, the issue of a new coinage, the appointment of royal justices: all this is characteristic of Henry II's restoration of orderly government, but all were measures already taken by Stephen following the peace settlement late in 1153. In governmental terms, therefore, the distinction between the close of Stephen's reign and the beginning of Henry II's should not be drawn too sharply. Thereafter, the political and military preoccupations which kept Henry II in France for more than half his first eight years as king inevitably curtailed his personal involvement in the administration of England: he could not respond fully to the lively demand for his intervention in lawsuits, and he had to leave the reordering of the exchequer to Nigel bishop of Ely and others. Even so, he did show some interest in judicial affairs: he decreed the protection of seisin and forbade unsupported criminal accusations in ecclesiastical courts, and he issued a host of writs providing for hearings before his justices in cases of default elsewhere, measures which helped to convey an impression of his overriding control. Then in 1163, following his return to England in January, there were a series of changes to the king's administration. Henry appears to have presided at an exchequer

---

[20] Henry did, of course, also offer protection to tenures in France, as held at the time he last crossed the Channel in the other direction: *RAH*, I, no. 397; II, nos. 657, 659.

session during the course of that year, when sheriffs were obliged to render their 'old farms' to him in person. The totals of sheriffs' farms attained new levels of accuracy and the 'assay' process may have been reintroduced to safeguard the quality of coin paid in. A concern to increase the king's sources of income is demonstrated by the attempt to add sheriff's aid to his revenues, although this particular proposal was dropped in the face of Becket's opposition. Meanwhile, fresh impetus was given to judicial administration, with royal justices sent out on eyre and criminals forfeiting their chattels to the crown. In the following year came the Constitutions of Clarendon, which (among other measures) addressed once again the handling of crime in ecclesiastical courts, and reserved for the king's courts procedure by recognition on whether land was held in free alms or lay fee. There was also a thoroughgoing enquiry into encroachments upon the royal demesne, which led to the first accounts of purprestures in the pipe roll of 1165. All this was to be the prelude to a new judicial eyre, the Assize of Clarendon, an assize concerning disseisins, the enquiry into knight-service and a (probable) assize of the forest, which collectively stamp 1166 as a year of assertive administrative achievement. The measures implemented at this time, including the despatch of itinerant justices and the use of juries of recognition in procedures available only in the king's courts, were to become familiar features from hereon and accordingly 1166 has often been seen as a watershed in the reign.[21] But the ingredients can already be discerned in earlier years, especially from 1163.

As far as England was concerned, the task of reconstruction was the dominant one for the king and his advisers in the early years of the reign, and accordingly most of this book has been devoted to the restoration of lands, titles and administrative processes. An observer of the early 1130s, revisiting in the early 1160s, would have found much that was familiar, not only in the structure of the king's government – household, financial system, sources of revenue – but also in the personnel favoured by the king, in the tenurial pattern and in the manner of royal intervention in lawsuits. The extent to which Henry II reconstituted the administration and restored the landholders of his grandfather's time should not be exaggerated,[22] but it is fair to say that, until 1163, the thrust of his policy was towards those ends. Thereafter, priorities shifted, and contemporaries duly took note. Among Henry II's early legislative measures was that

---

[21] E.g. Stenton, *English Feudalism*, 11; Warren, *Governance*, 105–6; Chibnall, *Anglo-Norman England*, 3–5; cf. Green, *Aristocracy of Norman England*, vii, 1. It is fair to add that the convenient span of a century from the date of the Norman Conquest has contributed to this treatment of the year 1166.

[22] See esp. ch. 3 for certain differences in the composition of the royal household and in types of sheriffs appointed, and also for cases in which the families of pre-1135 landholders were not restored.

referred to in the previous chapter, making provision for a vassal whose case had been delayed in his lord's court to have it transferred to the court of a higher lord. Although this was essentially a refinement of existing procedures rather than a major innovation, it clearly attracted comment: by the time we learn of its implementation in 1164, lords were apparently grumbling that they lost jurisdiction thereby, and the king was seen to have 'made a new constitution, which he thought would be very advantageous to himself'.[23] It is a pity that we do not have a more precise date for the introduction of this measure, for it encapsulates much that is characteristic of Henry's approach to the dispensation of justice in the early phase of the reign. The king was primarily concerned to improve the working of seignorial courts, rather than to increase business for his own: he facilitated the removal of a case from one lord's jurisdiction, on complaint of default of justice, so as to transfer it to that of another. Yet these provisions obviously had the potential ultimately to bring suits before the king and his justices, and by 1164 they were perceived to be doing so. By then, a deliberate expansion of royal justice had begun and – if Becket's later biographers are to be trusted on the mood of the barons at that time – it did not go unnoticed that substantial changes were afoot. A period which may fairly be categorised as one of political, administrative and tenurial restoration, dating back before Henry II's accession to the peace settlement of 1153, was already giving way to one of significant reform.

---

[23] *Becket Materials*, IV, 40–1 ('Anonymous I'); transl. in Cheney, 'Litigation', 15–16 and 'Decree of Henry II', 186; cf. *Lawsuits*, II, no. 420, esp. pp. 427, 431 (Guernes de Pont-Sainte-Maxence); Hudson, *English Common Law*, 128.

Appendix I

SHERIFFS' FARMS, 1130–65 and 1197

The financial year ran from Michaelmas to Michaelmas. In the lists below, a date refers to the twelve months ending at Michaelmas in that year (e.g. '1156' means Michaelmas 1155 to Michaelmas 1156). Against each total, the designations 'blanch', *ad pensum* or *numero* are taken from specifications in the pipe rolls; where sums were unqualified, as was sometimes the case in the early pipe rolls of Henry II's reign, allowances out have been assumed to be *numero*, but amounts paid in, owing or in surplus have been assumed as 'blanch' unless known to be otherwise. In calculating 'blanch farms', allowances *numero* have been converted to 'blanch' by subtracting at a rate of one shilling in the pound; this was the practice set out in *Dialogus*, 125, and (from comparison of calculations with stated totals) was clearly the method in operation in 1197 (9 Richard I), the first year when totals were given at the heads of each sheriff's farm account. Halfpence have been rounded up to the nearest penny.

Figures for several sheriffs' farms early in Henry II's reign have appeared elsewhere, notably in G. J. Turner, 'The sheriff's farm', *TRHS*, new series 12 (1898), 142–9, and in Amt, *Accession*, 198–204. Totals for 1130 were given in Ramsay, *Revenues*, I, 61, and for 1164 in W. Parow, *Compotus vicecomitis. Die Rechenschaftslegung des Sheriffs unter Heinrich II von England* (Berlin, 1906), 24–6. However, all figures shown here have been calculated independently.

The following information is given about each shire. (1) Totals calculated from the 1130 pipe roll. (2) Totals calculated from the transcript of the 1155 pipe roll in *RBE*, II, 648–58, and from the 1156 pipe roll. (3) Totals stated in the 1197 pipe roll, which were normally the 'standards' which formed the basis for earlier accounts. (4) Years (up to 1165) in which farms totals came to within 1s 0d. of the 1197 'standard totals', or (as, for example, in the case of Essex–Hertfordshire in 1159, 1160 and 1165) within 1s 0d. of a previous 'standard', subsequently changed. Years in which totals were within one penny either side of the 'standard' are underlined. Where totals appear to have missed the 'standard' only because of clerical error (such as that for Berkshire in 1160, where the figure was £542 8s. 2d. instead of the usual £541 8s. 4d.) the relevant years have been marked ★, although there is obviously room for disagreement over which totals should be so regarded.

BERKSHIRE

1130: £433 10s. 1d. *ad pensum* + £42 16s. 4d. *numero* + £45 6s. 9d. blanch
1155: £512 7s. 11d. blanch   1156: £541 8s. 4d. blanch
1197: £541, 8s. 4d. blanch
Standard farms of £541 8s. 4d. blanch in <u>1157</u>, <u>1159</u>, 1160★, <u>1161</u>, <u>1162</u>, <u>1163</u>, <u>1165</u>.
(Sheriff accounted for only three-quarters of the year in 1161; calculation based on full year's equivalent.)

BUCKINGHAMSHIRE, BEDFORDSHIRE

1130: £292 0s. 8d. *ad pensum* + £111 16s. 1d. *numero*
1155: no record   1156: £370 0s. 0d. blanch + £108 0s. 0d. *numero*
1197: £369 19s. 11d. blanch + £108 0s. 0d. *numero*
Standard farms of £369 19s. 11d. blanch and £108 0s.0d *numero* in <u>1158</u>, <u>1159</u>, 1161, <u>1163</u>, <u>1165</u>.

CAMBRIDGESHIRE, HUNTINGDONSHIRE, SURREY

1130 (all three together): £414 1s. 0d. *ad pensum* + £28 0s. 9d. *numero*
1155: Cambs: £200 0s. 0d. blanch; Hunts: £163 11s. 2d. blanch;
     Surrey: £183 3s. 3d. blanch
1156: Cambs.: £235 6s. 1d. blanch; Hunts.: £158 0s. 10d. blanch;
     Surrey: £184 5s. 11d. blanch
1197: Cambs.–Hunts.: £373 9s. 4d. blanch; Surrey: £174 7s. 0d. blanch

Standard farms of £547 16s. 4d. blanch (all three together) in <u>1161</u>, <u>1163</u>.
Standard farms of £373 9s. 4d. blanch (Cambs-Hunts) in 1164★, <u>1165</u>, and of £174 7s. 0d . blanch (Surrey) also in <u>1164</u>, <u>1165</u>.
(In 1155, the account for Cambridgeshire covered only a quarter of the year, that for Huntingdonshire only half the year; the figures above are equivalents for a full year.)

CARLISLE

1130: £56 2s. 4d. (not specified but presumably *numero*)
(No account under Henry II until 1158.)
1197: £114 0s. 4d. *numero*
Standard farms of £114 0s. 4d. *numero* in <u>1159</u>, <u>1160</u>, <u>1161</u>, <u>1162</u>, <u>1163</u>, <u>1164</u>, <u>1165</u>.

Appendix I

DEVON

1130: £205 16s. 8d. *ad pensum* + £7 16s. 0d. *numero* + £37 7s. 11d. blanch
1155: £98 10s. 2d. blanch
1156: £336 12s. 8d. blanch
1197: £312 7s. 0d. blanch
Standard farms of £312 7s. 0d. blanch in <u>1159</u>, <u>1160</u>, <u>1161</u>, <u>1162</u>, 1163*, <u>1164</u>, 1165*.

DORSET

1130 (including Wiltshire): £454 10s. 0d. *ad pensum* + £185 18s. 7d. *numero* + £83 2s. 7d. blanch
1155: £118 3s. 11d. blanch
1156: £120 0s. 0d. blanch
1197: £120 0s. 0d. blanch
Standard farms of £120 0s. 0d. blanch in <u>1157</u>, 1158*, <u>1159</u>, <u>1160</u>, 1161*, <u>1163</u>.

ESSEX, HERTFORDSHIRE

1130 (together): £420 3s. 0d. *ad pensum* + £31 17s. 0d. *numero* + £86 19s. 9d. blanch
1155: Essex: £503 17s. 11d. *numero*; Herts.: £46 13s. 4d. *numero*
1156: Essex: £503 12s. 10d. blanch; Herts.: £100 0s. 0d. blanch
1197 (together): £645 2s. 4d. blanch

According to Turner, farms of £645 2s. 4d. blanch for the two shires together began to be accounted for in 15 Henry II (1168–9). The Essex farm of 1156 was repeated in <u>1157</u> and 1158 and a standard of £644 17s. 2d. blanch for the two shires together was attained in <u>1159</u>, <u>1160</u>, 1165.

GLOUCESTERSHIRE (blanch)

1130: £222 13s. 0d. *ad pensum* + £73 11s. 2d. *numero* + £16 9s. 10d. blanch
1155: £332 13s. 8d. blanch
1156: £372 13s. 6d. blanch
1197: £372 13s. 6d. blanch
Standard farms of £372 13s. 6d. blanch in <u>1157</u>, 1158*, <u>1159</u>, <u>1161</u>, 1162*, <u>1163</u>, <u>1164</u>, 1165.
(The sheriff accounted for three-quarters of the year in 1155; the figure shown above is a full year's equivalent.)

HAMPSHIRE

1130: £484 4s. 2d. *ad pensum* + £11 8s. 5d. *numero* + £180 15s. 2d. blanch
1155: no record
1156: £606 2s. 8d. blanch
1197: £606 2s. 8d. blanch
Standard farms of £606 2s. 8d. blanch in <u>1157</u>, <u>1163</u>, 1164, <u>1165</u>.

Appendix I

HEREFORDSHIRE

1130: no record
1155: £164 16s. 4d. blanch
1156: £159 2s. 3d. blanch
1197: £164 16s. 5d. blanch
Standard farms of £164 16s. 5d. blanch in <u>1157</u>, 1158, <u>1159</u>, <u>1162</u>, <u>1163</u>, 1164, <u>1165</u>.
(The sheriff accounted for three-quarters of the year in 1155; the figure shown above is a full year's
  equivalent.)

KENT

1130: £260 0s. 0d. *ad pensum* + £182 14s. 4d. *numero* + £29 1s. 7d. blanch
1155: £427 6s. 1d. blanch
1156: £426 19s. 7d. blanch + £165 13s. 4d. *numero*
1197: £412 7s. 7d. blanch + £165 13s. 4d. *numero*
Standard farms of £412 7s. 7d. blanch and £165 13s. 4d. *numero* in <u>1158</u>, <u>1159</u>, <u>1160</u>, <u>1163</u>,
  1164*, <u>1165</u>.
(The sheriff accounted for three-quarters of the year in 1155; the figure shown above is a full year's
  equivalent.)

LINCOLNSHIRE

1130: £422 14s. 8d. *ad pensum* + £40 0s. 0d. *numero* + £293 17s. 7d. blanch
1155: £666 0s. 4d. blanch
1156: £836 1s. 7d. blanch + £140 0s. 0d. *numero*
1197: £836 1s. 8d. blanch + £140 0s. 0d. *numero*
Standard farms of £836 1s. 8d. blanch + £140 0s. 0d. *numero* in <u>1157</u>, <u>1163</u>, <u>1164</u>, <u>1165</u>.

LONDON

1130: £327 3s. 11d. blanch + £209 6s. 6d. *numero*
1155: insufficient detail
1156: £500 0s. 0d. blanch + £22 0s. 0d. *numero*
1197: £300 0s. 0d. blanch
Farms at a standard of £500 0s. 0d. blanch + £22 0s. 0d. *numero* in 1158*, <u>1162</u>, <u>1163</u>,
  <u>1165</u>.

NORFOLK, SUFFOLK

1130: £599 4s. 6d. *ad pensum* + £31 1s. 5d. *numero*
1155: £304 16s. 3d. *numero*
1156: £305 6s. 7d. blanch
1197: £790 2s. 0d. blanch
Farms at a standard of £749 13s. 4d. blanch + £50 0s. 0d. *numero* in 1160, <u>1161</u>, 1162*,
  1163*, and at £749 13s. 4d. blanch + £100 0s. 0d. *numero* in <u>1164</u>, <u>1165</u>.
(There were accounts for only half the year for Suffolk in 1155 and for Norfolk and Suffolk together in
  1157; calculations are for the full years' equivalents.)

223

Appendix I

NORTHAMPTONSHIRE

1130: £249 2s. 1d. *ad pensum* + £10 2s. 6d. *numero* (including Warwickshire and Leicestershire)
1155: £233 9s. 4d. blanch
1156: £250 2s. 2d. blanch
1197: £230 7s. 4d. blanch
Standard farms of £230 7s. 4d. blanch in 1163, 1164, 1165.

NORTHUMBERLAND

1130: £139 5s. 1d. *numero*
(No account under Henry II until 1158)
1197: £240 18s. 4d. *numero*
Standard farms of £240 18s. 4d. *numero* in 1164, 1165.

NOTTINGHAMSHIRE, DERBYSHIRE

1130: £10 7s. 2d. *ad pensum* + £25 2s. 4d. *numero* + £121 15s. 2d. blanch
1155: insufficient detail
1156: £359 5s. 11d. blanch + £40 10s. 0d. *numero*
1197: £279 5s. 11d. blanch + £40 10s. 0d. *numero*
Farms at a standard of £359 5s. 11d. blanch + £40 10s. 0d. *numero* in 1157, 1158, 1159, 1160, 1162*, 1163, 1164, 1165.

OXFORDSHIRE

1130: pipe roll damaged
1155: insufficient detail
1156: £327 12s. 9d. blanch
1197: £326 12s. 9d. blanch
Standard farms of £326 12s. 9d, blanch in 1157*, 1163, 1164, 1165.

SHROPSHIRE

1130: no record
1155: £395 5s. 0d. *numero*
1156: £264 14s. 1d. *numero*
1197: £265 15s. 0d. *numero*
Standard farms of £265 15s. 0d. *numero* in 1157*, 1159*, 1160*, 1163, 1164, 1165.
(The 1155 and 1165 figures are both full year's equivalents of sums covering only a quarter of the year; there is an account for the remainder of 1164–5 which gives a slightly different total, but it is clear from the pipe roll that £265 15s. 0d. was acknowledged as the standard total farm.)

SOMERSET

1130: no record
1155: £114 10s. 10d. *numero*
1156: £360 0s. 10d. blanch

1197: £360 0s.0d. blanch
Standard farms of £360 0s. 0d. blanch in 1157, 1158, 1159, 1160, 1163.
*(The sheriff accounted for only half the year in 1155; the figure shown above is a full year's
   equivalent.)*

STAFFORDSHIRE

1130: £119 18s. 9d. blanch + £4 3s. 9d. *numero*
1155: £134 17s. 3d. blanch
1156: £138 11s. 0d. blanch
1197: £140 0s. 0d. blanch
Standard farms of £140 0s. 0d. blanch in 1158, 1159, 1162*, 1163, 1164, 1165.

SUSSEX

1130: no record
1155: £40 0s. 0d. *numero*
1156: £40 0s. 0d. *numero*
Standard farms of £40 0s. 0d. *numero* in 1157, 1158, 1159, 1160, 1161, 1162, 1163, 1164,
   1165.
*(The sheriff accounted for three-quarters of the year in 1155; the figure shown above is a full year's
   equivalent.)*

WARWICKSHIRE, LEICESTERSHIRE

1130: for both, see Northamptonshire
1155: Warwicks.: no record; Leics.: £83 6s. 10d. blanch

1156: Warwicks.: £147 2s. 0d. blanch; Leics.: £115 5s. 10d. blanch
(totals together £224 7s. 10d. blanch + £40 0s. 0d. *numero*)

1197: Warwicks.: £128 2s. 0d. blanch; Leics.: £85 16s. 4d. blanch
(totals, together, £213 18s. 4d. blanch)

Standard farms of £213 18s. 4d. blanch in 1157, 1158, 1159, 1160, 1162, 1163, 1164, 1165
   (although the two shires were treated separately in 1157, 1158, 1159, 1164, 1165). An
   additional £40 0s. 0d. *numero* was charged in 1157, 1158, 1165.

WILTSHIRE

1130: see Dorset
1155: £537 4s. 6d. blanch
1156: £542 8s. 2d. blanch
1197: £542 9s. 10d. blanch
Standard farms of £542 9s. 10d. blanch in 1157, 1158, 1159, 1161*, 1162*, 1163, 1164,
   1165.

Appendix I

WORCESTERSHIRE

1130: no record
1155: £191 3s. 4d. blanch
1156: £215 10s. 4d. blanch
1197: £215 10s. 4d. blanch
Standard farms of £215 10s. 4d. blanch in 1159, 1161, 1162, 1163, 1165.

YORKSHIRE

1130: £233 5s. 6d. unqualified + £86 2s. 9d. *numero* + £125 8s. 8d. blanch
1155: £421 5s. 4d. blanch
1156: £444 9s. 3d. blanch
1197: £440 7s. 3d. blanch
Standard farms of £440 7s. 3d. blanch in 1158, 1163, 1164, 1165.
(The sheriff accounted for three-quarters of the year in 1155; the figure shown above is a full year's equivalent.)

Appendix II

PIPE ROLL 11 HENRY II (1164–5)

Calculations from this pipe roll mostly follow the conventions and criteria set out in Amt, *Accession*, 189, in order to ease comparisons with the figures set out *ibid.*, 190–7. In particular, payments in 'blanch' have been converted to *numero* by the addition of a standard 1/19, even though there would have been variability in the conversion rate by 1164–5 owing to the (presumed) reintroduction of the assay.

'Payments in' cover all recorded payments to the treasury and chamber in the financial year 1164–5; no attempt has been made to distinguish current year's accounts from those left owing from previous years, and no reference has been made to debts carried forward. It must be presumed that payments into the chamber were higher than the £877 10s. 4d. recorded in the pipe roll; damage to the pipe roll also conceals a few payments in Cambridgeshire–Huntingdonshire although sums involved were probably small. Expenditure incurred in advance on behalf of the king, and allowed to sheriffs and others when presenting their accounts at the exchequer, has been added to the amounts of 'payments in' to give total sums raised.

The category for 'Farms, etc.' includes not only sheriffs' farms but also those of manors accounted for separately, purprestures and escheats, cesses of woods and the farms of vacant bishoprics and abbeys (the last were treated as 'regalian rights' in the calculations from the 1130 pipe roll, Green, *Henry I*, 223–5). 'Taxation and other similar levies' is largely composed of payments on knights' fees for the campaign into Wales, but also includes lastage and contributions by moneyers and other craftsmen. 'Fines, pleas and amercements' includes reliefs and other offerings to the king as well as payments specifically in connection with crime and civil litigation. Many items do not specify their purpose, so it has been necessary to assign them to one category or another by reference to their character and placing in relation to others; obviously, some informed guesswork has been involved here.

In both tables, the first figure represents 'payments in', the second figure covers advance expenditure, and the third figure gives the total.

Appendix II

Table 1   Totals raised, by source

Farms, etc.:	£9,477 0s. 2d.	+	£3,405 7s. 10d.	=	£12,882 8s. 0d
Taxation and other similar levies:	£4,791 4s. 7d.	+	£52 0s. 0d.	=	£4,843, 4s. 7d.
Fines, pleas and amercements:	£2,939 10s. 8d.	+	£367 2s. 0d.	=	£3,306 12s. 8d.
TOTAL:	£17,207 15s. 5d.	+	£3,824 9s. 10d.	=	£21,032 5s. 3d.

Table 2   Totals raised from all sources, by Shire

Berkshire	£342 13s. 5d.	+	£224 4s. 4d	=	£566 17s. 9d.
Bucks.-Beds.	£1093 6s. 5d.	+	£30 13s. 9d.	=	£1,124 0s. 2d.
Cambs.-Hunts.	£620 14s. 0d.	+	£14 2s. 0d.	=	£634 16s. 0d.
Cumberland	£437 0s. 6d.	+	£2 8s. 7d.	=	£439 9s. 1d.
Devon	£268 19s. 4d.	+	£47 13s. 6d.	=	£316 12s. 10d.
Dorset–Somerset	£485 0s. 3d.	+	£29 6s. 8d.	=	£514 6s. 11d.
Essex–Herts	£898 5s. 10d.	+	£43 13s. 3d.	=	£941 19s. 1d.
Gloucestershire	£426 11s. 4d.	+	£110 16s. 9d.	=	£537 8s. 1d.
Hampshire	£1,060 5s. 8d.	+	£330 3s. 3d.	=	£1,390 8s. 11d.
Herefordshire	£25 19s. 11d.	+	£170 12s. 11d.	=	£196 12s. 10d.
Kent	£2,343 11s. 2d.	+	£406 0s. 5d.	=	£2,749 11s. 7d.
Lincolnshire	£1,711 19s. 5d.	+	£488 5s. 7d.	=	£2,200 5s. 0d.
London–Middlesex	£553 4s. 0d.	+	£411 3s. 7d.	=	£964 7s. 7d.
Norfolk–Suffolk	£2,200 3s. 0d.	+	£73, 13s. 6d.	=	£2,273 16s. 6d.
Northants.	£398 14s. 2d.	+	£255 11s. 4d.	=	£654 5s. 6d.
Northumberland	£384 2s. 7d.	+	£3 14s. 2d.	=	£387 16s. 9d.
Notts.–Derbys.	£784 7s. 0d.	+	£28. 4s. 10d.	=	£812 11s. 10d.
Oxfordshire	£202 14s. 10d.	+	£185 9s. 4d.	=	£388 4s. 2d.
Shropshire	£9 15s. 10d.	+	£336 2s. 6d.	=	£345 18s. 4d.
Staffordshire	£65 7s. 2d.	+	£54 7s. 0d.	=	£119 14s. 2d.
Surrey	£167 19s. 4d.	+	£52 3s. 1d.	=	£220 2s. 5d.
Sussex	£351 11s. 11d.	+	£1 6s. 8d.	=	£352 18s. 7d.
Warwicks.–Leics.	£329 18s. 1d.	+	£153 6s. 8d.	=	£483 4s. 9d.
Wiltshire	£342 1s. 10d.	+	£109 17s. 6d.	=	£451 19s. 4d.
Worcestershire	£64 1s. 3d.	+	£222 1s. 7d.	=	£286 2s. 10d.
Yorkshire	£1,639 7s. 2d.	+	£39 7s. 1d.	=	£1,678 14s. 3d.
TOTAL	£17,207 15s. 5d.	+	£3,824 9s. 10d.	=	£21,032 5s. 3d.

SELECT BIBLIOGRAPHY

MANUSCRIPT SOURCES

Cambridge, University Library

Add. MS. 3020 ('Red Book of Thorney': Thorney Abbey cartulary, vol. I).

Lincolnshire Archives Office

3 Ancaster 2/1 (Huntingfield family cartulary).
Foster Library P. 10 (transcript of Castle Acre Priory cartulary).

London, British Library

Add. charter 6037.
Add. MS. 30311 (transcript of Shrewsbury Abbey cartulary).
Add. MS. 35296 (Spalding Priory register).
Campbell charter ii. 2.
Cotton MS. Vespasian B. xxiv (Evesham Abbey cartulary).
Cotton MS. Vespasian E. xvii (St Andrew's Priory, Northampton cartulary).
Cotton MS. Vespasian E. xviii (Kirkstead Abbey cartulary).
Harley MS. 2110 (Castle Acre Priory cartulary).
Royal MS. 11 B. ix (St Andrew's Priory, Northampton cartulary).

London, Public Record Office

C. 47/12/4 (formerly Cartae Antiquae Roll OO).
C. 52/21 (formerly Cartae Antiquae Roll W).
C. 52/28 (formerly Cartae Antiquae Roll DD).
E. 372/1–6, 8, 9.
E. 401/1.

Oxford, Bodleian Library

Dugdale MS. 12 (SC 6502), pp. 111–72 (transcript of a Combe Abbey cartulary).

Peterborough, Dean and Chapter

MS. 23 (Goxhill Leger).

Select bibliography

PRINTED SOURCES

Acta of Henry II and Richard I, ed. J. C. Holt and R. Mortimer (List and Index Society, special series, 21, 1986).

Ancient Charters, ed. J. H. Round (P.R. Society, 1888).

Anglo-Saxon Chronicle: a Revised Translation, ed. D. Whitelock, D. C. Douglas and S. I. Tucker (rev. edn, London, 1965).

'Annales de Saint-Aubin', in *Recueil d'Annales Angevines et Vendomoises*, ed. L. Halphen (Paris, 1903).

Annales Monastici, ed. H. R. Luard, 5 vols. (RS, 1864–69).

Beauchamp Cartulary: Charters, 1100–1268, ed. E. Mason (P.R. Society, 1980).

'Belvoir Chartulary', ed. J. H. Round, in *Historical Manuscripts Commission Report on MSS. of His Grace the Duke of Rutland*, IV (London, 1905), 105–73.

Bracton, *On the Laws and Customs of England*, ed. G. E. Woodbine and S. E. Thorne, III (Harvard, 1977).

Brut y Tywysogion: Red Book of Hergest, ed. and transl. T. Jones (2nd edn, Cardiff, 1973).

'Burton Chartulary', ed. G. Wrottesley, in *Staffs Colls.*, v, pt i (1884), 1–101.

Calendar of Charter Rolls preserved in the Public Record Office, 6 vols. (London, 1903–27).

Cartae Antiquae Rolls, 1–10, ed. L. Landon (P.R. Society, 1939).

Cartae Antiquae Rolls, 11–20, ed. J. C. Davies (P.R. Society, 1960).

Cartularium Monasterii de Rameseia, ed. W. H. Hart and P. A. Lyons, 3 vols. (RS,1884–94).

Cartularium Monasterii Sancti Johannis Baptiste de Colecestria, ed. S. A. Moore, 2 vols. (London, 1897).

Cartulary of Darley Abbey, ed. R. R. Darlington (Derbyshire Archaeological and Natural History Society, 1945).

Cartulary of Launceston Priory, ed. P. L. Hull (Devon and Cornwall Record Society, 1987).

Cartulary of Missenden Abbey, ed. J. G. Jenkins, 3 vols. (Buckinghamshire Archaeological Society, 1939–62).

Cartulary of Oseney Abbey, ed. H. E. Salter, 5 vols. (Oxford Historical Society, 1929–36).

Cartulary of the Abbey of Eynsham, ed. H. E. Salter, 2 vols. (Oxford Historical Society, 1906–8).

Cartulary of the Monastery of St Frideswide, ed. S. R. Wigram (Oxford Historical Society, 1895–6).

Cartulary of Worcester Cathedral Priory, ed. R. R. Darlington (P.R. Society, 1968).

Chancellor's Roll for the Eighth Year of the Reign of King Richard the First, ed. D. M. Stenton (P.R. Society, 1930).

Charters of the Anglo-Norman Earls of Chester, c.1071–1327, ed. G. Barraclough (Record Society of Lancs. and Ches., 1988).

'Charters of the Earldom of Hereford, 1095–1201', ed. D. Walker, in *Camden Miscellany XXII* (Camden Society, 1964).

Charters of the Honour of Mowbray, 1107–91, ed. D. E. Greenway (British Academy, 1972).

Charters of the Redvers Family and the Earldom of Devon, 1090–1217, ed. R. Bearman (Devon and Cornwall Record Society, 1994).

'Chartulary of the Augustine Priory of Trentham', ed. F. Parker, in *Staffs. Colls.*, XI (1890), 295–336.

Chartulary or Register of the Abbey of St Werburgh, Chester, ed. J. Tait, 2 vols. (Chetham Society, 1920–23).

Chronica Regum Mannie & Insularum, ed. G. Broderick (Manx Museum, 1979).

Select bibliography

Chronicle of Battle Abbey, ed. E. Searle (OMT, 1980).

Chronicle of John of Worcester, 1118–40, ed. J. R. H. Weaver (Oxford, 1908).

Chronicles of Ralf Niger, ed. R. Anstruther (Caxton Society, 1851).

Chronicles of the Reigns of Stephen, Henry II and Richard I, ed. R. Howlett, 4 vols. (RS, 1884–9).

Chronicon Abbatiae Rameseiensis, ed. W. D. Macray (RS, 1886).

Chronicon Monasterii de Abingdon, ed. J. Stevenson (RS, 1858).

Collections for a History of Staffordshire, 18 vols. in 20 (William Salt Archaeological Society, 1880–97) [further series thereafter].

'Continuatio Beccensis', in *Chronicles*, IV.

Coucher Book of the Cistercian Abbey of Kirkstall, ed. W. T. Lancaster and W. P. Baildon (Thoresby Society, 1904).

Councils and Synods with other Documents relating to the English Church, I, ed. D. Whitelock, M. Brett and C. N. L. Brooke (Oxford, 1981).

Coutumiers de Normandie, ed. E.-J. Tardif, 3 vols. (Société de l'Histoire de Normandie, 1881–1903).

Cronica Jocelini de Brakelonda, ed. H. E. Butler (NMT, 1949).

Curia Regis Rolls (London, 1922–).

De Necessariis Observantiis Scaccarii Dialogus, ed. A. Hughes, C. G. Crump and C. Johnson (Oxford, 1902).

Descriptive Catalogue of Derbyshire Charters in Public and Private Libraries and Muniment Rooms, ed. I. H. Jeayes (London, 1906).

Dialogus de Scaccario by Richard fitz Nigel and Constitutio Domus Regis, ed. C. Johnson, corrections by F. E. L. Carter and D. E. Greenway (OMT, 1983).

Documents Illustrative of the Social and Economic History of the Danelaw, ed. F. M. Stenton (British Academy, London, 1920).

Eadmer, *Historia Novorum in Anglia*, ed. M. Rule (RS, 1884).

Earldom of Gloucester Charters, ed. R. B. Patterson (Oxford, 1973).

'Early Charters of Sibton Abbey, Suffolk', ed. R. A. Brown, in Barnes and Slade, eds., *Medieval Miscellany*, 65–76.

Early Scottish Charters, ed. A. C. Lawrie (Glasgow, 1905).

Early Yorkshire Charters, ed. W. Farrer and C. T. Clay, 12 vols. (Yorkshire Archaeological Society, 1914–65).

English Episcopal Acta I, Lincoln 1067–1185, ed. D. M. Smith (London, 1980).

English Historical Documents II, 1042–1189, ed. D. C. Douglas and G. W. Greenaway (2nd edn, London 1981).

English Lawsuits from William I to Richard I, ed. R. C. van Caenegem, 2 vols. (Selden Society, 1990–1).

English Register of Godstow Nunnery, ed. A. Clark (Early English Text Society, 1911).

'Extracts from the Cartulary of Haghmon Abbey', ed. W. A. Leighton, *Transactions of the Shropshire Archaeological Society*, 1st ser., I (1878), 173–216.

Facsimiles of Royal and Other Charters in the British Museum, ed. G. F. Warner and H. J. Ellis (London, 1903).

Feudal Documents from the Abbey of Bury St Edmunds, ed. D. C. Douglas (British Academy, London, 1932).

Final Concords of the County of Lincoln, II, ed. C. W. Foster (Lincoln Record Society, 1920).

Fouke le Fitz Warin, ed. E. J. Hathaway, P. T. Ricketts *et al.* (Anglo-Norman Texts, 1975).

'Fundacio Abbathie de Kyrkestall', in *Thoresby Society: Miscellanea*, II (Thoresby Society,

1895), 173–80.

Gervase of Canterbury, *Opera Historica*, ed. W. Stubbs, 2 vols. (RS, 1879–80).

Gesta Abbatum Monasterii Sancti Albani, ed. H. T. Riley, 3 vols. (RS, 1867–9).

Gesta Stephani, ed. K. R. Potter, intro. R. H. C. Davis (OMT, 1976).

Giraldus Cambrensis, *Opera*, ed. J. S. Brewer, J. F. Dimock and G. F. Warner, 8 vols. (RS, 1861–91).

Henry of Huntingdon, *Historia Anglorum*, ed. D. E. Greenway (OMT, 1996).

Herefordshire Domesday, ed. V. H. Galbraith and J. Tait (P.R. Society, 1950).

Historia et Cartularium Monasterii Sancti Petri Gloucestriae, ed. W. H. Hart, 3 vols. (RS, 1863–7).

Historical Manuscripts Commission Eleventh Report, Appendix, part vii (London, 1889).

Historical Manuscripts Commission Tenth Report, Appendix, part vi (London, 1887).

'John of Hexham, *Historia*' in Symeon of Durham, *Opera Omnia*, ed. T. Arnold, ii (RS, 1885).

John of Marmoutier, 'Historia Gaufredi Ducis', in *Chroniques des comtes d'Anjou et des seigneurs d'Amboise*, ed. L. Halphen and R. Poupardin (Paris, 1913).

John of Salisbury, *Historia Pontificalis*, ed. M. Chibnall (2nd edn, OMT, 1986).

Leges Henrici Primi, ed. L. J. Downer (Oxford, 1972).

Letters and Charters of Gilbert Foliot, ed. A. Morey and C. N. L. Brooke (London, 1967).

Letters of John of Salisbury, ed. W. J. Millor, H. E. Butler, C. N. L. Brooke, i (NMT, 1955), ii (OMT, 1979).

Liber Eliensis, ed. E. O. Blake (Camden Society, 1962).

Life and Miracles of St William of Norwich, by Thomas of Monmouth, ed. A. Jessopp and M. R. James (Cambridge, 1896).

Life of Ailred of Rievaulx by Walter Daniel, ed. F. M. Powicke (OMT, 1978).

Lincolnshire Domesday and Lindsey Survey, ed. C. W. Foster and T. Longley (Lincoln Record Society, 1924).

Magni Rotuli Scaccarii Normanniae sub Regibus Angliae, ed. T. Stapleton, 2 vols. (Society of Antiquaries, 1840–4).

Materials for the History of Thomas Becket, Archbishop of Canterbury, ed. J. C. Robertson, 7 vols. (RS, 1875–85).

Memoranda Roll 1 John, intro. H. G. Richardson (P.R. Society, 1943).

Monasticon Anglicanum, ed. Sir W. Dugdale, rev. edn. J. Caley, H. Ellis and B. Bandinel, 6 vols. in 8 (London, 1817–30).

Orderic Vitalis, *The Ecclesiastical History*, ed. M. Chibnall, 6 vols. (OMT, 1969–80).

Papsturkunden in England, ed. W. Holtzmann, 3 vols. (Berlin and Gottingen, 1930–53).

Peter of Blois, *Opera Omnia*, ed. J. A. Giles, 4 vols. (Oxford, 1846–7).

Pipe Roll 31 Henry I, ed. J. Hunter (Record Commission, 1833).

Pipe Roll 2–4 Henry II, ed. J. Hunter (Record Commission, 1844).

Pipe Rolls for subsequent years edited by Pipe Roll Society.

Pleas before the King or his Justices, 1198–1202, ed. D. M. Stenton, 4 vols. (Selden Society, 1952–67).

Ralf of Diceto, *Opera Historica*, ed. W. Stubbs, 2 vols. (RS, 1876).

Reading Abbey Cartularies, ed. B.R. Kemp, 2 vols. (Camden Society, 1986–7).

Records of the Templars in England in the Twelfth Century, ed. B. A. Lees (British Academy, London, 1935).

Recueil des Actes de Henri II, ed. L. Delisle and E. Berger, 4 vols. (Paris, 1906–27).

Red Book of the Exchequer, ed. H. Hall, 3 vols. (RS, 1896).

Select bibliography

Regesta Regum Anglo-Normannorum, II, ed. C. Johnson and H. A. Cronne (Oxford, 1956); III, IV, ed. H. A. Cronne and R. H. C. Davis (Oxford, 1968–9).

Regesta Regum Scottorum I: the Acta of Malcolm IV, King of Scots, ed. G. W. S. Barrow (Edinburgh, 1960).

Register of the Abbey of St Benet of Holme, ed. J. R. West, 2 vols. (Norfolk Record Society, 1932).

Registrum Antiquissimum of the Cathedral Church of Lincoln, ed. C. W. Foster and K. Major, 8 vols. (Lincoln Record Society, 1931–58).

'Richard of Hexham, *Historia*', in *Chronicles*, III.

'Robert de Torigni, *Chronica*', in *Chronicles*, IV.

[Roger of Howden] *Gesta Regis Henrici Secundi Benedicti Abbatis*, ed. W. Stubbs, 2 vols. (RS, 1867).

Roger of Howden, *Chronica*, ed. W. Stubbs, 4 vols. (RS, 1868–71).

Rolls of the Justices in Eyre for Gloucestershire, Warwickshire and [Shropshire], 1221, 1222, ed. D. M. Stenton (Selden Society, 1940).

Rotuli Chartarum in Turri Londinensi asservati, ed. T. D. Hardy (Record Commission, 1837).

Rotuli Curiae Regis, ed. F. Palgrave, 2 vols. (Record Commission, 1835).

Rotuli de Dominabus, ed. J. H. Round (P.R. Society, 1913).

Royal Writs in England from the Conquest to Glanvill, ed. R. C. van Caenegem (Selden Society, 1959).

Rufford Charters, ed. C. J. Holdsworth, 4 vols. (Thoroton Society Record Series, 1972–81).

'Rydeware Chartulary', ed. G. Wrottesley, in *Staffs Colls.*, XVI (1895), 227–302.

Sarum Charters and Documents, ed. W. D. Macray (RS, 1891).

Scottish Chronicle known as the Chronicle of Holyrood, ed. M. O. Anderson (Scottish History Society, 1938).

Select Charters and Other Illustrations of English Constitutional History to the Reign of Edward I, ed. W. Stubbs (9th edn. by H. W. C. Davis, 1921).

Sir Christopher Hatton's Book of Seals, ed. L. C. Loyd and D. M. Stenton (Northants Record Society, 1950).

'Staffordshire Chartulary, Series I, II', ed. R.W. Eyton, in *Staffs. Colls.*, II (1881), 178–276; 'Series III', ed. G. Wrottesley, *ibid.*, III (1882), 178–231.

Stoneleigh Leger Book, ed. R. H. Hilton (Dugdale Society, 1960).

Symeon of Durham, *Opera Omnia*, ed. T. Arnold , 2 vols. (RS, 1882–5).

Tractatus de Legibus et Consuetudinibus Regni Anglie qui Glanvilla vocatur, ed. G. D. G. Hall (2nd edn., OMT, 1993).

Walter Map, *De Nugis Curialium*, ed. M. R. James, rev. C. N. L. Brooke and R. A. B. Mynors (OMT, 1983).

William of Malmesbury, *De Gestis Regum Anglorum*, ed. W. Stubbs, 2 vols. (RS, 1887–9).

William of Malmesbury, *Historia Novella*, ed. K. R. Potter (NMT, 1955).

William of Newburgh, *The History of English Affairs*, I, ed. P. G. Walsh and M. J. Kennedy (Warminster, 1988).

'William of Newburgh, *Historia Rerum Anglicarum*', in *Chronicles*, I, II.

Select bibliography

SECONDARY WORKS

Books

Amt, E. M., *The Accession of Henry II in England: Royal Government Restored, 1149–1159* (Woodbridge, 1993).

Appleby, J. T. and Dalton, P., *Government, Religion and Society in Northern England* (Stroud, 1997).

Barlow, F., *William Rufus* (London, 1983).

Thomas Becket (London, 1986).

Barnes, P. M. and Slade, C. F., eds., *An Early Medieval Miscellany for Doris Mary Stenton* (P.R. Society, 1962).

Barrow, G. W. S., *David I of Scotland (1124–1153): The Balance of New and Old* (University of Reading, 1985).

Bishop, T. A. M., *Scriptores Regis* (Oxford, 1960).

Boon, G. C., *Welsh Hoards, 1979–81* (Cardiff, 1986).

Coins of the Anarchy, 1135–54 (Cardiff, 1988).

Boussard, J., *Le Gouvernement d'Henri II Plantagenet* (Paris, 1956).

Bradbury, J., *Stephen and Matilda: the Civil War of 1139–53* (Stroud, 1996).

Brand, P. A., *The Making of the Common Law* (London, 1992).

Britnell, R. and Hatcher, J., eds., *Progress and Problems in Medieval England* (Cambridge, 1996).

Chibnall, M., *Anglo-Norman England, 1066–1166* (Oxford, 1986).

The Empress Matilda (Oxford, 1991).

Complete Peerage by G. E. C., rev. edn V. Gibbs, G.H. White *et al.*, 12 vols. in 13 (London, 1910–59).

Cronne, H. A., *The Reign of Stephen, 1135–54* (London, 1970).

Crouch, D. B., *The Beaumont Twins* (Cambridge, 1986).

William Marshal: Court, Career and Chivalry in the Angevin Empire, 1147–1219 (London, 1990).

Dalton, P., *Conquest, Anarchy and Lordship: Yorkshire, 1066–1154* (Cambridge, 1994).

Davis, R. H. C., *King Stephen, 1135–1154* (3rd edn, London, 1990).

Ellis, R. G., *Earldoms in Fee* (London, 1963).

Eyton, R. W., *Antiquities of Shropshire*, 12 vols. (London, 1854–60).

Court, Household and Itinerary of King Henry II (London, 1878).

Farrer, W., *Honors and Knights' Fees*, 3 vols. (London and Manchester, 1923–25).

Garnett, G. and Hudson, J. G. H., eds., *Law and Government in Medieval England and Normandy: Essays in Honour of Sir James Holt* (Cambridge, 1994).

Gillingham, J., *The Angevin Empire* (London, 1984).

Green, J. A., *The Government of England under Henry I* (Cambridge, 1986).

English Sheriffs to 1154 (P.R.O. Handbook 24, London, 1990).

The Aristocracy of Norman England (Cambridge, 1997).

Haskins, C. H., *Norman Institutions* (New York, 1918).

Hollister, C. W., *Monarchy, Magnates and Institutions in the Anglo-Norman World* (London, 1986).

Hudson, J. G. H., *Land, Law and Lordship in Anglo-Norman England* (Oxford, 1994).

The Formation of the English Common Law (London, 1996).

Kealey, E. J., *Roger of Salisbury, Viceroy of England* (Berkeley, 1972).

Keefe, T. K., *Feudal Assessments and the Political Community under Henry II and his Sons*

Select bibliography

(Berkeley, 1983).

King, E. J., *The Anarchy of King Stephen's Reign* (Oxford, 1994).

Knowles, D. M., *Thomas Becket* (London, 1970).

Madox, T., *History and Antiquities of the Exchequer of England* (London, 1711).

Maitland, F. W., *Domesday Book and Beyond* (Cambridge, 1897).

Milsom, S. F. C., *Historical Foundations of the Common Law* (London, 1969).

The Legal Framework of English Feudalism (Cambridge, 1976).

Mitchell, S. K., *Taxation in Medieval England* (New Haven, 1951).

Morey, A. and Brooke, C. N. L., *Gilbert Foliot and his Letters* (Cambridge, 1965).

Morris, W. A., *The Medieval English Sheriff to 1300* (Manchester, 1927).

Pollock, F. and Maitland, F. W., *History of English Law before the Time of Edward I*, 2 vols. (2nd edn., Cambridge, 1898).

Poole, A. L., *From Domesday Book to Magna Carta* (2nd edn., Oxford, 1955).

Ramsay, J. H., *History of the Revenues of the Kings of England, 1066–1399*, 2 vols. (Oxford, 1925).

Reynolds, S., *Fiefs and Vassals* (Oxford, 1994).

Richardson, H. G., *The English Jewry under the Angevin Kings* (London, 1960).

Richardson, H. G. and Sayles, G. O., *The Governance of Mediaeval England from the Conquest to Magna Carta* (Edinburgh, 1963).

Law and Legislation from Aethelberht to Magna Carta (Edinburgh, 1966).

Round, J. H., *Geoffrey de Mandeville: a Study of the Anarchy* (London, 1892).

Studies in Peerage and Family History (Westminster, 1901).

Saltman, A., *Theobald, Archbishop of Canterbury* (London, 1956).

Sanders, I. J., *English Baronies: a Study of their Origin and Descent, 1086–1327* (Oxford, 1960).

Stenton, D. M., *English Justice between the Norman Conquest and the Great Charter, 1066–1215* (London, 1965).

Stenton, F. M., *The First Century of English Feudalism, 1066–1166* (2nd edn., Oxford, 1961).

Stringer, K. J., *Earl David of Huntingdon, 1152–1219* (Edinburgh, 1985).

The Reign of Stephen (London, 1993).

Sutherland, D. W., *The Assize of Novel Disseisin* (Oxford, 1973).

Thacker, A. T., ed., *The Earldom of Chester and its Charters* (Journal of Chester Archaeological Society, 71, 1991).

Victoria History of the Counties of England (in progress, London, 1900–).

Warren, W. L., *Henry II* (London, 1973).

The Governance of Norman and Angevin England, 1086–1272 (London, 1987).

West, F. J., *The Justiciarship in England, 1066–1232* (Cambridge, 1966).

Wightman, W. E., *The Lacy Family in England and Normandy, 1066–1194* (Oxford, 1966).

Young, A., *William Cumin: Border Politics and the Bishopric of Durham, 1141–1144* (University of York, Borthwick Paper 54, 1979).

Articles and papers

Amt, E. M., 'The meaning of waste in the early pipe rolls of Henry II', *Economic History Review*, 44 (1991), 240–8.

Archibald, M. M., 'Dating Stephen's first type', *BNJ*, 61 (1992 for 1991), 9–21.

Barnes, P. M., 'The Anstey case', in Barnes and Slade, eds., *Medieval Miscellany for Doris Mary Stenton*, 1–24.

Barrow, G. W. S., 'King David I and the Honour of Lancaster', *EHR*, 70 (1955), 85–9.

Select bibliography

'The Scots and the North of England', in King, *Anarchy*, 231–53.

Bates, D., 'The origins of the justiciarship', *ANS*, 4 (1981), 1–12.

Bearman, R., 'Baldwin de Redvers: some aspects of a baronial career in the reign of King Stephen', *ANS*, 18 (1996), 19–46.

Biancalana, J., 'For want of justice: legal reforms of Henry II', *Columbia Law Review*, 88 (1988), 433–536.

Blackburn, M., 'Coinage and currency under Henry I: a review', *ANS*, 13 (1991), 49–81.
'Coinage and currency', in King, *Anarchy*, 145–205.

Boorman, J., 'The sheriffs of Henry II and the significance of 1170', in Garnett and Hudson, eds., *Law and Government*, 255–75.

Bradbury, J., 'The early years of the reign of Stephen', in D. Williams, ed., *England in the Twelfth Century* (Woodbridge, 1990), 17–30.
'The civil war of Stephen's reign: winners and losers', in M. Strickland, ed., *Armies, Chivalry and Warfare in Medieval Britain and France* (Stamford, 1998), 115–32.

Brand, P. A., '"Multis vigiliis excogitatem et inventam": Henry II and the creation of the English common law', *Haskins Society Journal*, 2 (1990), 197–222.

Cheney, M. G., 'The litigation between John Marshal and Archbishop Thomas Becket in 1164: a pointer to the origin of novel disseisin ?', in J. A. Guy and H. G. Beale, eds., *Law and Social Change in British History* (London, 1984), 9–26.
'A decree of Henry II on defect of justice', in D. E. Greenway, C. Holdsworth and J. Sayers, eds., *Tradition and Change: Essays in Honour of Marjorie Chibnall* (Cambridge, 1985), 183–93.

Chibnall, M., 'The charters of the Empress Matilda', in Garnett and Hudson, *Law and Government*, 276–98.

Corner, D., 'The texts of Henry II's assizes', in A. Harding, ed., *Law-Making and Lawmakers in British History* (London, 1980), 7–20.

Cronne, H. A., 'The office of local justiciar in England under the Norman kings', *University of Birmingham Historical Journal*, 6 (1957–58), 18–38.

Crouch, D. B., 'Earl William of Gloucester and the end of the Anarchy: new evidence relating to the honour of Eudo *Dapifer*', *EHR*, 102 (1988), 69–75.
'The March and the Welsh kings', in King, *Anarchy*, 255–89.

Dalton, P., 'William earl of York and royal authority in Yorkshire in the reign of Stephen', *Haskins Society Journal*, 2 (1990), 155–65.
'Ranulf II and Lincolnshire' in Thacker, ed. *Earldom of Chester*, 109–34.
'*In neutro latere*: the armed neutrality of Ranulf II earl of Chester in King Stephen's reign', *ANS*, 14 (1992), 39–59.

Davis, H. W. C., 'The anarchy of Stephen's reign', *EHR*, 18 (1903), 630–41.
'Henry of Blois and Brian fitz Count', *EHR*, 25 (1910), 297–303.
'Some documents of the Anarchy', in *Essays in History presented to R. L. Poole* (Oxford, 1927).

Davis, R. H. C., 'King Stephen and the earl of Chester revised', *EHR*, 75 (1960), 654–60.
'The authorship of the *Gesta Stephani*', EHR, 77 (1962), 209–32.
'Treaty between William earl of Gloucester and Roger earl of Hereford', in Barnes and Slade, *Medieval Miscellany for Doris Mary Stenton*, 139–46.
'What happened in Stephen's reign', *History*, 49 (1964), 1–12.
'Geoffrey de Mandeville reconsidered', *EHR*, 79 (1964), 299–307.

Duggan, C., 'Richard of Ilchester, royal servant and bishop', *TRHS*, 5th ser., 16 (1966), 1–21.

Eales, R. G., 'Local loyalties in Norman England: Kent in Stephen's reign', *ANS*, 8 (1986), 88–108.

Eyton, R. W., 'The Staffordshire pipe rolls . . . to 35 Hen.II', in *Staffs. Colls.*, I, 1–143.

Fowler, G. H., 'The shire of Bedford and the earldom of Huntingdon' in *Publications of the Bedfordshire Historical Record Society*, 9 (1925), 23–35.

Gillingham, J. 'Conquering kings: some twelfth-century reflections on Henry II and Richard I', in T. Reuter, ed., *Warriors and Churchmen in the High Middle Ages* (London, 1992), 163–78.

Green, J. A., 'The last century of danegeld', *EHR*, 96 (1981), 241–58.

'"Praeclarum et magnificum antiquitatis monumentum": the earliest surviving pipe roll', *BIHR*, 55 (1982), 1–17.

'Anglo-Scottish relations, 1066–1174', in M. Jones and M. Vale, eds., *England and her Neighbours: Essays in Honour of Pierre Chaplais* (London, 1989), 53–72.

'Earl Ranulf II and Lancashire', in Thacker, ed., *Earldom of Chester*, 97–108.

'Financing Stephen's war', *ANS*, 14 (1992), 91–114.

Hill, R., 'The battle of Stockbridge, 1141', in C. Harper-Bill, C. Holdsworth and J. L. Nelson, eds., *Studies in Medieval History presented to R. Allen Brown* (Woodbridge and Wolfeboro, 1989), 173–7.

Holdsworth, C., 'War and peace in the twelfth century: the reign of Stephen reconsidered', in B. P. McGuire, ed., *War and Peace in the Middle Ages* (Copenhagen, 1987), 67–93.

'The Church', in King, *Anarchy*, 207–29.

Hollister, C. W., 'The significance of scutage rates in eleventh and twelfth century England', *EHR*, 75 (1960), 577–88.

'The rise of administrative kingship: Henry I', in *Monarchy, Magnates and Institutions*, 223–45.

'The Anglo-Norman succession debate of 1126', in *Monarchy, Magnates and Institutions.*, 247–71.

'The aristocracy', in King, *Anarchy*, 37–66.

Holt, J. C. 'The assizes of Henry II: the texts', in D. A. Bullough and R. L. Storey, eds., *The Study of Medieval Records: Essays in Honour of Kathleen Major* (Oxford, 1971), 85–106.

'Politics and property in early medieval England', *Past and Present*, 57 (1972), 3–52 and 65 (1974), 127–35.

'1153: the treaty of Winchester', in King, *Anarchy*, 291–316.

Hurnard, N. D., 'The jury of presentment and the Assize of Clarendon', *EHR*, 56 (1941), 374–410.

'Did Edward I reverse Henry II's policy upon seisin?', *EHR*, 69 (1954), 529–53.

Hyams, P. R., 'Warranty and good lordship in twelfth century England', *Law and History Review*, 5 (1987), 437–503.

'The charter as a source for the early common law', *Journal of Legal History*, 12 (1991), 173–89.

Jolliffe, J. E. A., 'The *Camera Regis* under Henry II', *EHR*, 68 (1953), 1–21, 337–62.

Keats-Rohan, K. S. B., 'The making of Henry of Oxford: Englishmen in a Norman world', *Oxoniensia*, 54 (1991), 287–309.

King, E. J., 'King Stephen and the Anglo-Norman aristocracy', *History*, 59 (1974), 180–94.

The parish of Warter and the castle of Galchlin', *Yorkshire Archaeological Journal*, 52

(1980), 49–58.

'The anarchy of King Stephen's reign', *TRHS*, 5th ser., 34 (1984), 133–53.

'Dispute settlement in Anglo-Norman England', *ANS*, 14 (1992), 115–30.

'Economic development in the early twelfth century', in Britnell and Hatcher, eds., *Progress and Problems*, 1–22.

Lally, J. E. 'Secular patronage at the court of King Henry II', *BIHR*, 49 (1976), 159–84.

Latimer, P., 'Grants of "Totus Comitatus" in twelfth-century England', *HR*, 59 (1986), 137–45.

Leyser, K., 'The Anglo-Norman succession, 1120–25', *ANS*, 13 (1991), 233–9.

Mack, R. P., 'Stephen and the Anarchy, 1135–54', *BNJ*, 35 (1966), 38–112.

Mason, E., 'The Mauduits and their chamberlainship of the exchequer', *BIHR*, 49(1976), 1–23.

Nightingale, P.,'"The king's profit": trends in English mint and monetary policy in the eleventh and twelfth centuries', in N. J. Mayhew and P. Spufford, eds., *Later Medieval Mints: Organization, Administration and Techniques* (Oxford, 1988), 61–75.

Palmer, R. C., 'The origins of property in England', *Law and History Review*, 3 (1985), 1–50.

Patterson, R. B., 'An un-edited charter of Henry fitz Empress and Earl William of Gloucester's comital status', *EHR*, 87 (1972), 755–7.

Reedy, W. T., 'The origins of the general eyre in the reign of Henry I', *Speculum*, 41 (1966), 688–724.

Richardson, H. G., 'The chamber under Henry II', *EHR*, 69 (1954), 596–611.

'The coronation in medieval England', *Traditio*, 16 (1960), 111–202.

Southern, R. W., 'The place of Henry I in English History', *Proceedings of the British Academy*, 48 (1962), 127–69.

Stenton, D. M., 'England: Henry II', in *Cambridge Medieval History V*, ed. J. R. Tanner, C. W. Prévite-Orton and Z. N. Brooke (Cambridge, 1929), 554–91.

Stephenson, C., 'The aids of English boroughs', *EHR*, 34 (1919), 457–75.

Stewart, I., 'Scottish mints', in R. A. G. Carson, ed., *Mints, Dies and Currency* (London, 1971), 165–289.

Stringer, K. J., 'A Cistercian archive: the earliest charters of Sawtry Abbey', *Journal of Society of Archivists*, 6 (1980), 325–34.

'State-building in twelfth-century Britain: David I, king of Scots, and northern England', in Appleby and Dalton, eds., *Government, Religion and Society in Northern England*, 40–62.

Turner, G. J., 'The sheriff's farm', *TRHS*, new ser., 12 (1898), 117–49.

Walker D., 'The "Honours" of the earls of Hereford in the twelfth century', *Transactions of the Bristol and Gloucestershire Archaeological Society*, 79 (1960), 174–211.

White, G. H. 'King Stephen's earldoms', *TRHS* 4th ser., 13 (1930), 51–82.

White, G. J., 'King Stephen, Duke Henry and Ranulf de Gernons, earl of Chester'. *EHR*, 91 (1976), 555–65.

'Were the Midlands "wasted" during Stephen's reign?', *Midland History*, 10(1985), 26–46.

'The end of Stephen's reign', *History*, 75 (1990), 3–22.

'Continuity in government', in King, *Anarchy*, 117–43.

'Damage and "waste" in Yorkshire and the north Midlands in the reign of Stephen', in Appleby and Dalton, eds., *Government, Religion and Society in Northern England*, 63–76.

Select bibliography

Yoshitake, K., 'The arrest of the bishops in 1139 and its consequences', *Journal of Medieval History*, 14 (1988), 97–114.
'The exchequer in the reign of Stephen', *EHR*, 103 (1988), 950–9.

THESES

Abbott, M., 'The Gant Family in England, 1066–1191' (University of Cambridge PhD, 1973).
Boorman, J., 'The Sheriffs of Henry II and their role in Civil Litigation' (University of Reading PhD, 1989).
Latimer, P., 'The Earls in Henry II's Reign' (University of Sheffield PhD, 1982).
White, G. J., 'The Restoration of Order in England, 1153–1165' (University of Cambridge PhD, 1974).

INDEX

Index

Cambridge Studies in Medieval Life and Thought
Fourth series

Titles in series